THE GUGGENHEIMS

Also by Harvey O'Connor

MELLON'S MILLIONS:
THE BIOGRAPHY OF A FORTUNE

STEEL—DICTATOR

MEYER AND BARBARA GUGGENHEIM

The Guggenheims

The Making of an American Dynasty

BY HARVEY O'CONNOR

NEW YORK

New York · COVICI · FRIEDE *· Publishers*

COPYRIGHT, 1937, BY HARVEY O'CONNOR

First Printing, August, 1937
Second Printing, August, 1937

PRINTED IN THE UNITED STATES OF AMERICA
BY J. J. LITTLE AND IVES COMPANY, NEW YORK
DESIGNED BY ROBERT JOSEPHY

CONTENTS

ILLUSTRATIONS

THE GUGGENHEIMS

1. SWISS FAMILY GUGGENHEIM

YOUNG MEYER GUGGENHEIM sat cross-legged on a bench in his father's tailor shop in Lengnau, looking out across the meadows and forested uplands. His native canton of Aargau was a pleasant sight, but he did not see it just then. Poised between horizon and cloud floated vague, grand America, where even Jews were free—free to travel from city to city, live where they pleased, enter what business they chose, grow wealthy. How different from Switzerland!

For almost two hundred years the Guggenheims had lived here in Ober-Lengnau and still they were "foreigners." Indeed, they had just outgrown the category of "tolerated homeless persons not to be expelled." Only in Meyer's own time had a Jew been permitted to enter a trade, and that he was obliged to pick up somehow at home. A Jewish youth could not travel to learn, nor enter a guild as a journeyman. In the census Jews were lumped together contemptuously among the occupational groups as mere "Hebraer." Peddling was allowed to them, yes. On any Sunday morning you could see scores emerging from their swarming hovels to start their rounds through neighboring cantons, not to return until next Friday sundown.

Was that a life for a human being? Young Meyer's eyes again sought the Zurich paper and its article on the American democracy beyond the seas. Just then father Simon tramped into the shop. Meyer, ashamed to be caught daydreaming, took up his needle.

For generations the only bits of soil in all Switzerland where Jews might live were these two small sections of the villages of Lengnau and Endingen—ghettos for the nation.

11

And these were established in the sixteenth century, when that region was Baden, under the Holy Roman Empire.

It was Christian fire and Christian swords that had driven out of Mainz, Worms, and a dozen other Rhenish cities the forbears of the families of Guggenheim, Dreifuss, Bloch, Gedeon, Weil, Wyler, Braunschweig, and the other Ober-Lengnau people. Massacre after massacre in town after town kept them wandering. Finally, roasting Jews alive went out of fashion; yet still Jews' homes were looted, and as late as 1662 Jews were being expelled en masse from the Swiss Confederation.

Seeking where to lay their heads, the wanderers sent emissaries to the embarrassed but greedy Landvogt of Baden. What a fine group to tax! But he could settle them in no city, for there resistance to the hated race was well organized. To Lengnau and Endingen he sent them, exacting heavy fees for his graciousness and calculating many yet to be levied.

No one will ever know exactly who were the forbears of the Guggenheims. The history of their race in the Middle Ages was lost in the never-ending sack of ghettos and synagogues. There had been a brief enlightened period before the hordes of the First Crusade swept down the Rhineland in 1096 to avenge the desecration of the Holy Sepulcher in Jerusalem. For ten centuries before that the ancestors of the Swiss family Guggenheim had lived along the German river, first in security as Roman citizens, later in precarious tenancy of whatever cellar the Holy Roman Emperor might grant them.

When Pope Eugene sent St. Bernard around Europe in 1146 to arouse another holy crusade, local authorities took it as a clarion call to stir up the peasants and landless against the infidels at home. St. Bernard, abashed by the hearty response which mistook Jew for Saracen, rushed messengers in all directions pleading for mercy. It was too late.

12

Thousands, trapped in synagogues to which they had fled, slew their wives and children and then each other as Crusaders broke down the iron-bound doors.

When the Black Death raged across Europe, the screws brought confessions. In Switzerland Jews had poisoned wells to cause this scourge! Like a second plague the "confessions" raced down the Rhine, with dreadful consequences to Jewish communities. In Strasbourg alone, two thousand men, women and children were taken to their cemetery and burned alive.

And why not? Had they not invited the Mongol and Turkish hordes to sweep as far into Christendom as Breslau and the gates of Vienna? "Accursed people—the unslaughtered Jews," inveighed a chronicler of the times. Henricus von Erfurt wrote:

> The pestilence like fury broke
> And took its thousands of our folk;
> The earth against us fiercely turned
> And many Jews were therefore burned.

Between Crusades and plagues, segments of the indefatigable race flourished here and there. In 1386, Wenceslaus, Holy Roman Emperor, discovered that although the Jews were a cursed people, many could not be distinguished from Christians. He urged his loyal subjects to see to it that all Jews wore Jewish hats, as of old, "so that, in accordance with equity, one may recognize a Jew among the Christians."

The pre-Guggenheims wandered from city to city. Perhaps they stayed a while in the village of Guggenheimb, now called Jugenheim, on the Bergstrasse between Darmstadt and Heidelberg. Who can ever know? But the name, or its variants, Guggenheimer, Guckenheim, Guckenheimer, Gougenheim, stuck to "die Juden von Guggenheimb."

The village of Lengnau must have seemed paradise to this wandering family, fleeing the horrors of the Thirty Years'

13

War, when both sides agreed only on killing Jews. Here in Baden was rest at last, and a chance to exist. They could ask no more. That the Jew was merely spat upon and cursed, not killed in the streets, was a demonstration of the broadmindedness of a Caesar of the Holy Roman Empire, who decreed that Jews were his personal chattels, existing for the greater glory of the Imperial Treasury. When Emperors were hard up, and that was often enough, more taxes were laid on the backs of "our" Jews. Louis of Bavaria, on critical occasions, would pawn a bunch of them with a noble friend to raise money. Specimen:

> We, Louis of Bavaria, announce that we are selling to the noble Jean of Rappoldslein, the imperial Jews of Ribeauville, for 400 marks silver, for which sum the Jews are to belong to him and his heirs, to enjoy them in accordance with the rights attached to this privilege, until the day when we or our successors in the Empire have returned to the said noble or his heirs the said sum of 400 marks.

The paradise of Endingen-Lengnau was really a lower rung of purgatory. Times grew bad in the sixteenth century, and the corpse of a Christian child was found in a church. "Der Jud Josel von Rosheim," under the screws, "confessed" and he and his family were burned "for the sanctification of the Holy Name."

Nevertheless it was recorded that the refugees in Lengnau and Engingen "increased like black beetles." It was an honest tribute to the tenacity of human beings. In 1678 Prefect Gallati felt obliged to prohibit the practice of beating Jews as they passed through other villages of Baden peddling their wares. And it took the threat of one hundred crowns fine to restrain Lengnau Christians from driving out the hated ones. The historian relates that the good burghers and peasants of Baden demanded expulsion of the Jews "only" three times in the century: 1641, 1658 and 1678. On no account would they tolerate the burial of a Jew on their soil. Wailing processions toiled along the road to the Rhine, where on Judenäule, an island bought from the German town of Waldshut, the dead were buried.

The first mention of the Swiss Guggenheims occurs in 1696 when the County of Baden recorded "der Jud Maram Guggenheimb von Lengnauw." A gaunt figure out of the mists of the early Swiss eighteenth century is Jacob Guggenheim, perhaps the son of Maram. In 1702 Jacob was standing before the court of justice accused of owning the house of the late Maram and of having kept possession of a vineyard on Wettinger Hill. (The law forbade Jews to hold real estate.)

Jacob and his brother Schmaul (Samuel) pleaded:

They do not know that they have made assignments in violation of the latest charter and beg most humbly to be spared from an inquiry into their letters and documents, because no one likes to show his estate and cannot exhibit it without endangering his credit. As to the house of Maram, they would have liked to sell it but there are no buyers; the vineyard was not bought by them but came to them through an auction [of the goods of a debtor?] and after they sold it, it was returned [by default?].

Deputies of the Diet of Zurich and Glarus admonished Jacob and Schmaul to observe the law. "However, all the actions contrary to the latest charter are hereby forgiven and forgotten," the deputies decreed, "but the inheritors of the Jew Maram are told to sell the house and its accessories as soon as possible."

In the same year, 1702, the houses of Jacob and Siseli Guggenheim were gutted in one of those periodic uprisings against the entire ghetto of Lengnau. Wretched mobs hotly pursued the Jews. Jewish homes were plundered and burned

15

to the ground. The Landvogt, fearful that the villagers would destroy "his" Jews, warned them to restrain their holy zeal, and emphasized his words by fining them sixteen hundred guldens for Jacob's house and three hundred for Siseli's. The wails of the Christians rent the air, until the Landvogt lightened the fine by letting them cut more trees from the common forest.

Every sixteen years the ghetto's charter expired. On bended knees the elders of the community beseeched renewal. The year George Washington was born, 1732, was critical: the charter ran out and the authorities, responding to popular pressure, decided that the time had come to expel the hated race. On August 8, one of Meyer's ancestors, Jacob Guggenheim, and Raphael Pickart appeared for the community before the Diet to "beg most humbly for the abrogation of these decisions."

Accused of impoverishing the canton through depriving honest Christian merchants of trade, of charging exorbitant interest rates on loans, of buying real estate, of reproducing themselves, Guggenheim and Pickart entered a sweeping denial of all charges, and counter-attacked.

The Jews of Lengnau-Endingen traded not only in the County of Baden but in Zurich, Winterthur, Brugg, Lenzburg, and other cantons. They plied the various fairs outside Baden picking up guldens from all Switzerland, which were brought to the homeland and spent there, or delivered to the tax-collector.

As for buying houses, they could obtain only those ready to fall. Was it not well known that the Jew's house had a straw roof and could only be described as a "Hauslein"? Even so, the wretched structures they acquired could be bought only after they had been offered at auction three times and no Christian would take them.

Jewish women were dressed in "splendor," the complaint had charged. But, swore Guggenheim, it was exceptional for their women to have decent dresses, and these, such as they were, came from Germany, were family heirlooms or were part of the bride's dowry.

The Diet was reminded that Jews must have cash money. They were not allowed to plant gardens, but must buy all their food for cash. They could buy no wood at all for building, nothing but old deadwood for kitchen fires.

As for the increase in population, Jacob Guggenheim declared that "they could not help it that the Good Lord and human nature contrive to replenish the human race."

"Humbly obedient, and on their knees," Jacob and Raphael begged the Diet to reconsider its decision. The councilors rescinded the expulsion order, decreed that Jews' interest charges must be limited to one pfennig to the florin, and forbade them to seize real estate in satisfaction for defaulted loans. The later effort of officials to expel Jacob, perhaps for his upstanding defense of the community, was defeated. In 1754 another Guggenheim, Salomon, was ordered banished but that, too, was rescinded on payment of a six hundred florin indemnity. Such expulsions were merely thinly veiled demands for more money, the ingenuity of the tax-collectors in imposing ordinary fees having become exhausted. Once, when Jacob Guggenheim protested that the Jewish community could pay no more, the Diet ordered the sheriff to "proclaim in the synagogue that the protection tax must be paid by a certain time; if not, public force will be used to get it; and those families that do not pay their share according to their means will be expelled."

Young Meyer Guggenheim had heard his grandfather's story of the harsh charter of 1760, accepted only because the alternative was expulsion. This charter sharply forbade the buying or selling of real estate. If the Landvogt were agreeable a Jew might obtain a "baulos Hauslein," but he must put it in good order and hold himself in readiness to sell to the first Christian who made an offer. The same char-

17

ter warned the Jews that they "should not marry nor allow marriages between poor persons, and that all brides coming into the county must bring a dowry of at least five hundred guldens."

Simon Guggenheim had seen the decade of enlightenment that followed the French Revolution. The Helvetian Republic had turned the county of Baden into the canton of Aargau, had lightened taxes on the Jews and accorded them a limited citizenship. The Christians' wrath knew no bounds. In 1802 the villagers and peasants sacked the ghetto (for the last time) despite the best efforts of Marshal Ney and his subordinates. With the collapse of the Helvetian Republic, oppression returned. In 1821 the canton decreed that the Jew was not to be considered a citizen, but rather a foreigner belonging to the category of tolerated homeless persons not to be expelled.

It was about this time that Samuel Guggenheim, young Meyer's uncle, distinguished himself by rescuing two sleeping children from the burning house of the Rueggers at Wyl in Zurich canton. The government rewarded Samuel with two ducats and a letter of praise; he declined the ducats. Aargau handsomely followed Zurich's example and complimented Guggenheim through the mayor of Lengnau.

Once again, though, it was the French, backed up by the Americans, who forced a more enlightened attitude upon Swiss authorities. Louis Napoleon threatened to bar the Swiss from France unless the Confederation accorded due rights to itinerant and emigrating French Jews. Occasionally American Jews trading in Switzerland found themselves in a humiliating plight which brought sharp reminders to Bern from the State Department in Washington.

Even so, it was not until the year of the Emancipation Proclamation, 1863, freeing American Negro slaves, that Switzerland's Jews attained citizenship. That act, too, was called the Emancipation Act, adopted only over the most

18

vehement opposition of Aargau and other cantons, which feared the ruin of small Christian shopkeepers and an influx of Jews from Alsace.

After the Emancipation, the Guggenheim clan spread rapidly—as feared by the bigots—throughout Switzerland, entered the professions, trades and businesses, and attained an outstanding name. By 1870 Leopold Guggenheim had become mayor of Gailingen, a post he held with high distinction for fourteen years.

Meyer Guggenheim, daydreaming in his father's tailor shop in Lengnau, could not foresee this, however. The hard reality that faced this ambitious youth was that he lived, by compulsion, in the ghetto of Lengnau, and that his father could live nowhere else in all Switzerland. All his life he would be a tailor, like his father. Wealth was forbidden, comfort hedged in by the exactions of the tax-collector and the hatred of Christians, education sharply limited by the meager facilities of the little Jewish school in Lengnau.

Father Simon agreed with his son's earnest plea that they quit unfriendly Switzerland forever. Here there was no future for a lively boy with ideas in his head, Simon admitted. He had no love for the country that had given grudging shelter to his family.

The widow Rachel Weil Myers beamed with joy when Widower Guggenheim mentioned America. The prospect of their marriage in Aargau seemed dim. One must obtain official sanction for the privilege, and the cantonal authorities were unanimous in their belief that there were too many marriages in the Jewish community: certainly it was straining the temper of a too generous Christian people to permit Jews who had already been married and raised families, to be united with the possibility of another increase in that unwanted population. Perhaps permission could have been obtained, but Simon was by no means affluent. In any event it would be better to sell the little property they had, pay

19

the inevitable tax levied even upon emigrants, and leave this cursed soil.

Surrounded by many sacks and carpetbags, Simon Guggenheim and his son, Meyer, and his three daughters, and Rachel Myers and her seven children, tossed a scant farewell to Switzerland in 1847 and sailed down the Rhine to board a sloop for America at Hamburg. Many a weary week later the ship rounded Cape May. Young Meyer Guggenheim and Barbara, third of Widow Myers' daughters, stood hand in hand watching joyously the Jersey and Delaware shores crowding in to narrow the waters into the Delaware River. Here, at last, was America and freedom, a chance to work, to prosper, to marry, and be happy. Far behind in another world was the hated heritage of six centuries of oppression.

That sunny day many-spired Philadelphia seemed to beckon Meyer and Barbara. Slowly the sloop was warped into her dock, the lines made fast, the gangplank placed. And the Guggenheim-Myers family walked into the land of promise, penniless, and were swallowed in the din of the busy port.

2. PEDDLER TO MERCHANT PRINCE

ALONG MUDDY LANES from shack to shack in Pennsylvania's dark and grimy anthracite region trudged young Meyer Guggenheim. The wind blew and the rain soaked through his brown beard, trickled down his neck, sopped into his socks. His pants sloshed against his ankles.

On he trudged, stooped under a heavy knapsack, bent to the elements, like his ancestors for centuries in Switzerland and Germany. At doors of wretched shanties he beseeched, in meager English: "Shoe strings, glue, lace, ribbons, stove polish, everything for your home I have with me, very cheap."

The rain blew into the barren room, the baby whimpered, the miner's wife frowned and banged the door. "The dirty Jews," she muttered, as had Christian housewives in Switzerland and Germany.

The slight, twenty-year-old youth sighed, walked down the path, and headed for the next door.

By Friday night he was back in the crowded little house in Philadelphia where lived his father, his three sisters, the Widow Myers—now Mrs. Simon Guggenheim—and her sons and daughters. In the glow of the candles he sat down to the ritual repast, next to his fifteen-year-old stepsister, Barbara. It was good to be back, sheltered, surrounded at last by friendly faces, cheered by the sound of a language he understood. Good, too, to be sitting next to Barbara, confidante of his hopes, whose warm faith in his worth buoyed him against the sharp realities of his working life. On the long voyage across the Atlantic they had planned their future: a nice house, friends, children, music, an end forever

21

to the haunting fears and the starved life of fettered Switzerland.

And what was happening? Over there, the Guggenheim family had escaped from peddling, the badge of the race, to a shop of their own. They sold it for a song to come to the land of opportunity, and here they were, back where they started. Pack on back, knocking at doors, scratching out a living.

True, they were alive, and shackled only by lack of money, not by laws and rigid racial barriers. They had arrived in Philadelphia nearly penniless, knowing no English, dependent on the helping hand of sympathetic fellow-countrymen. There was food on the table, for which all bent their heads in reverent gratitude. There was fire on the hearth. They had never had to take charity, except for some ceremonial matzoth given to Father Simon by the Hebrew Relief Association for his first passover in the strange land. But after a year's onerous work, with Simon at fifty-six peddling in the streets of Philadelphia and his son conducting forays into the outlying country, those bright pictures that Meyer and Barbara had painted in words and in unspoken hopes seemed badly blurred.

Not that Barbara cared too much about it. She sang as she bustled about the house which bounded her world. She was sorry that Meyer must work so hard, but the Good Lord and Meyer would take care of that some day. Every Saturday they went to the little synagogue in an old church on New Market Street, and there she prayed for his success. Later in the day they would walk along Front Street on the Delaware, watching the animated water traffic, or stroll down busy Market Street. Sometimes they would go to a quiet square and settle down to serious business. Meyer would pull out his little English-German word book and Barbara would catechize him, superior in her knowledge only because she held the key in her hands.

While she listened, patiently if not too attentively, Meyer described the life he saw in the back country. The poverty that surrounded him he brushed aside. What mattered was that plenty of people were well-to-do, had comfortable houses, lived in security. Some were even wealthy. Occasionally he dropped his burden to pass the time of day with little Jewish merchants in these back-country towns. Yes, they too had carried the pack in their time, but it was not hard in this country to prosper. Indeed, right in Philadelphia there were Jewish people who had come here as mere immigrants, without money or friends, and now were wealthy. The thought comforted Meyer as he dug his heels into the sod of the park and planned for himself and Barbara. As for Barbara, she doubted not at all.

Long before dawn on Mondays, the Guggenheim household was astir, preparing Meyer for his week-long sortie. Before it was light, Barbara was at the door waving him a farewell as he walked down the street, bent to his knapsack, bound for far regions where he could sell twice as much as Father Simon, plodding along Philadelphia's peddler-congested streets.

In this age of good roads and well stocked stores, even at the country crossroads, peddling as Meyer Guggenheim understood it is a lost way of life. But the general store of the 1850's in eastern Pennsylvania stocked only the fundamental staples—flour, sugar, dried beans and peas, a few bolts of cloth, thread, the simpler kitchen utensils. As often as not the housewife was told, "Sorry, but we're out of that," or "We don't carry that." It was before the day of rural free delivery and thousand-page farm catalogues.

From his pack, Meyer filled in the gaps. In its mysterious depths were shoe strings, scraps of lace, stove and furniture polish, ribbon, amazing new safety pins, odds and ends of spices, packages of needles. If the housewife was in a receptive mood and had a little spare cash, Meyer was greeted

23

not without respect. As he slung his pack to the floor, the children crowded about to peer into its awesome, delightful depths and reinforce his halting English with cries of joy. He left with his sack lightened—though his back couldn't feel the difference—and his purse heavier. In time housewives began to expect the monthly visit from the cheerful, friendly young Jewish peddler. Most of his fellow craftsmen grew apathetic or surly or could not slough off ways and mannerisms that seemed uncouth. But Meyer was a vigorous youth, even handsome, and refused to cringe. He believed in America's promise of equality and opportunity. He walked his rounds as an itinerant merchant, necessary and useful. He saw no reason for suppliance.

Nevertheless he detested the pack on his back, age-long stigma of his race. How could he get rid of it? As he jogged along, he schemed and planned, and poked, poked everywhere for light and guidance.

People made money from that sack, but not he. Manufacturers lived in fine Philadelphia homes along elm-bordered streets. Scores of immigrants like himself came to the backdoors of their establishments, paid out painfully earned dollars for assorted small-goods, and trudged through eastern Pennsylvania and New Jersey to gather pennies, nickels and dimes, most of which went back to the manufacturer when the pack was replenished.

Oh, for a horse, any kind of a horse, even one lamed and wheezy, Meyer complained bitterly. Why should a man do something a horse could do infinitely better? Why must he be a beast of burden? "How rich I'd feel if I had an old horse, any kind of horse," he told his friends. It became an obsession with Meyer, who dreamed of the day when he would possess one.

Plodding along, he reflected on his wares and the profits they contained. This little can of stove polish, for instance. He made a few pennies out of that can, and the manufacturer made thousands of dollars. He fingered the black, pasty stuff. That German chemist in Bethlehem would know what it was made of. Why not drop in and see him next time he was up there?

Meyer had thrown his knapsack in a corner of the chemist's shop. He produced the can of polish. The chemist smiled. Time was hanging heavy on a dull morning. Certainly he'd run it through a few tests for this fine-looking lad, who certainly was no ordinary peddler.

That Friday Meyer returned exuberant to break the good news to his father. Here—he waved a sheet of paper— is the magic formula that may buy me a horse. No more packs. Already he felt it an exertion to stand straight. His back was bending prematurely into the age-long curve, the Christian curse upon his race. But he smiled triumphantly as he remembered the meaning of his first name: The Enlightened.

After the evening meal Father Simon and Meyer huddled in a corner debating the most serious problem since they had decided to quite Swiss soil. A few hundred dollars had been accumulated. Should it be ventured on stocking supplies for this business? Point by point, his brown eyes flashing with eagerness, Meyer countered his father's objections and won him over to the new endeavor.

Young Meyer continued to peddle while his father mixed the stuff at home and supplied friends who came to the house with packs. The big difference in the peddling was in the percentage. Before he had made a penny or so on a dime sale: now he cleared seven to eight cents. After a time the young merchant abandoned his pack. But not for a horse as he had dreamed. Now he traveled far afield by train and horsecar, carrying a little satchel with samples of the polish and other lines he was adding.

It was time now for Meyer and Barbara to be married. He was twenty-four, hopeful, and on the road to success.

She was nineteen; and they say her auburn hair glowed in the sun, her skin was unusually fair, and her eyes had a special way of looking sometimes brown and sometimes a soft warm gray.

Downtown in gloomy little Keneseth Israel synagogue, the wedding was solemnized, Meyer in a new black frock coat, Barbara in a gown adorned with lace which Mother Myers had brought over from Switzerland. Many friends were there, a few Swiss from Lengnau and Endingen, more new ones, peddlers and small merchants with whom the Guggenheims had been associated. Barbara was a fine-looking girl, not beautiful perhaps, but energetic, cheerful, home-loving, the cynosure of admiring eyes as she stood beside her husband. Blessings were invoked on them and their progeny.

And who but the Widow Wiener, that masterly cook and incredibly honest caterer, welcomed the gay party to her commodious place for the feasting and dancing that followed. Next day the good lady sent over to Barbara's mother two chickens and some cookies "that were figured in the bill and not eaten up last night." A little duty the guests had neglected to finish, absorbed as they were in the wine.

On this happy occasion Meyer's keen wit fairly crackled in the bluff, hearty give-and-take of the jesting. "That'll be a jolly household," said more than one. Even old friends were surprised at the new assurance and gayety of the business-like young fellow.

As profits from his stove polish piled up, Meyer tried his hand at other businesses. Once he started a tailor shop, and once he had a grocery store. But such shops required a great deal of his time and had a small turnover. It was when he joined hands with friends in downtown Philadelphia in a partnership wholesaling household products that he began to make real money. The family moved into a bigger house. It was needed. Every two years Barbara gave birth to a son, first Isaac in 1854, then Daniel, Murry, and Solomon.

Meyer's peculiar gift was his combination of caution and boldness. The panic of 1857 failed to shake him, and his business marched up toward a war-time climax in 1862. Barbara and the boys saw little of him as he darted about Philadelphia's commission district, buying and selling for his partnership and speculating himself in foodstuffs needed for the Army of the Potomac.

Particularly in demand was his coffee essence, a flavor apparently to be found only on the Guggenheim shelves. It was ideal for the Army: a little essence, some hot water, and the elixir of life was ready. Meyer used chicory and the poorer grades of coffee beans, superintending the roasting, grinding, boiling, and bottling. What the stuff lacked in fine aroma it more than made up in strength. Many an officer and private rejoiced in the stimulation of Guggenheim's essence, and the money rolled in.

Barbara sighed when she thought of her youngest and favorite brother Benjamin Myers, who rushed off to fight for the Union when scarcely turned twenty. Philadelphia was not far from the lines. By that time the Guggenheims had servants for their growing family, so she was not completely house-bound. But on those rare occasions when she did go out it was no pleasure to see the well-formed young men, hollow-faced from suffering, who stumped about on crutches, or, still worse, to happen on the unloading of a dozen stretchers at one of the emergency hospitals. Even at home in the neighborhood certain dreaded official notices struck like lightning. It took courage to face the mail. Barbara, however, was not of a brooding temperament, and her lively boys and constant new babies filled her life. Not for her the nervous drive that must spend itself in nursing, rolling bandages, or entertaining the men on leave.

In 1864, in the heat of epic conflict, the feminine portion of Philadelphia was set a-quiver to the edge of its hoops by the simultaneous announcements of two rival firms regarding "the new duplex elliptic steel spring skirt! Can be folded as easily as muslin in a crowded assembly, railroad car or church pew! A lady having enjoyed one for a single day will never afterward willingly dispense with them!" Ladies of fashion talked of little else, though there was a big battle that week. But Barbara probably never bought the new contraption. Everything was for her children. She never wanted anything for herself. Still she found the time to observe when a neighbor needed help, and the wherewithal to give it.

Stirring days those were to live in, and seventy years later they were to stand out as the "most vivid childhood memory" of the boys. Young Murry at six was overwhelmed by the great black drapes hanging on every house after the assassination of Lincoln. Sol was never to forget the joy of hearing of Uncle Ben's return, and his excitement as his sturdy four-year-old legs pounded down Franklin Street to embrace the tired, dusty, bearded young man from the 130th infantry.

Meyer's business throve, and one of his steadiest customers was Charles Graham, a Quaker from Germantown, who was also riding the war boom.

Discreetly in the background, Barbara presented to her rejoicing husband four more children, Jeannette, Benjamin, and the twins, Simon and Robert. Each confinement was in a different house and with a different doctor. Meyer's restlessness? Perhaps. More probably it was the outward sign of his rapid rise in the world. Certain it is that the house at 619 Franklin Street where Jeannette was born was not so commodious as 1423 Franklin, where Benjamin gave his first yell in 1865. As for 443 Green Lane, Roxborough, where in 1867 Simon and Robert greeted the world, it had a broad piazza with square pillars and fancy white woodwork, and a large yard both in front and in back for the children to play in. It must have seemed in every way worth the effort of moving with six children a few months before the twins came. In any case, not a word of complaint passed Barbara's lips.

But despite the pleasant yard with the fruit trees (fine climbing for the boys) Meyer must have found the nine-mile trip downtown too long for his rushing business in those busless, subwayless days. And so William, the eighth and last son, found them back in the city on Franklin Street (a little more uptown than before) when he came along, a seven months baby, just eleven months after the twins.

Short as was the Guggenheims' stay in Roxborough, it made its impression. "They were quite an excitable family," said the landlord's wife. And how could there fail to be excitement, with seven boys in the house and the European background of self-expression instead of Anglo-Saxon stiffness? Bright, friendly, young Dan won the landlady's heart. And their teacher, Miss Thomas, many years later, in writing the history of the Roxborough elementary school, the oldest in the township, did not fail to mention that "the copper kings once studied there."

Meyer, constantly seeking new lines of profit and new outlets for his energy, became a merchant of spices. Besides his redoubtable coffee essence he dealt in peppers, condiments, and strange products brought over to Philadelphia on swift clipper ships from Amsterdam, whither they had come from the East Indies.

In those days most families carefully saved pieces of fat and when a mess was accumulated boiled their own soap, for which lye was an essential ingredient. The Pennsylvania Salt Company had a monopoly in lye. Meyer's roving eye picked up an option from England on a caustic alkali, much cheaper than the lye being sold, and needing only melting to equal it. He imported it and packed it in small convenient packages. Unable to stop the sale of the Guggenheim product, the Pennsylvania Salt Company bought out his lye busi-

29

ness eventually at a fine profit. Meyer chuckled as his bank balance grew. The family's surplus was first recorded publicly in 1867, when Meyer became a regular five dollar member of the Jewish Foster Home Society.

"Ach, son, son," Father Simon used to say, "it's hard to believe you came here without a penny." The old man's rugged face looked beautiful and tranquil when they laid him away in Frankfort cemetery in 1869.

Two years later Meyer moved his family still further uptown to 1430 North Seventeenth Street, where Rose, first called Rosetta, was born. A true measure of Meyer's progress was that the doctor, a new one as usual, spelled his name right on the birth certificate this time, whereas previous doctors had been content to approximate with "Guggenheimer" and "Gougenheim." Next year the family moved a block nearer Broad Street. Even here, however, on spacious tree-lined Sixteenth, the division between affluence and modest circumstances was apparent. There were palms in the parlor windows on both sides of the street, but those on the west side were larger and fancier, and the curtains more elegant, than the east. The west side stoops somehow seemed to look down on their humbler brothers to the east. And east was the Guggenheims' side. Here, at 1417, Cora was born in 1873, the last of buxom Barbara's contributions to the House of Guggenheim.

Never had there been the slightest suggestion of purple passion in the simple romance that united Barbara and Meyer. For her, marriage was life's supreme business. There was little time and no inclination for outside frivolities. It was not unusual even in well-to-do families to lose a child or two in infancy, but Barbara's eleven all grew strong, although Barbara got prematurely gray looking after them. In her kitchen or nursery she was happiest; surrounded by her growing family, she felt no need for outside interests.

Life was by no means somber. "There were so many of us,

we made our own fun," the boys remembered. Many a charade, apt or far-fetched, was concocted for the mirth of the family and great was the reward when Meyer, whose mind even at home hummed with business problems as automatically as a musician's hums with tunes, was moved to join in with his full-throated roar.

Meyer brought his partners and their wives home occasionally, and there would be wine or beer and oysters, songs of the old country, even sometimes dances—the quadrille, the waltz, the lancers.

Such occasions started early, with a few friends invited to dinner in the big Guggenheim dining-room, where talk was mostly of business, business men, development of the West, bad news from the old countries, the goings-on in the local Jewish community. Dinner over, other friends began to arrive, the women retired to the kitchen to supervise the girls and exchange local news, and that done, returned to the two big connecting rooms that were dining-room and parlor for the evening's amusement.

Little distinguished the Guggenheim parlor from others of the period. A bit on the stuffy side, perhaps, from the modern point of view, but modest, its walls brightened with the usual quota of appropriate mottos embroidered in canvas or on perforated paper board, hanging among chromos.

Often Meyer stayed downtown for the evening, engrossed in a game of solo whist or pinochle in the back of some friend's shop or his own back office, or catching up on his work, or chastising negligent clerks. The ladies of this circle, for their part, frequently entertained with a Kaffee Klatsch in the afternoon, the guests bringing the handiwork of their own ovens to demonstrate their skill. Barbara's boys say she didn't have this kind of party. Why?—she was shy, she was Swiss and she was busy. The Swiss, they say, did not go in for social life as much as the Germans.

But it is hard to believe that the Guggenheim house was

not open, those famous New Year's Days, when all the men of each family dressed in their best and went calling around, and the women stayed home to serve them punch. It would be the height of rudeness to refuse to drink at each call, and if a man had a dozen good friends, the result might be "very unusual weather."

Rarely, Meyer would take Barbara down to the little German Theater for a sentimental reminder of the old country or to the Opera at the Academy of Music. Music was his soft spot: he had never been trained in any branch but he labored vigorously to produce a small orchestra out of his family . . . and failed ignominiously. He herded them into the basement at six in the morning—best hour of the day, he said cheerfully, and leaves plenty of time for school and errands. There the two violins and cello squeaked while the piano pounded scales above. A neighbor had married an old maid . . . late. "She had a fence eight feet high, and still she complained of the noise," recalls one of the willy-nilly musicians. "She had father brought before the alderman, several different years." (Meyer was nothing if not persistent.) The boys (and how many others!) felt mercifully relieved when he finally gave up the fight, except Sol, who really played his cello until he had to ride out over the rough trails of Mexico.

Though Meyer read English hesitantly, he made it a point to go over the papers every day, and friends recall he was as well posted as any man in the city on business matters that interested him. His letters on these subjects were vigorous and to the point.

He did not mix extensively in the feverish professional Jewish activities of Philadelphia. He was too busy and contented building up his family's fortune, and did not feel the need of social recognition. Barbara was deeply religious, and Meyer attended Keneseth Israel temple, then at Sixth and Brown Streets, more for the sake of his family

32

than himself. The boys went to Sabbath school. The congregation had introduced some reforms as early as 1852 and adopted more and more until at Rosh Hashana in September, 1881, a year which Meyer had particular cause to celebrate, Keneseth Israel was described as "the most lax of all: men take off their hats, sing hymns in English and German, curtail prayers to the utmost, celebrate only one day to each festival, and sit with the women." Meyer considered it no sacrilege to do business on the Sabbath; these and similar rules he held to be formal trappings, unrelated to a man's duty to advance himself, protect his family and see that his sons grew up to be useful business men. Nevertheless he was occasionally seen in the congregation and pledged support at the annual meeting. In later years when he had grown prosperous generous contributions were common. Others who had known the younger Guggenheim marveled to themselves as they tugged at their beards and related to awe-struck wives: "Believe it or not, that man who can hardly sign his own name" [an exaggeration] "gave a thousand dollars to the temple this year." Gifts of two hundred and fifty dollars had been considered quite respectable for the successful business man. One donation went for something close to Meyer's music-loving heart: a new organ.

The Jewish community in Philadelphia was sharply divided in Meyer's earlier years between the aristocratic and strictly orthodox Sephardic branch, many of them Portuguese and Spanish in origin, who attended the city's first synagogue, Mikveh Israel, and the recent German group who followed the Ashkenazaic ritual. The Germans, at first dirt-poor, founded Rodeph Shalom and Keneseth Israel in cast-off Christian churches suitably cleansed. By the end of the civil war they too were prosperous and Rodeph Shalom came into its glory by calling Dr. Marcus Jastrow from Warsaw where he had been imprisoned by Czarist police, and giving him the fabulous salary of four thousand dollars, raised to five thousand dollars the next year.

The year Guggenheim arrived in Philadelphia, the community barely counted twenty-five hundred souls, Sephardic and Ashkenazaic combined. But it had been established long before the Revolution. It is recorded that Haym Solomon gave twenty-five hundred dollars to General Washington's forces and lent three hundred and fifty thousand more, which also became a gift because of the casual attitude of the new government. Solomon was the opposite of a Shylock: indeed James Madison wrote of him, "The kindness of our little friend in Front Street is a fund that will preserve me from extremity, but I never resort to it without great mortification as he obstinately rejects all recompense."

Despite this long and honorable history, in Meyer's time Philadelphia synagogues still had to import their learned men from abroad to keep the faith alive. In 1848 the Hebrew Education Society was formed to rescue the youth from being engulfed in alien ways. The school gave afternoon courses in Hebrew and some of the Guggenheim boys actually went on Mondays for a time. For regular schooling, strangely enough, they attended the Catholic Day School at Broad and Columbus for a while, because it was well managed. They went to the public high schools. Meyer from 1884 on gave twenty-five dollars a year to the Hebrew Education Society, mostly for the industrial school fund. He always bought quantities of benefit tickets . . . for the Catholic Charities or the Fireman's ball, whatever came along. Absorbed as he was in work, he usually passed them on to friends . . . "Here, if you have a free evening, take 'em and enjoy 'em!"

In the late seventies when a vast new surge of immigration fled from the pogroms in Slavic lands, Meyer, remembering his younger days, contributed to help the new arrivals, in common with other prosperous, once penniless German-

34

speaking Jews. Something departed as they came, however —the spirit of jolly, democratic homogeneity that had begun in the sixties when the group was small and all the families had attained modest prosperity. Jewry was split again, with hordes of new poor, strictly orthodox, who spoke only Slavic and Yiddish.

Meyer Guggenheim was never an outstanding personage in this community. He shrank from wide public contacts, was too engrossed in his own business, had no appetite for crowds. He was small and unimpressive. He could be bluff and genial, but in his face a natural kindliness was shielded, for public purposes, behind a cold mien. He trusted the motives of few men, was ever on the alert for the ulterior purpose of friend and foe. He told a good story, but outside the circle of intimate friends, he spoke little and kept his own counsel. It was a dog-eat-dog world and he did not propose to be eaten.

Given his tenacity and curiosity, Meyer was the predictable product of his hard life. The harsh years of his youth under Swiss tyranny, the fear of oppression, the feeling (only too well justified by his experience and teaching) that safety lay only in money, the strange environment of a new world and his own successful rise in the teeth of obstacles, molded his character into an amalgam of self-assurance, cynicism, and wariness. It was he and his family against the world, with no quarter and little mercy expected on either side. None had ever been shown his forbears. He intended to wrest from the world as much as his intelligence and strength would permit. He felt little obligation to strangers, although he appreciated the free spirit of enterprise in America.

Business was the breath of life. Business, not only for its own sake and his own, but for his family's. He had gone far; his sons must rise much further.

To this end, he was unsparing of discipline and the rod.

His word in the tight little world of Guggenheim was law, irrevocable and unquestioned. Infraction was a personal challenge and met with physical punishment, the instrument being any suitable object at hand, strap, stick or rod. His boys must be prepared for the hard discipline of life. That meant study, a ready knowledge of figures. As they grew older they were introduced to the fundamentals of business practice: every penny, hard won, must be spent cautiously. Outsiders must never be trusted. The seamy side of every proposition must be examined for the lurking danger; every promise carried its hidden threat.

That the boys did not grow up to be narrow misanthropes was Barbara's glory. She was the perfect foil to Meyer. Where he criticized unceasingly, commanded without end, applied discipline's lash, she was the refuge in time of sorrow, the lamp of love in a world that seemed at times dark and bitter. On her lap they wept for consolation. Her gentle nature, while it failed to ward off disciplinary blows, softened their sting. To them Barbara interpreted Meyer's harshness as a sign of his devotion to their future.

Meyer himself found no little satisfaction, not acknowledged to them, however, in the progress his sons made. The boys grouped themselves into older and younger clans. Isaac, Dan, Murry, and Sol herded together, and Ben, Simon, Bob, and Will. Surrounded by sisters and the softer life of North Sixteenth Street, the younger boys had lost something of the rough fiber of the old days, when life was stern and Meyer's arm more sustained in chastisement.

Even with advancing prosperity, Meyer declined to foster in his boys any delusion that money came easily. There was no weekly allowance; it took hard drilling to extract a few pennies from their father's pocket, and these were necessarily spent with the precision toward maximum results that Meyer himself used in looking into every outlay in his spice business. Long they stood at the candy counter, trying to choose between licorice, sour balls and all-day suckers.

The only note of luxury that crept into the Guggenheim way of life was the fulfillment of Meyer's passionate love of horses, a love bred of the days when his own aching muscles cried out for a beast of burden. By now his business required a stable of horses to draw his spice wagons around the city and into the suburbs. When he needed solitude and a breath of fresh air to solve a perplexing problem he would summarily take over the reins from a driver and himself set out about town on deliveries. On Sundays he would hitch up a favorite mare to the family carriage and trot out toward Roxborough with Barbara and the girls.

His love of the open country found expression, in congested Philadelphia, in flowers cultivated about his house. These he watched with eagle eye, not only for their beauty, but to see to it that all buds snipped off were duly accounted for in vases on the family table.

The spice business was running along comfortably in 1871. A carefully built routine had relieved Meyer of drudgery. His curious soul felt uneasy. The unusual calm was a signal to him, not of approaching danger, but that he was not driving his faculties to their utmost. There was more money to be made, but not in spices. In this unexciting field, he had about reached the limits of his market. Merchants as vigorous as he, and with greater capital, bounded him toward New York and Baltimore. The profits, while substantial, could never place him on a high pinnacle of business life and he could not be satisfied with less. He was now forty-four, in the prime of life, with boys approaching the threshold of manhood and business.

It was about this time that an uncle of Barbara's in Switzerland started a factory for embroidering by machine. Until then the finer scalloped edgings had to be done by hand and were very expensive. Uncle Myers wrote Meyer that he had produced too much for sale in Europe that year and was sending him a consignment of goods, billed at a small advance over the cost, in the hope that his nephew could find an American market for it.

The spice merchant was perplexed. He knew nothing of embroidery, beyond the fact that inordinate quantities were being used on the undergarments of stylish ladies. He dropped in on his old friend, Abraham Goldsmith, for consultation. Goldsmith, cloth merchant, had his clerks look up the principal outlets. Samples, accompanied by glowing letters on the merits of the new machine process, went out to the trade. Claflin, the largest firm in New York, took the entire consignment, at a handsome profit to Guggenheim, and asked for more.

Meyer was all alertness. This business, though, would require frequent crossing of the ocean, and the ninety days he had spent on a small sailboat between Hamburg and Philadelphia had given him all he wanted of that. The boys, smart as they were, could not take the responsibility in their teens. There was Morris Pulaski, an ambitious young fellow: he proved that when he rushed out of the spice business because he feared the Guggenheim boys would be favored there. Still, he was reasonable . . . he showed that when he came back. Meyer had danced at his wedding a year ago at the big Dreyfus house, where the handsome young man married Lena, daughter of another of Meyer's partners. On that occasion the hook that held the bridegroom's boiled shirt down came undone and Meyer, ruddy and beaming, hurled sallies that belied the dignity of his mutton chop whiskers. Seriously, now, he reflected that young Pulaski was eager to better his position and would work hard.

Meyer invited him to join in the new venture and they formed the partnership of Guggenheim and Pulaski, Meyer putting up most of the money. Meyer was all the more willing to shoulder the financial burden in the partnership because he was worried about his growing sons. In the spice business he could see little to stretch their abilities. Driving a wagon might be a useful apprenticeship, but what could lie beyond that? Just a humdrum life, a modicum of respectability, satisfaction at a lower level than Meyer's curiosity and ambition could tolerate. Isaac had left school at seventeen to work in his uncle's wholesale grocery business and was about to go on the road as a commercial traveler. The other boys, with the possible exception of Dan, the second in line, seemed all too content to fall into an acceptable routine. Dan was a shrewd youth who already showed an ability to look down a row of possibilities and size up the right one. But one and all they hated school, particularly Philadelphia high school, which condemned them to classical studies having nothing to do with business.

When Pulaski sailed for Switzerland, to line up the new enterprise, Dan went with him, to finish up his education, acquire a working knowledge of German and look into the lace and embroidery business. The boy, only seventeen, did all three jobs with relish. Murry and Sol, too young yet to be of much use to the firm, begged nevertheless to be sent abroad, to finish school at least. Meyer approved of their impatience; he liked his children to see the world and knock off their prejudices. In due time Sol was placed in the Institute Concordia at Zurich, a strict and efficient school, and Murry went to St. Gall, the embroidery center, to help his brother Dan hold the fort when Pulaski was in America. Soon a New York office was opened. There were a number of factories at St. Gall which worked on commission for Guggenheim and Pulaski, and later another one in Pfauen, Saxony.

Orders poured in and the boys often had to work a ten-hour day. On Sundays, however, Sol and later Ben and other American friends would come over from the Institute and they would all hike up some lovely mountain trail, with an inn at the top like all well-regulated Swiss Alps, where Dan and Murry would treat the eager schoolboys to a delicious dinner. They also enjoyed the Continental theater occasionally.

The only mystery in the new business was why the dainty embroidery and cut work—rows and rows of which had to adorn ladies' pantalets, petticoats and summer dresses— were called "Hamburg edgings." There is a rumor that when a big customer in America asked Dan where they came from that wily youth answered "Hamburg" to throw him off the scent and maintain the Guggenheim primacy. In any case, "Hamburg edgings" they remained: in 1887 Wannamaker's was still boasting "dainty Hamburgs white and colored—new cases broken in every day."

This enterprise left seven children at home, Jeannette, Ben, Simon, Robert, William, Cora and Rose. That divided the Guggenheim brothers even more sharply into two sets, the older and younger. Then active young Robert fell off a horse and died soon after of what is believed to have been a ruptured appendix. The first real sadness in their healthy lives, the untimely death drew the younger brothers closer together.

Meyer paid passing attention to these three boys; theirs was not the rigorous training that had gone into the first four. As for the girls—well, they didn't count for much in the Guggenheim plans. Boys were important.

Meyer found the new business such a gold mine that he wondered why there were not more firms in it. In time others did enter this field, but Guggenheim and Pulaski was first and held its lead. Profits rolled in. The Guggenheims moved across that line down the middle of North Sixteenth Street that divided the wealthy from the well-to-do. The younger boys had to restrain themselves from war whoops as they carried the furniture triumphantly over to the west side. Meyer bought a new horse and a fine surrey. He was one of the few Jews of Philadelphia to possess such a thing, and loved to drive his friends out for a treat.

3. GREATEST BONANZA IN THE MOUNTAINS

A SLIGHT MAN, stoop-shouldered, frock-coated, stood on the main street of Leadville in 1881, watching the unbelievable stream of life that boiled around him. Motionless he stood, absorbed; only his brown dundreary whiskers waved to the sharp blasts from the 14,000-foot Continental Divide.

Meyer Guggenheim shook his head, amazed at the wildest, most disorderly sight he had ever experienced. And yet civilization had made great strides in Leadville since 1878, the year silver was discovered in a dying gold camp. The board walks, for instance, three feet above the muddy street . . . Progress! Dozens of two- and three-story buildings, and new mirrored bars. Even a few churches.

Singing incoherently with a crowd of friends, a six-footer in a ten-gallon hat and chaps lurched against the little figure in the bowler and long black frock coat. "Pardon, Señor," roared the giant with exaggerated courtesy. "Come along and have a drink." Guggenheim smiled politely and shook his head. "Hey, maybe you think I can't set 'em up till tomorrow morning? Maybe you think I didn't sell my claim? Look at that!" He shook a bag in front of Meyer's nose. "Ten thousand duros! Yassirree!" and he gave a wild whoop. His tones were loud and clear, and so many bystanders surged around him to accept the invitation that Meyer was forgotten. Wincing as the big fellow drew his gun and took three shots at the moon, Meyer crooked his arm around a hitching post and held his ground, until his part of the block became relatively empty as the crowd drained into the "Bucket of Blood."

42

But it was only for a moment. New hundreds strode, sauntered, staggered down Harrison Avenue, pushed each other off the boardwalk into the muddy roadway, sang, shouted, cursed, roared with laughter, elbowed their way through the milling crowds into overburdened barrooms, gaming dens, sporting-houses; shoved on sullenly toward work, from work, to mines, to shacks, to bare little cubicles in clapboard boarding-houses to sink into a bed warm from the previous occupant. The sidewalk was too small for the people, and the street was too small for the endless riders and the wagons which seemed to be always in a hurry with their crackling whips and panting, stumbling horses. For once Meyer's self-assurance was jolted.

Other gentlemen in frock coats, buffeted by the swarming horde of rough-clad miners, made their way as best they might to their destinations, but Meyer Guggenheim clung fascinated to his hitching post, watching astonishing creatures, old men, young men, occasionally a highly painted woman, flicker past him in the pale glow of lamplight from saloons, cafés, and hotels. An unseemly waste of time, this loitering by a sedate Philadelphia merchant on fantastic Harrison Avenue, but the Cloud City did stranger things than that to men.

Other fabulous camps there have been in the fitful history of Western mining, before and since, but none quite matched the mad days when a washed-out gold town found itself turned into the greatest silver city on the face of the globe. No other camp ever produced so many millionaires per square mile of magic sand and rock or catapulted so many adventurers into high positions in the United States Senate and the Governor's mansion. A good-natured, shiftless grocer within six months found himself, without benefit of even shovel or pick, wealthiest man in Leadville, its mayor, and a year later lieutenant-governor of Colorado. Miners who could neither read nor write sold their interests in shafts for hundreds or hundreds of thousands of dollars and lived to see ten million dollar Wall Street corporations straddled over their former property. Thousands came who could not have told the difference between country rock and a-thousand-dollar-a-ton ore, took a chance, and a few struck it rich. Restless spirits poured in from all America and Leadville became, for a time, the biggest city in Colorado while Mayor H. A. W. Tabor grandiosely offered a mountain top, free of charge, for a site for the yet undetermined State Capitol. Politicians came hat in hand from the lowlands of Denver, Colorado Springs, and Pueblo to offer U. S. Senatorships and other favors in return for cash.

And all the while that tide of humanity swept up and down Leadville's main street, at all hours of night and day, for the camp could never quit, even for an hour, its mad digging for the silver and lead under its world-famed Carbonate Belt. Midnight was as busy as noon and the theaters —spaces cleared in the backs of saloons—were open until six in the morning, with table service unflagging. Some of these places had balconies divided into private booths, with curtains that could be drawn when the spirit moved. Sudden-rich Leadvillers were particular about their culture, too: the best was none too good for the Cloud City. Even the premier danseuse of the Metropolitan Opera Company of New York climbed the mountains by stage-coach to perform for the wild men who paid so lavishly.

Outside, wagonloads of ore rumbled by at all hours, bound from the mines up in California Gulch down to the smelters, whose all-pervading smudge dimmed the city in broad daylight.

Meyer reached for his pipe, one familiar object in a crazy world. A little white-haired fellow, face deep-carved by sun and wind, asked him for a light.

"Lively town you got here," muttered Guggenheim.

"Oh, it's right quiet now, stranger," drawled the old man.

"Wait till a bit later in the evening, and the bullets will begin to fly. My nephew keeps a saloon down yonder . . . buries fifteen or twenty every Saturday night. He never knows half their names, just digs a hole and covers up the box." The old man spat into the mud three feet below.

"Well, good evening, guess I'll be going along," murmured Meyer.

Was there a glint in the old man's eye? After all, though, it didn't hurt to be careful in a strange town.

Exhausted in mind and body, he pushed and caromed his way as best he could among the hulking bull-whackers up a side street toward his boarding-house.

And now what? At the window of a notorious brothel sat a girl in a rocking chair, demure in her little house-cap, knitting. On the wall was a motto twined with pink flowers and green leaves: "Home sweet home."

Meyer's soundless lips formed words and he trudged on to his lodgings. He slept uneasily and was up at dawn. His friend and fellow-Philadelphian, Charles Graham, was already seated at the long table in the dining-room. Graham was a big man with a white beard, refined and distinguished. A Quaker from Germantown, he had a most worldly flair for speculation, and a will many younger men might envy. A wave of ill-fortune had broken on him after the Civil War, rolled him spinning into failure . . . and here he was back on silver mines, the trickiest bronchos a man ever tried to ride.

"What a place," mumbled Meyer, half in awe, half in disgust. "God help you if there is no million dollars in that mine. For no other reason could you ever get me here to such a place." Graham guffawed and Meyer smiled wryly while the housekeeper slammed down ham and eggs and coffee, grand staples of Leadville's breakfast.

An hour later they were climbing into a precarious straddle cart, which pitted its two high wheels against the pool-pocked road that led to the mines. Within ten minutes they were on the frayed outskirts of the town. In the honest light of early morning Meyer could see the reality of the Cloud City, the towering Saguache range to the left that directed waters to both the Atlantic and the Pacific, and the lower but still snow-capped Mosquito Range to the right. Below them lay Leadville, a few ornate three-storied structures standing out of a plateau of two-story, false-fronted frame stores, bars and rooming-houses, and a flatland of thousands of miners' shacks. These were the characteristic buildings of the boom city, thrown together from rough-hewn boards or logs, that housed twenty thousand miners, laborers and teamsters. A wood stove, a table, some cooking utensils—frying pan, tin plates, tin cups and cutlery—and as many cots and straw-strewn bunks as the remaining space could absorb were the typical furnishings. Here and there a curtain, to betray the presence in camp of hardy women who followed their menfolks even into this godforsaken end of the world; but there were few children to be seen.

The straddle cart careened past the first mine, up the hillside. Hoisting engines groaned as cables snapped taut under their burden of rock. A weather-beaten shed housed the engine and shaft, a lean-to served as office and sampling shed—a typical mining property whose owner by now perhaps disdained Leadville for the velvet splendors of the Windsor in Denver or the effete comforts of Chicago. Behind these buildings, or alongside, or almost completely surrounding them was a growing hill of mine refuse.

Meyer was in famed California Gulch. Here, in 1860, Abe Lee had panned gold from the Arkansas River. "Damn me," legend reports Abe, "there's more gold in this gulch than in all Californy." Whereupon the Gulch was named, and its golden sands poured into the Washington Treasury to keep the Union armies in the field. Oro City, cabin and shack town, flourished, then declined after the richest of the

46

sands had been panned and miners went off to South Park and over the Divide through Tennessee Pass, seeking pay dirt.

Billy Stevens and A. G. Wood formed the Oro Mining Ditch and Fluming Company in 1875 to sluice the sands and gravel of California Gulch for remaining gold. They found some, but Billy cursed at the heavy sand that clogged his sluice box and made it hard to get the gold through. Wood, a metallurgist of sorts, sent some of the stuff to St. Louis for assay. It was silver-lead carbonate, assaying as high as four hundred dollars to the ton. Stevens and Wood followed the sands to veins farther up the gulch on the hillsides, located a mine and later sold out to Levi Z. Leiter of Chicago. First of the million-dollar fortunes to come out of California Gulch, he founded a dynasty that interlocked with British nobility and vied with the grain barons in the Chicago pit.

The discovery of silver ended the poor man's sway in Colorado's mining camps. The gold miner needed only his pan, sourdough, and the physique of a Missouri mule. A silver mine required capital. Five years after the discovery of silver in the Gulch, Leadville saw the first of those savage capital-labor wars that were to range up and down the Rockies, adding chapters, yet unwritten, of heroism, desperation, violence, of cold, calculating brutality, to the annals of American labor history.

Colorado's gold never turned a miner into a millionaire. By the dint of his own labor, he could never hope to pan that much by himself and before he could wash out enough gold dust to turn capitalist, the gravel had been exhausted of its values. Nor could he hire others to work for him. Who wanted to work for wages when there was more gold up the creek? Silver was different.

"There's the Little Pittsburgh," roared Graham, flicking his whip toward some sheds up the hillside, and shouting above the hubbub of the bull-whackers as they lashed and cursed their teams. "That's Mayor Tabor's mine and now he's a millionaire and Lieutenant-Governor. He grubstaked a couple of Germans. They're gone now, but Tabor and Dave Moffat, his partner, are rich and Moffat's building a railroad into Leadville."

"Up yonder is the Chrysolite, another Tabor mine. He bought it from Chicken Bill for a thousand dollars. Joke was Chicken Bill had dug a shaft and found nothing. He 'salted' it—scattered some real ore from another diggings over the bottom of his shaft and laughed like hell when Tabor, the grocery store man, handed over ten hundred-dollar bills for it. Then Tabor went deeper and took out fifty thousand dollars worth of silver a month."

Tabor's partner in Chrysolite was Marshall Field, one-time partner of Levi Leiter. When the partners sold out for $1,200,000 (Marshall Field's investment was $500), Wall Street interests capitalized the new company at $10,000,000 and cleaned up, not so much on the silver in the Chrysolite as in the gold that changed hands for stock certificates.

Two ore wagons had collided on a narrow, muddy stretch and Graham adroitly maneuvered his cart on the shoulder of the road. Forty feet below foamed the yellow flood of the Arkansas. Looking up the stream, Meyer saw gold-panners bending, in hip boots, over the gravels of a bar. "Not much there," said Graham. "They're lucky to get a few dollars a day now. But they're their own bosses." The wagons had been disentangled to the yelling and cursing of teamsters whose bedlam of godlessness shocked Meyer's sober ears.

"There's the A. Y.," sang out his companion as they turned a bend. Meyer peered in the direction of the whip, but there was nothing to distinguish the A. Y. from other diggings in the Gulch. Another motley collection of sheds

48

and loading platforms. As they drove nearer, it became obvious that this mine was different; there was less turmoil and confusion. As a matter of fact it was barely operating. The shaft was down seventy feet or so, but the water came in faster than the wheezy pump could suck it out. A few men loitered about the building, expectantly, for the announced inspection of the mine by one Mr. Guggenheim, of Philadelphia.

"What next?" one of the loiterers inquired, aiming his remark at the sky and the gleaming Rockies. "Even the sheenies are coming in now. This camp's about done for."

Meyer jumped off the cart, his frock coat sailing up around his ears. "Here she is," announced Graham, waving his hand vaguely up the hillside. Meyer looked up the steep side of Iron Hill and tried to calculate how far a claim of 1,400 feet might extend. He entered the dim shed, looked at the old hoisting engine and the ancient pump. He peered down the blackness of the shaft.

"Well, there's a hole there, anyway," he observed, drily. So much he had to show for his money. A hole in the ground a few miles away from the crest of the Rockies. This was how one made millions in Colorado?

The hoist had been raised to the surface. The surface man hauled a car, sopping wet with rock, off the platform.

"Want to go down, Mr. Graham?" asked Supt. Sam Harsh nodding at a pile of rubber coats and boots in the corner and two bruised hats. The shaft was dripping wet from melting snow. "We'll drop you in the ore bucket."

"No, thanks," exclaimed white-bearded Graham. "Walk the tight-rope on that scaffolding down there? No. But maybe Mr. Guggenheim would like a look. He's never been in a mine." He glanced down at the younger man.

"No, no," answered Guggenheim. "For what? What can I see there? No, this is enough. I know there is a mine here. More I cannot know."

And so the cable uncoiled and the ore bucket dropped away without them, down, down, down. Meyer felt a sinking feeling as he watched. Graham shouted, then tossed a small chunk of rock into the inky recesses. They heard a splash. "That's the trouble with this mine. But the new pump will fix that," he explained.

On the way back to Leadville, Meyer chewed reflectively on his mustache. The rest of the day he spent with Graham and his figures on the costs of new engines, equipment, estimates on payroll. And all for what? He munched on the end of his pencil and muttered: "What a damned fool I may be. $25,000, and not a penny more. Ach, what a gamble is this! But must engines cost so much? Why, I can get good men in Philadelphia for a dollar a day. Why so much for these people?"

It all hinged on whether A. Y. Corman, bearded patriarch of California Gulch was right. He said there was a rich vein of silver-lead ore that ought to pass under his claims. Hadn't Uncle Billy Stevens and A. B. Wood traced their heavy sands, their lead carbonate, up the gulch to outcrops on both sides just west of the Colonel Sellers? And there was no denying the Colonel Sellers adjoined his own claims, the A. Y. and Minnie. Corman didn't claim to know much about geology, but it was just inescapable that his mines, as yet undug, were rich.

The A. Y. was the oldest claim in the Carbonate Belt. When the gold flurry was dying out, Corman and a group of miners staked it out on October 20, 1869. That was before there was any such spot on the map as Leadville, before the little smelters poured their black fumes over the valley. Dozens of cabins and shacks in Oro City were boarded up; others had already collapsed under the weight of snow, or in the spring floods; miners were leaving for other gold camps. His partners, too, drifted on but Corman remained, panning a little gold out of the gulch, nothing much, hang-

50

ing on, dispirited, in his little cabin. Year by year he did the assessment work required by the mining law, poking here and digging there. His main shaft went down a few feet a year but it was hard work lining it with timbers and most of the time the water filled his hole. In 1877 Corman relocated the claim in his own name and staked out another, named for his wife, Minnie. It was just a routine matter. No one was interested. Then the great carbonate discoveries were made. Corman hung on.

One day in 1879, a Philadelphian appeared in camp, Charles H. Graham. He had a few thousands to invest. Associated with him were George F. Work, a fellow-Philadelphian, and some Leadville miners on whom he relied, as he knew nothing about mines. They dug up A. Y. Corman, oldest resident of California Gulch and showed interest in his A. Y. and Minnie. They offered him a few thousand.

Corman recoiled in indignation. "Not a penny less than $25,000," said he. "It's sheer robbery at that price." Graham's associates had a good laugh out of that and suggested that now they talk business. They knew that the fellow owed everybody in Leadville, but principally the grocer. Merchants had vowed not to extend another cent of credit to the shiftless creature up the gulch. There was plenty of work in Leadville; but Corman preferred to putter around the creek with his pan, or cheer his flagging spirits in Leadville saloons rather than pay up his honest debts.

Minnie, who years ago had given up the fight, sat in the corner eying the strangers hopefully. "Don't be a damned fool, Corman," she broke in. "Talk business with those gentlemen." It had been many a long year since Minnie had worn a decent dress.

The miner took $4,000 and signed over the A. Y. and the Minnie.

That night the patriarch of California Gulch—patriarch even though his beard was still black—stood beside the door of his beloved cabin under the bright mountain stars and tears came to his eyes. For ten years he had held on to his claim, hoping great hopes. Some day he would be rich and move to Denver, or perhaps even Chicago, and buy a great house for Minnie and live like many another who had struck it rich. For that he had lived on the verge of starvation.

And here was the end of his hopes . . . $4,000 down in the bank in Leadville. That was the pot at the end of his rainbow. Well, it's more than a lot of other fellows ever managed to get, he reminded himself. He could buy a house down on the flats at Malta, get a new suit and buy some gowns for Minnie. Shrugging his shoulders, he opened the door and went in to plan with the jubilant Minnie on the disposition of his new wealth. She had tucked the boy in bed and was singing an old ballad. Far into the night they talked of their future. At last she would have some decent companionship, an amenity California Gulch lacked. Down at Malta they could live in style, she could entertain respectable women in her home, the boy could go to school. Perhaps her husband could even get a job in the smelters.

Corman died a few years ago, poor as ever, down in the shadow of the Malta smelter owned by Meyer Guggenheim's sons.

Graham bought into the Colonel Sellers and the Ricawill, adjoining claims, sold out to others and had the A. Y. and Minnie free of charge. Now back to Philadelphia went the white-bearded Germantown speculator to get some money.

To Guggenheim he went. Meyer always had ready cash on hand. He had no faith in banks and bankers. He preferred to lend his money personally. It paid more than the banks did, and he considered himself a better judge of loans than bankers, whose grinding of private axes landed their institutions too regularly into financial crashes. Meyer trifled around, too, with stocks and bonds on the Exchange. He found it more exciting than the embroidery business, and far more profitable. What with loans and speculations, backed by his solid interest in his merchandising, Guggenheim was a rising capitalist. He listened to Graham and smiled over his lamb chop. "A silver mine it is now? And you should want me to sink my good money down one of those things?"

Leadville silver mines were all the rage in the East. The dazzling rise to glory of H. A. W. Tabor in one short year had become a legend; and there were dozens of Tabors up in the Cloud City; and hundreds of Tabor-like mines that would pay as soon as the shafts had been sunk. The glittering prospectuses littered the wastebaskets of judicious investors. And here was another one, another acre of the Colorado Rockies that beckoned Meyer Guggenheim down a silvery road to fortune.

He drew a little package of Tarragona pepper from his pocket and sprinkled the dust over his chop. "Yes, yes, tell me more. We shall all be millionaires, but how much will it cost me? And what makes you think that there is silver in this ground of yours? Everybody can't get rich."

The dishes removed, Graham spread his map of California Gulch on the table of the little Philadelphia restaurant. "Here is where the proved vein leads. This mine has been developed and is rich. And this one and this one. See how the vein runs? Well, doesn't my mine stand right over this line, which marks the continuation of the vein? Of course I can't guarantee that it does. We must dig, but was ever money ventured better?"

Meyer passed his napkin over his carefully parted whiskers, folded the napkin neatly, and said: "If the mine is as good as you say it is, I won't lend you a penny. But I will take a partnership."

And that was the start of my finish, thought Meyer ruefully as the stage-coach bumped him down the mountain from Leadville. Not much he had tied up at first, but all these engines and expenses! Yet without them, how would he ever know if riches lay below?

Back in Philadelphia, friends noticed a slight nervousness in the generally confident Guggenheim. He was used to stretching his sinews in the market, making money by his own judgment every day. Mining was different. All he could do was sit and wait. Wonderful stories about Leadville appeared in the papers. From Harsh, however, all he got was a long rambling letter: this had gone wrong, that had been more expensive than planned. But next month looks like we'll hit it. All we need is a little more money.

Meyer dropped into his friend Goldsmith's store. "You're a lucky man," he cried. "You have more sense than to put money in Colorado mines. Look at this," waving Harsh's latest report. " 'Send me another thousand'! What does he think Meyer Guggenheim is made out of—dollar bills sprouting out of the pockets?"

"And the thousand dollars?" asked Goldsmith.

"Yes, I know. I suppose I must send him the thousand. But, believe me, this is the last thousand. You can take all your Colorado silver mines. It's just throwing good money after bad."

Guggenheim's temper did not improve as sweltering August came upon Philadelphia. He went perfunctorily about his tasks in the embroidery company. Once he was in New York to see how Isaac, now married and in charge of the office, was getting along. But there was little for him to do in the affairs of Guggenheim and Pulaski. The junior partner was over in Switzerland supervising business affairs and keeping an eye on Dan and Murry's progress in the business. Orders came in at good prices without much trouble. Even up in Leadville, Meyer noted with some little grim satisfaction, a merchant was stocking up on some Guggenheim and Pulaski embroideries. "And that's about

54

all I'll get out of Leadville," he muttered as he spread his handkerchief across his face, mopping up the sweat.

That was the trouble with the Leadville business: there was nothing Meyer could do about it. It was just a matter of extending money and hoping for the best, trusting that the manager was honest.

A messenger entered the office. "A telegram for Mr. Guggenheim."

Meyer went over to the counter and took it. What bad news is that, he grumbled as he slit the envelope carefully. He opened the paper:

RICH STRIKE FIFTEEN OUNCES SILVER SIXTY PERCENT LEAD HARSH

The telegram fell to the desk. Slowly Meyer reached into his back pocket and produced his handkerchief again. A little dazed he bent over to re-read the announcement.

FIFTEEN OUNCES SILVER

He grabbed for a pencil. $19.35, read his notation. In every ton of rock $19.35 worth of silver. To say nothing of the lead.

Meyer Guggenheim was a millionaire!

Not that he believed it. The figure couldn't be believed. Why, at that rate, the A. Y. was the richest mine in the Rockies. When he got the equipment, a mere 50 tons a day would mean $1,000 in silver. That was beyond Graham's wildest calculations. Perhaps it was just one of those crazy pockets he had heard of. As soon as they got out of that spot they'd be back in lean ore.

He waited impatiently for Harsh's reports, which began to come in more frequently. The lead content was fluctuating, sometimes as low as 20 per cent. But occasionally the silver jumped to 30 ounces a ton, the assay and smelter reports showed. Looks like we can pay expenses from now

55

on, wrote Harsh, if we can just get a better pump and keep the water out, so that we can produce in quantity.

Meyer sent him some more money and heaved a sigh of relief. Then all work stopped in the first strike in Leadville. The sudden prosperity of tuppeny-hapenny Colorado capitalists—whose investments consisted of grubstakes to starving miners or a few thousand dollar bills dangled under the eyes of a drunken digger—did not please Eastern financial interests. This was no way to make money, or rather the wrong people were making it. The proper way was to float companies. In that way the Eastern financiers could cut in on the silvery wealth of the Rockies. After three or four years' operations, the rich carbonate vein was being exhausted and Leadville was wondering just what it could hang on for future prosperity. The "second contact" of rich sulfide ore was still unknown.

A fire was engineered in the bottom of the Chrysolite. With the Chrysolite ruined, the stocks on the New York and Denver Mining Exchanges would be depressed, and the financial ring could step in and grab them up cheap. But the fire was not a complete success. Fortunately for the Wall Street bears, the Leadville operators played into their hands. The Denver and Rio Grande and the Denver and South Park had just shoved narrow gauge lines into the camp. Where the stage coaches had brought dozens of job-seekers each day, the railroads brought hundreds. Soon Leadville was overrun by destitute men. An auspicious time to cut wages. Silver was higher than ever but that did not stop the operators. They met at the Clarendon—Sam Harsh, the A. Y. manager, among them—and voted to post a $2.75 scale for the 12-hour shift. Wages for common labor had run between $3 and $5 a day, with more for experienced men. The Miners Union, whose organization the year before had marked the end of the golden days and the coming of millionaire and proletarian into the new silver camps, indignantly rejected the cut. They pointed to the owners' profits, so great that they stirred the whole nation to envy. The strike deadlocked: the editor of the leading daily whipped up frenzy for a "law and order" committee. Tabor called out his Light Cavalry to protect the mines while the older Wolf Tone Guards, made up almost entirely of miners, protected the union halls. A great parade of miners, marching silently and with folded arms, filled Harrison Avenue. The Law and Order Committee combed saloons, incoming trains, and dives for a counter-parade whose rear was brought up by a hundred girls conscripted from the sporting-houses. When no issue seemed likely from the protracted test of strength, Governor Pitkin found occasion to leave the state and Lieutenant-Governor Tabor ordered in the troops. The strike was broken; thousands of miners in disgust left for other camps. But old Haw Tabor who had grubstaked many a miner without hope of reward in the old days of Oro City, could no longer saunter down Harrison Avenue, hailing miners by their first names. He was a capitalist now, hated. The golden days were gone and grim industrialism was pressing in.

The strike vexed Meyer. He wanted to get on with the exploration work, to find out what lay beneath the surface of the A. Y. He could see no rhyme or reason to men rejecting $2.75 a day; in Philadelphia that was a good wage for an experienced mechanic, and the Leadville men were mere pick and shovel men. He backed up Manager Harsh and congratulated himself on his good judgment in sticking with the operators for the new scale. Workingmen always got the wages they deserved and efforts by these new-fangled unions that were appearing here and there were a menace to a man's solvency. Say what they pleased about the millionaire operators, he was none. The A. Y. was just an expense to him, and a dubious one at that.

Meanwhile water filled all the mines of the district. Meyer's hopeful A. Y. did not produce at all the first six months of 1881. How he must have chewed his nails! A millionaire he was . . . maybe . . . and nothing to show for it. Was that man Harsh as honest as he looked? Surely there had been smelter statements, though he had to take it on faith what that rigmarole meant. But even if the ore was good, who could tell how much was down there? Not Meyer. He had not even taken the giddy drop in the bucket to look at his property. Couldn't an unscrupulous superintendent "salt" a mine, just like Chicken Bill, in order to keep his job going on and on?

Graham was more experienced in those things, but Meyer had heard whispers along Third Street that his Iowa Gulch Mining Co. was not all it was cracked up to be. Mines! The best thing to do was keep his funds turning over as fast as he could in other businesses and forget it. But how can an ambitious man forget something that may either bring him millions or cost him thousands? Cool though Guggenheim was, he found more and more uphill dreams diluting his slumber. Barbara's forbearance was taxed by his temper that summer, and the youngsters got a taste of the old-time discipline.

Worst of all were the days when the inevitable letters came asking for more money. He would wrestle with himself, think it round and about, and finally send it off: "Might as well be hung for a sheep as for a lamb!"

September came, and another letter from Leadville. His fingers shook with annoyance as he opened it. "The A. Y. is producing ten tons a day now and this is paying expenses. I hope to have a good sized checks for you and Mr. Graham next month." Well! At last!

All the hopes he had repressed for months seized him and his impatience was immense. If ten tons a day, why not fifty? Why not take in a thousand dollars a day? Something must be done, at once!

Meyer Guggenheim was off for Leadville, and with him, infected by his enthusiasm, were friends who had also put money into holes in the ground after the A. Y. showed its quality the year before.

Few noticed him in Leadville because few knew his connection with the mine. The lone Jew among the operators, Meyer had no relish for notoriety, for fulsome stories headed, "Leadville's Newest Silver King," or to be pointed out on the streets and gawked at. But back in Philadelphia, to the financial reporters, he had grown overnight in stature. As he returned from the Cloud City, he was interviewed. He told how "he and another gentleman bought the mine for about $4,000," and "his individual profits during September were exactly $17,231.52, or over 800 percent on his original investment."

"Is your mine for sale, Mr. Guggenheim?" asked the reporter.

"No, sir, the mine is not for sale," he answered with some asperity. "I would not sell my share for half a million cash money. I have made a thorough investigation of the property and if what the geologists tell me is true, we could get three or four millions cash money out of the mine. I think it is better to work such a property myself than to form a company."

"If his luck continues," concluded the newspaper, "Mr. Guggenheim will soon rank as a genuine Bonanza King."

Bonanza King, indeed! Meyer grunted as he finished the story. But a swift picture passed before him. Only thirty-three years before he had landed in America, penniless. He had packed a knapsack to get his foot on the first rung of the ladder to success. He had worked hard but he felt no need to gloat. After all it was luck that dumped the A. Y. in his lap. He had been blessed: a good wife like Barbara who had presented him seven good boys, good health, a good country, that had given him every opportunity.

59

Bonanza King! The title didn't seem to fit the stooped shoulders of the little man who walked with a perceptible limp, reminder of early peddling days. But Meyer liked it anyway.

"Barbara, let us have a grand party. All our friends, to celebrate the good news. Invite them all, and see that we have plenty of wine and oysters."

When the mail got back to Leadville and local papers reblazoned the interview, laconic Manager Harsh rushed into print to explain that the $17,231.52 was the total gross proceeds of the mine up to October 1, 1881. Had Guggenheim's exuberance run away with him or was Harsh beset with too eager creditors?

No matter. Within six months the A. Y. was yielding $2,000 worth of silver a day.

The reputation of the A. Y. and Minnie spread through the West. Legend had it that from one stope $1,000,000 in pure silver was extracted. More plausible is the report that that stope gave up $181,000 in pure silver, deposited through the ages in fissures of the rock, and gathering in bird's nest formation, soft like feathers. No smelter was needed for such discoveries, they went straight to the mint. Meyer brought home a bunch of it, so resilient that he jigged while he drew it in and out, accordion-like. His friends shook their heads in amazement: old Guggenheim, whom they had known for years, was making $1,500 a day and the only exertion it required was his signature on the checks.

Leadville papers were hard put to it to describe the beauties of the A. Y. and its companion mine, the Minnie. The *Herald-Democrat* chanted:

Of the endurance of the magical foundation which Leadville awoke to find beneath its giant cradle, of the fullness of the breast from which she was nourished in infancy and of the permanency of those vaults from which she has derived her parentage amid a wave of tumultuous, if not riotous, approval, she has no better assurances to offer than those which are exposed in the massive blocks of mineral, those pyramids of ore that stand like glistening rows of tenements upon the various levels of the A. Y. and Minnie in California Gulch. . . . At this day there is no greater bonanza in the mountains.

By 1887 it was estimated that 9,000,000 ounces of silver and 86,000 tons of lead had come from the vitals of the two mines. In the next two years $1,383,000 had been realized clear, of which 1889 accounted for $617,000. Two miners in a single 12-hour shift pulled down enough ore to pay the mine's expenses for a day. And there were 130 men at the works, in mine and mill.

The *Herald-Democrat*, statistician of the camp, calculated that the Minnie alone held $11,000,000 in silver and lead, worth a clear $5,000,000. The Minnie, with the older A.Y., was still valued in 1890 at $14,556,000. All of which, by that time, belonged to Meyer Guggenheim alone.

Ten thousand tales embroidered themselves upon Leadville's tangled, hectic history, to the dismay of the present-day recorder of its fantastic past. Fact and fable mingled everywhere, and above all in the story of how a Philadelphia merchant became owner of Leadville's richest mines.

Old Philadelphia friends, intimate with Meyer and his sons as far back at the spice epoch, declare that he took the A. Y. and Minnie for a bad debt of five to six thousand dollars. They even quote the debtor's words: "Guggy, I'll never be able to pay you. I've got a share in a silver mine—don't believe it's any good. But take it—maybe it's better than nothing." And Guggenheim, they say, took it, uncomplaining; he was bluff and unpolished but he had a good heart.

"That's what we always heard in the family," a granddaughter agreed. Similar stories were told in the magazines early in the century about a friend "caught in the sudden panic in 1881." Alas for this last version, Guggenheim had been in on the mine since 1880. T. A. Rickard, honored historian of American mining, declared the Philadelphian was "an involuntary participant in the mine," having lent five thousand to A. J. Graham (his first name really was Charles) who in turn lent it to Harsh and Carey, owners. When they failed Guggenheim and Graham became owners.

Meyer's sons in the great offices of Guggenheim Brothers on Broadway—Murry, Solomon and Simon—are equally emphatic now that their father chose the mine as an investment. Sam Harsh, needing capital, asked Graham to sell for him and keep a half interest. Graham lacked capital and asked Guggenheim for a loan but he said he preferred to take a share. They gave him a third and he paid "between ten and twenty-five thousand for it and had to advance a hundred thousand before it was any good." Son William states a different version: that Graham and Meyer each put twenty-five thousand into the mine, as fifty-fifty partners. Son Benjamin's story, as quoted thirty years after the event in a magazine article, is a compromise between the bad debt and the purchase versions and placed Ben at the center of the story. A merchant in Leadville failed to pay a bill to Meyer and Ben was sent there to find out why. The merchant had an option on a share of the A. Y. and Minnie for five thousand dollars and offered it to Meyer for twenty-five hundred. Ben reported favorably and so Meyer came out to check up. Leadvillians saw a tenderfoot with a thick accent, hailed him as an easy mark, a sheep wool-laden. Intoxicated with the wealth of Leadville, Meyer found himself paying the merchant twenty-five hundred instead of collecting a bill. When he got home, runs this apocryphal story, Meyer promised each of his seven sons that they would be millionaires. Benjamin went down with the Titanic in 1912 and his story went with him.

The fact that Guggenheim had once been a peddler preyed on the imagination of local citizens through the years until now you can find a number of old men in Leadville who "saw him here with a pack on his back selling lace." A fine occupation in 1881 for the head of a big importing business with offices in Philadelphia, New York and Switzerland! Or they saw "Si and Benny selling lace curtains here in 1878." Lace curtains were undoubtedly just what Leadville needed in 1878! Unfortunately this fact was ignored by the thousands of people who kept moving into this incredible camp, ten thousand feet high, which had been all but deserted the year before. Water was five dollars a barrel. Candles were a quarter apiece and had to be ordered a week ahead. A man was glad to find any corner to flop in: building was far behind population and lumber was a hundred dollars a thousand feet. Beds were in constant use in three shifts and one lodging house had three tiers of bunks—"lowers reserved for Governors and Mayors," said Landlord Agnew jovially. Lucky was the newcomer who could find a chair for himself in a saloon for a night; scores were glad to sleep on the floors. Two mail lines and twenty-five six-horse coaches came in each day, besides the hacks and freight wagons. They were but a drop to the mighty thirst of Leadville's thousands for goods, and only the most vital needs could be imported. The mere checking of baggage cost a dollar, unless you could persuade the baggage man you were a better shot than he and meant to prove it. It took several days hard driving to get up from Denver. A few who had already cashed in on the wealth of the mountains could have paid for lace curtains. But their minds were on other things.

It was hard to see how all Leadville's merchants combined could have run up such a bill for unneeded lace in a rough

63

mining camp that Meyer would have been justified in sending Ben two thousand miles to check up on it. And anyway Ben was only fourteen years old in 1879 and Simon was twelve.

Another tale had Meyer buying the mine from his brother-in-law. All these versions cancel each other out. And Meyer, unmindful that fifty years hence men would want to know exactly how the greatest mineral fortune in all history got its start, never sat down to write the official version.

4. SMELTERS PAY BETTER THAN BANKS

MEYER FROWNED and tapped his pencil softly on the desk. Another confounded smelter statement! Look at those penalties slapped on the A. Y. and Minnie's zinc sulphide ores! What was he in business for? To hand over profits to a set of greedy smelter owners who had stationed themselves astride Colorado's ores? There were millions in mining, it was true—if you had luck. But in smelting all one needed to do was fly the jolly roger and levy toll.

The owner of the A. Y. and Minnie was not a lone voice. Every operator cursed the greed of the smelter magnates who skimmed the cream off their ores. Beggary lurked around the corner, they complained bitterly as they ordered another round at the bar, watched the wheel spin in the gaming-house, or gambled in back rooms at the Vendome. Meyer never joined this bitter chorus, but then the Vendome never saw him, except for some business engagement and that was quickly dispatched in low-voiced conversation.

The observer might have charged Guggenheim with snapping at the heels of Fortune for complaining about his smelter statements. His two mines were the greatest in all the Rockies. But he was not the kind to be easily content with some profit, when more profit lay within grasp. He believed in driving profit possibilities to the limit. Anything else was sheer laziness, a violation of the spirit of enterprise, an acquiescence in complacency. What if his actual take out of Leadville was a quarter of a million a year? If smelter charges were reasonable, he would net a third of a million instead of a quarter. Further, his mines grew poorer each year and some day would be gutted of their rich silver and lead. This smelter business would stand some looking into, he concluded, for at least two good reasons.

By this time Meyer was greeted in the Cloud City with no little respect and some envy. "There goes the Jew Guggenheim," citizens would inform newcomers. "Damned smart fellow. Struck it rich and means to hang on to it. No foolishness there."

Amazing legends grew up about him. He was a wealthy Jew from Holland. He was a Philadelphia merchant who had gone broke and had come to Leadville to invest his last five hundred on a forlorn hope. He was a dupe whom clever tricksters had set upon, but what they thought an empty gold brick turned out to be solid silver. His first trip to Leadville had been as an itinerant seller of laces and embroidery.

The legends attested Guggenheim's taciturnity. Aside from his mine manager, and the small Jewish community, there was not a person in all Leadville who had more than a bowing acquaintance with him and a "Good morning, Mr. Guggenheim" to say. He mixed not at all in the business or civic life of the community, and permitted his manager power to represent him in the Operators Association. Although not a pious man, he was glad enough, in that strange and frenzied city, to drop in occasionally in the little synagogue on a back street, for the feel of familiar ways and a bit of business gossip. Its architect had grand ideas; obviously he conceived a structure in stone and brick, with rounded pillars and curved domes, but alas, had nothing but straight boards to work with.

In only one quarter was Guggenheim's name mentioned without awe. In miners' cabins you could hear harsh words about the owner of the A. Y. and Minnie. You could hear just as bad or worse about the other operators, so even here Guggenheim held no special distinction in Leadville. A class war was being waged between the propertied few and the

66

MEYER GUGGENHEIM AND HIS SEVEN SONS

working many and in Colorado mining camps it was fought at all times, bitterly and without much mercy. The owners were represented solidly in their Operators Association, a one hundred per cent closed shop union. The miners tried desperately to maintain their own union, but what with the "card system" and blacklists, they had varying fortune.

In the golden age of Oro City, a miner threw up his cabin wherever he pleased on the mountainside. The gulches leading up from Leadville were spotted with shacks on which no rent was ever asked. It was a man's privilege, there in the Colorado mountains in the days of gold, to live where he pleased, ask no man's permission, and defend his cabin, if need be, with his gun. There, by the towering peaks of the Rockies, it seemed presumptuous to insist on real estate claims. Meyer thought it highly irregular but he fell in with the custom of the country, anxious not to give offense.

But the time came when the tailings from the A. Y. and Minnie mill threatened to overflow the low crib over the road. Cribs must be built farther up the hillside. The miners were ordered to leave their shacks. When they refused, Meyer Guggenheim's name did not appear in the court case of "Charles H. Graham et al." filed for writ of possession in ejectment. Graham "et al." won their writs but the sheriff of Lake County was none too eager to serve them. He could see no reason for unseemly haste, just to please some mine owners. Anyway, miners cast more votes than operators.

Among those who stood their ground was Mike Winters, who claimed a plot twelve by twenty feet on the Minnie claim. Writs availing not, Mine Manager Thomas L. Weir and a crew of his stalwarts boldly advanced on the shack and "forcibly and violently entered into and upon said premises and ejected the plaintiff therefrom and cut, broke, tore down and entirely destroyed said dwelling house." For which Winters asked restitution, $1,500 damages and cost of suit. Rucker and Ewing, Guggenheim's attorneys, answered "ambiguous, uncertain, and unintelligible" and asked removal of the case to federal court because Guggenheim and Graham were not citizens of Colorado. A useful subterfuge, of which Guggenheim availed himself repeatedly. The state courts were sufficient unto his needs to bring suits against others, but he declined to enter as defendant outside the pale of federal district court. It was unlikely that mere miners with limited resources could afford the expense of a Denver or Pueblo trial, and few ever pursued him that far. In like fashion Guggenheim shifted into federal court a claim for $6,989 by the contractor who built the Minnie mill.

In fine handwriting, with many a flourish and scroll, the records of Lake County courthouse also relate the bitter fight Guggenheim waged against what he considered avaricious extortion practiced on him by the county commissioners, sitting as the board of tax equalization. They presumed to boost the valuation on his mines from $20,000 to $68,500 each. True, the mines turned in a profit of $683,000 that year and two years later were to be valued, not for tax purposes, at some $14,000,000. But Meyer stood on his rights: if the machinery and equipment were worth a penny over $20,000, he challenged the board to produce the buyer. Nevertheless a tax of $5,821 was levied on him. To Meyer it seemed that the commissioners were merely greedy politicians seeking what they could devour. He had no protection from Lake County: when he wanted to reclaim property rightly his, he had to rely on his own armed men to dispossess squatters. As for public improvements—well, the less said of that the better. The only public improvement he knew of was the road up California Gulch and that was kept passable only because the operators took care of it.

Meyer was in no special category in Leadville because he fought doggedly for his rights. No operator acted otherwise. Boomers all they were, in godforsaken Leadville only as long as the silver held out: after that, who knew? Already there were "ghost towns" in the mountains above Denver, camps which had no silver after the gold rush had petered out. Each operator for himself and a community of interests only when a common front was needed against the miners, the railroads, the smelters. Get while the getting was good, then get out.

Railroad rates . . . that was another subject which angered Meyer every time he thought of it. No one knew just what a rate was: it could change overnight, it was always too high, there was caprice and favoritism, cars could be denied, and an operator brought to his knees pleading for transportation at any price. He had Weir bring the subject up in the Leadville Operators Association. They entered suit in the courts against the discrimination which was "strangling" Leadville and ruining the camp. The case dragged along and after a while was forgotten when some new menace touched the operators' pocket nerve.

Guggenheim had some satisfaction from private concessions wrung from the railroads, and turned to the smelter problem. With Weir's aid, he managed to interpret the mysteries of the complicated schedules. The straight smelter charge was not, in itself, exorbitant, Meyer admitted. But what were these damned penalties for treating his rebellious ores? An even sorer point was the arbitrary price paid for silver and lead. Meyer pondered that curiously. The gold, silver, lead, copper and zinc you handed over to the smelter, imprisoned in rock and sand, was yours. And yet after the smelter extracted your metal from your rock, you had no power whatsoever over the product of your own mine. You could not haul away your silver and gold and lead. The smelter claimed possession, paid you its price and proceeded to market the metal. It made one profit on the business of smelting, and another, highly speculative, on selling metal. Then, too, your ore might contain appreciable copper

69

values, considerable zinc and other minerals. But the settlement sheet failed to mention them; indeed might even heap additional penalties and deductions on you because of their presence.

The small mine operator took the smelter's word for it as to whether his ore ran rich or lean in silver and lead. Larger mines had their own agents in the smelter's assay office and when disputes arose, both sides agreed on an umpire whose word was final. But the operators swore that the smelters owned the "empires" body and soul.

It was all a hopeless mystery to Meyer. The secrets bound in the bosom of Mother Earth and in the fiery crucibles were not for him to fathom. As a matter of fact, few of the metallurgists even knew how to handle the tricky Leadville ores. The first smelter in the West had been built only a few years before in Leadville by Captain Nathaniel P. Hill. Others followed quickly, but their methods were so crude that only the cream of the ores paid a profit. Years later mill tailings and smelter dumps were to be worked over, to the rich profit of concessionaires who availed themselves of new techniques.

If Meyer, in his late fifties, could not hope to pierce the complex secrets of his zinky ores, he was not a bit abashed. He had seven sons, and their peculiar usefulness was to serve as his instruments in building the foundation for the House of Guggenheim. The four older boys, whom he had established in Guggenheim & Pulaski, were now all living in New York, whither Meyer had packed Barbara in 1888, closing the Philadelphia chapter in the family's history.

Barbara was lonely in the new house up on West Seventy-seventh Street. Isaac, Dan, and Murry were married and had their own homes in New York; Jeannette, her oldest daughter, had died in childbirth; Cora and Rose were both in Paris at a Catholic convent school, being "finished"; Simon was in Spain, studying and tasting the delights of

70

Continental life; Ben was in Leadville serving as his father's ears and eyes at the A.Y. and Minnie; Will was a student at the University of Pennsylvania. Sol lived with his mother, and she took Jeannette's little girl-baby to her heart. Murry had a gate cut through from his West Seventy-sixth Street home to connect with the back of his mother's house.

The four older boys fitted nicely into grooves which led them to mix in the upper circles of New York Jewish society, go abroad regularly with the seasons, move freely through the cultivated international freemasonry of Jewry. No mere upstarts they in business, but men who had been launched on commercial life as able sons of a now wealthy father who had spared nothing in their education. They watched their father with a mixture of admiration, awe and concern as he plunged into Colorado mining, gambled successfully on the Exchange and refused doggedly to fit into the grooves they found so acceptable. In merchandising, they followed a way of life which was part of their racial heritage; the strange business out West interested them only as a tour de force in which their father showed his versatile courage. At best though it could only be a flash in the pan. Like all mines, the A. Y. and Minnie some day would be gutted, deserted, a mournful reminder of the millions that had been blasted from the earth's interior. But the demand for embroidery and laces could be served forever by the firm of M. Guggenheim's Sons, which had succeeded Guggenheim and Pulaski.

So Meyer used his younger sons to serve him in the West. Ben, the oldest of these, entered Columbia in 1882, the first that Meyer had been able to entice into academic life. Meyer deflected his interests to metallurgy. In the summer he was out in Leadville, clerking, peering into the depths of mining, visiting smelters to check his theoretical training against practice. He did not finish at Columbia. Impatient of the folderol, he persuaded Meyer to let him go West and plunge into practical mining and metallurgy on his own.

71

For Ben it was a great lark, not only to escape Columbia but the stuffy offices of his older brothers in downtown New York. Prosy embroidery indeed, when life beckoned in the great Rockies where millions were to be made with the greatest fun!

Simon whittled his father out of the university notion, went to business school, studied and polished in Spain, and headed for Leadville. Will, youngest of the boys, was the only eager college student. He entered the University of Pennsylvania in 1885. He loved oratory, the theater, and aimed at becoming a Philadelphia lawyer. But his father had little love for eloquence for its own sake, and Will switched to the Wharton School of Business and Finance for a while, sheering over later into metallurgy when the head of the House of Guggenheim had reached another critical decision in his life.

Edward R. Holden was the man who helped Guggenheim make his decision. He was a born promoter who tired of running an assay office in Leadville. In 1886 he persuaded C. B. Kountze, the Omaha banker, and Dennis Sheedy, Irish-born pioneer in western wagon-trading, who sold his 32,000 head of cattle to buy control of the Colorado National Bank in Denver, to finance the West's biggest smelter. Even so Holden was not happy. The smelter bore his name, but he was only a minority stockholder. So he was gracious to the unimposing little scion of the House of Guggenheim whenever Ben was in Denver. Ben had free run of the smelter, was wined and dined at the Windsor, and gained the impression that Holden's genius plus his father's money would mean a new era in western smelting and a solution to the woes of A. Y. and Minnie.

These views, as Holden had hoped, were sent east. Meyer was interested. He cared little for Holden's ambitions, much for an insight into the mystical recesses of the smelting business. Undoubtedly it was Holden's smelter which was robbing him of a good share of the wealth of his mines. As there seemed to be no escape from that, why not go into this business and join the merry pirates who battened off honest operators? Meyer cautiously inserted $80,000 into the Holden smelter and insisted that Ben have a job there. The job itself was inconsequential—$100 a month or so—but he instructed his son to keep his eyes open and report regularly. As for Meyer, he studied the financial statements of the Holden Smelting and Refining Company with undisguised interest.

He broached his plans to the older boys. He was looking now down the broad avenue of the years, to the time when he would no longer be a factor in the House of Guggenheim. The fast-growing West, with its untold mineral resources, seemed to him an invitation to adventure and wealth. Why shouldn't the firm of M. Guggenheim's Sons be extended into this profitable field? There were millions out there in mining and smelting waiting to be plucked by a firm which could introduce efficient business methods into the slipshod, haphazard industry which had just grown, Topsy-like, under the guidance of itinerant metallurgists and ignorant capitalists. M. Guggenheim's Sons should expand to enter this business and admit the three younger brothers, who were to be the operating heads of this new activity.

It might seem unfair to the older boys, he admitted. But he wanted all his seven sons on an equal footing in the family's undertakings. If some were too young now, well, some day the situation would be reversed and the older brothers would be relying on the younger. And at this point shrewd Meyer Guggenheim strummed another string. There was not only equality of the brothers to be considered, but harmony among the sisters-in-law. Inequality would gall them more than their husbands; if one sister-in-law saw another with something that she could not buy—well, Meyer wouldn't give much for the harmony of such a family group. As his clinching point he cited Aesop's fable of the bundle of sticks. If they were separate, they could easily be broken, but if all seven stuck together, no power could break them, and in smelting they might lead the world.

The members of M. Guggenheim's Sons were aghast. Enter an unknown, speculative, uncertain business two thousand miles from the well-worn grooves of New York? Admit three youngsters, one of whom was still in university, into a partnership which they had done nothing to enrich? Risk all their assets in an undertaking which could absorb millions and wreck the partnership?

A wild scheme. Their father would have to admit that the A. Y. and Minnie venture was a lucky break. Had he not invested in other mines that were merely holes in the ground? Had not friends in Philadelphia, excited by his fantastic somersault into millions, staked their own thousands in mines that had returned them only heartaches, broken fortunes, and disaster? Why should he not be content with this one fortunate adventure into the unknown West, invest his money, and be satisfied? Now he was wealthy but catastrophe could overtake not only him but the partnership and plunge them all into ruin.

Isaac, in particular, objected to the proposal to admit the younger boys into the partnership on equal shares. As the senior partner, he felt that the youngsters might well serve the tutelage in business which he had undergone before hoping to share and share alike. After all they could bring neither experience nor capital to the partnership.

Meyer sat silent during this avalanche of expostulation and dire foreboding. Yes, he reflected bitterly to himself, if they had started out peddling, they would still be peddling, competently, efficiently, but still—peddling. He himself had formed the partnership of M. Guggenheim's Sons, had bought out Pulaski's interest and turned the entire business over to the boys. He was not a member of the firm although his was the only name in it. To himself he had reserved the right of moral leadership. Anxious to be rid of the details of a business which had become humdrum, he had installed the boys in full charge when Isaac was twenty-eight, schooled and tested in business, Dan twenty-six, and the others finished with their schooling abroad and thoroughly acquainted with embroidery.

Meyer had bigger fish to fry, and far more lively. In 1882 the A. Y. was pouring its silvery profits into his lap, the Minnie was being developed, he was shuttling from Philadelphia to New York, Denver and Leadville, and worrying about how to keep the A. Y.'s profits turning over satisfactorily. He had little patience with banks and so-called securities. Life was a game, played with dollars and human beings. If you got the right combination, the returns made the sober 4 per cent on tested securities seem not worth while. Much better to size up a man, entrust him with $10,000, enjoy 10 per cent and the satisfaction that you had helped him and vindicated your own judgment. Much better, too, to keep an eye on the market and gamble sagely.

That had been his practice for years. An early example was the corner in Hannibal and St. Joseph common stock in the fall of 1881. This Missouri railroad in the sixties had held a practical monopoly in traffic through its territory to Kansas City. It was a pretty little road that rewarded its Boston promoters up to their expectations. But in the seventies when other roads were built across Missouri, the Hannibal and St. Jo failed to hold its own. Dividends were passed monotonously and the common descended to 22⅞ on the Stock Exchange in 1880. A crowd of New Yorkers, engineered by the astute Elihu Root, got control. Jay Gould, building up his railroad empire, decided that the St. Jo would come in handy as a link for the Wabash and the Union Pacific, and went out to buy up control. Guggenheim, who followed railroad shares with a hawk-like eye, quietly laid in 2,000 shares at $42.

A dazed Stock Exchange watched St. Jo shoot up September 6, 1881, from 96 to 130 and 150 and then leap on succeeding days to 200 and 225. The newspapers cried out against the merciless operation, which was reducing the shorts to beggary. *The Commercial and Financial Chronicle,* staid oracle, could not suppress its surprise and quiet indignation. "Corners," it commented, "have not been in vogue for the past ten years or so. We believed that consolidations and watering were more in fashion." It quoted the more respectable brokers as deploring such tactics among the railroad kings. Meyer watched the struggle between the two groups, and sat tight. As the stock rose, brokers besieged Meyer for his shares. He only smiled and shook his head. Russell Sage, it was rumored September 7, was short 8,000 shares and had to draw a check for $750,000 to settle the account. Total losses to bears, all big New York financiers, were estimated at $2,500,000. But Meyer handed his shares over at $200 on September 8 with a fine glow of satisfaction. Wild rumors got about among Philadelphia friends that the Leadville Silver King had engineered the corner by himself. It was true that he had made nearly a third of a million by holding out till near the top, but the corner was not of his designing.

This and later speculations he conducted on his own account. He drew no profits from M. Guggenheim's Sons. Occasionally he borrowed from his sons' partnership, at 6 per cent, and more frequently he lent them money, at the same figure. By 1887, his reserves had far outgrown the limit that his sons could profitably use and, truth to tell, were greater than Meyer's own strength to invest at what he considered an inviting return. He was approaching sixty and felt it tiring to be scrutinizing the stock market day by day, interviewing borrowers, tracing down credit ratings. He was eager to tie his money up in a new enterprise that his sons could manage and extend.

Meyer bridled his impatience at his sons' timorousness. Eagerly he sketched to them his picture of America developing, of vast fortunes yet to be accumulated, of whole industries to be brought under the sway of the capitalist.

"And you?" he asked reproachfully. "You wish forever to be respectable lace importers? Very fine! But who wants to sell lace forever? Who will ever hear of the Guggenheim brothers?

"My boys, I can see great things coming in this country. Watch those railroad men! They are taking little railroads and tying them together. The little roads fight each other and nobody makes much money. They join, and there's millions, and you hear of Vanderbilt, Fisk, Gould, men of many, many millions. The time is coming in this fine country of ours when all these businesses will be big. Either big, or nothing at all. You will be gobbled up there, in your little business. America is growing. You must grow with it. Forget about your little laces. Many years ago I carried a few yards of lace with me up and down Pennsylvania and New Jersey, selling a little here, a little there. I saved money, I forgot about peddling and went into a bigger business. Ever since I have gone into bigger businesses. And now I intend to go into the biggest business of all. Maybe it will cost me a million dollars. And what is a million in a country like this? Nothing!

"Don't be satisfied so easily. You are living nice, you are doing well. And you are satisfied. Why? Don't you see there are millions to be made? You shall all be great men, not little merchants. Don't think your father is becoming a fool because his hair is turning white. I have studied this business, I know it will succeed."

They agreed. The old business of M. Guggenheim's Sons would be kept separate; the younger brothers would be admitted when they showed their responsibility; but in the new smelter they would share equally, and Meyer would finance that himself and take the loss, if there was a loss.

That decided, Meyer was off for Denver to see Holden and start work on the new smelter. Holden bubbled over. Unbeatable game, this smelter business. The smelter works day and night, while you sleep and while you're in church, and all the time the gold and silver pours out of the furnaces. Better than the banking business, because you deal with money itself, in the raw. The ore rolls in, and the money with it. The Denver Smelting Company, with $500,-000 capital was incorporated in January, 1888. Meyer, Holden and Ben were in daily consultation, Simon was up in Leadville representing the family and Will had hastily changed his curriculum at the University of Pennsylvania from business to metallurgy.

Denver, Leadville, Pueblo were canvassed as smelter sites. Denver was too far from coal, coke and lime supplies. Leadville suffered too much from high railroad rates, high labor costs and lack of balanced ore supply. Pueblo looked better. The ore from Leadville and Cripple Creek could roll down to Pueblo, at the foot of the mountains. Pueblo was on through lines east and west, north and south. The ores of the Southwest and Mexico could be hauled there.

Pueblo agreed enthusiastically. The town, hemmed in between mountain and parched plain, was in the throes of a boom to establish itself as the smelting capital of the West. Without smelters, it was only a railroad junction and a dream in the mind of the boomer.

Holden was polite but mentioned that Denver was being considered seriously. "Denver?" cried all honest Pueblans, in high indignation. Denver indeed! All Colorado hated Denver, and Pueblo claimed highest hate honors. Denver was the great leech that sucked Colorado's life blood: if a man made money anywhere in those mountains, he was off to Denver to enjoy it, to invest it, to add to Denver's luster. And all the while cities far better located (in the eyes of their own boosters) languished because selfish Denver must have the Capitol, must have the wealth, the pomp and the glory. And by what right did Denver think it was also the smelting capital of Colorado? Pueblo would show its rival some civic spirit.

Mr. Holden's next trip to Pueblo was a grand affair. The Policemen's Band tootled with all its might as the train rolled into the station and Mr. Holden alighted, derby in hand, his face wreathed in smiles. The mayor, the board of county commissioners, the bankers and merchants and real estate boomers were there to greet him. Up the street swung the parade, marching for the greater glory of Pueblo.

All the town's notables turned out at the Opera House March 29, 1888. Two bands were on hand, so the music might flow without interruption. The local chorus sang a new song to "Marching Through Georgia" in which Holden and golden were ringing rhymes. Speeches galore, eloquence without end, a few modest remarks by Mr. Holden himself.

The great moment was at hand: collection of the $25,000 fund which was to bring the Holden smelter to Pueblo. "Please accept my $100," announced the mayor. "And who'll be next?" cried the chairman, "next in this great enterprise to make Pueblo's position as the smelting center of our great Western country unassailable for all time. Who will be next?"

"Governor Adams wishes to subscribe $500. Three cheers for the Governor! Another $500? Thank you! And another, and another!"

The band blared, the citizens cheered, the chairman reached for dizzier heights of adulation for the great Mr. Holden, and the money poured in. Volunteers were asked to canvass every block of the city, and dozens of eager hands shot up. Glowing with civic pride, the citizenry retired to their homes happy in the thought of a fine day's work. Canvassers pressed the good work, and not only $25,000 but a free site down on the flats a little distance from town was obtained for the new smelter. The city council, in special meeting, waived all taxes for the next ten years, and the county commissioners matched them. Edward R. Holden was the hero of Pueblo. None noticed the little fellow who accompanied him here and there. All big men had secretaries. This secretary happened to be Ben Guggenheim. As for old Meyer, he was nowhere to be seen. He didn't care much for public acclaim, and as for the $25,000, well you couldn't build much of a smelter with that. Yet he couldn't deny being pleased by the cordial reception given his company.

Except for one feature, which Holden mentioned quietly. The Pueblans didn't care much for the name, Denver Smelting Company. Hadn't they better change it? "One city's as good as another," answered Meyer. "We'll call it the Philadelphia."

While the six-stack smelter was going up, the Opera House burned down. One good turn deserving another, the Philadelphia Smelting and Refining Company donated $3,500 to its rebuilding and subscribed generously to the Board of Trade, which had engineered the $25,000 gift to the smelter. A cyclone swept over Pennsylvania, and the Philadelphia, Pueblo and Colorado smelters each donated a 50-ounce silver brick, to be auctioned off in the stock exchanges in Philadelphia, New York and Pittsburgh for the benefit of the sufferers.

The smelter was scheduled to start October 1, 1888, but there were embarrassing delays with the furnaces, houses had to be built for employees, and it was decided, midway, to add extra stacks. Once the smelter got into operation, the amount of silver and lead recovered from the ore fell far below expectation. There were appalling losses, as much as

80

$50,000 a month, and the more the Philadelphia smelted, the more it lost.

At that point stories vary. One is that Meyer didn't like the idea of paying royalties on the orthodox types of smelting apparatus. Wasn't there some way to short-circuit these royalties? The smelter superintendent, according to this version, was a mechanical engineer innocent of much metallurgical experience. A new type of hearthless furnace was devised. The melted metal and slag were run outside the furnace into a large pot with partitions. The heavy lead sank to the bottom and passed under the partition where it could be dipped out readily. But the furnaces "froze" and the new process led to heavy losses of metal in the slag.

The superintendent had another story to tell. The trouble was too much Meyer and Benny. "Wherever I turned," he related plaintively over his whiskey in later years, "there was a Guggy in the way. I feel nagged now every time I think of it. If we had ever been able to put all their ideas into practice, you'd have had a smelter that looked like something in the funny papers."

Ben defended the new-fangled furnaces in an emphatic letter to the *Engineering and Mining Journal*, oracle of the industry. He denied that the foundations of the fine, spacious engine room were sagging already, and that the company had been loaded up with contracts for refractory ores that other smelters wouldn't take. Nevertheless it seemed for a while as if the Philadelphia smelter would go down in history as Guggenheim's Folly. The brothers in New York were appalled. Meyer himself was abashed. He capitulated on the royalty question and ordered orthodox equipment. The furnaces began to work satisfactorily, and then the price of silver tumbled from $1.30 an ounce to $.93. Meyer hadn't foreseen that the Baring Brothers Bank in London would get into trouble and that metals, most sensitive of commodities, would register the international distress.

There was a somber meeting in New York around the big council table of M. Guggenheim's Sons. Meyer conceded things weren't going any too well. Holden apparently wasn't much of a smelter man, Meyer had concluded, and let him go. The promoter, who joined the former superintendent in feeling that there were "too many Guggies" under foot, was glad to pull out with a little profit from a venture that promised only disaster. So "multifarious business activities" lured him into a smelter project at Glenwood Springs.

Into the gloom in the Guggenheim council Meyer shot some rays of hope. Silver had hit the bottom. A new superintendent had been secured. It was always to be expected that such a complicated mechanism as a smelter would falter at the start. The older brothers decided to install one of themselves to supervise matters in the West, and Murry was dispatched to Pueblo as president, replacing Holden. Ben was made general manager, not that he was an expert metallurgist, but it was thought better to have someone bearing the family name wielding the authority.

Job's seven plagues were reproduced, smelter-wise, before the Philadelphia swung out of the red. One hole after another was plugged: delayed construction, faulty design, lack of good metallurgists, falling silver prices, badly balanced ore supply, and flighty management. The final coup was a strike which tied up the works in the early fall of 1889. The furnace men in June had asked for an eight-hour shift, claiming that the terrific heat of desert-bound Pueblo compounded with the furnace heat made the twelve-hour shift impossible. Facing the loss of good smelter men to the furnaces up in Leadville, where it was cool in summer, the demand was granted, with an appropriate wage cut. But by September the furnace men decided the eight-hour shift was desirable the year round. The Guggenheims blamed the agitation on a union which had gotten into the works, and protested that many of their employees had been "forced into it by intimidation." After a few weeks' shutdown, the works reopened with the twelve-hour shift victorious.

By this time the doughty Will had received, in 1889, a certificate of proficiency in metallurgy and mining from Pennsylvania and was attached to the smelter as assistant to the superintendent. Will, in the full bloom of his academic metallurgical lore, found fault with the superintendent's conduct of the furnaces, and so the second man to hold that job also quit in high dudgeon, swearing likewise that there were too many Guggies under foot to make life bearable. Up to Leadville he went, to the competing Arkansas Valley smelter, to regale old hands with tales of how a bunch of Jews were trying to run the Philadelphia. They roared with laughter and agreed that it was the funniest incident in all the ups and downs of western smelting.

The Philadelphia nevertheless turned the corner. Will always maintained that it dated from the time that he, a youth of twenty-two, was advanced to be superintendent. Others said it was because the Guggenheims employed August Raht, "prince of lead smelters," to take charge of the furnaces. It was he who devised an economical system of smelting the A. Y. and Minnie's zinky lead ores. He was a graduate of famous Freiberg School of Mines, Europe's outstanding metallurgical institute and the mother of America's early furnace wizards. It was this grave German, with his short clipped white beard and long drooping mustaches, who rescued the Philadelphia and began to turn in profit statements of $50,000 a month to happy old Meyer Guggenheim. Raht was to remain the keystone in the Guggenheim smelting enterprises, the man on whose shoulders rested the destiny of the House of Guggenheim. It gave Meyer a twinge to pay him the price he asked, but it turned out to be one of the best investments that sage speculator ever made and established a guiding principle for the family: that success for capitalists lay in hiring the best brains available, no matter what the price.

Murry, as president, began to spend more of his time supervising smelting finances and less in the embroidery business. He became a director of the American National Bank in Pueblo. Ben, secretary and general manager, joined in promoting a railroad to Silver Cliff to tap new mines. Simon, made vice president, scouted ore up and down the Rockies and found use for his Spanish in Mexico in tying up a good part of the output of the rich Sierra Mojada mines. Capitalization was increased to $1,250,000, six new furnaces and a refinery were built, and the fame of the Philadelphia spread up and down the western mining regions.

A group of English capitalists, scouting the West for good investments, looked over the A. Y. and Minnie mines and the Philadelphia smelter and offered Meyer $4,000,000 spot cash.

"No, thanks," said Meyer. "I'll take $10,000,000, but even then I'm not anxious to sell."

5. DON PORFIRIO'S CONCESSION

A USTED, Ciudadano Gobernador, encarecidamente suplicó se sirva otorgarme la gracia que solicitó."
—Daniel Guggenheim.

This supplication, if turned from Spanish into German, might well have been uttered by Jacob Guggenheim of old in begging a charter for the Lengnau ghetto. Actually it was his descendant asking a Mexican governor for a concession to build a smelter in Monterrey.

To Bernardo Reyes, puissant General and Governor of Nuevo León, Daniel Guggenheim's fine words were formal husks of a juicy concession which could convert his state from a wilderness of mesquite and cactus into a thriving industrial center. Viceroy in all the Mexican states that faced the Rio Bravo, General Reyes was the strong right arm of Porfirio Díaz. As *Jefe de Operaciones* he brought the "iron peace" to rule the wild marches of northern Mexico. With fierce, ungloved hand he put down banditry, silenced the stirrings of rival *políticos*, nipped audacious revolts against the serene person of President Díaz.

Not content was he to rule over a starved desert land and unnourishing mountain wilderness, to act the role of strutting despot over an impoverished region. The sand and barren rock and scraggly brush were the unpromising lid to northern Mexico's treasure chest, that lay deep in the earth. Given tranquillity, these hills would yield their wealth, Nuevo León and its bedraggled capital, Monterrey, would become rich and mighty, and he, General Bernardo Reyes, would hold the power and the purse strings.

To the American railroad men he gave right of way, placing his mounted *rurales* at their service, impressing reluctant peasants into the toiling army that laid mile after mile of tracks across the hot, parched plains and the rugged mountains. Following the railroad came, as Bernardo Reyes had hoped, a vanguard of prospectors who scoured the hills and returned to Monterrey reporting promising veins of silver and lead. Men with money ventured south from San Antonio to seek personal interviews with General Reyes, to gage the tranquillity of which he boasted, to invest, cautiously, in mines which yielded quick and easy returns. The good news of the iron peace and golden profits spread rapidly. By the time the Philadelphia's furnaces were ready for ore in Pueblo, the mines of northern Mexico had become an important factor in the location of the Kansas City Smelting and Refining Company's new smelter at El Paso, on the very border.

One day the operators hailed the advent of the El Paso smelter as a godsend; the next day they were cursing its exorbitant charges—the old familiar pattern of smelter-operator relations. When David Kelly announced at the Foreign Club that he was now agent for the new smelter up in Pueblo, eager mine owners refused to let him buy a drink for a week. Right in the heart of the Kansas City company's territory he picked up contracts for rich Sierra Mojada ores, needed to balance the Guggenheim smelter's ore supply. Long trains of gondolas rumbled and swayed through the El Paso yards, in the shadow of the Kansas City Company's tall stack, and up the Rio Grande bound through New Mexico to the Pueblo smelter.

As for the Guggenheims, all that Holden had ever said about smeltering's golden stairs to affluence had come true, and with a rush. Congress had passed, in 1890, the Sherman Silver Act, boosting the Treasury's purchases from 2,500,-000 ounces a month to 4,500,000. The silver states of the West were wild with jubilation; mining towns closed down all work and celebrated in a burst of enthusiasm that emptied warehouses of whiskey; farmers saw the doom of the Money Trust in the ever broadening stream of silver that poured down from the Rockies to ease the credit situation and usher in the day of cheap money. The price of silver, under the compulsory demands of the Treasury, floated up to $1.25 an ounce.

The Guggenheims were not given to public demonstrations of joy, but in the end it proved that they and their fellow-smelters were the only lasting beneficiaries of Congressional largesse intended for the miner and farmer. As silver boomed they made bigger profits on its sale than its smelting, and the smelting profits were respectable enough.

Meyer sat back in the Philadelphia Company's board meeting, stroking his sideburns, and chuckled as his sons recounted their triumphs in the Rockies. Lace and embroidery now be damned, they cried, as the money fever mounted. Isaac, who stayed close to New York, kept an eye on the old business and the other three members of the firm of M. Guggenheim's Sons occasionally devoted odd moments to it. Dan, second oldest, became field marshal of the new venture, chief planner and eastern head of the smelting firm. Murry, third in line, divided his time between New York and Colorado Springs, which was as close as he cared to live to Pueblo. As president of the smelting company, he supervised the financial end in the West and wielded the authority of the House of Guggenheim in spot decisions. Sol, genial good fellow, was traveling salesman for the Philadelphia's metals, operating out of the New York office. These four, bound together in the M. Guggenheim's Sons partnership, carried the financial responsibility for the smelter.

On the operating end were the younger boys. Ben was in charge of the smelter and its personnel. Simon worked up and down the rocky backbone of the continent, buying ores, leasing mines, acting as western contact man for the Guggenheims. Will was metallurging at Pueblo in between

87

dances, theatricals and inspections of the relative merits of Denver's hot spots and Pueblo's humbler Row.

Meyer had noted the frolicsome tendencies of his younger sons, and proceeded to care for them in the methodical, Continental manner. No telling what messes they might get into! A smart girl, a good time, and some young Guggy might wake up to find himself legally tangled to *her* profit. Meyer had his own idea about marriages worthy of the rising House of Guggenheim: they must unite the name of Guggenheim with that of New York's established families. Why aim low, ever, and particularly in the all-important business of marriage?

No puritan himself, Meyer quietly arranged the business in Pueblo much to the amusement of the town's wiseacres, who noted the family surrey frequently bound for the Row. Ben in keeping with his position as chief of staff of the Pueblo Guggenheims, visited the Opera House with the Madame herself, who, bedizened in his diamonds, blew kisses in all directions to her many customers. At the time it seemed like a prudent investment, but probably old Meyer later on wondered whether his experiment had justified itself.

Across this blissful idyl of life in Pueblo blew a dark cloud from Washington. Congress had responded to the uproar of western mining men against the "flood of peon-labor Mexican ore that threatened to overwhelm the great industry of the Rockies." An embargo was inserted in the new tariff of 1890 that effectively bottled up Mexico's minerals. To the Guggenheims it meant more than loss of lucrative ore contracts; it seriously hampered the operation of the smelter itself. Colorado ores were too "dry," lacking in lead. They created special furnace problems, as Meyer had found out when he read the penalties imposed in the eighties on his A. Y. and Minnie ore.

"But why give up Mexico?" Meyer asked his sons. "Our

government is very foolish. If we can't bring Mexican ore to Pueblo, let us take a smelter to Mexico. I hear there are no smelters there? Very well, Mexico is ours for the taking."

Dan looked at his father quizzically. Another of his wild ideas, no doubt. But his boldest ideas were usually the best. Why not take a look around down there, anyway? Simon had some glancing knowledge of the country. Kelly, their Monterrey agent, was an old hand in the Sierra Madres and even knew useful people in Mexico City.

The discussion was continued into the evening at Meyer's house up on West Seventy-seventh Street. Mother Barbara's face clouded as she heard mention of Mexico. What, go down among those bandits and be shot? Her boys laughed long and loud about that and recounted a tale or two of occurrences north of the Rio Grande. The old lady withdrew, protesting that she wanted to hear no more of such outlandish ideas, and why couldn't the boys and old Meyer stay in New York safe and sound instead of gallivanting around the country and getting into such awful places. Business talk interested her little anyway.

It would be interesting to speculate that on that very evening a conference not so different was under way in Mexico City. Perhaps in another dining room, much more ornate than the rather dowdy one presided over by Mother Guggenheim, distinguished gentlemen discussed, in very fine Spanish save for Creole variations, the problem raised by the action of the American Congress in shutting out Mexican ore. Time aside, it is certain that such discussions proceeded, perhaps at the home of the Secretary for the Promotion (*Fomento*) of Industry. At his table sat lawyers, economists, business men, politicians. It was, in a way, the Supreme Junta of the *Científico* Party—Porfirio Díaz' brain trust. These men had evolved a theory of national progress for Mexico, dependent on Don Porfirio's strong right arm. Given pacification, they held that Mexico's fu-

89

ture depended on foreign capital's creating modern transportation and industry. Some may have seen it as a recrudescence of the ancient Aztec blood sacrifice: the people must suffer that progress may come. The *Científicos* had little tolerance for such philosophizing. The nation could be shaken out of its age-old apathy, indolence, and indifference only by an injection of foreign capital. Then Mexico could join the parade of the modern industrial nations, with capitalists and proletariat. That would also mean luxury and poverty confronted, but the *Científicos* answered that all Mexico was poverty-stricken now. They were practical men, not perfectionists.

It was this group, cashing in on Díaz' law and order, who had enticed timid foreign capital to venture into the land, build railroads, textile factories and mercantile trade. It was this group that considered coldly, scientifically, the new American tariff law locking up Mexico's mineral wealth. To them it seemed a blessing conferred unwittingly by the tariff-greedy American Congress. If now they could entice foreign capital into a domestic smelting industry . . .

At that very time the Guggenheims yearned telepathically for a concession to create a Mexican smelting industry. Colonel Joseph Robertson, who was building a railroad from Monterrey to Tampico, urged Simon to bring his older brothers below the border to see for themselves the wealth that was theirs for the taking. Mine owners begged the Guggenheims to come, to relieve them from the oppressive monopoly of the Kansas City Smelting crowd and their El Paso smelter. Indeed it was by watching the rival Kansas City company that the Guggenheims learned as much as they did about Mexico. The two companies were sole rivals for Mexican ore.

Dan and Murry Guggenheim and Dave Kelly crossed the border bound for Mexico City. On the dusty, monotonous ride across northern Mexico, Dan looked across the barren

plains, dotted by grotesque Joshua-trees, toward the purple
shadows of the western mountains. Did he see there high
stacks which forced plumes of ink across the horizon and
poured silver pesos without end into the vaults of the House
of Guggenheim? The train stopped occasionally at a miserable collection of adobe huts. Women clustered about the
car windows, handing up tamales, tortillas, roast kid. Peasants in rags lounged about the railroad station, the only
presentable building in sight. Otherwise there was no life in
the shimmering town. In more pretentious places a Gran
Hotel Nacional across from the station warned foreigners
that it was far better to endure the miseries of the hot, dusty
train than to venture into primitive caravanseries innocent
of bath, toilet, and running water, overrun by flies, hotels
in whose ample courtyards burros punctured the starry
night with raucous calls.

Stories of bandit outrages seemed unreal to Dan among
a people so apathetic and across a country where desolate
mile after mile passed in empty review. The armed guard
of untidy soldiers in the front coach and the revolvers carried in unobtrusive holsters by trainmen testified to the
contrary. By dawn the train climbed up on the plateau and
Dan felt better about the country. Lofty mountain and
deep valley, cities and towns seen across distant vistas, green
fields in the bottom lands, wiped out his melancholy reflections of the previous afternoon. After all, he thought, and
smiled at the idea, was he not another Hernán Cortés,
come almost alone, to knock on the gates of proud Chapultepec, to demand that the wealth of Mexico be laid at his
feet, a foreigner, who sought only the riches he could wring
from the land?

But one didn't go about getting concessions quite that
way. Dan and his brother were off to see Emeterio de la
Garza, who had handled a few small matters for them already. De la Garza, suave, energetic attorney, enjoyed the

finest connections with the *Científicos* and even passed the time of day occasionally with Don Porfirio himself. He believed in foreign capitalists with all his heart. For hundreds of years his country had wallowed in stagnation, ignorance, disorder. The Mexican people, and particularly the numerically dominant Indian, he held, lacked the initiative ever to lift themselves from their unprogressive ways. The country was poor, frightfully poor, so poor that few ever acquired real capital of the kind that could build railroads, open mines, develop ports. And these few refused flatly to venture their funds in their own country, which they knew to be notoriously unstable. Their liquid funds went abroad to serve a twofold purpose: to supply dependable dividends and to serve as a sea anchor when things got too stormy at home.

Ergo, foreign capital was the savior of Mexico. And he, Emeterio de la Garza, was its adviser, who made the way smooth for its entry. He longed for the day when trains speeding on time from the City to the most distant state would bind the country into a nation, factories pour smoke across the national capital, hundreds of thousands of Indians be wrenched from their agrarian indolence and put to work in establishments owned by Frenchmen, Spaniards, Germans, Englishmen and Americans. That was progress. And an attorney who knew the right people was the indispensable tool of progress, and would die wealthy.

De la Garza speeded on his errand, with all requisite composure and punctilious attention to formality. His message from the Guggenheims to the *Científicos* was not unexpected. In *Científico* circles foreign capitalists were watched with all the eagerness a *zopilote* devotes to a bloated carcass in the fields. The first appearance of Guggenheim agents in Nuevo León, scouting for ore, had been reported to the City. General Reyes' secretaries had forwarded items from time to time. The Guggenheim name may well have

92

been mentioned in *Científico* conclaves. While the Guggenheims were introduced to the floating wonders of the Xochimilco gardens and the dark serpents of Teotihuacán, De la Garza was working in the Secretariats.

Followed conferences, dinners, neatly arranged tête-à-têtes between the distinguished North American *capitalistas*, the functionaries of the government and leading members of the *Científico* group. Machinery was to be imported free of duty—a notable concession—and the silver tax on the smelter's output was waived—an even greater victory. On October 9, 1890, the concession was signed, with many bows, handshakes and eloquently phrased encomiums on the liberal and eminently progressive Government and the far-sighted, enterprising, and most distinguished New Yorkers. Daniel Guggenheim was authorized to undertake *"la exploración y explotación de minas de todo especie y la construcción de tres haciendas metalúrgicas"* either "personally or through one or more companies to be organized in this Republic or abroad."

Daniel enjoyed every minute of his stay in Mexico City. The deference shown him by highest officials of the government contrasted pleasantly with his near-anonymity in New York and with the rough manners of Pueblo. He loved agreeable music, fine wine, the flattering attention of a Creole beauty, cosmopolitan conversation with his host. He and his brothers were no uncouth merchants, no rough miners. In their youth the older brothers and Simon had been schooled abroad, had lived as young gentlemen absorbing culture agreeably, knew Venice, Florence, the Riviera, as well as Paris and Switzerland. As they grew into manhood they became foreign representatives of Guggenheim and Pulaski and were accorded the respectful consideration of Swiss, German, and French merchants. Later they were abroad, sometimes twice a year, as representatives of the importing firm of M. Guggenheim's Sons. In any company they were the courtly gentlemen, at ease with elegance, and thoroughly in tune with the manners of the Mexican aristocracy, with whom they felt more at home than with the business élite of New York City.

As for the Mexican uppercrust, Dan and Murry Guggenheim were something of a surprise. In an American they expected a certain brusqueness, an eagerness to be on with the business, a badly concealed contempt for Mexican business manners. The added touch of Jewishness had not excited any hopes: the city of Mexico was overrun with Jewish merchants of all degrees, from owners of bustling emporiums to peddlers, whom the Spaniards and Creoles despised and taxed to the limit.

Dan left Mexico City triumphantly with his concession from Don Porfirio tucked securely in his bag. Now he and Murry must negotiate with state authorities for local tax concessions. Rivals already intended to build smelters in Monterrey so the Guggenheims went up to Saltillo, beautiful and complacent capital of Coahuila, the state in which lay most of the coveted lead-silver mines. The Governor of Coahuila was in no hurry to have smelter smoke blowing over his somnolent city, still wrapped in the glories of its past as capital of all northern Mexico and Texas. The modern views of the *Científicos* did not impress him, nor did he consider it worth while to shower concessions upon foreigners.

Back to Monterrey went Dan, to negotiate with General Reyes, who had noted the trip up to Saltillo with amusement and had waited, sure of his prey. There were not so many formalities attendant on negotiations in the simple frontier city. General Reyes himself was a man of action, happier on horseback than at a desk, more agreeably entertained on a foray into the mountains than in the tenuous social life in his shabby capital. He and Dan reached a set-

94

tlement quickly. Its terms, proclaimed on Dec. 12, 1890, read:

By virtue of the power conferred upon me by Article 1 of Law No. 8 of the State Congress, dated Nov. 22, 1889, it is decreed:

Article 1: Exemption from all municipal and state taxes is granted Sr. Daniel Guggenheim and the company or companies he may organize, on the capital he may invest in the establishment of a smelter in this city.

Article 2: The concessionaire must complete this plant, to cost not less than 300,000 pesos, within 18 months.

Article 3: In order to guarantee compliance with the provisions of Article 2, the concessionaire must deposit 4,000 pesos in the State Treasury, in a bank or commercial house of this city, or with any competent person, to the satisfaction of the Governor, this amount to be forfeited to the revenues of the State in case the concession is not fulfilled."

Other concessions had already been granted to Joaquin Maiz, a Spaniard, and Samuel Lederer, a Hungarian, for the Nuevo León Smelting, Refining and Manufacturing Company, and to the *Compañía Minera, Fundidora and Afinadora de Monterrey*, with Mexican capital. Dan hastened to organize the *Compañía de la Gran Fundición Nacional Mexicana*—the Great National Mexican Smelter Company.

Dan and Murry dashed off to New York to report to Meyer and consider finances, while Sol was sent to get the construction work started. He and Kelly and Henry Dieffenbach, who had quit his Monterrey agency for the Balbach refinery in Newark, N. J., tied together plots of land in the low country a little beyond Monterrey, found enough water to cool the furnaces—most difficult of smelter jobs in arid

95

Mexico, rode horseback up into the hills to scout ore, shot rattlesnakes without end, slept on mats in adobe huts, ate tortillas for days in their quest. Getting ore was arduous work. Díaz was just pushing through his Congress a law revising the fundamental concept of mineral rights in Latin countries. He proposed that owners of land enjoy the subsoil rights. That resulted in a boom in mining lands, but the competing smelters being built in Monterrey and the powerful Kansas City smelter interests also had their agents scouring Nuevo León, Coahuila, and Durango.

The Yankee invasion poured in on General Reyes' dingy capital. Electric lights, just installed, were the only modern feature of the town. Neither sewers, nor horse cars, nor comfortable hotels were known. A few main streets were cobbled with small boulders: if anything the dusty clouds of the unpaved streets were preferable to the jolting on the paved. But a new hotel was rising near the central plaza; along the railroad corrugated iron sheds, sure sign of advancing industrialism, were being erected. There was even talk of an iron foundry, the first in northern Mexico, and General Reyes fondly hoped that the day would come when he could entice American capital in to tap his great Iron Mountain to create a domestic steel industry.

The *Gran Fundición* arose slowly from the plain. Its stack leaned so badly that workmen refused to go near it until Will Guggenheim, who had been transferred from Pueblo, climbed half way up its interior to still the workmen's fears. The furnaces were ready and a superintendent was needed. Ben and Si recommended that Alfred Geist, their Pueblo metallurgist, be sent down. With a partnership, yes; otherwise no, he answered. Not for wages did he intend to give up family and home to face the hardships of a foreign land.

There was some point to his protest. Van Yngling, the construction engineer, who had been slashed to death with

96

knives as he lay sleeping in his bunk, was an example. The American workers were all for leaving. Sol and Will summoned the police and General Reyes sent out a detachment of troops. Next day he told Sol that four men had been shot. "Were they found guilty?" asked Sol. "Oh, we didn't bother about a trial," answered the General. "They were vagabonds anyway." After that Sol was careful to have a revolver on his belt but he was thankful that he never had to use it.

The question of Geist's partnership was considered by M. Guggenheim's Sons. The answer was "No." To which Meyer echoed, "Let it always be so. The firm must always remain a family partnership. Outsiders can contribute nothing which we cannot buy, and they would drain the profits."

To keep an American staff in Monterrey, Sol and Will found it essential to build comfortable quarters, recreation halls and a sports field. General Reyes was invited to the grand opening, a ball and fiesta in the style of both countries. The Governor of Nuevo León was invited to open the new bowling alley. He had never encountered such a sport before, but with a quick fling he sent the ball thundering down the alley to knock down all ten pins. Amid cheers, General Reyes was invited to throw a second ball but he warily declined to dim his perfect record.

The recreation hall served another purpose: to afford Will Guggenheim scope for his suppressed oratorical ability. He had wanted in his vealy days, to be an actor and then a lawyer. In metallurgy there was no scope for histrionics but Will compensated by calling together his working force frequently and giving them long speeches. The words were soon forgotten but old-timers in the West still recall the curious spectacle of the earnest young smelter manager haranguing his audience on a range of subjects worthy of an encyclopedia.

Wonderingly, Sol and Will ran into the Mexican Indian's

aversion to monotonous toil. Labor in Monterrey was getting twenty-five centavos a day, so gradually the brothers stepped up the pay to a peso. But the higher the wage, the fewer days the Indian worker needed to work to satisfy his meager commercial needs, and the more time he had for delightful leisure in the sunshine. A final concession was a rent-free house to the men who would work twenty-five days a month. Burdened with money, the men, Sol said, gambled their money away on roulette wheels that spun ceaselessly in broad daylight on the streets of Monterrey.

For their own amusement, the brothers dropped in at the Casino, one of Monterrey's few splendors and the center of whatever social life the frontier city boasted. Will became the cynosure, he admitted, of dark eyes but warily avoided the entangling alliances which designing Spanish and Creole fathers plotted for him. The bullring was Monterrey's only other amusement, but its bloody sacrificial rites held little interest after the novelty wore off.

The smelter was but half completed when a wail arose from the throats of Mexican silver producers as they realized the import of the Guggenheim concession. Their plaints ascended to the *Científicos* themselves, in whose ranks were many wealthy silver mine owners, and even penetrated to Chapultepec Palace. All very well it was to encourage foreign capital, but must it mean the ruin of Mexican producers who still stamped silver out of ore with the hooves of mules in the ancient patio process? On such silver, wrung through their slow, wasteful process, the domestic producers paid a 5 per cent mintage tax, but the Guggenheims' base bullion could be exported without a penny of tax.

It was an occasion for astute de la Garza's utmost patience and tact. The concession was suspended; machinery for the smelter reached the border and stayed there. After two months of finagling, the concession was reinstated with a provision that the 5 per cent tax was to be levied on all silver in the Guggenheim base-bullion assaying over 204 ounces to the ton. The machinery was to enter duty-free as stipulated.

Another six months, and the furnaces of the *Gran Fundición Nacional Mexicana* began eating into Sierra Mojada's ore. The first month's profit was reported at sixty thousand dollars. In less than a year all capital expenses had been realized.

Back in New York, old Meyer Guggenheim listened to his seven sons' reports on the operations of the Pueblo and Monterrey smelters, their purchases of mines in Mexico and Colorado, their plans for expansion into copper-smelting at Aguascalientes, their acceptance in the highest sectors of Mexican society. After Dan had finished, he sat wrapped in his own thoughts as he fingered the gold links of his heavy watch chain. At last he looked up.

"My boys, you shall all be millionaires," he said, "millionaires many times over. This is something for which I have hoped for many years. Now I can see no reason why this firm, which I have built, shall not grow and grow. Today we have smelters in Pueblo and Monterrey, and many mines. And why should we not have smelters all over the West? But can we be satisfied with only this? The day is coming when only the most intelligent, the most powerful, can run these businesses. Mark my words, some day there will only be one smelting company in America, and it will be the Guggenheims'.

"I feel that I have done enough. I have told you how to grow. You must never be satisfied. As for me, I think I have done enough. I feel tired with too much work and I want to rest. I have all the money I want, and more. It was not just money that I wanted but to protect my family, to see that they shall be honored and respected as they never were in the Old Country, to see you stand high in America, as high as you please."

99

Meyer kept his desk in the big office where the four brothers kept theirs. Occasionally he came down, to see after personal matters, to talk over new developments with the boys, or just for the love of seeing his business prosper. But in the winter months he and Barbara went to Florida, where he lay for long hours in the sunshine. A few of his old Philadelphia cronies, grown prosperous, were there too, and they talked of the good old times over their beer and pinochle.

Sol and Will bought the Tepezala copper mines in Mexico, superintended the erection of the new *Gran Fundición Central Mexicana* at Aguascalientes while Ben came east to oversee the erection of the Guggenheim refinery in Perth Amboy, New Jersey. The firm was integrated from the mine-mouth to the finished metal. And always in the background stood quiet, modest August Raht, metallurgist par excellence, dragging the Monterrey smelter out of its preliminary tantrums, supervising the delicate processes in the new Perth Amboy refinery, the man on whom all the growing Guggenheim enterprises depended for profitable operation.

Neither M. Guggenheim's Sons nor any of the firm's mines or smelters published financial reports. But mining men who had scoffed at Meyer Guggenheim and his seven sons a scant decade before, changed their tune. They grew respectful toward the Philadelphia–New-York Jewish family which by 1895 was skimming at least a million a year in profits from its mines and smelters.

6. SHAKING DOWN THE SMELTERS TRUST

I T WAS as if the nineteenth and twentieth centuries were conscious, willful entities. The nineteenth century had ordered that in its span of years individual men by free enterprise should build up their own businesses, carrying proudly at their mastheads the names of their proprietors— Guggenheim and Pulaski, M. Guggenheim's Sons. The twentieth century willed otherwise. The names of sturdy individuals and partners were to give way to National, Consolidated, Intercontinental impersonalities—Molochs which devoured the names, doings and accumulations of thousands of petty entrepreneurs. The land, overnight, became too mighty to permit names of mere men to appear in the titles of corporations.

The cleavage between fashions of the nineteenth and twentieth centuries was starkly visible from 1899 to 1901 as New Jersey Chancellors sanctified the appearance of dinosauric agglomerations of capital. Manufacturers threw their factories, names, good will into the cauldron, promoters from Wall Street emptied into it small vials of yeasty, effervescent stuff such as dreams are made on, and solemn-jowled lawyers uttered legalistic incantations. There was a tremendous spluttering, bubbling, boiling, and churning; attendants in witchcraft known as brokers rushed hither and yon with buckets which had caught some of the precious stuff—known in the cant of the Street as "water"—and peddled this to a yawping citizenry.

As if in preparation, the last years of the nineteenth century recorded the downfall of western populism, Bryanism and anti-monopolism, and the rise of the fat complacency of Mark Hanna politics attended by the spread-eagle victory of a pinfeather imperialism over a decrepit Spanish navy. Wall Street, emerging victorious over the menace of sixteen-to-one money, hailed the inauguration of William McKinley as the curtain-raiser for the Twentieth Century Financial Follies.

Lower Manhattan was the stage, the entire nation the audience, and none more interested than western smelter men as they gathered in the heavy opulence of the Brown Palace in Denver to comment on the incredible scenes of this drama. Among them were veterans of the old Leadville carbonate camp, men who had grown up in the hurly-burly of Colorado's pioneer days, who had built smelters and operated them by test and trial, who had themselves developed the black art of metallurgy on the rickety foundations of whatever technical knowledge was at hand, but mostly out of their own costly experience.

Of such caliber was Anton Eilers, dean of American lead smelters, who had changed smelting from "a rule of thumb to an exact science." A native of Nassau, Germany, and a graduate of Goettingen, Eilers spoke and ate German at the mess table in his Pueblo smelter, was a prince of good fellows and one of the few metallurgists who combined shrewd business judgment with technical knowledge. August R. Meyer, who came nearest to being a smelter magnate, headed the powerful Kansas City Smelting and Refining Company, with smelters at El Paso, Argentine, Kansas, and Leadville. A graduate of the famed Freiberg School of Mines in Saxony, he was one of the three founders of Leadville and later a figure in Kansas City realty. James B. Grant, also a Freiberg graduate and one-time governor of Colorado, built one of Leadville's earliest smelters and when it burned down, built another in Denver and later organized the Denver National Bank. Such men as Eilers, Meyer, and Grant were anxious to escape the rugged individualism

102

by which they had risen to fortune, tired of the uncertainties of free enterprise. Eager and envious, they sat watching in the stands while that master of financial legerdemain, H. H. Rogers, killed competition in the mines at Butte with his Amalgamated Copper Trust.

How often these very men had met in the dim recesses of the Denver Club to achieve the same result, and failed! They had had "clearing houses," combines and even the pretentious Smelters Association of Colorado to peg the price of ore. When the Association smashed, early in '95, smelting charges sagged to five to six dollars a ton, against the standard ten. Lone wolf Meyer Guggenheim shed no tears: he placed slight trust in the word of his fellow-smelter men and believed in a fair fight to the finish. Again in November, 1897, the smelter men were meeting in Denver, and the bait of secretaryship was dangled under young William Guggenheim's nose, but he cagily declined. Under a terrific din raised by the Mine Owners Association, foe to the death of these abortive "smelter trusts," the combine collapsed early in 1898 with attractive concessions to the bigger mine operators.

Alas for the weakness of the human spirit and the sordid greed of the mine owners! The smelter men rarely agreed among themselves, and when they did, one or the other would yield to the blandishments of some big ore-shipper. On the occasions when agreements were reached and sealed at the bar of the Brown Palace, the tribunes of the people wrote flaming editorials aimed at the horrid head of the "western smelting trust" which had reared itself over the rim of the Rockies to strike terror into the hearts of all honest mine owners.

Wherever old-timers gather now in the West to chin about times gone by, you hear the story of how the Guggenheims outsmarted the Smelters Association of Colorado and still kept within the bounds of their agreement. All the

Colorado smelters had agreed to divide the market amicably. None abided more scrupulously by the bargain than did the Philadelphia smelter. But when the time grew near to renew the agreement, Ben and Simon Guggenheim bowed themselves out of the picture. They would go it alone next year. With this blow to the Smelters Association, the other companies sent their buyers out pell-mell to sign contracts for ore.

"Sorry, but I'm signed up with the Guggenheims," answered the men with the best ores. Rivals cursed the "Guggies" but the Philadelphia turned in its million or more profit that year to M. Guggenheim's Sons.

It was apparent to Eastern observers, and particularly to H. H. Rogers, "piston rod of the Standard Oil engine" and genius of Amalgamated Copper, that these wild sons of the Rockies could not achieve that "perfect and permanent harmony" which Elbert H. Gary held to be the shining goal of business enterprise. They were a bit too primitive, these mountain men. It would need the slick hand of an Eastern co-ordinator to bring order to the troubled gold-silver-lead industry.

Many slick hands reached out. All during the winter of 1898-99 these hands manipulated the smelter men, dangling glittering prizes before their fascinated eyes, urging upon them the surer beauties inherent in 7 per cent preferred stock, the fearful prospect of continued competition.

The Easterners needed no credentials, least of all Henry H. Rogers, the Fairhaven, Massachusetts, grocery boy who had pioneered in oil refining in Brooklyn with Charles Pratt and had thrown his business in with the Rockefellers in 1874. With William Rockefeller, Rogers had become the financial dictator of that empire of oil millions that seemed destined, at one time, to buy up the entire United States.

Envious silver-lead mine owners and smelter men alike had watched in amazement his manipulation of Butte and

Boston, Boston and Montana, and Anaconda, to build up the $75,000,000 Amalgamated Copper Company, first of the great trusts of the McKinley period. Loud was the outcry when he paid $37,000,000 for the Butte copper mines and then floated Amalgamated. "Ruthless watering," economists cried; "Unconscionable," editorialists said of his quick $38,000,000 profit. That fazed Rogers not at all. He was the perfect fashion plate for a Wall Street dramatic villain. Tall, handsome, distinguished in manner, he was cold as steel to the world; to his intimates, a delightful raconteur with hypnotic charm of personality. Smashing banks and foes to grab control of Boston's utilities, he showed an intuitive regard—a generation ahead of his time—for the possibilities of gas and electricity, and forged the New York Consolidated Gas. Not forgetful of humble origin, he showered gifts on Fairhaven which still catch the eye of Cape Cod-bound autoists, and he provided the old whaling town with an industrial backbone in Atlas Tack.

The idea of a silver-lead monopoly to back up his copper trust appealed to Henry Rogers, and his hands were heavy with Standard Oil profits. He called in the Lewisohn brothers, who sold his copper in the London market and had a bowing acquaintance with the western smelter men. Armed with preliminary data, he summoned Grant Schley, only brother-in-law of formidable George F. Baker of First National, and John Moore, the Western Union and Chase National magnate. These two, operating as Moore and Schley, were known as the market's most astute "movers," the confidants of the Havemeyers, Rockefellers, Morgan, and Whitney in their devious maneuvers. Moore was about to cover himself with glory among his masters by getting the federal income tax law declared unconstitutional.

Moore and Schley obtained the co-operation of E. W. Nash, who had risen from a bookkeeper to be president of the Omaha smelter, and Barton Sewell, whose interest in smelters dated from the time he bought jewelers' sweepings, refined them in a tiny crucible, and sold the gold and silver to dentists. Nash and Sewell spent the winter of 1898 leading fellow-smelter men into temptation. Eagerly tempted, they found it necessary to visit New York to gain a truer perspective on the evils of monopoly. They were even led into the presence of the great Rogers, who added to his fund of amusing anecdotes stories of the jealousies and bickerings among these mountain men as they listed reasons why a $250,000 smelter was worth at least $2,000,000 and why a competitor's plant was ready for the junkheap.

By March 7, 1899, Moore and Schley were ready to announce the creation of the American Smelting and Refining Company, capitalization, $65,000,000, half in 7 per cent preferred, half in common, a total of 650,000 shares, all duly authorized by the State of New Jersey, "incubator of trusts and corporation frauds."

To mine owners, the announcement came like the crack of doom. Economists shook their heads. Defeatists, as ever, proclaimed the entire affair fantastic and sure to fall of its own paper weight. The staid *Engineering and Mining Journal* wrote of "this momentous event, of the realization of which we have been somewhat incredulous." An old hand in the industry, A. H. Danforth—he who had donated land for the Guggenheim smelter at Pueblo—asserted that $11,500,000 would duplicate all of the smelters and refineries which had been thrown into the trust. If true, that left $53,500,000 to be charged up to "good will" and showed that Rogers had improved on his technique since forming Amalgamated Copper. Only half of Amalgamated had been water, but in the case of American Smelting it seemed that none of the common and only a third of the preferred represented anything tangible.

Even Rogers hardly ventured to say that a $100 share was worth $100. Moore and Schley offered 10 shares of preferred and seven of common for $1,000. The syndicate —Rogers, the Lewisohns and Moore and Schley—held on to 3/10ths of the common, nominally $8,100,000, to reward them for their foresight.

The promoters had a ready answer for the cavilings of the small-minded. The trust would be in control of the lead and silver markets. Lead could be boosted a cent easily and silver several cents. That alone would take care of the preferred. The smelters, individually, had realized $3,000,000 in 1898. Who would say that $6,000,000 profit for the largest silver producer in the world was fantastic? Then there were operating economies possible. Jittery mine owners were assured that the trust had only the kindliest feelings for its source of supply. Smelting charges, quite definitely, would not be raised.

Fascinated by the assurance of Standard Oil backing for the smelter trust, investors and speculators rushed into the market and laid their checks on Moore and Schley counters in such abundance that the promoters had to announce, by mid-March, that subscriptions were closed, many applications rejected and allotments reduced. Selling rights in the still-to-be-issued stock were quoted at $115-125. American Smelting common opened at 40, preferred at 91, and even after two months, the preferred had sagged only to the 80s while the common stuck in the 40s, so astutely had Moore and Schley taken care of the market.

Jubilant smelter owners, pocketing some $19,000,000 in stock, planned, the older ones, to retire, were off on long-promised trips to the Riviera, Egypt, the Orient; the younger ones assembled in shiny, new offices of American Smelting in New York to consider the problem of conducting a trust 2,000 miles from the scene of operations.

That small community known as M. Guggenheim's Sons watched the creation of the Smelters Trust with cautious, designing eye. The Lewisohns had invited them in and been met with curious interest but no enthusiasm. Moore upped the ante but the brothers were dissatisfied. Their business, they told the promoters, was a family affair and had prospered as such. Very definitely (although they didn't say so) they had no relish to be at the mercy of H. H. Rogers and his tricky, fast-moving Standard Oil gang.

Rogers was annoyed. Moore grunted in disgust. The Lewisohns pronounced the Guggenheims insane. They wouldn't even name a price! But the price was there just the same—Guggenheim control of American Smelting and Refinery. And for what? For one lone smelter out in the Rockies, their only one in the United States, and two down in Mexico, plus a refinery in Perth Amboy. The refinery interested the Lewisohns particularly. It was the only copper refinery owned by interests in the silver-lead business. It enabled the Guggenheims to enter the European copper market as an important factor independent of the Lewisohn selling agency. Decidedly the refinery had key importance and the Guggenheims were undoubtedly the major factor in Mexico not only in the silver-lead-gold market, but also in copper. Their Tepezala mines and Aguascalientes smelter, plus Perth Amboy, interferred with Amalgamated Copper's plans; their dominance of Mexican silver-lead production threatened the Smelters monopoly; the Pueblo smelter could play hob among the Colorado ore-sellers by providing the single independent outlet.

What price Guggenheims? Ruefully the promoters admitted it was too high. But as a standing invitation, $11,000,000 stock was left in the treasury, against the time when the racalcitrant family might change their mind.

Old Meyer Guggenheim chuckled as he rocked back and forth in his chair at his sons' office. "You see, every time Rogers opens his mouth, he says another million," he cried, jovially. "With such a business as he is cooking up, some day he must come to us and say, 'Here it is, we need you.'

"For $11,000,000 in their paper we should give away our smelters," he snorted. "What is $11,000,000 in a country like this? And what are we without our smelters, mines? Not worth two cents. And anyway, who knows what good their stock is?"

Meyer chuckled again and smoothed his gray whiskers. In the back of his designing mind he already saw American Smelting and Refining crawling to the Guggenheims, begging unity. Too happy to sit still on that pleasant spring morning, Meyer grabbed his hat, went uptown, had his top-buggy harnessed and went driving in the Park.

Dan Guggenheim did not share his father's mirth. Old Meyer could go driving light-heartedly behind his fine horses, but it was up to the Guggenheim brothers to make three smelters and a refinery survive the onslaughts of a Rogers-Rockefeller trust. Of course, there was the plan he and Meyer had talked over before. He called up his friend Samuel Untermyer and arranged for lunch together.

If lawyers were an inevitable nuisance, Guggenheim preferred this young Virginian, two years his junior, keen, and with a prodigious appetite for corporation work. It was said that he had tried more cases in a single year than any other lawyer at the New York bar. Associated with him was his half-brother, H. Randolph Guggenheimer, and phenomenal Louis Marshall, fresh down from Syracuse with a state record for number of appearances before the august Court of Appeals and a growing national reputation as a Constitutional expert.

Dan liked the firm of Guggenheimer, Untermyer, and Marshall. No pomposity or starched prestige, but the driving force of two exceptional men who managed to have their fingers in every important pie. Similarity in racial tradition was a help, too, in the confidential relations that existed, necessarily, between lawyer and client.

Guggenheim and Untermyer, over their coffee, continued

sketching the scope of their strategy against the Smelters Trust. Keystone in the plan was the yet unborn Guggenheim Exploration Company, which was to thrust the family's interest into every corner of Mexico, seeking out every profitable mine and hitching it to a Guggenheim smelter and refinery. The Mexican field lay open for intensive exploitation. Aside from Kansas City Smelting and Refining (August Meyer's company, now part of the trust) Mexico's mines were still being exploited helter-skelter. Free-lance prospectors, engineers, and promoters roamed the country seeking what they could devour. Everyone said Mexico was a rich land, but few reputable engineers, backed by large funds, had ever been given free scope there. Here was virgin territory open to the Guggenheims upon peculiarly favorable conditions, thanks to their friendly relations with Porfirio Díaz. Let the Smelters Trust monopolize the United States, the Guggenheims would base fame and fortune on the undeveloped riches of the Sierra Madres.

A necessary ingredient in venturesome companies were men of large fortune who could afford to lose hundreds of thousands on the high probability that millions could be made eventually. It was this angle of Guggenheim Exploration that Dan and Untermyer were considering, and particularly the personality of William C. Whitney, one-time Secretary of the Navy, inheritor of millions of Oliver H. Payne's Standard Oil money, manipulator with Thomas Fortune Ryan and P. A. B. Widener in the Broadway street car franchise scandal back in the eighties.

Whitney had a flair for high society; an appetite for fine houses in many places, just one of which was the Italian Renaissance palace at Fifth Avenue and Sixty-eighth Street built for his second wife; and a vaulting ambition to place his son, Harry Payne, in a firm where the high-spirited fellow could surge forward.

Mines in Mexico? Backed by the established Guggenheim

firm? And fighting the Rogers crowd? All three points appealed to Whitney and he agreed. On June 10, 1899, Isaac and Murry Guggenheim and Dr. E. P. Mathewson, metallurgical manager at the Perth Amboy refinery, filed papers at Trenton, New Jersey, as incorporators of the Guggenheim Exploration Company, capitalized at $6,000,000. Its announced business was to prospect, explore, and deal in lands, mines and minerals.

Formation of a $6,000,000 company was nothing to excite New York in 1900, but mining men and particularly the heads of American Smelting looked upon the notice with real interest. The newcomer's title imitated that of the Exploration Company of London, it was evident. As far back as 1891 Jacob H. Schiff, who regarded the Guggenheim boys as coming figures in the Jewish world, arranged an introduction between Dan and Hamilton Smith, Jr., manager of London's Exploration firm, whose capital, too, was Jewish—Rothschild. For years those international bankers enjoyed 20 percent dividends on their firm, whose scouts found themselves at home in wastelands of Siberia and Australia and knew every inch of the Witwatersrand. They had opened the great Kimberley diamond mines in South Africa, and had managed Alaska's Treadwell gold mine and Anaconda's copper.

Well, the Guggenheims are pretty smart, admitted Smelting's officials. But there's nothing we can do about it. We're not in the business of buying mines, or managing them either. This is the smelter trust and we've got to hitch together a score of plants and make them work somehow.

Headaches a-plenty there were for President Nash. It wasn't just the physical co-ordination of plants, but the co-ordination of a jangling board of directors. Rogers was notorious for leaching firms from the inside; and now he and the Lewisohns were cooking up a United Metals Selling Company, which would relieve American Smelting of the trouble—and a good bit of the profit—of selling its metals in London. There was nothing that a conscientious smelter man could do about that, either. Rogers and his partner, William Rockefeller, and the Lewisohns were in on this deal and it was not politic to question their ethics. The Guggenheims noted the maneuver and thanked themselves once again for their good sense in shying clear of the Rogers promotion.

There were pettier troubles, too. So-and-so's nephew had to be taken care of, and Mr. X's son had to be pushed ahead. Some smelters were to be scrapped and whole communities howled madly. The news from Colorado was even worse. Dan got quite fascinated, contemplating the Smelter Trust's feet of clay.

Franklin Guiterman, manager of the trust's Durango, Colorado, plant, and the kind who liked to come to New York, cock his feet on the radiator and regale his select audience at the Rocky Mountain Club with tales of how smelter and mine owners dealt with their labor, had succeeded in precipitating a strike that was spreading to all the trust's plants in Colorado. The state legislature at last had passed the eight-hour law which the unions had pushed for twenty years. The law went into effect June 15, 1899, and on that day Guiterman posted a notice at the works that employees were "at liberty" to work as many hours as they pleased. Hereafter all employees were to be paid by the hour, and work above eight hours would be calculated as overtime. Under the new wage scale, a man still had to work twelve hours to make his usual pay. "The men employed at the smelters," summed up the *Engineering and Mining Journal,* "are urgently invited to break the eight-hour provision of the new law and are assured protection in every way." Their main protection, it developed, was the trust's court action questioning the law's constitutionality.

Soon every trust smelter in Colorado was closed. Simon
112

Guggenheim decided to offer the men in the Pueblo smelter a temporary eight-hour day, contingent on the success of the strike in competitors' plants and on the fate of court action.

Mines closed as smelters were unable to take their ore. That is all except the mines which shipped to the Guggenheims. The Philadelphia smelter rode high. President Nash of American Smelting rushed to Denver to quell the strike but stuck on the demand for union recognition. It was not in a western smelter boss' blood to tolerate the Western Federation of Miners—"a lot of damned anarchists." As for the Federation, it returned the compliment with pointed reference to the trust's own defiance of the eight-hour law.

The strike dragged on through July and ended in August with a 10 percent increase for key men . . . and the twelve-hour shift. The Colorado Supreme Court later upheld the trust's contention that the law was unconstitutional.

As for the Guggenheims, they rode high with the labor men. True, they didn't abide by the eight-hour law either, but at least they had made a decent gesture of compliance. These amiable sentiments had cost the brothers not a penny, in fact had brought extra profits during the existence of the walkout.

The year 1899 was decidedly a Guggenheim year in Colorado. Their names leaped into the newspapers; Republican politicians cozened up to millionaires who had snapped their fingers at the Smelter Trust; mine owners, burning under the outrage of eastern monopoly brought home to the pit mouth, hailed them as sturdy outposts of competition, men who refused to bend the knee to Wall Street.

From every section of the populace came praise. Mine owners and miners forgot their bitter warfare in fighting the common enemy, the trust. The famous cartoon which pictured Rockefeller's bald pate and beady eyes as the head of an octopus was reproduced in Colorado papers with tentacles that wrapped themselves around the peaks of the Rockies. Charley Thomas, the Silver-Fusion governor, sponsored a bill forbidding the Smelter Trust to function in Colorado, but legislators who fulminated against the trust in speeches, quietly accepted money from the trust's henchmen and killed the bill in committee. A bitter editorial writer sighed: "Perhaps it is as well that the Legislature stifled the Governor's bill. If it had passed, American Smelting and Refining would have had to buy over the State's judicial department—merely an account in another shop."

Back of public agitation was the somber reality of "ghost towns." In the little "Republic of Gilpin" up behind Denver, a dozen mining camps decayed. Central City's famous opera house and proud three-story brick and iron buildings of the seventies and eighties were boarded up, or just abandoned to the elements. Hundreds of mines, some large, some just gopher holes, were closed. American Smelting had raised charges, had flatly refused grades of ore its furnaces didn't need, had turned down small lots of ore as a nuisance to handle—and thereby had placed the seal of doom on scores of mining communities. Smaller smelters were to be dismantled. The trust was living in the twentieth century. It had no use for small units, for small mines. The little mine owner was free to do as he pleased; but his freedom was sharply limited by the fact that, aside from the Guggenheims, there was no smelter in all Colorado to take his ore if the trust turned it down.

Guggenheim ore agents were hailed as the hope of the mining industry. They in turn were instructed by the three junior Guggenheims, Ben, Si and Will, to be liberal in terms, to recommend the advancement of loans to hard-pressed operators, to subscribe to stock to help develop promising holes. The Guggenheims had the pick of the ore.

Nothing brought the family louder huzzahs among the mine owners than their posted notice to pay $20 an ounce

114

for gold. The mint price was $20.67 but the trust smelters paid operators only $19 an ounce. "Bigger robbers than Jesse James," cried the operators, because it was *their* gold for which American Smelting was paying them $1.67 below the price the U. S. mint at Denver paid all comers. Grudgingly the trust conceded the $20 price, to meet Guggenheim competition. That little piece of Guggenheim strategy cost American Smelting a million dollars.

In Utah, the *Engineering and Mining Journal* reported, "there is no competition and mines must comply with the conditions imposed by the smelters or go out of business." Salt Lake like Denver, seethed with revolt. There was talk in the press of new smelters to be built, and the Guggenheim name was hopefully mixed with these rumors. The brothers saw no reason to deny reports they had not sponsored—that the Guggenheims were to build a chain of smelters across the Rocky Mountain region.

The Smelters' board in New York grew apprehensive. Vice-President Barton Sewell was rushed west to quell the insurrection. Yes, it was true, he conceded, that rates had been raised, but it was merely a temporary measure to iron out inequalities under the previous setup. Liberal terms would be offered large shippers with three- to five-year contracts. Good treatment would be accorded small interests. "All posted mining men," observed the oracular *Engineering and Mining Journal*, "look on the Smelting Company's announcement with suspicion."

Well pleased with matters in their old territory, the Guggenheims turned to the Missouri soft lead district. Missouri was independent of all the traditions and conditions that ruled the Rockies. Its lead was not argentiferous. Different processes were used. Monopoly had not yet had time to favor the Missouri lead mines with its blessings. M. Guggenheim's Sons invested $2,000,000 in the Desloge properties, to add to other properties already held. Their buyers circu-

115

'lated through the district. Suddenly in the summer of 1900, the price of lead dropped. The Guggenheims had dumped large supplies of their own from Mexico and had induced the Missouri operators to break away from American Smelting's fixed price.

It was a blow below the belt and the Smelter Trust flinched. Many of those millions in watered stock were justified only by the trust's ability to shove up the price of lead another cent. Trust agents were forced to concede a buying price of 4.125¢ to reconstruct their control of the market among the big Idaho, Montana, and Colorado producers.

In Mexico the Guggenheim smelters worked to capacity, 24 hours to the day and 365 days to the year; heavy-laden Guggenheim ships took the bullion from Tampico to Perth Amboy to be refined; Guggenheims occasionally dropped down to Mexico City to see José Limantour, the secretary of finance, Joaquin Casasús, leader of the *Científicos*, and be honored guests, on occasion, of the Dictator himself.

Against the stone wall of court influence enjoyed by the Guggenheims, the trust's agents in Mexico got nowhere. The *Científicos* feared the Rockefeller company; they preferred to pit competing interests of various nationalities in the scramble for the nation's resources.

Smelting's statement brought a smile at Guggenheim offices. Profits of $3,500,000 were reported. M. Guggenheim's Sons published no statements but it became known later that their profits for the same year were $3,600,000, and that on three smelters and a refinery, contrasted with the Trust's twenty smelters and refineries!

The smaller company, tightly managed, adroit, hard-hitting, had outpointed the Trust. The Guggenheims had broken the code during the strike that tied up the Trust plants, had undercut on the price paid for gold, had spiked the hoped-for monopoly profits at a dozen points, had broken the Trust's fixed price for lead, were dominant in

116

Mexico, and, worse than all else, remained a focus around which anti-Trust sentiment in the West might rally to extend a chain of rival smelters throughout the Rockies.

American Smelting and Refining ran up the white flag in December, 1900. Shortly before Christmas the board called a stockholders' meeting to authorize an increase of $35,000,000 in capitalization. The negotiators lifted the curtain to disclose that all the "smelting and refining plants appurtenant to the properties and business of M. Guggenheim's Sons" were to be turned in to the smelters trust for $45,200,000 in American Smelting and Refining preferred and common. In return, the Guggenheims were to hand over to the financially hard-pressed trust $6,666,666.66 in cash reserves and $9,000,000 in cash or credits. This left $30,000,000 in Smelters stock for the brothers. As the common was quoted at 60 and preferred at par, the actual cash value paid the bright sons of Meyer Guggenheim was about $20,000,000—for smelters and refinery which could be reproduced for $5,000,000. The brothers kept all their mines in Colorado and Mexico, the Tampico-Perth Amboy steamship line, and the Guggenheim Exploration Company. And became the largest factor in the trust, besides.

It was a signal victory won cleverly by the weaker side —and largely by posing as the people's champion against monopolistic oppression. All in all, it was a good year's work, and Meyer invited all his boys and their sisters, Cora and Rose, and all the wives and husbands and whatever grandchildren there were up to the brownstone house at 36 West Seventy-seventh Street for a grand party. One little aspect of the victory tickled him immensely: the adroit bookkeeping down in Mexico which had shown a $2,000,000 profit for the year for the Monterrey and Aguascalientes smelters. To do so, the bookkeeper had arranged things so that the mines showed no profit at all, but there was no need to bring that out during negotiations as the trust was not buying the mines.

Rogers, the Lewisohns, and Schley had taken little part in the negotiations for the merger. Rogers had bigger fish to fry; the grandiose billion-dollar steel trust had been conceived, and he left details of the American Smelting and Refining deal to its officers. The full import of the Guggenheim victory did not dawn on American Smelting and Refining promoters until Dan, in a public statement justifying M. Guggenheim's Sons' action in putting their smelter and refinery interests in the trust, mentioned casually that among the economies to be expected was the trust's use of the Guggenheim selling connections abroad.

The Lewisohn brothers jumped. Dentist Dan had drilled into their tenderest nerve, United Metals Selling Company. They ran to Rogers, their partner in the company. He blew up. Dan and the American Smelting and Refining officers were called on the carpet. What was the meaning of this treachery? Treachery? they repeated, incredulously. Why, they meant to save the company money, big money, perhaps a million a year. American Smelting and Refining would need every penny. The meeting broke up in a grand row. In the calm after the storm, Rogers, Schley, and the Lewisohns sat down to see what could be done. It was then they realized that the Guggenheims controlled the Smelter Trust. The promoters, among them all, had only a minority interest.

Rogers' cold eyes snapped. He who had said: "All meetings where I sit as director, they vote first and talk after I am done," felt outraged. He called in David Lamar, Wall Street's wrecker. Smash Smelters stock, he commanded. The next day, February 11, 1901, 100,000 shares of American Smelting and Refining were dumped on the market. Quotations sagged from 62 to 55. At the low points buyers entered. Dan had talked the situation over with Bill Whitney,

118

and the Guggenheim interest in Smelters stock rose. Rogers, Lewisohn, and Schley resigned from the board.

The stockholders met February 16 amid a frightful hubbub. The *New York Times* reported the doings on Page 1: "The millionaires of American Smelting and Refining are in a snarl grave enough to threaten sensational consequences." The motion to increase the company's capital stock to $100,000,000 to acquire the Guggenheim properties was about to be put, with an easy majority in sight. Ed Lauterbach, Rogers' handy man in legal matters, rushed to Vice-Chancellor Stevens' chambers for an injunction, and dashed back to the stockholders' meeting, waving the document. Sam Untermyer thereupon raced over to see Stevens and came back with permission for the stockholders to vote, merely as an expression of their desire. They did, with all but 27,000 shares recorded for the increase in capitalization. The meeting was adjourned, subject to call, to let the lawyers get to work in earnest.

Richard Vliet Lindabury, specialist in the intricacies of New Jersey corporation law, was called in by Rogers. Lindabury had sprung into fame when he and Joe Choate defeated the state in the Singer Sewing Machine tax case. Successfully he had defended Thomas Fortune Ryan's American Tobacco Company when New Jersey sought to break up the combine for violation of the state's anti-trust law. Of him it was said that no other lawyer ever represented and counseled so large an aggregation of capital investment. Most of the new trusts were New Jersey corporations, and New Jersey law differed in striking ways from the New York. Lindabury established his offices in Newark and scorned ever to move across the Hudson.

It was his job to paint Rogers and his associates as wronged minority stockholders fighting for the integrity of American Smelting and Refining against a group of outside despoilers. Giving the Guggenheim properties an outside

119

valuation of $10,000,000, Lindabury appealed to Chancellor Stevens: "Will your honor believe that the good will is worth 4½ times as much as the real property?" As for the working capital to be put up by the brothers, "Your honor must remember that it was not to be drawn from their own pockets by the Guggenheim brothers, but was to be obtained by the sale of a portion of the $45,000,000 in new stock which they were to receive."

Lindabury, tall, elegant, defender of the promoter of Amalgamated Copper and the Smelters Trust, launched into queer language: "No arrangement," said he, "can be good business that consists of watered stock. If this is an attempt to water stock to the extent of $30,000,000, the harm that will result is incalculable. Everyone knows that the statutes of New Jersey have become the plaything of Wall Street; that under them on the merest pretext or baldest excuse fictitious stock is being constantly issued. If the directors of American Smelting and Refining acted in good faith, they exceeded their powers; if in bad faith, they are guilty of fraud."

Sam Untermyer entered the fray with great gusto. Who was to say what is water, other than the court? Could it be said that properties which had earned $3,600,000 in the preceding twelvemonth were unreasonably valued at $45,000,000? Untermyer produced his pencil and pad and figured that Guggenheim smelters and refinery earnings were 8 per cent on the valuation; and that, he assured Chancellor Stevens, was a pretty good return on any stock. The question at issue was the determination of "worth," and he insisted that earnings were the real test. The inanimate buildings might be valued at $5,000,000, or $10,000,000, or $100,000,000, but the test of their worth was their earnings.

Lindabury smiled contemptuously, and attacked from a new angle. Smelters' board of directors had been corrupted, he charged. What would learned counsel have to say to the testimony of Mr. Rogers that he had been quietly offered 2,500 shares of preferred, selling on the market at par, for an inside price of 80? Mr. Rogers had indignantly spurned the offer—which was suggestive of the "preferred lists" of the House of Morgan to be exposed a generation later. Adolph Lewisohn quoted President Nash to the effect that the Guggenheims agreed to pass $10,200,000 in stock around among the 15 directors, the prefered at 80—a $20 profit—and the common at 50—a profit of $10. Chancellor Stevens nodded his head and agreed that the statute governing "conscious overvaluation as a basis for fraud" applied to this case.

Testimony developed the fact that no one except the Guggenheims had a very clear idea as to what their plants were worth . . . and possibly they were prejudiced. A motion at a directors' meeting for a subcommittee to examine the value of the properties had not been carried. Lewisohn added that the Trust staggered under a debt load of $7,000,000 which it had no way of paying. He conceded that Smelters was badly in need of fresh capital. When it was organized, everyone had overlooked the need of working capital, it seemed, in the dash for grabbing what they could.

To all of which Untermyer answered: "The Guggenheims will make no more sacrifices. They will call the deal off if there is further delay."

Chancellor Stevens on March 11 denied the application for a permanent injunction, ruling that the plaintiffs had failed to prove that $45,000,000 was an excessive price for the Guggenheim properties. He upheld Untermyer's contention that earnings equivalent to 8 per cent indicated that the properties were not over-valued.

Lindabury appealed to the Court of Errors and Appeals at Trenton, which, March 28, reversed Chancellor Stevens,

9-5, and enjoined American Smelting from issuing the disputed $45,000,000 in new stock.

The *New York Times* cheered the New Jersey Court of Appeals. After criticizing "those adjustments so convenient to the promoter and the speculative vender, which will not stand the rude test of a serious and expert appraisal," it continued:

> Not only New Jersey but the investing public generally can be congratulated upon a decision which will add to the strength of those fortifications which it is the interest of conservatism, looking to the future rather than the immediate present, to build more and more solidly about the undertakings which are to develop the resources of the country and distribute the products of wealth, labor and inventive genius. This Smelters case will rank as a significant precedent.

"The decision will not prevent a union of the two interests," stormed Untermyer. "The desire of the stockholders is almost unanimous in favor of this trade." He revealed that Guggenheim profits by now were at the rate of $4,500,000 a year while Smelters was earning, thanks to the entente cordiale, at the rate of $5,900,000. All told the earnings he said were equivalent to 30 percent on the common after paying the 7 percent preferred dividend. Sweet uses of monopoly!

Court action, he added, "may furnish stock raiders who are trying to cover short accounts an opportunity to frighten weak holders and get some cheap stock." Under the persistent hammering of Rogers' wrecking crew headed by Dave Lamar, preferred had been pounded down from 96½ to 90⅛ and common down to 52. Lamar was unquestionably an expert in pounding and boosting on the market. He had co-operated profitably with Russell Sage against the Union-Pacific–Government settlement, had supervised the fireworks in the Third Avenue Railroad scandal, and he manipulated the leather trust, boosting its common from 6 to 40, at the behest of young John D. Rockefeller, Jr. Wall Street saw Standard Oil behind the attack on Smelters, both on the Stock Exchange and in the New Jersey courts.

Inspired stories appeared in the press that Standard Oil might sponsor a new smelters trust. Financial commentators suggested that American Smelting would find itself out on a limb. Denver and Salt Lake newspapers caught all stray items and greedily flared them under red headlines. The *Engineering and Mining Journal*, in an uncomfortable position, nevertheless ventured that there could be "little doubt that $100,000,000 capitalization is far too large for the intrinsic value of the properties. . . . The abnormal profits of a busy year are not a safe basis for the permanent capitalization of a company of this class." The *Journal* was cynical about the new trust. Undoubtedly mining men would welcome the competing smelters, but ultimately one of the trusts would absorb the other "and pass the costs off on the public through more capitalization."

Untermyer advised retreat in the face of the powerful Standard Oil attack. After all the Guggenheims had won astounding victory in taking the Smelters Trust into camp, and if Rogers and Lewisohn demanded that their United Metals Selling Company must be cut in on the gravy, it would be wise to compromise. At some later date the selling agency business could be straightened out.

All day April 8 the principals in the negotiations, Rogers, Leonard Lewisohn, and Daniel Guggenheim, were closeted in Untermyer's office. That evening they adjourned to Delmonico's to ratify the treaty of peace. Both sides emerged with honor. Lewisohn and his United Metals were reinstated as the Smelters sole selling agency abroad with a 1 percent commission on all metals handled. The Guggenheims were conceded to be undisputed masters of the Trust. Reporters, thrown off the trail when the conferees switched to Delmonico's, laid siege to the Rogers, Lewisohn, and Guggenheim houses. Waylaid late that night as he entered his home at 12 West Fifty-fourth Street, Dan admitted that the merger had been approved. An official statement next day confirmed that "to avoid any further complications, the new stock has been issued and delivered to the Guggenheims."

Peace news hit a buoyant market in which brokers sweated in a "consolidation fever" that shot all stock, good and bad, to unheard-of levels by mid-April of 1901. The first two weeks of that month were recorded as the "most profitable for speculators in history," and Rogers was in the midst of it, happy in the success of the United States Steel flotation, his pockets bursting with new millions.

Smelting common leaped from 52 to 65 on April 9, with 48,000 shares traded. By June the preferred was above par. The only losers in the two-months warfare among Smelting's insiders were the little fellows not privy to the secrets. They had been shaken out by Rogers' gloomy seal of doom on their company. Richer by millions however were the Guggenheims and their ally, Whitney, who were said to have picked up $6,000,000 in American Smelting and Refining stock, in addition to the $45,000,000 delivered to them by the company.

The long-adjourned stockholders' meeting was held April 22. The purchase of the Guggenheim properties was approved. The board was enlarged from sixteen to twenty-one, to accommodate the new members, Isaac, Daniel, Murry, Solomon, and Simon Guggenheim. Daniel was elevated to the newly created position of chairman of the board; Simon became treasurer. Two seats were left vacant, in case Rogers and Lewisohn were interested.

The new board met April 27 and elected Dan chairman of the executive committee. His four brothers likewise mounted to commanding seats. Against that solid block of

124

DANIEL, HEAD OF THE HOUSE OF GUGGENHEIM

Photo by Wide World.

five were the six who had been the Smelter Kings of old:
E. W. Nash, president; Barton Sewell, vice-president;
Dennis Sheedy, A. R. Meyer, Anton Eilers and J. B. Grant.

Smelter kings no more were they, but dukes of the Guggenheim Empire, subordinates of the sons of old Meyer, the penniless immigrant and peddler of shoelaces and ribbons.

7. GOLDEN AGE OF THE GUGGENHEIMS

HAVING JUST MISSED a rendezvous with death on a Boer gallows, John Hays Hammond, whose nose could "smell a gold mine a thousand miles away," was happy to return to America, eager to cash in on the headlines which had made him, for a few months, this nation's most noted resident in foreign parts.

Standing in the dock in the hot, crowded Pretoria courtroom, Hammond had understood perfectly the penalty for treason against the South African Republic as the prosecutor screamed, "Hangen bij den nek." The American engineer was one of the junta of Uitlander capitalists who plotted armed insurrection against the Boer government so that they could run the famed gold camp of the Witwatersrand and its capital, Johannesburg, as they wished. Trapped by Dr. Jameson's premature raid, they had been clapped into a stockaded jail compound built for Kaffirs.

After the American Senate had petitioned Oom Paul Kruger for mercy, and when it became apparent that the British Government would not tolerate extreme penalties against its own subjects, the death penalty was commuted. Cecil Rhodes paid Hammond's fine of $125,000 out of commissions he had earned. The famed consulting engineer of Consolidated Gold Fields, Limited, shook the dust of South Africa from his heels, agreed in London to become representative in America for the Venture Corporation, splitting fifty-fifty on mines, and returned to his homeland to enjoy his triumph.

Hammond was outstanding among that venturesome company of American engineers who roamed the globe for mines in which pudgy capitalists in New York, London, Amster-

126

dam, and Frankfort might sink their surplus funds. Enduring the hardships of the prospector's life in frontier lands, clambering up and down shafts and stopes in just-opened mines, bending over assay tables in clapboard shacks, such men courted discomfort, danger, and disease to see for themselves exactly what the earth hid in its black recesses. Clad in corduroy breeches, grime under his fingernails, a pack of cheap cigarettes in his shirt pocket, the American engineer became a familiar figure in outposts of the mining world and the despair of his Continental brother, who fastidiously disdained the hardships of first-hand investigation.

His examination of a mine completed, the engineer, a few weeks later, would be cast in the role of diplomat and negotiator, in conference with native landowner, minister, or ranking dignitary; a few months later, would be dining in New York or London with his employers, laden with facts which he himself knew to be facts, showing maps which he himself had drawn, analyzing assays which he himself had supervised. Men of the type of John Hays Hammond and Herbert Hoover were admitted to the choice circle of financier-promoters as blood brothers. Their fat salaries reinforced by generous shares in the companies for which they explored, they talked as equals with president and money-master, traveled in the pomp of an Indian Prince.

Hammond, adventurer, raconteur, prince of mining engineers, found all doors open upon his return to America. No money king of Manhattan was too proud to boast that he had had John Hays Hammond as dinner guest, and none entertained him more than Bill Whitney, partner in Guggenheim Exploration. Over cigars in Whitney's Fifth Avenue palace, the engineer proposed a union of his nose for mines with his host's pocketbook. The cream of the new discoveries in the West and in Mexico was theirs; Whitney would meet the expenses of his mining staff and put up the money for development work.

Scorning the status of employee, Hammond would treat with Whitney as fellow-gentleman and fellow-adventurer. There would be no salary: at the end of two years the capitalist would pay the engineer what he thought was due. Whitney was agreeable: association with Hammond humored his itch for recognition, promised rich returns, and offered an avenue of high adventure for his spirited son, Harry Payne.

The frown on Dan Guggenheim's face was as dark as the bold wing mustache that swept past the corners of his tight mouth. The short, pudgy man stiffened.

"But, Mr. Whitney, we are partners in this business of mining development," he expostulated. "Is it possible for one member of our partnership to go off by himself on a parallel business? And is it advisable, for your own best interests? We have built up in Guggenheim Exploration this country's best mining organization. We have contacts everywhere on this continent, most favored relations with our own American Smelting and Refining Company. Wouldn't Mr. Hammond be more valuable to you as consulting engineer for our own company?"

Hammond, being sought at the moment to umpire the War of the Butte Copper Kings raging between H. H. Rogers' Amalgamated and F. Augustus Heinze, shrugged his shoulders when Whitney passed on Guggenheim's proposal. "I prefer to deal with you," he answered. "There's a pack of Guggenheims, and I'd be falling and tripping over them." Nevertheless, he agreed to meet Dan.

"Mr. Guggenheim, this is Mr. Hammond, the man I've been urging you to get for our Exploration Company," said Whitney, introducing the two over a luncheon table at the Midday Club. "He is worth any salary he may ask."

That afternoon the engineer spent in the Guggenheim offices in the Empire Building overlooking Old Trinity, examining the scope of "Guggenex" and its mines, scattered all along the backbone of two continents from Alaska to Chile. Then he and Dan talked business. And what business! Out of it came a contract that dazzled the world, crashed the name of Guggenheim into the front pages of every newspaper, and lifted the matter-of-fact House of Guggenheim from its prosaic foundations up to the misty cloudland of High Finance.

The contract set Hammond's salary at $250,000 a year, for five years, and a quarter interest in all properties recommended to Guggenex. It was the biggest salary ever paid a man and was to stand out even in the lush decades after 1902 as a mark for top-flight executives of billion-dollar corporations. In the first year, Hammond was to make $1,250,000. The papers were full of homely illustrations of the vast salary. In 2½ hours, calculated one journalistic statistician, the engineer was to make as much as the average worker did in a year; in 5 weeks as much as the President of the United States. Every hour of his working time, it was figured, was worth $277.77 and it cost the Guggenheims 75 cents every time their general manager and chief engineer said, "How do you do?" His garage full of $10,000 automobiles and his 200-foot steam yacht with a crew of 32 were to be favorite copy to whet the anger of mining men in the West and to preach a true success story to the millions. Small wonder that Hammond referred to Guggenex as "my company."

The Sunday supplements marveled at the suddenly discovered potentates who could pay Hammond his fabulous salary. The Guggenheims were found to be Smelter Kings and Silver Princes, and their name became a byword in American homes for wealth and power. Perhaps Hammond was, in reality, underpaid. On his great prestige companies yet unborn were to be launched to the tune of tens of millions in stocks and bonds. Under his management, Guggenheim Exploration was to become the greatest of all mining

129

ventures. When he and Dan Guggenheim placed their signatures to the famous contract February 9, 1902, neither could name the names later to be emblazoned on the investment sky—American Smelters Securities, Nipissing, Yukon Gold, Esperanza, Kennecott, Utah Copper, Nevada Consolidated, Ray Consolidated, Braden and Chile Copper—and yet these were to be the fruit of Hammond's collaboration with the Guggenheims.

Hammond seated on his right hand young Alfred Chester Beatty, twenty-nine-year-old graduate of Columbia School of Mines who had been understudying the master for the past three years. The bargain for Hammond's services included Beatty, who was to receive the "princely salary" of $27,000 a year plus an option of some 2,000 shares of Guggenex at $100 a share. For only part of that option, Guggenex a few years later paid the young man $80,000.

If that seemed a staggering compensation for an assistant general manager, the Guggenheims demurred not a moment. The brothers were financiers, not engineers. A mine offered for their purchase might eventually be gutted of $10,000,-000 for Guggenex's greater glory—or it might cost a million dollars to find that it was a dry hole. Neither Dan, nor any of his brothers, would ever be able to tell which was true. The fate of their vast investments rested solely on the judgment of Hammond and Beatty. Trusted with the company's "most secret information," participants in all its plans, vested with all responsibility and authority in mining operations and yet unchecked by supervision, these two men must necessarily regard their relation to the Guggenheims as one of "meticulous loyalty, the most scrupulous fidelity, and a delicate sense of honor." They must assume a "primary obligation to eschew every form of temptation" that might lead them to divert their employers' profit to their own private gain. To aid them in this laudable aim the

130

money-wise Guggenheims diverted their ace employees from temptation by generous salaries.

Beatty was sent out on his rounds while the chief proceeded to sift through the assortment of mines into which the Guggenheims had dumped their Smelters profits. $5,000,000 had been put into a group of Durango mines, $10,000,000, all told, was to be spent on Velardeña. On the other hand, Veta Grande, bought for $200,000 was later to turn in $5,000,000 net. It was the Guggenheim policy to take options on all promising mines, examine them at leisure, and buy the choicest.

Murry Guggenheim explained the family's key to success. "We did very little prospecting," he said. "That would have been too much of a gamble. We picked out the best mines in Mexico, Colorado and South America and then bought them outright. This gave us a steady supply of ore for our smelters. It also gave us a variety of ores so that we could combine them in such a way as to produce the best results." It also gave the Guggenheims some highly unprofitable mines, as Hammond discovered in thumbing through Guggenex's portfolio. There were Velardeña, a $10,000,000 headache in Mexico, and the Silverton mines in Colorado.

Over both the successes and the failures it was the habit of the brothers to spend long hours in conference, to which Hammond was invited. But the great engineer, another of that lustrous company of Freiberg graduates, was not amused by the brothers' comments on mining affairs nor did he relish listening to a none too expert discussion on the shortcomings of a mine which he himself might have scouted ten years before, whose owners and managers he knew by their first names. Lengthy reports were read from wordy managers who covered their failures under a blanket of explanations.

These board meetings, at which he had voice but no vote,

were convened at almost any hour of the day when Dan discovered an empty spot on his calendar. Messengers scurried about the building, poking their heads into the offices of American Smelting and Refining, Exploration, and M. Guggenheim's Sons to round up the brothers and Hammond.

The engineer blew up one fine day when a report was read from a manager who constantly miscalculated his budget at the beginning of the month and spent the rest apologizing.

"Good Lord," he cried. "Don't you realize that your entire investment in this mine would only pay my salary for about a month? I'd be saving money if I bought it myself and shut it down, yet you are taking up half of my time in these endless discussions. These port-mortems are just a waste of my valuable time and yours. I can't get anything done if you insist on talking trivialities."

Dan smiled, and agreed. From then on Guggenex meetings were held monthly and Hammond attended if he had time.

It was not much later that Hammond was back in New York from scouting a big lead proposition in Missouri. Embarrassed, he asked Dan to call a meeting. Burdened with maps and statistics, he began his analysis of the property. Dan toyed with his watch charm and examined the ceiling. Isaac sauntered over to the window overlooking Trinity. Murry took up the morning paper. Nobody even glanced at the maps, much less listened to the report.

In the midst of a Hammond sentence, Isaac broke in: "How much money is involved in this transaction?"

"About a million," answered Hammond.

"Well, J. H. H.," broke in Murry, "why are you spending so much time on such an insignificant matter? If you recommend its purchase, we should buy it without further delay and not waste precious moments of your 'valuable time.'"

Dan guffawed and Hammond realized that the joke was on him. He stowed away his maps and took the brothers over to Delmonico's for luncheon, regaling them with stories of the Missouri lead fields that were much more interesting than his formal report.

First fruits of Hammond's entry into Guggenex was the decision to increase the stock from its modest $6,000,000 to $17,000,000. Backed by the Hammond prestige, its value stepped up briskly, never sinking below 200 and rising as high as 325, despite a mere 7 percent dividend. The option to buy Guggenex at 100 was the prize Dan held out before his engineers, the reward he offered them after a remarkable coup, such as Beatty's negotiation of the American Congo contract with the King of Belgium. This gilt-edge security became the bellwether of the mining shares; a favorable report on a Guggenheim mine sent it up for 5 to 25 points, adverse news pegged it down. And small wonder! Under Hammond-Beatty direction, Guggenheim Exploration rivaled the Geological Survey in its knowledge of the mineral wealth of the Americas; became the center of all information, financial and technical, on the bonanzas, the focus toward which converged European capital seeking remuneration in American mining.

By 1904 Dan felt confident that his Exploration Company had seized control of nearly every promising mine this side of Tierra del Fuego that could be had for a price. He saw a new sun rising over the mining world, the coppery sun of the great porphyries, demanding tens of millions for their development. Why not tuck the silver-lead mines into another company, the sale of whose securities would give Guggenex free millions for the new coppers?

Dan was facing criticism from minority interests in American Smelting and Refining who said that the interests of mine owner and smelter owner were necessarily divergent. They wanted to know whose interests the Guggenheims were furthering, those of the Smelters Trust or of Guggenex's mines? Some charged flatly that Guggenheim mines wrung special concession from Trust smelters, to the detriment of American Smelting and Refining dividends.

A third problem faced him. The Coeur D'Alene district in Idaho, rising into importance in the lead market, was outside the Smelters Trust's ambit. The Idaho operators sent their ore to non-Trust smelters on Puget Sound. These smelters must be controlled if the Trust was to maintain its silver-lead monopoly. But it was unwise to add, at the moment, to the Trust's topheavy capital structure.

Dan concluded that the neatest solution to his problem would be to toss Guggenex's lead-silver mines into a special corporation whose control would be vested in the Smelters Trust. A successful flotation of this character would give Guggenex and American Smelting and Refining millions in cash, and the mines transferred to the Trust would still be under Guggenheim control. Dan would eat his cake and have it, too.

So he sought out his old friend and financial counselor, Jacob Schiff, of Kuhn, Loeb and Company. Their problem was to tie up the Guggenheim mines in a package attractive to European investors wary of American mining stocks. Schiff and Dan set out for London to see the great Sir Ernest Joseph Cassel, the international banker who floated loans for Mexico, China, Uruguay, who owned Swedish iron mines and was the British Government's financial ambassador to all those Mediterranean countries from Turkey to Morocco which flew the Crescent flags. Sir Ernest was the financial adviser and intimate friend of Edward VII, a collector of *objets d'art* ranging from the great paintings to tiny miniatures, a patron of horseflesh. He belonged to that company of Jewish financiers which included the Rothschilds, the Schiffs, Warburgs, and Guggenheims who, a generation later, were to be pilloried as the "international

Jewish bankers." This greatest of London's Jewish bankers had turned Catholic, a fact viewed tolerantly by Dan, whose own sisters had been educated in a Catholic convent school in Philadelphia and "finished" in another convent academy in Paris.

Guggenheim and Schiff were welcomed to Sir Ernest's mansion in Grosvenor Square, which he preferred to the business-like offices in Old Broad Street for entertaining distinguished overseas guests. They concocted a preferred "A" 6 percent cumulative stock issue of $17,000,000 but with no voting power for the first two years, nor thereafter unless the dividend was passed. It was to be guaranteed, not by Guggenheim Exploration, but by American Smelting and Refining, which was to keep a majority of the common stock. It was very much like a bond, and the Banque de Paris, the Bank of Amsterdam, and the Cassel-Schiff houses in Cologne and Frankfort absorbed the new issue so greedily that "we could hardly give the most serious of the applicants a half of what they wanted," Schiff reported to Dan.

With flotation an assured success, Dan regretted his decision to christen his new $77,000,000 child American Smelters Exploration Company. People might confuse its common stock, of which American Smelting and Refining carried $17,751,000 on its books at $1 (the rest being in Guggenex's portfolio), with the common stock of Guggenheim Exploration, then selling for upward of $300 a share. It was renamed American Smelters Securities. Dan tucked away most of the preferred B stock (5 percent guaranteed cumulative) in Guggenex's vaults after consenting to exchange 25,000 shares with American Smelting and Refining for $2,302,270 cash which the Trust had on hand and didn't know what to do with.

The transaction was a happy one for all parties involved. The Trust had, in effect, increased its capitalization by $77,000,000 and had voting control of the new company;

the Guggenheim brothers had replenished their coffers with some $22,000,000 for new investment; the mines they had sold to Smelters Securities were still theirs, but merely shifted to another account; the European bankers had made a neat commission; and the Trust was now in a position to step out and smother alarming competition in the West.

Smelters Securities set out in 1905 to add the Pacific Slope to the American Smelting and Refining domain. Key to Coeur D'Alene, the Pacific Northwest, and the Far North was Bill Rust's smelter in Tacoma. He came along from Colorado in 1890, just a year after Dennis Ryan, the St. Paul lumberman, had built the Tacoma smelter, and bought a partnership. With the Yukon gold discoveries, his plant became prosperous and after the development of the Idaho lead mines, it boasted a steady stream of 10 per cent dividends.

According to the story current in Tacoma, Smelters Securities offered Bill Rust $1,000,000 for his smelter and the feudal domain called Ruston. Rust laughed long and loud. "It's yours for $4,000,000," said he. Then the Securities agent laughed, and Rust ruffled. Shaking his finger under the Guggenheim man's nose, he bellowed: "And you tell Dan Guggenheim that he can have it now for $6,500,-000." The price paid was $5,500,000, and Bill Rust had the last laugh, for it represented 1,100 percent profit on capital.

The true story was a bit subtler. It involved Dan Guggenheim, a mysterious Wall Street operator named Bernard M. Baruch, and old Darius O. Mills, with intriguing Rockefeller agents lurking in the background. Secrecy was of the essence in this deal, and that perhaps is why Dan called in Baruch, a tight-lipped young broker who had got his early training under Jim Keene, king of stock manipulators, and had operated for Thomas Fortune Ryan, E. H. Harriman, and the Guggenheims.

Baruch was dispatched to the Coast, incognito, as it were, to get options from Mills on his two key smelters. None but the Guggenheims knew for whom he was acting. Rust fell in with Baruch's plans, the more so as he was generous in promises. Dan heard in New York at that point that the Standard Oil crowd was nosing around the Coast. He wired Baruch to close immediately on the seller's terms, if necessary. The price paid for the Tacoma smelter was indeed $5,500,000, most of which represented hopes of future monopoly profits, and part of which was the toll paid to the Rockefeller scare.

Half the Smelters Trust's prosperity rested on smelting profits, the other half on the sale of metals. The Guggenheims set out quite deliberately to control the lead market. Their $25,000,000 United Lead not being equal to the job, they acquired $30,000,000 National Lead, Baruch being in charge of operations. He retained Harry Content to do the actual buying on the Exchange. So quietly did the operation proceed that none knew the Guggenheims were buying in, and when it was all over, the Guggenheims denied that they had purchased a single share. Baruch's work was finished when Dan and Murry stepped into National Lead's board in 1906.

None could say Baruch was a sentimentalist. It was not long after he had superintended the National Lead deal that he was advising his friends to sell American Smelting. This stock was a plaything of the market and very sensitive to rumors. A new contract signed, a new mine opened, a slight upturn anywhere in the price of metals, and American Smelting marched up. It was just as susceptible to adverse rumors. There was always something doing in Smelters, much to the delight of the speculators. At the center of this vortex of speculation stood the Guggenheims, who alone knew which rumors were true and which unjustified.

When Smelters common climbed to 120 in the summer of 1905, Baruch advised his friends to clear out. It wasn't the very best advice, for early in 1906 this stock, which originally had represented nothing but a hope in H. H. Rogers' bosom, was selling as high as 174. When the stock tumbled considerably in February, Baruch was supposed to have his hand in it, pushing it down ever lower.

To cement its control of the lead market, the Trust signed a long-term contract with Federal Mining and Smelting, controlling half the Idaho output. Later Smelters Securities bought a dominant interest from the Rockefellers, who agreed to stay out of Idaho mining.

Federal shares flew up from 40 to a top of 199. Dividends sustained the quotations but after the Knickerbocker panic in 1907, Federal slid down as rapidly as it had risen, passed its common dividends and was quoted with the cats and dogs. A terrific howl rang through the mining speculative crowd that the Guggenheims had bilked them, while Federal's preferred stockholders declared the company was being milked by the Smelters Trust. The preferred would be paying 7 per cent and the common 10, they claimed in court, if the iniquitous twenty-one-year smelter contract could be modified in Federal's interest. The contract, it was revealed, required the Trust to pay Federal for only 90 percent of the lead extracted from its ores, and at a 10 percent deduction from the New York price, when lead was selling up to 4.1 cents a pound. Over that, the Trust and Federal split the difference in profit.

Federal's plight was plastered across the papers as an example of Guggenheim finance. M. Guggenheim's Sons formally denied they had traded in the stock. Garet Garrett, writing in *Collier's*, declared the brothers could not so easily evade responsibility for investors' woes. The stock, he said, had soared on the strength of the Guggenheim name, and if they didn't know that, "they were the only seven men in the world of finance ignorant of it. If they did not know that they were either selling themselves or being sold at a fantastic price valuation, then there is no accounting for the fact that M. Guggenheim's Sons has got rich in mining and smelter shares."

In that lush period that lay between the Spanish-American War and the panic of 1907 was the Golden Age of the Guggenheims. In that decade they rose from provincial miners and smelters to be Lead Barons and Silver Princes. Their own fortune had shot up from a few millions to at least $50,000,000, drained from the Rockies and the Sierra Madres, and siphoned from the pockets of an investing public confident of the good name of the Guggenheims and the worthwhile character of the $200,000,000 in securities behind which stood their corporations.

Where now were the defeatists who had predicted ruin for the Smelters Trust when it thrust another $35,000,000 in paper into the Guggenheim pockets in 1901? Never, never, predicted those Jeremiahs, could dividends be paid on all that $100,000,000 in shares listed on the Stock Exchange ticker under the symbol "AR." The lordly march of "AR" earnings proved that they had underestimated the power of monopoly. Those earnings were:

1900	$ 1,979,000
1901	3,828,000
1902	4,861,000
1903	7,576,000
1904	7,905,000
1905	8,898,000
1906	10,161,000
1907	11,509,000

From the 1907 earnings, $7,000,000 had been paid in dividends and a surplus of $13,397,000 stood in the treasury. And dividends were being paid, to boot, on American

Smelters Securities Preferred A and B stocks and on Guggenheim Exploration stock. Goodly portions of all three streams poured into the pockets of M. Guggenheim's Sons, the center of the vast network of mining and smelting enterprises that covered the North American continent.

Looking at those dividend figures, western mine owners wailed: "The name of Guggenheim is Juggernaut." To which King Daniel answered: "We have kept up the price of lead and we propose to do the same thing with silver. The American Smelting and Refining Company now controls the silver output of South America, Central America, British Columbia, Mexico and the United States, which is nearly 80 percent of the output of the world."

The key to a substantial part of those millions in dividends was the Guggenheims' control of lead. Roughly, that netted American Smelting and Refining a cent a pound on smelting and another cent on the sale. With lead selling at four to five and one-half cents a pound, it was an impressive tax collected by these monopolists.

Twice a year Dan Guggenheim and his brothers and his corporation servitors covered part of the circuit of their far-flung possessions, which included no fewer than ninety-three Trust properties. No brass bands greeted them as they surveyed the West. Suspicion, fear, hatred lined the way. The Trust had closed a dozen smelters, bringing disaster to entire communities. The Trust, on a mere order from New York, could close a hundred mines by the simple expedient of refusing to accept their ore. The Trust was not interested in small mines or in small offerings of ore. Little men who owned "gopher holes" scattered across the western mountains, "sagebrushers" hoping to earn a modest living from their small mines, interested the Trust not at all. The blight of "ghost towns" spread across Colorado's mountains. "Disorder, riot and bloodshed" swept the state's mining and smelting centers as the Trust closed smelters and doomed

140

President Roosevelt Has Ordered an Investigation of the Smelter Trust

mines. Now the name of Guggenheim was anathema; the Attorney-General of Colorado filed an anti-trust suit to bar the Trust from operations, but that broke upon the State Supreme Court's stern reprimand that the Trust was not to be deprived of its property rights, no matter what happened to the rights of hundred of small independents.

True to their father's injunction, the Guggenheim brothers were not satisfied. They looked beyond their lead and silver domain for a new empire, and found it in the great porphyry copper fields which were about to astound the mining world with a flow of dividends that made the Smelters Trust's seem parochial. On the threshold of this new era stood the firm of M. Guggenheim's Sons and Guggenheim Exploration with millions in cash, stripped for action. The Silver Princes and the Lead Barons were about to become Copper Kings.

8. IMPERIAL FAMILY

AFTER MEYER GUGGENHEIM retired, the fortunes of the House of Guggenheim rested on the shoulders of his second son, bold, dynamic Dan, assisted by his brothers, Murry and Solomon. This was the triumvirate that encompassed the American Smelting and Refining coup. They were the dominant figures in M. Guggenheim's Sons and in Guggenheim Exploration. And at the center of this triumvirate stood stocky, jovial, ebullient Dan, his head full of ideas and his restless energy eager to transmute ideas into money.

All three had similar training. They were the apples of their father's eye, coming into young manhood before Meyer made a million dollars and slackened the reins on his three younger sons. The older boys he packed off to Europe to learn, to observe, and to work. They studied German and French with zest, threw themselves into the Continental way of life, and gained a cultured polish. Dan, as oldest of the three, went to St. Gall, where the embroidery which his father sold was manufactured. He was treated with the deference due the son of a prized customer.

His European apprenticeship ended, Dan understudied his father in the Philadelphia office of Guggenheim and Pulaski and soon took complete charge of the routine. Meyer was delighted: he believed utterly in the need for efficient routine, and detested it. Now he was free to speculate in railroad shares, to supervise his investments and to become involved in Leadville. Hardly had Dan settled into the job than his father turned over the entire business to him, reorganized as M. Guggenheim's Sons. That was in 1882, when Murry was Swiss representative of the firm, Sol was studying in Germany, Ben was in Columbia and the two younger boys were still in high school.

Perhaps the leadership of the House of Guggenheim would have been Isaac's had he not been the only one of Meyer's seven sons to strike out into business for himself. At the age of seventeen, Isaac went to work in the wholesale grocery firm of M. Myers and Company, owned by his uncle, and by 1876 he had launched his own business, Guggenheim and Company, dealing in oil. In that year he moved to New York, married Carrie, seventeen-year-old daughter of Jonas Sonneborn, a fancy goods dealer, and became interested in wells in Petrolia, Ontario, near Detroit.

Isaac, a stout fellow somewhat taller than his younger brothers, looked for all the world like a prosperous restaurateur. They say he lacked the imagination of his brother, Dan, that he had acquired a conservative cast of mind and looked askance at some of Dan's bolder strokes. All that mattered nothing, however, in 1882 when he joined Meyer's new firm of M. Guggenheim's Sons and watched after its New York office. In the days of the Smelters Trust, Isaac became the trustworthy office manager and counterweight to his younger brothers' dashing flights into finance.

It was natural that Murry and Sol, when they returned from their European apprenticeship, should look up to Dan. Isaac was too busy with his oil affairs to give full attention to the embroidery firm and perhaps, too, his lack of the European background the younger boys had picked up, rather alienated them. It fell to Meyer's second son, Dan, to deploy Murry and Sol into the search for ever greater markets for the firm's embroidery goods. Sol in particular proved an excellent salesman. He was genial and hearty and enjoyed his heritage of Meyer's shrewdness.

When Meyer handed over the Philadelphia smelter to his four older boys, it was Dan who took the New York leadership, Murry watching over the Pueblo smelter, and Sol

144

over the new Monterrey works. In this period, when the four older boys were already wise in the ways of business, the three younger brothers were still in school. Ben was nine years younger than Dan; Simon, eleven, and Will, thirteen years. This trio was looked down upon, naturally, as the "babies" of the family, to be taken under the tutelage of the older members of M. Guggenheim's Sons. As soon as Ben and Will finished short metallurgical courses at Columbia and Pennsylvania, they were sent out West. Ben helped his father in Leadville and in the moves toward establishing the Pueblo smelter. Later he took over charge of the Philadelphia when Murry was satisfied he was experienced enough to take hold. Will was stationed at Monterrey as family representative.

Simon, alone of the younger brothers, enjoyed European schooling and training. He was not burdened with the need for mixing business with pleasure, and chose Spain for his *wanderjahr*. Because he could speak Spanish, he was useful later in Mexican contacts. By the turn of the century, when his three older brothers, stationed in New York, were busy with the high financial moves involved in the capture of the American Smelting and Refining Company, Si was installed as western representative for the Guggenheim mining and smelting interests.

By that time Ben and Will were in disfavor with the triumvirate. Ben had been taken East and placed as family representative in the nearby refinery at Perth Amboy. Will was withdrawn from the West.

Old Meyer delighted in telling his friends that his family was a unit. He used the old Aesopian fable of the sticks, easily broken when separate but unbendable together, to illustrate his point in pleading with his sons to maintain a united front to the world. But the differences in age, experience, training, and temperament could not be disguised. The younger brothers, who had had to fight, with Meyer's assistance, for equal position in M. Guggenheim's Sons with the others, winced under the position of lasting inequality. The break came when Dan decided to organize Guggenheim Exploration. Ben and Will smarting under rebukes, said that it was a mistake to take outsiders such as the Whitneys into the family business. They argued that high finance should be left to the Morgans and the Rogers; the Guggenheims should confine themselves to the straight business pattern of extracting their profits from their plants rather than the pockets of the investing public.

In those exciting years from 1899 to 1901, which saw the House of Guggenheim transformed into one of the nation's leading monopolies and placed high on the pinnacles of Frenzied Finance, Ben and Will decided on a policy of non-cooperation. Will was put in charge of the Smelters Trust's supply department. Such a dreary humdrum job Will interpreted as a slap in the face, and he withdrew, with Ben, from all active participation. Ben entered the mining supply business and headed International Steam Pump until his unsuccessful venture into independent business was tragically cut shore by the iceberg that ripped open the *Titanic* on April 14, 1912. Ben made no effort to get into one of the all too few lifeboats and went down stoically with hundreds of others. His brothers assigned Sol to salvage the affairs of International Steam Pump, which had to go into a receivership.

Simon was dissociated from the New York financial maneuvers by virtue of his position as western representative of the Guggenheim interests. The distance between Denver and New York satisfied him, and he turned to politics as an outlet for the superabundant vitality that Meyer had transmitted to his sons.

Just what happened to Will, Dan probably neither knew nor could understand. But he turned up in Hoboken on November 30, 1900, with a marriage license and wedded

Grace Brown Herbert, a divorcee out of California, resident in New York since 1894. Will was afraid to break the news. He was living at home with his father, Barbara having died in the spring of that year. He kept a parlor down on West Forty-fourth Street near Tenth Avenue, but Grace continued to live at the Waldorf, where she had moved after meeting Will. He assured his bride that, although his brothers would be furious when they heard of his marriage to a Gentile, eventually she would be accepted into the family.

To say that Dan was furious when Will broke the news to him was merely to illustrate the inadequacy of words. When the storm was over, Will was faced with this alternative: divorce Grace or be disowned.

In later years, on the witness stand, Grace gave a vivid account, in short, breathless sentences, of what took place one January 2, 1901. Dan came up to the parlor to confront Grace and demand her compliance in the plan he had carefully devised with his family counsel, Samuel Untermyer. She must go to Dakota immediately and get a divorce. The Guggenheims would see to it that she was taken care of. According to Grace, she told Dan that she didn't care a farthing for the Guggenheim's money. She loved Will and would stay with him whether he had money or not. But the prospect of a penniless future didn't please Will in the least. During the entire session, he sat silent while the Wall Street money master and the woman from out of California fenced.

"Go away and leave us together," implored Grace, according to her story in court. "I don't want your money." Dan was firm. "Will," Grace quoted him as saying, "is nothing but a weakling. You will thank me afterwards for taking him away." Grace stood her ground and Dan announced that his youngest brother would take the next boat for Europe and would stay there until she agreed to a divorce. And in the meantime she wouldn't have a penny.

Dan impressed Ben into service. He interviewed the redoubtable Grace in her fortress. Later she denied that Ben had taxed her with living with other men and had named that, and not religion, as the real ground for the family's alarm.

Will sailed for Europe January 4 with his brother Ben. They headed for Monte Carlo while *Maitre* Untermyer maneuvered to obtain Grace's consent to a divorce, with suitable compensation. This was forthcoming by the end of January. Only it couldn't be a New York divorce. There would be too much scandal and trouble to that. The scene of separation would be Chicago. She must swear that she was a resident of Chicago. A cable to Will brought him speeding back from Europe to attend to his share of the unpleasant formalities in Chicago. That done, he departed immediately for France by way of Florida, Nassau, and New York, motored through Europe, dallied with a Baroness, and further justified his title of "Charming Prince Willie."

Judge Edward F. Dunne, later to be Mayor of Chicago and Governor of Illinois, granted the divorce March 20. Grace's lawyer attended to the alimony details in Untermyer's office in New York. Untermyer handed over a check for $150,000, in lieu of monthly payments of $500. Grace's attorney blithely took a $12,500 cut on that in addition to $25,000 from the Guggenheims. By Christmas Grace's spiritual wounds had healed to the extent that she married Jules Roger Wahl, a Frenchman several years her junior, and they were off for a grand tour of Europe and South America. Back in New York, they departed for Mexico. Back again in New York, they set off for Japan. By the time they were in New York again, the $150,000 was gone. Young Wahl discreetly took the boat for France and later obtained

148

an annulment of the marriage. In the same year, 1904, Will married Aimee Lillian Steinberger, a friend of his sisters, Rose and Cora, and three years later William Guggenheim, Jr., was born.

Grace found penury not a bit to her taste. Inspired by developments in Ben's life and a desire to be back in the Guggenheim money once again, she sat down and wrote Will:

> *I would take the time to read this if I were you.* The enclosed speaks for itself, further explanation is not necessary. *I may not ask you for anything,* nor has Mr. Werner [the attorney] anything further to do with this affair. As your brother [Ben] that feared notoriety a few years ago seems to have gotten his share a few days ago from the accounts in the various papers, I too may go and tell my story as I can get money enough from a certain newspaper to get my jewelry. Not that I want them to wear, but first to redeem them. I may sell them for their full value, and use the money to put a roof over my head. The thousand dollars I still have as I intend to take a rooming house this fall. I am stopping with friends. You will no doubt remember my marrying you was all your doing and thank God I have letters to that effect. You ought to be ashamed of yourself, a man with your money to allow me to want for money enough to support myself. In the past I have kept quiet. Now the world shall know it all.

Grace was willing to settle for $250,000, Untermyer discovered. Dan snorted and decided to fight. On October 31, 1908, Grace's new attorney, William M. Seabury, filed suit for annulment of the Chicago divorce. It was a fraud on the Illinois courts because neither she nor Will had been residents of Illinois, he contended. Consequently, Will was living in bigamy and his child was illegitimate. Justice James

149

W. Gerard of the New York Supreme Court, whose admiration for Dan Guggenheim led him to include Dan's name in his famous list of the fifty-nine men who rule America, upheld the referee's report against Grace.

The case hinged on one point: Was Grace a resident of Illinois when she got the divorce? Untermyer pointed to her sworn statement that she was, in the divorce bill. Against that was the evident fact that she had been living in New York since 1894 and had never lived in Chicago. Untermyer excitedly asked that such testimony be "expunged from the record."

Grace swore "absolutely before God" that she had lived "unaccompanied" in New York, that she had not been divorced in California for adultery.

The courts—Gerard's, the appellate and the Court of Appeals—all declined to go behind the Illinois divorce to establish whether it had been obtained fraudulently. Grace's only recourse, judges agreed, was to go before the Illinois Court. But when she did that, Will's second wife dashed into New York court and obtained an injunction from Gerard restraining Grace.

With fine scorn Untermyer denounced Grace:

> The defendant seeks to open the grave of the past, in which she herself has buried her dead, and now brings forth the corpse to the plaintiff's undoing . . . Her motive is foul and her object blackmail . . . Her conduct is void of conscience, and is immoral and shocking.

To which Seabury answered, at another stage of the proceedings:

> If there is to be an examination into the comparative moral status of the parties, apart from the legal aspect of the case, the respondent cannot stand the test. . . . To do so he must first break the chains that bind him and his own immoral past.

150

Grace appealed against Gerard's injunction. Fighting for her right to enter the Illinois courts, her counsel argued:

Thus the court will see that through all the able efforts of appellant's counsel, the defendant is first prevented from giving her testimony in the New York court, counsel states that the courts of Illinois are the only courts which can receive such testimony, and then, when defendant presents the facts to the Illinois courts and finally files her bill and that court is about to extend to her the privilege and right to be heard, the same resourceful counsel, to prevent even a hearing upon its merits, does two things:

He first broke his promise and violated his stipulation by failure to appear in accordance with its terms and then, lest the facts should, in spite of the broken promise and agreement, be proved, and the conspiracy to which, it is charged, Mr. Untermyer was himself a successful party, be established, this plaintiff [Mrs. Guggenheim] became and was made the convenient instrument and shield both of Mr. Untermyer and Mr. Guggenheim.

Grace succeeded in having the injunction dismissed, and proceeded with her Chicago case. On July 16, 1913, the Circuit Court there refused to annul the divorce, but thundered a denunciation of the Guggenheim case. "Colossal fraud," said the three judges, and recommended that State's Attorney Hoyne conduct a "searching investigation and prosecution of all those who took part in the fraud." Neither Grace nor Will was a bona fide resident of Illinois, the court held. "The decree of divorce . . . was obtained as the direct result of frauds and the procuring of said decree was an outrage against the laws of the state of Illinois and a fraud upon the Circuit Court in Cook County."

Fortunately Untermyer was not in the Chicago court room which heard this excoriation. The Guggenheim lawyers

151

disregarded the thunder and hugged to their bosoms the victory. "It's just another decision for Mr. Guggenheim," they said. "We have beaten them at every turn."

As for State's Attorney Hoyne, he was not at all impressed by the court's fury. In fact, he asked that all records in the case be expunged, and when that was refused, said it would be a waste of time to look into the conduct of attorneys involved.

Early in 1914 Guggenheim attorneys offered Grace $78,000 in alimony, at the rate of $500 a month since her divorce in 1901. Undeterred, she prosecuted her appeal, but the higher court held that she did not come with clean hands. Guggenheim money, and not her fair name, was held to be the real motive for the action. An anti-climax was afforded when Guggenheim's Chicago counsel sued the six brothers for $20,000, the difference between their fee and the $5,000 actually paid. The curtain closed on *Guggenheim* vs. *Guggenheim* with Grace in court again, claiming that the four senior brothers had promised to pay her $42,-500 back alimony and $500 a month for life, the ex-Guggenheim Chicago attorneys backing up her story, and Will found guilty of contempt of court for refusing to answer questions which, he claimed, might incriminate him.

After the divorce in 1901, Will stayed abroad for an entire year. Returning, he found affairs in M. Guggenheim's Sons no better to his liking than ever, with his brothers spreading out in varied enterprises which seemed to him a far cry from mining and smelting. So he plunged into philanthropy, suggested a united publication for the Christian and Jewish charities organizations which became the *Survey*, joined the board of the Christian Charity Organization Society as well as the United Hebrew Charities. Later he threw himself into the activities of the Pennsylvania Society, becoming its treasurer, and into the University of Pennsylvania Club.

Will's was the only divorce in the second generation of the Guggenheim family. To his older brothers, divorce seemed an unpleasant extravaganza, without excuse unless one made a bad mistake, like Will. For themselves, they had all married into respectable, well-to-do, and even wealthy Jewish families, were rearing children, and if they made any pleasurable excursions they regarded that as their own business and not the State's. In this they differed markedly from the third generation.

Another marked difference was the size of families. Barbara bore eleven children, eight of them boys. But neither Isaac nor Sol nor Ben had any sons at all and each had three daughters. So eager was Isaac to see his own name continued, that he persuaded his daughter Beulah to name his oldest-born grandson Isaac Guggenheim II. Only two sons were to be born on the male side of the House of Guggenheim able to carry on the family's business, one of them Dan's and the other Murry's. It was a cruel trick that cast an ominous shadow, even by the end of the nineteenth century, across the future of the family's fortunes on which Meyer had lavished so much care and so many sons.

Dan married Florence Shloss of Philadelphia in 1884 and soon after the birth of his first-born, Meyer Robert, moved to New York, where Harry Frank and Gladys were born. Murry went abroad to marry Leonie, tall and stately daughter of Jacques Bernheim of Mulhouse, Alsace, in 1887. He courted her on lovely Lake Lugano. Leonie still treasures the first box of chocolates her suitor gave her. They had two children, Edmond and Lucille. Murry's name was signed indifferently Murry or Morris throughout his life. At least once in his youth it was Morris, Jr.

Sol married Irene, daughter of V. Henry Rothschild, a New York merchant, in 1895. Like Isaac and Ben, he had three daughters and no sons. Jeannette married Albert Gerstle in 1888 and died in childbirth. Her daughter,

Nettie, was brought up by Barbara, who was glad to have a youngster about the house once more.

Ben's wedding in 1894 ushered in the magnificent period of the Guggenheims, the period of society weddings and lavish displays of wealth. The bride was Florette Seligman of the celebrated banking family.

Simon in 1898 married Olga, beauty, and daughter of Henry Hirsh, a realty operator. Will was best man, and the couple honeymooned in the Orient. They had two sons, one of whom died in his youth and the other was not in good health. Will's son by his second marriage was likewise in poor health.

Because they do not carry the name of Guggenheim, the children of Rose and Cora have been all but neglected in recording the family's third generation. Rose married well, to Albert Loeb, scion of another New York banking family with whom the Guggenheims in later years were to have close financial ties. Meyer helped young Loeb set up a brokerage office downtown. Rose had three sons; but being on the distaff side, they apparently didn't count. In 1899 Cora married a partner in the Loeb firm, Louis F. Rothschild. Cora had one son and two daughters. Only a year later—so little disparity was there in their ages—Cora's niece, Edith, daughter of Isaac, married another partner in the firm, Louis M. Josephthal.

Totaled, the ten Guggenheim brothers and sisters had twenty-four children, ten sons and fourteen daughters, averaging a trifle under two and one-half children, as compared with Barbara's magnificent accomplishment.

As the family entered its golden age, old Meyer, who in his youth had cursed the pack that bent his back and had prayed for a horse, any kind of a horse, now drove his carriage proudly up Central Park West, out quiet, suburban Seventh Avenue, or into Riverside Drive. On more formal occasions his coachman harnessed the victoria and Meyer took Barbara driving through the Park.

The boundless curiosity that drove him in his earlier years from one business into another, was diverted into quieter channels. He delighted to read history and to weigh his own experiences against the current political and social follies. Occasionally he went to the Opera to hear Wagner, and more frequently to musical comedies. He liked particularly the satiric works of Gilbert and Sullivan and Victor Herbert's tuneful pieces. At home his love for music found diversion in the pianola which Will or Nettie pumped patiently for him.

Two or three times a week he took the elevated downtown to drop in at M. Guggenheim's Sons, located in the early nineties at 30 Broad Street, and later at 2 Wall Street. His old roll-top desk waited uncomplainingly for him, but he had little business to transact. Monthly he opened his royalty statement from the A. Y. and Minnie mines. He no longer operated the mines directly but leased them out and drew juicy profits from the dumps, rich with zinc ore, which encumbered the side of Iron Hill. He took little part in directing his sons' enterprises. They had grown to puzzling complexity and the old man lost touch with them. There were dozens of hired men taking care of the business, and Meyer had no faith in hired men.

Happier was he to drop in at the office of his son-in-law, Albert Loeb, whom he had helped to set up as a broker. There was a concern simple in essence and easily grasped, and Meyer's sage advice was as helpful to young Loeb as his capital. His son-in-law provided him with a small office, with desk, reclining chair, and lounge. Often Meyer had his lunch there and then dozed off in the early afternoon hours while Albert was busy on the Exchange.

Only once in those years did Meyer break the routine of his days. When the Black Hundreds inspired the terrible

155

pogrom in Kishinev early in 1903, Meyer was shaken. Having felt the blessings of life in a nation free from the cruder manifestations of anti-Semitism, he yearned to extend a helping hand to the suffering Jews in czarist ghettos. Through Dan's connection with the Whitneys, he was able, it was said, to interest former President Grover Cleveland in speaking at a great Carnegie Hall outpouring at which Mayor Seth Low presided. A hundred thousand dollars was pledged to the relief of the Kishinev community.

Continuing an old custom, the children gathered each Friday at their parents' home at 36 West Seventy-seventh Street, just off Central Park, in a quiet, middle-class section. That was all right in the years directly after the Guggenheims left Philadelphia, but as more boys and girls got married, Barbara could no longer take care of them all on Friday evenings, and so only half the children and their mates came each week. It was the high point in Barbara's week, and all day she busied herself with instructions for cook and maid. She found week-days rather lonely. Before his marriage, Sol stayed with her, and when Will returned from the West in 1899, he made his home there. Murry's house was directly in the rear, at 35 West Seventy-sixth, and he cut a gate between the two gardens so that he could drop over and chat with his mother in the evening. Her two daughters lived next door to each other only two blocks away, and Isaac also lived nearby. But it was on Friday evenings, traditional reunion night among Jewish families, that all the children and the in-laws met.

There was no particular religious significance to the custom. Meyer never had approved of orthodox Jewish observances, which he held tended to set Jews apart. He believed sincerely that America was a land of equality which offered opportunity to all and he opposed customs and observances which interfered with a man taking his place unostentatiously as an everyday American. In New York he

156

hardly ever went to a synagogue, except to humor Barbara, who was no fanatic either.

The men and women sat at different tables, not from any religious precept, but because their interests diverged so sharply. Relaxation to a male Guggenheim meant to talk business. To a female Guggenheim it meant dresses, babies, servants. So it was all silver and lead and mines and smelters at one table, with merry stories of dumb mine managers, outwitted competitors and smart deals, while at the other table the merits of Dressmaker McNally's latest creations were subjected to sharp analysis, and the bright sayings of each mama's child were held up for applause.

Meyer and Barbara rarely had outsiders in at the house. All their old friends were in Philadelphia and they had not bothered much about new ones in New York. It was fatiguing to get around such a city and anyway a couple with nine children, nearly all married, and a crop of growing grandchildren felt little need for outside human contacts. Barbara was in constantly worse health. Worn out by a lifetime of childbearing, she suffered from diabetes before the day of insulin. The disease took a turn for the worse early in 1900. Ben and Will were in Europe when the news was cabled them. Both took the next boat home. Barbara died March 20, 1900, at the age of sixty-seven. Never was a mother mourned more sincerely and deeply: her life had been for her children and for them only. Tenderly they laid her body away in the big mausoleum Will had designed only the year before in Salem Fields, Jamaica, Long Island.

As a memorial to their mother, the brothers gave $200,-000 to Mt. Sinai for a wing for paying patients, to increase the hospital's income. Meyer added a final $60,000 to his long list of gifts to the Jewish Hospital in Philadelphia. Will gave the United Hebrew Charities $50,000 toward a permanent endowment to be known as the Barbara Guggenheim Memorial Fund and promised another $50,000, matching his dollar against every five given to the fund. The income went to aid poor Russian Jews. As President Henry Rice of the Charities explained:

"If we find a Hebrew workman in a factory where he has contracted consumption and where he is no longer able to pursue his usual work without menace to his life, we purchase him a lemonade stand or a fruit stand or something of the sort so that he will be able to remain outdoors and thus have a chance to preserve his health." About 150 were thus set up in business for themselves each year, and Rice was hopeful that Will's generosity "would arouse other Hebrews to like munificence."

Old Meyer felt the chill of the sere years gathering in his bones. His trips downtown became fewer and when he went driving in the Park, his coachman held the reins. The Friday evening reunions were no longer held on Seventy-seventh Street. The New Year's celebrations remained the high point of the family's year, and Meyer's seventy-fifth birthday the grandest of all such high times. During the day he had received only perfunctory greetings, but early in the evening he was taken over to Isaac's house, to be greeted by the House of Guggenheim, nine children, seventeen grandchildren, and a dozen parents of various sons: and daughters-in-law. Two great-grandchildren could have been there too, had it not been past bedtime.

The greetings over Meyer was seated in a great chair in Isaac's salon, and the program was on. Bob, Harry, Edmond, and Nettie acted in a satiric skit on Wall Street, "U Ketchum and I Skinem", written by William Spiegelberg, Isaac's son-in-law and himself a Wall Street broker. Meyer, ever ready for a good joke, laughed until the tears rolled down his cheeks. Spiegelberg sang parodies of popular songs; Helene, Isaac's daughter, sang the Coquette Song from "The Mocking Bird," and Nettie recited. After the family entertainment was over, there was a musicale by a professional orchestra, and then dancing.

What thoughts must have gone through Old Meyer's head as he sat there in his big chair watching the merriment in his honor. How the world had changed in the fifty-six years since he had come down the gangplank at a Philadelphia dock, penniless, friendless, ignorant even of the language of the country. He had done the most menial of all labor, selling odds and ends carried on his back, he had gone hungry, had lived in wretched hovels in Philadelphia alleys.

And yet his younger sons knew nothing of that life save as a story told by the evening fire, and even his oldest boy, Isaac, had known comfort, if not luxury, from childhood. To them business was a sporting game, with opportunity thrust under their noses on a silver platter, and not a bitter struggle against hunger itself. He wondered if they were made of as tough stuff as he, whether they would have had the courage, the patience, the humility to face life as he had.

Never mind, it didn't matter a bit. He was proud of his boys as of himself. Thank God they did not need to go through the hardships of his own youth. He built for them and they carried on magnificently. They understood well his oft-repeated proverb: "Roasted pigeons do not fly into one's mouth." On the basis of his lone smelter out in Pueblo they had reared the American Smelters Trust. He knew that he couldn't have done that. In the first place, no one man could have; in the second, the world had changed so much in the past fifty years and particularly in the last ten, that the rules of the business game had already become strange to him.

What mattered was that his boys were equal to the great opportunity. They now ranked with America's biggest Big Business. He had made them millionaires; they had made themselves multi-millionaires.

At last old Meyer Guggenheim was satisfied. He beamed on his grandchildren (the boys, big lusty six foot fellows, towering over their fathers), joked with his daughters-in-law, quipped with their parents, and went to bed happy.

A strange case clouded Meyer's last years. Hanna Mc-Namara, forty-five, sued for $100,000 for breach of promise. He was fighting mad and offered $10,000 reward to anyone who had ever seen them together. Indignantly he denied that she had ever worked at his house. But Hanna stubbornly contended she had been in "constant intimate association" with Meyer for twenty-five years until 1904. Soon after Barbara's death, she said, Meyer promised to marry her, but kept putting it off and now she was afraid he might up and die on her. So she asked that her suit be put on the preferred calendar. Meyer's physician deposed that he was good for at least five more years. It turned out that the doctor was wrong and Hanna was right, about that aspect of the case.

Old friends of Meyer, while they might know nothing of the facts in the McNamara case, nudged each other and remarked that Meyer had always been a gay dog. Unencumbered by puritanism, Meyer held an Old Testament view of marriage which forgave much so long as a man reared his family honestly, gave his wife the affection due her, and comported himself with dignity in public life.

On Thanksgiving Day of 1904 Meyer submitted to the third of a series of operations. It was typical of him, old-fashioned in his ways to the last, to shun a hospital. The surgeons urged him to take an anesthetic, but Meyer declined. "You can't sell a Jew anesthetics or life insurance," he remarked, as he settled down on the table. While the surgeons worked over him, he called nonchalantly for a cigar. The knife cut deep and Meyer winced. Turning to a nurse, he asked her to play a record on the phonograph, and the operation was ended to music, Meyer puffing his cigar all the while.

He failed to make a complete recovery. Weakened by a bad cold, he was taken to Palm Beach early in March, 1905. After a few days at the Royal Poinciana, he took a turn for the worse and a cottage was rented on Lake Worth. Dr. Edwin Sternberger rushed down to Florida, part way by special train, to attend the failing capitalist, but he died quietly March 15, aged seventy-eight.

As became a leading figure in Jewry, Meyer Guggenheim's funeral service was held in splendid Temple Emanu-el on Fifth Avenue. Old friends such as Jacob Schiff and the Seligmans, all the members of his family, including by now four great-grandchildren, ranking officials from his sons' many enterprises and the luminaries of the Jewish world were there to do homage. The cortege entered as the Kol Nidre was intoned.

"His ideal of success", said Rabbi Joseph Silverman, "was achievement by building up—not by tearing down. He rose not upon the prostrate forms of others. Simplicity of thought and action characterized his every movement. Consideration of others which characterized his life is one of the highest virtues of man and I would esteem it greater than that charity which is so often tendered by us after we have caused our fellow-men pain and suffering."

The simple services over, the great organ of Emanu-el —Meyer's main reason for attending services during his life—played Chopin's Funeral March, the cortege withdrew, and the body was placed beside Barbara's out in Salem Fields.

His will revealed a fortune of about $2,250,000, of which a third was in American Smelting, nearly $500,000 in railroad bonds and substantial amounts in American Tobacco and Tennessee Iron. The bulk of his estate he gave to his two daughters and his granddaughter. To Rose he gave

161

$500,000 in a life trust administered by Murry; to Cora he left $100,000 in cash and $300,000 in a life trust; to Nettie, $500,000 in a life trust but with a proviso that she could have $200,000 in cash from it on her marriage. To his housekeeper he left 100 shares of American Smelting, valued at some $12,000. He bequeathed $20,000 each to the Hebrew Benevolent and Orphan Asylum in Philadelphia, to the Montefiore Home for Chronic Invalids, to the Mt. Sinai Hospital, and to the Jewish Hospital in Philadelphia.

Jewish leaders in Philadelphia and New York joined in encomiums upon Meyer's virtues, his modesty, simplicity, scrupulous honesty, and fair dealing. Said an old associate: "I never saw a man of the same degree of persistence and fortitude." Said another: "I like to think of him as a man who got ahead without walking over the graves of others."

The tributes were justified. He was the pushful man par excellence, but not for him was the ruthlessness of monopoly nor the cleverness of those who manufactured their own money by issuing millions of shares of stocks and floated bond issues to finance undertakings in which they held sole control. In those achievements of corporate business his older sons amply made up for Meyer's backwardness. His were the virtues of a simpler time, but on them the House of Guggenheim would never have gained pre-eminence above ten thousand other modestly successful fortunes.

As a memorial to him, his boys built an asylum for the aged, in his birthplace, Lengnau, Switzerland, It was the only recognition they ever gave their Swiss origin; apparently the history of the Swiss Family Guggenheim was too distasteful to dwell upon.

His last summers Meyer had spent with his boys at their summer places along Long Branch, New Jersey, where Dan had built a rambling, flower-decked summer home called Firenze, a tribute to his wife, Florence. Israel Zangwill stayed at Dan's place one summer and other notables in the

Jewish world also visited him there. Murry had a Moorish castle nearby and Sol a place called The Towers. Dan dallied at being a gentleman gardener, particularly in drug plants. He pioneered in introducing belladonna into American cultivation.

In town Dan lived with the magnificence expected of New York's wealthiest Jewish family, at 12 West Fifty-fourth Street, just off Fifth Avenue and only a few doors from John D. Rockefeller's mansion. For neighbors he had John D., Jr., just across the street, Morton F. Plant, Chauncey M. Depew, and Mrs. John Jacob Astor. But while none rose up to deny Dan's right to live among the first, he himself tired of the swagger. He was no poseur, and the plush elegance of the Fifties bored him. Neither he nor Florence cared for society life and after a few years they moved to the St. Regis. Isaac established himself at 763 Fifth Avenue, Sol at 743, Murry at 998, William at 833. They belonged to the Lotos Club, which patronized the arts, and the Criterion. They patronized art even more directly; Dan had his Corots, Daubignys, Isabeys and Homer Martins, and Simon cherished a Rembrandt.

The brothers' association with the Whitneys, Thomas Fortune Ryan, and others in Guggenheim Exploration, brought them into business circles not directly affecting mining and smelting. Thus Dan became a director of Continental Rubber, Gimbel Brothers, Morton Trust, and the National Bank of Commerce. Isaac was a director of the National Park Bank, Plaza Bank and International Banking Corporation. Sol was interested in Interborough-Metropolitan traction and Metropolitan Street Railway. Murry was treasurer and trustee of the Baron De Hirsch fund, which aimed to settle refugee Jews on farm lands.

Men who held such eminent position in Jewry owed a multitude of debts to various enterprises that cherished the faith. It was characteristic of wealthy, non-religious Jews

163

that they gave open-handedly to both traditional and liberal Jewish creeds. Jacob Schiff, for example, took hold of the run-down Jewish Theological Seminary, bought it a fine site at One Hundred and Twenty-third Street and Broadway, a few blocks from Columbia and adjacent to the medieval pile of Union Theological, and launched a drive to endow it. Dan and the four brothers who always acted jointly with him—Isaac, Murry, Sol and Simon—gave $50,000 to this stronghold of arch-conservatism. Their gift came from no conviction that the tenets of orthodoxy were correct and certainly they were little interested in the scant handful of young rabbis turned out each year. It was pride of race that forbade leaving a Jewish institution bedraggled. Some years later the brothers gave $25,000 to Hebrew Union College in Cincinnati, the seat of the reformed faith, following an appeal by their friend, Adolph Ochs, proprietor of the *New York Times*.

Dogmatism sat no more heavily on Louis Marshall, legal confidant of the Guggenheims, who was coming more and more into leadership of American Jewry. A liberal, he cheerfully became chairman of the board of orthodox Jewish Theological and President of reformed Temple Emanu-el, the "Cathedral of Israel," the richest Jewish temple in all Christendom. The roll of Emanu-el's trustees became the highest Social Register of the American Jewish community, and Dan's name was duly inscribed.

Isaac, although oldest of the family, gladly yielded the spotlight to Dan. He was a quiet, aloof fellow who made friends none too easily. He, nevertheless, was a warm admirer of Mayor Gaynor and was critical when Mayor Mitchel removed Gaynor's police commissioner, Douglas I. McKay. To McKay he sent $1,000 for the Legion of Honor fund for the families of policemen killed on duty. His daughters long remembered Isaac's trip to Europe for treatment after a nervous breakdown. "But why did you come to

Europe for treatment?" asked the amazed German physician. "All I can do is give you the treatment evolved by your famous Philadelphian, Dr. Weir Mitchell."

Isaac's desire to keep out of the public eye was taken as a command by his wife, Carrie, who stepped out of the matinee one afternoon to find her chauffeur under arrest for blocking the street, defying a policeman and violating other rules in his eagerness to be at the theatre door at the exact moment Mrs. Guggenheim needed him. Carrie pleaded with the policeman to forget about it, and then jumped in the auto to make the trip down to the police station. There she refused to give her name, but confused, signed a bail bond for her driver. When she realized she had given away her name, she broke into tears, tore up the paper and stamped on it. More amused than angry, the lieutenant telephoned her husband who smilingly rescued his wife and chauffeur. Isaac consoled Carrie, telling her he hoped his name would never appear on the police blotter for a worse crime.

Dan's flair for publicity—he liked to keep the scales tipped in his favor, or at least balanced—was illustrated by his prompt dispatch of an order for $50,000 on an Oakland bank after earthquake and fire had destroyed much of San Francisco. Two drays bore the money to the stricken city and Dan wired General Funston: "No red tape. Give it to the people at once."

To supplement their other lordly gifts to Mt. Sinai, the five brothers gave $165,000 to add to the pavilion which was a memorial to their parents. The pavilion was to be seven stories high and to extend two hundred feet along Fifth Avenue, overlooking Central Park, from Ninety-ninth to One Hundredth Streets.

Such gifts emphasized the wealth of the Guggenheim family and brought them the malignant attention of bombers. The firm of M. Guggenheim's Sons and Jacob Schiff each received a bomb one day in 1905. Their enemies were too crude: to escape detection, they had cut the letters of the alphabet they needed from newspaper headlines. Forewarned, Guggenheim clerks doused the package in water and fled the room. There was a muffled roar. "Anarchists," muttered the police as they examined the bundle of powder, sandpaper, matches, and sulphuric acid. The theory saved them thought.

Only one Guggenheim gift failed to be appreciated. In 1909 Kaiser Wilhelm II gave a statue of Frederick VIII to the United States through his good friend and admirer, Theodore Roosevelt. Wishing to return the compliment, Dan Guggenheim thought it would be nice to give a statue of George Washington to Germany. German diplomats felt that the Guggenheims without warrant put themselves on a plane with the All-Highest by the exchange gift, and perhaps, too, they hardly approved of Washington's anti-monarchistic achievements. The statue was never presented.

Dan's own sense of humanity and his knack of doing the right thing was never better illustrated than when his car ran down a little Italian boy in Lafayette Street, the crowded thoroughfare between uptown and downtown New York. Dan took the boy in his own arms and asked a policeman to accompany him to the hospital. From there he called the boy's parents to come to the hospital, waited till they arrived, and then comforted them. He of course took care of all hospital expenses and gave friendly help to the family. Another man of affairs might have shrunk from the publicity involved and the time wasted, contenting himself with instructing his chauffeur to take care of the child.

Unlike his father, who paid little attention to his clothes, Dan was the faultless dresser. Not for him was Meyer's casuistry: "If they know me, it doesn't matter; and if they don't, what does it matter?" He astonished reporters in the trials in which he was a central figure by pulling a different suit out of his wardrobe each day. On one occasion he faced

166

his examiner for three days running, cool and collected, remembering little and forgetting much ("I don't clutter up my head with details"), sipping vichy water and milk by the quart as a cure for indigestion. Urbanely he deprecated a comparison of his wealth with that of a New England millionaire who knew not how many automobiles he had. "I have only four," said Dan.

For himself and his brothers, Dan always insisted on at least two months off in every year, summer and winter. It was his contention that if a man worked twelve months of the year, the value of his labor was cut in half. This theory was never tried out on Dan's laborers. The Guggenheim brothers were likely to be found at the summer homes in late spring and early summer, in Europe later in the summer, and in the south in the winter. Sol, whose lordly manner approached Dan's, developed a ranch out in Idaho which was a suitable refuge any month of the year, for hunting, fishing, riding, and plain loafing.

Dan had his own ideas about offices. One was that office boys must not be kept waiting. "Their time is just as valuable to them," he said, "as mine is to me." That was an exaggeration but it showed Dan's executive conviction that every unit should be kept usefully working.

His oldest son, Meyer Robert, inherited Dan's grand manner. Still a student in Columbia School of Mines, he married Grace Bernheimer November 30, 1905, and took over his father's mansion in West Fifty-fourth Street. The first-born was named Daniel II. When he was graduated in 1907, some thirty years after his Uncle Ben, the newspapers announced that he would start work in the Guggenheim enterprises at the bottom of the ladder. Bob didn't waste much time with the ladder, the more so as he found dogs far more entertaining than mining and metallurgy. Despite that, his father gave him directorships in American Smelting

167

and Refining and Guggenheim Exploration and waited prayerfully.

Bob showered sparks wherever he went. His dad was interested in Alaska at the time of the Seattle Alaska-Yukon-Pacific Exposition in 1909, and so what better than for Bob to sponsor a Guggenheim cup race from the East to Seattle? The contest was highly spectacular as roads were few and far between in the West. It was a gala day when the cup-winning Ford raced up Seattle's Second Avenue and out to the Exposition grounds to the clanging of street fire alarms and police sirens. Bob had the best of good times in Seattle that year and wound up overdrawn $25,000. His father came to the rescue.

At great expense that year, he said, he brought a team of Alaska Huskies to the Westminster Kennel show in Madison Square Garden. Harnessed to their sleds, the dogs were the feature of the show. Bob kept kennels out at his summer home in Roslyn, Long Island. English bulldogs were his hobby, and his prize pups he listed invariably with the first name "Frenzi"—could it have been in some devious homage to his mother, whose name, italianized, graced Dan's summer home? He added Russian greyhounds and fox terriers to his kennels, was a judge at the Bulldog Show of America and was considered an authority on canine rather than business affairs. His Uncle Isaac, who had paid as much as $1,000 for a dachshund, looked on in amusement.

It must have been a biting disappointment to Dan that his oldest son showed no greater interest in the Guggenheim firms. He dropped out of Guggenheim Exploration in 1909 and out of American Smelting a year later. Something was happening to the House of Guggenheim that neither Meyer nor Dan had foreseen. The third generation, Dan was to find out, either lacked the ability or the desire to take their place in M. Guggenheim's Sons. Why after all should Bob renounce the pleasures of life to concern himself with piling up more millions? He had all he wanted and what more was to be gained by hard work? The itch to accumulate which had driven Meyer on and on had spent itself so soon.

Fortunately for Dan, his second son, Harry, showed a more serious turn of mind. And his daughter Gladys was keen-minded. It was too bad women didn't count in Guggenheim business affairs, for many said that Gladys was the most capable of Dan's children. But eighteen and just out of Rosemary Hall, she became engaged to Roger W. Straus, just out of Princeton, while they were with their parents in Europe, in the fall of 1913. Her wedding to the son of Oscar S. Straus, former Ambassador to Turkey, former Cabinet member, and biographer of Roger Williams, was the highlight of society interest in January, 1914.

The ceremony was solemnized at the St. Regis, where Gladys' parents lived, by Dr. Joseph Silverman, who had buried the girl's grandfather. The bride and groom walked down a long aisle of gilt standards garlanded with flowers and ribbon the length of the ballroom to a temple of flowers at the south end. There eight great columns of silver held up a dome of white roses and smilax.

Present were the Guggenheims and the Strauses—Oscar, Nathan, Jesse—and Mrs. Theodore Roosevelt, Mrs. Nicholas Longworth, Mr. and Mrs. James Speyer, Mr. and Mrs. Andrew Carnegie, Mr. and Mrs. Louis Marshall, Dr. and Mrs. Judah Magnes, the Seligmans and other notables. Messages were received from Sir Ernest Cassel, Earl Grey, Ambassadors Merrick, Page, and Morgenthau, and from Baron Edmond de Rothschild.

Another of the famous Guggenheim weddings—westerners grumbled that it cost a Guggenheim as much to marry off his daughter as to pay a miner for half his life's work—was that of Lucille, daughter of Murry, to Frederic A. Gimbel, graduate of Phillips Andover and Yale. That wedding, too, was solemnized at the St. Regis, on December 15, 1914. Thousands of roses, camellias and lilies bloomed in natural beauty in a setting of rich green in the marble ballroom, made over into an Italian garden. In a large pergola at the south end of the ballroom was a dense growth of smilax and roses as a background to camellias intertwined with ropes of green, festooned to represent a curtain. A string orchestra was hidden behind bay trees, while an organist played softly. The aisle was a garden path of dark green velvet scattered with rose petals. Killarney roses graced high standards connected with streamers of white satin ribbon. Walls of the ballroom were screened with smilax, baytrees, and fruit-laden orange trees.

The wedding cake was three feet high and surmounted by little cupids and doves.

9. MEXICAN EXTRAVAGANZA

MINE OWNERS eager for Guggenheim cash, prospectors who had stumbled across riches in ravines five hundred miles from civilization, scheming promoters armed with options which cost them little or nothing, laid siege to 71 Broadway, wandering from office to office, waiting for long hours to see a Guggenheim underling, living in cheap hotels against the time when a secretary would nod and give an appointment.

Rarely did they see a Guggenheim, unless he was darting down the hall. Dan's invariable rule forebade such familiarity with the president of Guggenheim Exploration. The most that the promoter could hope was to see a Hammond assistant. The day before Christmas of 1902 one such, Brad Barnar, who had prospected, mined, and promoted all over the West on a shoestring, had progressed far enough through the wickets of Guggenex to see Ed Rogers, Hammond's predecessor. He had an option, he explained, on a Mexican bonanza, the Esperanza, next to the famed El Oro gold property. Rogers, as a matter of routine, asked for maps and figures, and bade his visitor a Merry Christmas.

Barnar dashed to the telegraph office to inform dour old August Sahlberg that he had buyers for Esperanza. In a covering letter he urged strictest secrecy on Sahlberg: "The question of the sale of a mine is, as you know, of as delicate a reputation as that of a woman, and no talking."

Sahlberg, suffering from a floating spleen and sick at last of his rugged life in a shack 9,300 feet up on the flanks of El Oro, opened the telegram and then threw it on the floor and spat. Why did he ever let a fellow like Brad Barnar pester him? Bitterly he reviewed his life for Esperanza, his

171

hopes when he dangled it under the nose of Exploration of London, the begging he had had to do in Mexico City to get suspicious, flinty Mexicans to put a few thousand pesos into development work, the price they had exacted from him— 70 per cent of the share capital. Would he ever live to see the day when he could sell his mine and retire to Florida to mend a rebellious body and pass his last years in peace and the companionship of his own people? He picked up the telegram from the rough board floor.

SEE EDWARD DOERR, GUGGENHEIM AGENT, MEXICO CITY

Damned if he'd see a Guggenheim man; let him come and look at it if he wanted to. He wrote to Doerr, who answered, propounding a list of questions that staggered Esperanza's manager. In a mine operating with benefit of accountants and clerks, the questionnaire would have been routine: but Sahlberg sat in his shack, his choler mounting every time he glanced at the catechism.

"Judging from your letter," he wrote Doerr, "the interest of your company in buying Esperanza is not what letters from New York have led me to believe. If it was, either yourself or another of your company's bona fide examining engineers would go to El Oro, where all the necessary data would be given. As it is, I do not feel justified in going to all the trouble that the information which you require entails. I shall wire New York immediately that the proposed transaction is off."

To Brad Barnar, chewing his fingernails in New York while this deal on which he hoped for a 10 per cent commission hung fire, Sahlberg wrote, in high dudgeon, that Doerr "wants to go into ancient history and for that life is too short. When a man wants to examine a mine of the magnitude of La Esperanza by proxy while sitting in his office, and he wants the proxy to be yours truly, I respectfully decline—which I did to Mr. Doerr."

172

Barnar borrowed more money from his Vesey Street friend, Dennis Harris, and frantically wired Sahlberg by all means to come to New York. As Esperanza's manager was going to Chicago to buy more mining machinery, he grudgingly came East, met Chief Engineer Rogers and Secretary W. W. Porter of Guggenheim Exploration, laid his own beautifully thorough maps before them.

"$3,000,000, gold," said Sahlberg, curtly when asked his price.

Rogers reminded him that Guggenex bought only on the basis of a minimum 18½ percent return from a mine and that according to his own figures, the mine's value would be $2,000,000. Sahlberg grabbed his hat and stamped out of the office. The figure of Brad Barnar, crushed, disappeared from Guggenheim offices, never to return.

A month later Rogers was out and Hammond was ensconced as general manager of Guggenheim Exploration. After his preliminary survey of his new company, he hitched his private car, Kya Yami (Zulu for "One of My Homes") to a Pennsylvania express and was off for Colorado. On April 13 he left Colorado Springs for Mexico City.

Hammond sent a flunkey with his respects to President Díaz. The president sent his military attaché with a command for dinner at the Palace. Three years earlier, after his Boer experience, Hammond had dropped down to Mexico armed with a letter of introduction from Secretary of State Hay. The dictator and the engineer had become fast friends, Díaz twitting Hammond on his revolutionary proclivities, and Hammond responding that such activities were not needed in Mexico, under Don Porfirio's beneficent sway. Thereafter the man who became the Guggenheim's representative in Mexico was treated with more deference than the American Ambassador himself: after all, the Ambassador was a shadow of a shadow but Hammond was envoy plenipotentiary of Yankee power.

Social courtesies out of the way, the engineer addressed himself to the task at hand: La Esperanza, which he himself had scouted on his first visit and which was still on the market. The Kya Yami and a special train bearing his staff were off for El Oro, in the neighboring State of Mexico. Among them was E. A. Wiltsee, who had been with Hammond on the Rand, and to whom Hammond handed over his Venture connection when he joined Guggenheim forces.

For Sahlberg it was now or never. The spleen grew worse and the world fuzzed before his eyes every time he came up out of the mine. For once he was deferential, in the presence of Hammond, Wiltsee, Beatty, and Doerr who among them represented as much of mining engineering and finance as were ever likely to be seen in this camp. Hammond, for all his lordly airs, recognized a kindred spirit in the tough old engineer whose faith had pried into the depths of Esperanza and brought up, almost unaided, $752,000 in gold ore in 1902, and laid bare $4,000,000 more.

"Yes, sir," boasted Sahlberg. "You can't beat La Esperanza. It costs us $12 a ton, mex., to get this ore out, and we get $12 a ton, gold, for it."

On the other side of the ledger was the drop in Esperanza quotations from 1,700 pesos a few years before to 1,100, because of adverse reports. Hammond concluded that Esperanza now showed enough paying ore to justify negotiations so he left Beatty at the mine to continue assay tests and Wiltsee in Mexico City to negotiate with the major owners of *La Compañia Minera La Esperanza y Anexas*. Venture's representative met Don Luis Mendez, venerable lawyer whose record for honesty, in the midst of the temptations abounding in the capital of a rickety land, was notable throughout the Republic. Don Luis represented, as trustee, the estates of the late owners. Dan Guggenheim himself conceded that he was a man "of the highest class in every respect, as a gentleman and a scholar and a lawyer."

174

Don Luis was stubborn in backing up Sahlberg's contention that their mine was worth $3,000,000 and negotiations lapsed. Splenetic Sahlberg, disheartened by the drag, went down into his mine once too often and was carried to the surface, dead. His dream of retirement and declining years in Florida had been his only consolation for Esperanza's hard years.

Wiltsee saw his chance. Manuel Calero, later Ambassador to Washington but then attorney for Wiltsee and Venture, hatched up a pretty scheme to scare old Don Luis into action. Sahlberg's executor was anxious to wind up the engineer's estate, and agreed. "You go to Don Luis," Wiltsee instructed him, "and get very angry with him and tell him if he does not join with you in the option that you will put your entire 30 per cent of the stock on the market and clean up and come to the States." The trick brought old Don Luis around, and he signed an option to sell the mine for $2,025,000.

Hammond made a beeline to Dan Guggenheim's office bursting with the news that Mexico's greatest gold mine was theirs for a song. Dan listened impassively, waved Beatty's report and Wiltsee's telegram to one side, reached for other papers on his desk and informed Hammond that he was busy.

The engineer was astounded. He strode into his own office, fumed, grabbed his hat, and darted down to the subway. Unable to compose himself after he reached his Fifth Avenue home, he rang up Bill Whitney, and dashed out to his Long Island place.

"Is Dan Guggenheim crazy?" he bellowed, as he greeted the financier.

"Not from what I know of him," answered Whitney.

Rapidly Hammond sketched the Esperanza, its history and prospects.

"All right, we'll take it up together," concluded his

friend. "No use letting things like that get by us. I'll see Dan tomorrow and find out what's the trouble, and if he won't go along, we'll take it up together."

Dan was out of town and did not return till Monday. The three had lunch that noon and Dan seemed surprised at the astonishment of his partner and his engineer's impatience.

"Why, if you think Esperanza's that good, of course Exploration will take 51 percent," he said.

Hammond stared at his employer and lapsed into silence. In later years he said charitably that "at the time Mr. Dan was diverted by trivial schemes."

Beatty went to London to report to Venture on its 49 per cent share and help "prepare the market" for the flotation of Esperanza, Ltd., capitalization £455,000. Esperanza struck a bonanza vein, and so enthusiastic became L. Hirsch and Company, London specialists in mining stocks, that the shares rose to 300. Hammond, touchy in that early period concerning his own firm's reputation in the market, cabled London that the Guggenheim stock would be dumped to break the market if Hirsch boomed Esperanza any higher. Hirsch replied that they would handle no more Guggenheim ventures. Hammond shot back a hot retort that they would never have a chance to.

Esperanza's profits rose from $24,000 a month to $143,000 and by 1906 reached, for a few months, $350,000. Dividends that year were 160 percent on capital. So enamored was Dan of the mine which he had coolly turned down of a Friday afternoon, that it was the sole property maintained when Guggenex dumped its mines into American Smelters Securities in 1905. Esperanza paid $6,000,000 clear before it was abandoned.

The epilogue to this extravaganza in Guggenheim finance was played in New Jersey courts when Dennis Harris, who had grubstaked Brad Barner in Manhattan while he tried

176

to sell his Esperanza option, entered claim to $202,500. Brad, who testified that he had spent his whole life "doing things for others for nothing," had signed over his claim to the seedy old promoter of mines whose hopes were infinite and accomplishments nil. Harris asserted that the Guggenheims had bought Esperanza because of Brad's salesmanship.

Both Brad and Harris were dead before the case had dragged its way through New Jersey's legal labyrinth. A gentleman from King William County, Virginia, who had never heard of Esperanza before, presented himself as executor of Harris' estate, and demanded $202,500 with appropriate interest. Even the New Jersey courts wearied of this, and rang down the curtain.

10. CONGO INTERLUDE

LEOPOLD II was about to lose control of the vastest domain ever yet to fall into the private ownership of a single mortal. Emile Vandervelde, fiery young Socialist, was hammering the aging monarch as a man whose conscienceless cupidity had reduced the Congo Free State into the world's prize slave-pen. The Belgian Parliament, stung by Vandervelde's eloquence and the international scorn heaped upon Leopold's gray head, was about to transfer interior Africa from the monarch's private purse to the nation's public charge. Cagey Leopold, aware of his loyal subjects' intentions, greedily cast about for suitable concessionaires to whom he could sell the remaining undeveloped parts of his black empire. He struck up an alliance with the "most adroit, suave, and noiseless man" in American finance, Thomas Fortune Ryan, hero of New York's traction scandals, of Equitable Life and the Tobacco Trust.

The King, approaching the end of his years and increasingly devoted to his amours, had one last and favorite corporate child for which he sought a legitimate father. He hoped, before Parliament intervened, to organize a company to develop the rubber and gold of the Kasai River, which rose in the southwestern part of the Congo Free State and ran northerly to the Congo. From America had come the bitterest criticism of his inhumanities and so to America he sent Count Kowalsky, hired for 100,000 francs to defend him and scout for American capital. Kowalsky scored not too brilliantly with President Roosevelt; but he reported to his employer that Thomas Fortune Ryan, inordinately rich, a Catholic peer beyond reproach, and an endless hunter for lucrative investment, was the King's man. One thing that attracted the Belgian monarch's attention was the Lawrence process for extracting rubber from the guayule plant. Ryan and Senator Nelson Aldrich, the Republican leader, owned the Lawrence patent. Leopold summoned the six-foot American potentate, then sojourning in Europe, to confer with him in Brussels but Ryan was in no mood for business. The astonished King thereupon dispatched a personal envoy, and Ryan interrupted his vacation to hie himself to the Belgian capital.

Leopold and his financial man Friday, Jean Jadot, governor of the *Société Générale*, suspected that there was more than rubber on the upper reaches of the Kasai, and he appealed to Ryan to send in American engineers to explore. Ryan remembered his friend, Dan Guggenheim, whose Exploration Company specialized in doing just that. He cabled Dan. Alfred Chester Beatty, number-two man of Guggenex, grabbed the next boat Europe-bound.

The royal concession, signed November 9, 1906, gave to the new *Société Internationale Forestière et Minière du Congo* (*Forminière* for short) the right to prospect for minerals in the entire unassigned public domain—forty-five times as large as Belgium—for six years, with the proviso that mines exploited could be worked for ninety-nine years. *Forminière* was capitalized at 10,000,000 francs, half put up by Ryan and his friends, a quarter by the *Société Générale*, the King retaining a quarter interest.

As the concession placed the Guggenheims in control of mineral exploitation of all the undeveloped Congo save only that given to the *Union Minière* (where Katanga's copper was later discovered), Beatty was given a hearty welcome when he reported to Dan at the St. Regis. Another block of Guggenheim Exploration was set aside for him on option at $100 a share. (The stock was selling at about $300.)

Dan went up to see Thomas Fortune Ryan in his Fifth Avenue palace. Ushered into a great room lined with palms, with a fountain playing in the court, Dan for once lost his self-assurance. He thought it was Ryan's famous private chapel and he did not understand chapel etiquette. His host roared with laughter and assured him it was only the library. Ryan, a leonine figure with a bellowing voice and a magnificent pearl pin stuck in his cravat, towered over the soft-spoken little mining financier.

Ryan and Guggenheim produced from their conference the American Congo Company and the Intercontinental Rubber Company, the latter a $30,000,000 promotion controlled by the Ryan-Aldrich Continental Rubber Company. Bernard M. Baruch and others were invited in to make something out of Intercontinental on the market; later the company developed a big business in handling the rubber extracted from the guayule.

Dan named his engineer, Beatty, as vice-president of American Congo and installed him as chairman of *Forminière's* technical committee. Guggenheim engineers went up the Kasai for gold and copper while Ryan's men scouted for the rubber possibilities. But the development of the Malayan rubber plantations was beginning, so the coveted guayule process was never tried out in the Congo. And as for the mining technicians, they found something even more interesting than gold, namely, diamonds in alluvial deposits that extended over the Belgian border into Angola, the Portuguese West African colony.

Guggenex engineers ran into the same trouble that had led Leopold's men into the infamies of the Free State days—scarcity of labor. Men and women there were plenty, but one and all they had more agreeable ways of spending their time than digging for pieces of pure carbon that weren't even pretty. The Belgians had found that money wages were meaningless to these people, who had few commercial needs: the lash, the saber, the pistol, and the concentration camp were needed to provide incentives.

180

The scourge of world criticism had rendered these methods impracticable; the Belgian Parliament salved its conscience by imposing a labor tax, payable by the Congo people in the only wealth they possessed, their own labor. *Forminière* abjured the use of this forced labor and formed the Kasai Labor Exchange which recruited thousands of men each year—11,000 in 1924 alone. Peculiar conditions were imposed on recruiting: the company had to furnish each recruit a blanket; the men could only be walked thirty kilometers a day; there had to be one day's rest after six days' marching. The Governmental official responsible for enforcing the labor code was also the manager of the *Bourse du Travail*, paid by *Forminière*.

Forminière alone of the big corporations in the Congo boasted that it built villages in native style into which hundreds of families moved voluntarily, established half a dozen farms stocked with seven thousand cattle, kept store prices low even during the World War. Wages of a dollar or two a month, plus free salt, calico and trinkets were maintained until recent years. Now wages run about five dollars a month.

Fortunately for *Forminière*, the Congo people, unlike the Kaffirs, did not understand the value of the diamonds which they recovered from the Kasai. So it was unnecessary to house them in barbed-wire compounds, as in South Africa, to post armed guards over them in both working and leisure time, and to keep them two weeks after their discharge to recover swallowed stones.

To Thomas Fortune Ryan, his Congo Company, too, was a pet corporate child, and the last of his fruitful life. Dismissing charges in the American press that he was profiting from black slavery, he assured reporters:

"I sleep like a baby. I don't remember ever having been in better health or spirits. Of all my business concerns, that which most interests me now is the Congo development. The

181

mines in which I am interested are just north of those known as King Solomon's Mines. The outlook for gold there is probably unsurpassed anywhere in the world. I am interested not only in the industrial development of the Congo but also in its social and moral conditions. The solution of the Negro problem there is perhaps the one which deserves the greatest attention. The great exaggerations to which currency had been given have not in any way changed the firm purpose of those responsible for the future of that region to correct any abuses that have heretofore existed."

Unabashed by criticism, *Forminière* proceeded with its work of civilization, establishing a "Little America" at Tshikapa, bringing the blessings of honest toil to 12,000 Congo laborers, pushing over the border to bigger concessions in Angola, where the diamonds were even heavier and thicker. The Ryan-Guggenheim company took over the Kasai Company's diamond concession.

The Ryan-Guggenheim enterprise in 1921 surrendered to the Belgian government its monopoly on the produce of 1,200,000 hectares in exchange for full property rights over 100,000 hectares to be selected anywhere in the Congo-Kasai province. It gained exclusive mining rights for 99 years in all mines it had discovered before 1926 on ground extending over 1,000,000 hectares.

To Dan Guggenheim, his American Congo Company was a minor province in the great mining empire that was slowly encompassing half the world. By 1906 his companies had become the ruling powers in the United States and Mexican mining and smelting fields; he had extended a tentative feeler into Chile, had stridden boldly into the Congo. His attention shifted, for the moment, to the mineral wealth of Canada.

11. TO HELL WITH NIP AND GUGGENHEIM

WHEN JOHN HAYS HAMMOND walked down the Silver Sidewalk at Cobalt, midway between Toronto and Hudson Bay, the stock of Nipissing Mines Company jumped five points, and the Curb went wild on all mining shares. Nipissing became the magic word among speculators from London to Shanghai as word spread that the Guggenheims were back of it and Hammond was to be president of the company. As many as 250,000 mining shares changed hands daily and exhausted brokers forced the Mining Exchanges in Salt Lake and San Francisco to close so they might catch up. The market value of Nipissing soared from $4,000,000 to $40,000,000 within a few months. The *Wall Street Journal* pronounced it "one of the most extraordinary events in mining finance."

That inveterate promoter, William Boyce Thompson, was back of the market with 240,000 shares of Nipissing. No man in Wall Street however was more surprised than he when "Nip," which he had taken on option at $3.45 and fed into the market in May at 4, nursing it along to 5½ at the end of July, jumped to 15. The week when Engineer Hammond and his entourage marveled at the streak of silver ore on the earth's surface, 6 to 28 inches wide and 600 feet long, which was guarded night and day by armed guards, Nip jumped to 25.

It was a triumph of the promoter's art, and not the least artistic touch was Hammond's appearance on the scene. Dan Guggenheim, complaining bitterly to his brothers that Guggenex had not been in on the ground floor, grumbled permission for his chief engineer to make an Ontario sortie.

183

Hammond left, surrounded by a party which included a fastidious chef, a willing wine steward, and a flock of reporters. Thompson's own press agent, in charge of the expedition, himself took care of the *New York Sun* and *Harper's Weekly*. When he dutifully offered to turn over the checks from these molders of public opinion to Thompson, the promoter airily waved them aside and presented him with 1,000 shares of Nip.

Hammond and his entourage arrived in Cobalt in a happy frame of mind and the great man, touched by the homage accorded him on all sides, grew enthusiastic about Nip's obvious riches, even to taking a flier on 10,000 shares for himself.

With the "Go" sign from their chief engineer, the Guggenheims, on November 1, 1906, signed on the dotted line with Thompson for 400,000 shares of Nip on option at $25, laying $2,500,000 on the counter and receiving 40,000 shares, the remaining 60,000 staying in Thompson's hands as a forfeit in case they should change their minds about going through with the rest of the $10,000,000 transaction.

Hammond had left Pope Yeatman up in Cobalt to continue researches. He pursued Nipissing's most famous vein down twenty feet, found it pinched, and communicated privately with his chief. Hammond was annoyed and later alarmed. The day was nearing when his employers were to put another $2,500,000 on the counter. Nip began sliding down, down, down, slowly, from the high 30s to 28, 27. The day before the second payment was due Dan asked Thompson for a conference on Nipissing's titles. He had heard there was some question about their validity. The promoter assured him that the titles were perfect and guaranteed by both the Canadian Land Department and the company. Dan was dubious and arranged a second meeting at ten A.M. December 1 at Sam Untermyer's office.

Thompson was there on the stroke of ten, sent in his card,

184

FORMER SENATOR SIMON GUGGENHEIM

Photo by International.

was told that Untermyer was in conference. He watched the minutes tick off on the office clock, heard Trinity chime the quarter and half hour, watched the hands move on toward eleven. The market would close at noon and every hour Nipissing sagged more. At eleven Dan and Untermyer were still closeted. Thompson grabbed his hat and raced for a telephone. By noon he had sold 80,000 shares and the end had begun for Nipissing.

Next Monday there was pandemonium on the Curb with 200,000 shares traded and the afternoon press screaming of a "new panic" as "Nip" tumbled to the depths from which it had but lately risen. The cellar opened when the Guggenheims announced that the deal was off because Nipissing had refused a thirty-day extension to permit an examination of titles.

A roar of indignation bellowed from the throats of investors and speculators the country over, for in Nip's wake a hundred other mining stocks dived for the bottom.

Appalled by the public reaction, Dan and Murry declared that their company would reimburse the 150 clients who had put down money on Nip through Guggenheim Exploration, even though it cost the company $1,300,000, in addition to the $1,000,000 lost on the forfeit on the shares held for members of the family personally. This brought forth a cry of rage from the thousands who had bought Nip on the market instead of through Guggenheim Exploration and the tens of thousands who suffered from the smashing of the mining market.

Beginning his generation-long policy, Adolph Ochs of the *New York Times* loyally defended his friend, Daniel, in an editorial on The Moral Law in Wall Street, referring to the Guggenheim offer to reimburse Guggenheim Exploration customers. But the *Wall Street Journal* and the gambling fraternity suspected that they had been made victims of a bunco game. What the Guggenheims had deliberately

185

pushed up, they had torn down, and without a penny loss to themselves because, it was said bitterly, they had cleared out before Nip had passed 25 on the downward path.

Clarence Barron, writing in the *Boston News Bureau*, rose to inquire who were the Hydes and who the Jekylls in M. Guggenheim's Sons. The question revolved about Isaac's curious statement of October 21: "You can deny that report *in toto*. We are not negotiating for a big block of Nipissing stock, nor have we contemplated doing so. There is not the slightest grain of truth in all these reports." But on October 30 the option on Nipissing was signed.

The *Boston News Bureau* continued:

If they fooled the public concerning their entry into Nipissing, would they not fool it concerning their exit? . . . The Nipissing mines had no great value with the public until John Hays Hammond and the Guggenheims became identified therewith. There was great market value in their entry and exit.

It made the gamblers no happier to see American Smelting and Refining stock going up as Nipissing descended. It was said that the fateful Saturday morning conference, when Thompson was watching the clock tick off the minutes, was concerned not with Nipissing's titles to its claims but with Guggenheims' efforts to gain a controlling share in a mine they knew to be rich.

The Guggenheims, one and all, stoutly denied that they had speculated in Nipissing, or indeed in any of the securities they promoted. Against the impression, held almost unanimously by the speculative fraternity, that the brothers were first and foremost speculators and promoters and only secondarily the operators of mines and smelters, must be placed that categorical denial and their announced pledge that they felt they were not entitled to speculate in their own shares.

186

To one of his legal staff, Dan Guggenheim said: "I want you to remember that you aren't here only as our legal adviser. If you ever see any of us or any of our lawyers doing anything unethical, come to me and wave the red flag." That was in 1919 and this legal consultant said that he had waved the flag only once or twice.

John Hays Hammond reported a conversation with Sol while they were walking up and down a western railroad station waiting for a train connection. The malodorous suit between H. H. Rogers and F. Augustus Heinze over the rich prize of the Butte mines was being heard, to the accompaniment of crimson charges of bribery, corruption, and blackmail. Even Mighty Morgan had said to Hammond: "It reflects on every business in Wall Street and it ought to be stopped."

Hammond had been asked to step in as umpire, and he was talking it over with Sol. "I can't understand," said Sol, "why Rogers keeps up such a dirty mess. He may get a few millions out of it, but he'll only give it right away to charity. Wouldn't you think he'd have more sense than to sacrifice his good name for that? I think it is a damned shame!"

"I agree with you, Sol," said Hammond, "and I'm glad to hear you've such a high ideal of business ethics. In the future I'll never have to worry about any rumors of sharp practices connected with your enterprises."

In later years Dan said, apropos of Nipissing, that "some members of M. Guggenheim's Sons had been willing to risk and perhaps lose their own money but were not willing to hazard the money of their friends and that they did not wish to associate others with them until such enterprises had been rounded up and were practically certain to be successful undertakings."

This "association" of the Guggenheims with investors was through bond issues and not through stocks, which the Gug-

187

genheims usually held themselves. The eagerness of the investing public to buy these mining bond issues proved that the investor believed Dan, and that the bonds appeared only after the risks had been conquered and the mines seemed sure to pay.

A syndicate took hold of Nipissing and it became one of the jewels in the coffers of International Nickel. Edmund C. Converse of Bankers Trust; E. P. Earle, the first to confirm Nip's riches after a railroad construction crew blasted silver ore out of a hillside; Captain Joseph Delamar, the old mine adventurer; and Ambrose Monell, for whom a famous alloy was to be named, took leading roles in the syndicate. The ground for which Earle had paid $200,000 turned in dividends of $29,940,000.

The star of the "greatest mining engineer of his time" was somewhat tarnished by the Nipissing episode. The *Canadian Mining Journal* cried: "He stands unique, alone, the man with the largest salary in the world, the man who capitalized his proboscis from the Rand to Mexico, and from Siberia to Cobalt, where lies a mine called Nipissing."

Stories got around that Hammond was about to resign from Guggenheim Exploration. This was formally denied. "There is no mining company or set of mining engineers that is infallible," Dan explained. The properties Hammond had recommended and developed had brought in "enormous profits—enough to triple the losses sustained in the Nipissing deal." Nevertheless the *Wall Street Journal* quoted an "intimate friend" as saying that "I have received the most direct information that he has been considering retiring. . . . Notwithstanding his magnificent income, Mr. Hammond has fretted under it."

The engineer himself admitted that the family "stood loyally by me" and "publicly stated that their confidence in my judgment had not been shaken by the error."

Nipissing nipped the craze in mining shares which had

188

diverted some $150,000 from the Exchange to the Curb, much to the annoyance of the big interests. Some said that the Money Power had forced the Guggenheims to destroy the Nipissing boom because it was leading speculation into channels over which it had no control. Dan himself stated that there had been "too much wildcat mining speculation." All that was little consolation for the little fellow who had picked up Nipissing as a bona fide investment with Guggenheim backing and found that it was only another wildcat. One wailed, in trochaic tetrameter:

> Tell me not in mournful numbers,
>> That I've only had a dream;
> Must I wake from pleasant slumbers,
>> Finding things not what they seem?
> I had hunted out earth's chances,
>> Seeking for a "dead sure" thing;
> Only one thing caught my fancies—
>> And I bought some NIPISSING.
>
> Up from "twenty-five" it started,
>> Bounded on to "thirty-four";
> Through the push I madly darted—
>> Yelled, "It's good, give me some more."
> I had visions of a pocket
>> Bulging out at Christmas time;
> How I'd buy a mine and stock it.
>> Whoop! For NIP and Guggenheim!
>
> "Deal off?" Thunder! What's this crashing?
>> Is it something that I bought?
> Everything to smash is smashing;
>> I'm a "sucker"—I've been caught.
> "Life is real,"—but this vision
>> Lasted only a short time;
> If you want my last decision—
>> To h—— with "NIP" and Guggenheim!

189

12. BACKDROP FOR YUKON GOLD

A HUNDRED MILLION in gold had been panned out of Bonanza Creek's gravelly bed by 1905 when Alfred Chester Beatty, Hammond's right-hand bower, stood upon its banks with Arthur N. C. Treadgold, Yukon sourdough-promoter out of London, and and O. B. Perry, Guggenheim Exploration's crack hydraulic mining expert.

Another hundred million remained imbedded in the sands but that gold could never be recovered profitably by the swishing pans or crude cradles of the solitary gold miner. If giant dredges, however, were put to work sucking up those sands, if rivers of water could be hurled against those barren, treeless hills . . .

From the frontier station of Hootalinqua, Y. T., clicked the following telegram:

GUGGENEX NEW YORK TOTAL NET RECEIPTS ABOUT ONE MILLION PER ANNUM BEGINNING WITHIN THREE YEARS STOP POSSIBILITIES OF LONG LIFE VERY GREAT STOP PROBABLE PRODUCTION WILL BE NINE MILLION PROFITS WITH POSSIBILITIES BEYOND THIS STOP GRADE OF GRAVEL HIGH AND YARDAGE WIDE STOP GRANITE.

Hammond stroked his beard as he read this message, signed with Beatty's code-name, and decided the business merited a trip to Dan Guggenheim's summer camp.

In Treadgold's cabin, down where the Bonanza emptied into the Klondike, Beatty and Perry bent over maps of the creek. The promoter slid his fingers down the claims he had hitched together, options from old miners who still clung to their gravel, waiting for the day when Big Capital would enter the Yukon, toss them a few thousand dollars for

190

their few hundred feet of frozen soil, and ring down the curtain forever on that short but heroic chapter of history when the sourdough tramped across the stage of Yukon gold-mining.

A new era would begin when the hydraulic engineer would be boss of the Klondike, his employer a company of capitalists in far away New York or London, his miners a gang of day laborers directing the nozzles of huge hoses against crumbling hillsides, working the machinery of great dredges which swallowed tons of sand and mysteriously and profitably extracted ounces of gold. For that artificial rivers would be flumed, siphoned, pumped across the arid wastes, rough camps would rise at the mouths of creeks, men and machinery would work feverishly under the long summer sun in the few months when the ice left the top layers of the earth.

Water, water, water! Treadgold had worried about that for two years, devising schemes to get water into the Bonanza Valley to loosen the sands quickly. The winter before he had gone to the States to lay his proposal before Hammond. The engineer, puffing contentedly on a cigar in his suite at the Auditorium in Chicago, had rejected in a half hour the scheme Treadgold had built in a year. "All you've got there, my friend, is a water-selling proposition, and not enough water at that. You get the claims, all of them, and we'll take care of the water."

Treadgold returned to the Arctic.

And now the short summer was back again, he had the claims, and still there was no answer to Beatty's telegrams. He looked suspiciously at the engineer. "Damn the Guggenheims," he muttered. "Do they want it all for nothing?"

Another conversation was proceeding at about the same time in another cabin—Dan Guggenheim's summer lodge in the Adirondacks.

"So he wants 40 per cent?" asked Dan Guggenheim, looking out across the green mountains. "Well, you can't say Treadgold isn't being generous with himself. All we do is put up the money, the machinery, the brains, the organization, and he wants 40 per cent."

Hammond looked at his chief appraisingly. "Well, maybe you're right, Mr. Dan. Let's hope the Englishmen don't get to him. I've got an idea the old fellow will be down here this fall and anxious enough to talk business with us."

"You'd better send Beatty a wire, J. H. H., that we don't think the business is attractive on the basis of money returned and $9,000,000."

Treadgold, worn out by anxiety, the short summer months quickly sliding away, broke down when he heard that Guggenex had rejected his proposition. Alternately cursing and weeping, he stamped up and down the narrow cabin, almost on the verge of insanity. "The damned Jews," he screamed. "They're trying to squeeze me, they want to strip my bones." He flung himself out of doors, and the two Guggenheim engineers sat down to see what could be salvaged from the ruins of a summer's work.

With the fifteen claims toward the mouth of the creek they sketched a hydraulic scheme that could be swung for a quarter of a million. Perry, the hydraulic expert, would furnish the brains and a little cash, but it was up to Beatty to turn in at least $100,000. As chief consulting engineer for Tom Walsh's (*Father Struck It Rich*) Campbird and Stratton's Independence mine at Cripple Creek, Beatty figured that he could scrape together enough to get a dredge into the Bonanza while Treadgold and Perry took care of the water. He agreed to advance $35,000 immediately so that Treadgold could hold together the options on which importunate miners and small-time speculators in Dawson were demanding action. Before the two engineers floated dreams of a clear $2,500,000 profit from their minor Bonanza Creek scheme.

"But what will Dan Guggenheim say?" asked Perry. Perry could ask with clear conscience; his relations with the mining magnate were on a percentage basis; but Beatty was on straight salary and under relations which lawyers describe as *uberrima fides*—utmost faith. "What can he say?" countered Beatty. "We're holding together the basis of a $9,000,000 proposition for the Guggenheims. If he changes his mind and decides to go through with the development of Bonanza Creek, I can either be repaid for this money or take it out in shares."

Beatty left for the States and it was up to Perry to deal with the frantic Treadgold, who was corroded with suspicion that the Guggenheims intended to freeze him out of the Bonanza. Perry finally got him to put his signature to a contract to hold together the claims of the lower Bonanza and Beatty rushed the money to pay off insistent miners, anxious for cash on options about to expire.

Beatty, back in New York, reported to Dan. The conversation, according to Beatty, went like this:

Guggenheim: "Mr. Beatty, are we going to get some business there in the Klondike?"

Beatty: "On this contract we have got something good for you."

Guggenheim: "Get together with Mr. Hammond on the business and present it to me and I will pass on it."

Following Beatty came Perry, with detailed information on the hydraulic features. Following Perry, as soon as the frost had bitten the Bonanza, came Treadgold, drawn by that mining lodestone of the Western Continent, Guggenheim Exploration.

Treadgold walked high, wide and handsome, once he got to the metropolis. Hammond was affability itself, spending long hours with him, trading stories of California's placers with Treadgold's yarns of the Yukon, extracting from him in bits the essence of the Bonanza business. The

Yukoner was pleased as punch to be introduced to Sam Untermyer himself, the famous lawyer, through whose brother he had first borne a letter of introduction to Hammond. For days he was closeted with Louis Marshall, Untermyer's partner, drawing up carefully the terms of agreement, and the clauses in the corporation which was being created under his eyes out of his claims—Yukon Consolidated Goldfields, a corporation whose name suggested the famed South African Rand Company. The millions danced before the old man's eyes—$5,000,000 in common stock of which he was to get 30 percent; $3,000,000 in preferred, which was to rest in Guggenex vaults. On paper his share worked out to $1,500,000. A millionaire at last! With $160,000 cash to his credit for his claims, Treadgold was off for London on the next boat.

Of all that long, frostbitten, hungry, gold-fevered line of heroes who toiled over Chilkoot Pass and braved the terrors of the Arctic from 1897, he alone, it seemed, was to climb to wealth on the frozen sands of the Yukon. Other fortunes had been made in the Yukon; but it was a byword that the saloon-keeper, the professional gambler, the merchant, the whoremaster and the promoter, not the miner, was the beneficiary of the Goddess of Fortune who whirled her wheel in the Frozen North.

That winter the section of Guggenheim Exploration in charge of Yukon Consolidated Goldfields bustled with activities. A million dollars in supplies must be waiting at Dawson in late spring to be taken to the mouth of Bonanza Creek. Dredges, machinery, hydraulic apparatus, food, fuel. Perry left for the Yukon as soon as formalities were out of the way, to establish headquarters in Dawson, to get Guggenheim sawmills working on lumber to be cut from Guggenheim forests, to have Guggenheim depots built, and to lift a Guggenheim river across the wilderness.

The enterprise stirred the Guggenheim brothers as had

194

no undertaking since the days of the building of the Philadelphia smelter in Pueblo some thirty years before. In the summer of 1906 Dan left his lodge in the Adirondacks for Troy, New York, to board his private car for an inspection of his Yukon domain. He picked up Sol in the west, and accompanied by Beatty, he steamed up the Inside Passage to Skagway, went over the White Pass and Yukon and down the rivers to the goldfields.

From Skagway on, Dan and Simon saw evidence of the Goldfields project: machinery being swung off the steamer at the pier; the railroad cars loaded with supplies for the Goldfields; river boats churning along the Yukon basin bound for the Bonanza. Engineers were rushing work along the sixty-two miles of flume, ditch, and pipeline that transported the waters of the Tombstone River through an absolute wilderness to the Bonanza workings. They were erecting a two thousand horsepower hydro-electric plant whose juice was to run thirty-six miles by high-tension wire, and throwing a barrier of earthworks across the upper Bonanza to impound spring waters.

Dan stood on a ridge and looked across the Klondike and the vast waste land of the Arctic, useless to man. Below his men toiled, erecting barracks and worksheds, installing machinery, putting together jigsaw-like a big dredge that had traveled five thousand miles in crates to its destination here. Who but the Guggenheims could have done this, he asked himself. Who but the Guggenheims could have unlocked the wealth of this Frozen Empire, have introduced the age of electricity, machinery, big-scale production, to the Yukon and Alaska? Little men might shout all they pleased about the evils of great wealth and the dangers of monopoly, but how else was the wealth of the world's out-of-the-way places to be exploited? By the little men themselves? They had been here, in the thousands, panning gold from this very creek, but where were they now? Gone, leaving tens of millions behind them that they could never recover. Pioneers? Yes, in a small, plundering way. The Guggenheims themselves now were the real pioneers of a new order. They were to show the world that the North could be developed industrially, that hundreds of thousands could live here, nourished permanently by the land's mineral wealth.

Intoxicated by his dream as he stood there on a hill by the quiet-flowing Klondike, surveying that empty, silent land, Daniel Guggenheim, the little Napoleon of the mining world, saw himself Emperor of the North, life-bringer, torchbearer, who would summon industry and prosperity to rule over the brooding wilderness that no man claimed.

What could be done here in the Yukon could also be done in neighboring Alaska. All this forbidding, slumbering northland could be wakened into life, its mines probed of their wealth in gold, copper, and coal, its forests hewed, railroads built, the sea seined for its teeming salmon. And it was he, Daniel Guggenheim, who would summon that life by waving the magic wand of his millions. .

13. ALL THAT GLITTERS

THE WINTER of 1907-8 was the coldest in Dan Guggenheim's life. After the Knickerbocker panic had knocked paper values on Wall Street into a cocked hat, its underlying causes became visible everywhere in restricted buying power, business failures, and pitifully long breadlines. The sensitive copper market sagged, lead demand dropped like a plummet, and American Smelting and Refining shares fell from 174 to half that.

Dan Guggenheim sat alone in his study at the St. Regis, staring out at the snowflakes dropping slowly through the pale glow of a winter evening which saw no sunset. Powerful bear interests were knocking on the door of American Smelting and Refining, depressing the shares, circulating rumors that the Guggenheims were embarrassed. As quotations dropped, these bear interests quietly bought American Smelting and Refining. It was the Rockefellers.

Dan needed money, needed it badly. Yukon Gold was still being developed; so far not a penny had been realized from those creeks along the Klondike. His new copper properties were encumbered with high development costs, and their output was selling in a world market riddled by panic and deflation. Against all Guggenheim tradition he had floated second mortgage bonds against his copper properties. He wanted, prudently, to conserve his resources but the Rockefeller and Morgan interests demanded that American Smelting and Refining meet its dividends in order to buoy up the market.

All the West had broken out in one of those periodic eruptions of anti-Guggenheim fury. The American Mining

Congress, laying all the blame for lower prices and reduced production at the door of the unholy Smelters Trust, was demanding Congressional investigation. The Montana Mine Owners Association was passing the hat for cash to build an independent smelter; the Utah Mine Owners Association was in open rebellion; in Colorado, fortress of hatred against the Smelters family, mine owners, miners and a state plunging into near ruin raged against the Trust. When the smelters refused ore, mines closed and threw thousands of men and dozens of communities into want; the smelters themselves cut wage rates and laid off hundreds, biting sharply into the normally meager incomes of workmen.

"All kinds of rumors have been flying around," reported the *Engineering and Mining Journal,* somberly. "In spite of repeated denials, these have reiterated that the controlling interest of A S and R has passed from the Guggenheims. Some say Standard Oil, others Amalgamated [Copper], others John D. Rockefeller." All of whom, the *Journal* might have added, were substantially one and the same. Alarmed by the Guggenheim entry into coppers, the Rockefeller interests pounded down A. S. and R, a steady payer on its 5 per cent common, to 65 on a wild, cold day when 128,000 shares changed hands.

In this crisis Dan called in his closest and most trusted adviser, Sam Untermyer. Together they went through the Guggenheim portfolio, but Dan, stubborn and possessive, could find nothing more that he would toss to the wolves. He had sold as much American Smelting as he dared. The coppers, just bonded, were out of consideration. The two men's eyes rested on Yukon Consolidated Goldfields. Dan shook his head. The market for speculative mining shares had fallen on evil days since the Nipissing fiasco and the panic had sent them into the cellar. Perhaps . . . highly seasoned and served with hot sauce Yukon could be converted into a tasty morsel for a jaded market. But who could trim up Yukon? Who, indeed, but William Boyce Thompson, hero of a hundred mining promotions, specialist in the coppers, the wisest head in the crazy "Nip" boom?

Thompson dropped into the St. Regis to see his old friend. His head was buzzing with ideas for a super-Amalgamated, a Consolidated Copper, the greatest of all the copper flotations, the answer to the Rockefellers. His Consolidated, redubbed Copper Mines, Inc., was to be a $60,000,000 job, including Utah Copper, Nevada Consolidated and Cumberland-Ely. That dream got short shrift, for the time being, from Dan who was absorbed in Yukon. Thompson agreed and listened to him paint a pretty picture of the goldfields.

It was the promoter's turn to cast a lackluster eye on this scheme to take the public in on a gold mine stock. "Somehow people don't take a shine for those gold and silver mines the way they used to," he sighed. "And as for those $100 shares you're talking about, haven't you been reading the papers lately? You might sell some $5 shares, but $100 shares, not now. How much money do you need?"

"Three and a half million."

Dan talked and Thompson labored over pencil and paper. At the end of it all they had a new $25,000,000 company, Yukon Gold, of which $17,500,000 was to be issued, and $3,500,000 in 700,000 shares was to be sold. The rest would remain with Guggenheim Exploration.

"Very neat," said Thompson, feeling better and better. "The public gives us $3,500,000 to develop Yukon Gold and we give them 20 per cent of the profits. Very neat. I'll take a chance on 700,000 shares. If I can sell anything, I guess I can sell a real gold property with you and Beatty back of it. I'll need about a hundred thousand dollars for the advertising campaign and of course you'll underwrite the expenses of the promotion."

But the more Thompson thought about Yukon Gold, the

less stomach he had for it. What chance was there that investors would ever realize their principal on such a scheme? Someone else would have to sell this package, he needed his own reputation. A happy idea struck him, and he smiled.

"Hello, Tom, that you?" he called over the phone. "Can you come up tonight? Got something you might be interested in."

Tom Lawson, he of the piercing eye, the bold manner, and the fancy vest, bustled, red-faced, into Thompson's room. "What's up?" he asked, his eye roving over the room. The hero of Frenzied Finance was humbled and repentant since his dashing exposé, three years before, of ways financial in *Everybody's Magazine.* This uneasy genius had thought up Amalgamated Copper, had sold Rogers on the idea of a copper trust, and had been bilked in the end. The *Everybody's* series, which was the sensation of the year, was his answer to Rogers and the Oil Trust, but apparently it hadn't mattered much. Standard Oil went on and on. Lawson concluded that reform didn't pay, and, anyway, promoting was more exciting.

"What's up?" asked Lawson, his eye lighting on Thompson's desk.

"Guggenheim," answered Thompson. Tom grunted.

"Dan needs a little money and we've got to make a market for his Yukon Gold."

Lawson whistled. "What a nice little job," he remarked softly. "When do we start?"

The contract signed, Dan was off for Europe, his cabin on the *Aquitania* smothered with an immense bouquet of Lawson pinks. Dan had no stomach either for what was to come. Engineer Beatty had turned over his report on Yukon, and he too was off, for Bermuda. Sol and Murry stayed to face the music.

200

Lawson slipped his imagination into high gear, and on March 25, 1908, announced to the world that the days of Frenzied Finance were gone forever. In a flamboyant ad, headed in fine, bold type,

FAIR FINANCE 1

he addressed himself to four audiences:

TO PRESIDENT ROOSEVELT:

I respectfully point to "Fair Finance 2" and "Fair Finance 3" which will be in this space in the leading dailies throughout the world this afternoon and tomorrow. Also to the most extraordinary statement, "Gold for Sale," which will follow No. 3. The only reason for flagging your attention is that you may have positive proof of a result your work has produced.

TO THE PEOPLE:

I earnestly ask that every thinking man and woman throughout America and Europe will read what will appear in this space—in the press of the world—this afternoon and tomorrow and the day after that.
What you will read will be mighty interesting—otherwise I would not consume your time and my own. It will be even more than interesting; it will show one of the people's most perplexing problems solved.

TO CAPITALISTS:

This is a notice to you, wherever located, that in this space—in the press of the world—this afternoon and the two following tomorrows, will appear news—good news—which will cause you to sit up—straight up—and take notice.
That these notices cost over $100,000 should be proof positive that the news will be news.

Reserve this space for this afternoon and the day following and double this space for the next day following. Copy will be mailed to the eastern press, telegraphed to the press of the West, South and Canada, and cabled to Paris, Berlin, and London daily. This notice inaugurates a publicity campaign—a three section campaign of $17,500,000, $60,000,000 and $225,000,000. It will call for an advertising expenditure of $1,000,000, and it will convey to the people news of import. You might print each day on your front page a notice something to this effect: "No reader should fail to absorb and digest Thomas W. Lawson's Fair Finance printed on Page ———.

If you decide the text merits, post it daily on your bulletin boards. As to additional notice, reading or editorial comment, your decision will be my conclusion.

THOMAS W. LAWSON

Boston, March 25, 1908

Public appetite having been whetted, next day's Fair Finance 2 was addressed:

TO EVERY MAN AND WOMAN WITH SAVINGS:

Up to four years ago the people of America invested their savings in Wall Street or in stocks created in, or controlled by, Wall Street. They bought what the Captains of Finance told them to buy. They were not equipped to know the worth of what they bought. The people annually brought to Wall Street millions of their savings and—left them there. A further result—a few score of men became possessed of fabulous wealth.

Lawson related how the people had forsaken the stock market and, as a result, a panic had overtaken Wall Street. It was only then that "the great Captains of Finance asked my advice, and, upon receiving it, my co-operation.

202

I said to the Captains of Finance: "The people have been educated to the old game. They will not again, blind-folded, send their hard-earned savings to your market place. If the people will not buy their flour, their sugar or their woolens without first being shown they contain no chalk, no sand, no shoddy, why should they buy grossly adulterated stocks or good stocks at grossly manipulated prices? . . .

Then I agreed to act as salesman, but upon my terms, which were that I be first actually shown the value of the goods to be offered, and in a way that would enable me to prove the values to the people so that they, too, would actually know them.

As a result of "pawing over" the "goods of the Street," Lawson was now offering to investors: "First, millions of gold; second, scores of millions of copper; third, hundreds of millions of (to be named later)." He explained:

Men and corporations of great wealth and business re-sponsibility have been induced to contribute 20 per cent of one of their most important investments to the public at 50 per cent of its actual sure worth, or 25 per cent of its perhaps worth, for the purpose of proving to the public, in an unmistakable way, that from now on the people are to get a square deal in American finance. . . . In thirty-eight active years in finance, I have never known of an investment which combined safety—government bond safety—with unusual dividends or unusual profits. In that time I have never known of any investment where large dividends were combined with sufficient safety to justify an honest man who really knew finance in advis-ing, say, a woman of ordinary means, to exchange her Government bonds or savings bank deposits for it. . . . In this Gold case, all the above heretofore unmet with

203

conditions surround and control the investment which will be offered.

"What's come over the Guggenheims?" men asked. The market-wise nodded significantly, and American Smelting and Refining shares continued to fall.

"Fair Finance 3" explained more. Lawson announced that 700,000 shares were to be offered at $5 a share; 2,800,000 shares were not for sale "at any price"; the entire 3,500,000 shares were owned by a holding company whose capital stock (Guggenheim Exploration) had been selling at $300. The stock was owned and controlled by "the most successful group of mining capitalists in the world" whose corporations aggregated $300,000,000.

On March 28, every major paper in the country and many abroad carried an advertisement which filled nearly a complete page. In box-car type it announced:

FAIR FINANCE   YUKON GOLD   FAIR FINANCE

Leading all was an excerpt from a letter signed by Alfred Chester Beatty:

> . . . I believe that the gravels owned and controlled by the Yukon Gold Company in Yukon Territory should yield upwards of $50,000,000 in gross value, and when the properties are thoroughly equipped, I believe that Mr. Perry's estimate of $36,000,000 net profit, with possibilities beyond this, will be realized.

Followed excerpts from reports by Perry and Tread-gold, a list of the Guggenheim companies, of the Guggenheim directors, everything but pictures of the Guggenheim brothers themselves, and they were omitted only because the picture era was just a-borning. Lawson's feverish announcement continued:

The only reason that makes it possible to secure any of this stock now is first, because it is now a completed success, and second, because the group have been convinced that just at this time, when people are filled with distrust of all things corporation-wise, it will be of inestimable value to the whole investment and corporation structure to spread through the land into the hands of thousands of small and large investors a fraction of the stock of this enterprise at less than its actual worth.

Although besieged, he said, by bankers and brokers to sell them the stock privately, Lawson had resisted all temptation. Every share would be offered on the Curb at not less than $5 and not more than $7.50, so that all the people might profit. Every last share could be sold right now, what with orders from London for 50,000, et cetera. Unissued shares already were being traded at 8½ to 10½. "Unquestionably if I allowed it, the trading would begin Saturday at $10 and above. If I permitted such a course, my consent would give the lie to my pledge that Saturday would inaugurate Fair Finance."

Lawson surveyed the results of his golden artistry on the eve of Saturday, March 28, the great day of Fair Finance and Yukon Gold, and he felt none too confident. His office was ablaze far into the night as telephones rang, clerks shouted, brokers dashed in and out with last-minute instructions.

March 28—the day of the "Yukon Gold Rush"—was the biggest day in all the history of the New York Curb, bigger than that Black Monday which saw the Nipissing "panic," wilder than the day when United Copper broke. The Curb was due to open, as usual, at ten, but long before, groups of brokers had formed in Broad Street and by opening time hundreds of brokers and messengers created "a scene of excitement such as seldom has been witnessed even on the Big Board," the *Wall Street Journal* related. The crowd blocked Broad Street from curb to curb, brokers dashed pell-mell from one to another of the ten trading groups in Yukon Gold, knocking each other down, cursing, shouting, as they sold blocks at marginal profits and dashed elsewhere to buy or sell again. Customers came directly to the Curb to give orders, unable to do business by telephone. All the office windows overlooking the market were open, most of them filled with excited men shouting orders to their representatives or throwing them down on bits of paper. In Boston, Exchange Place, too, was the scene of a shouting mob of frenzied brokers and speculators.

When trading ended in the two-hour session, Lawson fell exhausted into his chair. Recovering an hour later he dashed out to inform one and all that the 700,000 shares had been sold. But as Curb brokers reviewed the extraordinary morning, and eyebrow-tilted observers of the Exchange looked it over, Lawson had nothing to be excited about. The stock which was to open at $10 and soar, actually closed at 6½, and few believed that Lawson had dared to dump more than half his holdings. An interested onlooker from the sidelines was William Boyce Thompson himself. Skeptical from the start, he frankly advised his friends not to touch Yukon. "It's dynamite," said he, confidentially, "but don't quote me." Harry Content of the Stock Exchange firm dashed into print to deny that he was in charge of Yukon. Use of his name in Lawson ads was without his authority or consent and "in contravention of my position as a loyal member of the New York Stock Exchange." "Rain fell for two hours in Broad Street Saturday," said a *Wall Street Journal* columnist. "It started at ten A.M. and left off at noon."

One Broad Street wag summed it up in a phrase that flew through the financial district:

206

"Sometimes," he said, "Yukon, and sometimes you cawn't."

Monday saw Lawson back in the market, buoying up the great flood of paper shares that had descended upon the Curb, fighting desperately to keep the "Government bond" stock from sinking below 5.

Riding the storm up on the bridge of Guggenheim Exploration paced the unhappy Murry and Sol, bending before blasts of criticism from astounded friends and enemies, watching helplessly their sister ship, American Smelting and Refining, being hounded by bear raids backed by an outspoken campaign to the effect that the Guggenheims were on the verge of bankruptcy. Sol, as president of the frail Yukon bark, spoke out, but few listened, and they smiled to hear:

In view of the misleading reports regarding our attitude with respect to the marketing of the shares of the Yukon Gold Company, I consider it but just to ourselves and to all concerned that we make our position plain.

The arrangements for the sale of 700,000 shares of treasury stock were made by our Mr. Daniel Guggenheim just before his departure for Europe. We have no criticism or complaint as to the manner of marketing the stock, and have never attempted to repudiate any of the statements published by Mr. Lawson concerning the property.

We have absolute faith in it. Every statement of fact contained in the publications is fully justified by the reports of our experts. Our judgment is based not only on their reports, but on a personal examination of the situation made by my brother Daniel and myself in the summer of 1906. It was after that visit that I accepted the presidency of the company, which I now hold, and we have never sold any of our shares.

Lawson, abashed by the shaky condition of Yukon after only two days of trading, brazened it out with a flaring ad:

FAIR FINANCE—YUKON GOLD $10

"Never before in the history of stocks," he began a pane-gyric over the sale of the 700,000 shares.

In spite of the great, good-natured mob which trampled upon rules and regulations, and swept aside the police detailed to Wall and State Streets, my program went through on schedule time. . . . The buying will advance to the price of 10, perhaps to 15, its actual worth now—and later to whatever price is justified by the splendid dividends it will pay.

Almost everybody was happy, almost everybody was glad, even the brokers, who had "made $250,000 to $350,000." All except a few sourpusses.

While Wall and State Streets had a wild time of it, as they always must have when the great public, bent on real business, visits them, it was such a good-natured, jolly time that their hats should be in the air along with their huzzas, but instead a section of both localities are surly at my success, as they always have been and probably always will be.

These marplots were saying that Yukon would not go above 8 "for some time to come," so Lawson had decided to remain in the market another week. The day would come when the "great public" would clamor for some of the Gug-genheims' remaining 2,800,000 shares which "Daniel has assured me will not be sold but at much higher figures than now prevail."

But such flights of the fancy failed to break the Curb's apathy on Yukon. "After the storm comes the calm," remarked the *Wall Street Journal*. "At one moment on Tuesday the celebrated Yukon crowd consisted of a boy with a sandwich board and two brokers busily quoting the stock to one another. . . . What significance can this silence have?" Everybody, including Lawson, knew very well. Yukon Gold had "blown up." The frenzied promoter was beside himself with rage and fear. Toppling with Yukon was his effort to "come back" as a big-time speculator; already he could see his Copper Mines, Incorporated, in which the public was to have "tens of millions," and his unnamed venture, that castle in the clouds with "hundreds of millions" for widows and orphans, dropping into the grave of Tom Lawson's hopes.

Beatty, off in Bermuda, opened the New York paper, several days late, to scan the news. And there, facing him in bold, black type, were his name and an excerpt from his Yukon Gold report. The newspaper clutched in his hand, he raced for the cable station:

GUGGENEX GIVE FOLLOWING CABLE SOL GUGGENHEIM ASTOUNDED TO HEAR THAT LAWSON HAS PUBLISHED LETTER I GAVE YOU IN MODIFIED FORM PERIOD YOU PROMISED ME THAT SAME WAS NOT TO BE PUBLISHED PERIOD I INSIST THAT I SHALL NOT BE QUOTED BY LAWSON WITHOUT AN OPPORTUNITY TO SEE HIS ADVERTISEMENTS BEATTY

Lawson was insolent. "I signed no contract with Beatty," he shouted. "And I'll stand for none of his criticism. My contract's with Mr. Dan and it stipulates that I can use Beatty's report any way I want to." In a tangled mess Sol could do no more and disconsolately he filed Beatty's cable in a folder for Dan's attention on his return from Europe.

As Yukon slid beneath its par value, Lawson shook his head in an ad titled YUKON AND WALL STREET. "Wall Street, as I have said so many times, is a queer place—very, very queer." But also "fascinating" to one who knew "every hair on its beautifully combed head." Wall Street is like a "rosy-cheeked kid." It "pouts." It was "mad" at Tom for driving up in a jamcart and letting everybody help himself instead of letting capitalists selfishly keep the good things for themselves. Not only was it mad at Yukon, "but upon my word if it didn't proceed to lambaste Smelters. Now what a childish performance. I have no Smelters, more's the pity. . . . Just think of it! Smelters, the greatest metallurgical property in all the world . . . paying 4 per cent and selling at 68 . . . Truly it's a joke."

This was too much for Sol and Murry. Not content with dragging the Guggenheim name into the mud of the curb and foozling the Yukon deal, Lawson was now coupling American Smelting and Refining with unhappy Yukon. The promoter was told, short and to the point, to quit his useless advertising.

With Yukon down to 4½ and with the smarting reprimand from the Guggenheim brothers ringing in his ears, Lawson gave rein to that erratic impulse that had caused him to burst forth in Frenzied Finance in *Everybody's*. Another chapter in Fair Finance, subheaded Startling, appeared in the papers of April 7. Lawson proclaimed:

Something happened on Saturday [the day of Yukon's launching] which was not on the program. What was it?

Something did happen Saturday, a startling, astounding something. I thought it best for all interests concerned to keep what happened from the public. I have now decided it will be better to let sunlight through it. Therefore I will describe the happening in the press of the world tomorrow.

The "great public" was doomed to disappointment. The Guggenheim brothers most emphatically objected to Lawson's brand of "sunlight" in a memorable interview the night before the ad was to be published. Lawson, emerging triumphantly from the interview, hastily drafted an ad addressed "To Yukon Shareholders" informing them that he "had decided that publication of my statement at this time would be unwise and perhaps, to some, unfair." Yukon would advance to 10. He denied that extra shares had been dumped on the market on that memorable Saturday.

But the *Engineering and Mining Journal* was not so sure. Several weeks later it reported:

> It has been gossiped for several weeks that when the stock was going like hot cakes on the memorable Saturday, there appeared on the market large offerings of stock other than the treasury stock, which alone was supposed to be on sale. Some owners could not resist the temptation. . . . The trouble was that previous to the public offering, about 200,000 shares of Yukon stock were distributed privately at $5 and $5.50 per share, and this stock Lawson had to take back in the open market.

The *Journal's* finger pointed unerringly at the Guggenheims, only possessors of stock not sold through Lawson. But Sol denied categorically that the family had disposed of any privately. The fact was that 2,800,000 shares stayed in Guggenheim Exploration's treasury and so could not have been available for dumping.

"All is Not Gold That Glitters," read the caption of an ad for the *New York Evening Post*, stodgy organ of High Church Finance.

> The *Evening Post* is the ONLY paper that rigidly and persistently excludes from its columns all kinds of financial advertisements which fail to measure up to the high standard it has established. . . . Among the advertising the *Evening Post* DECLINED, which was printed in

every other New York daily newspaper, were all the famous Yukon Gold announcements of T. W. Lawson.

The *Engineering and Mining Journal* declared flatly that Yukon Gold was no bargain at $5. The *Journal* reminded its readers that Yukon had been carried on Guggenex books at only $8,222,000. Even if claims of $36,000,000 net profits proved correct, when that was discounted over the period of years needed under conditions in the Frozen North and the principal returned to the stockholders, there would be no amazing profit left.

The *Journal* wondered not a whit at Lawson's advertising technique, but "the amazing thing is that the Guggenheims should have appeared in association with him." The worst aspect was that an "attempt has been made to dispose of unproved property at a good deal more than its actual value."

> Criticism may be more properly leveled against the engineers, who failed in their reports to call attention to serious difficulties, which have already been experienced in working the Yukon placers, and avoided any particular reference to the time required for extracting their gold . . . a factor of supreme importance in determining the value of the property.

Hitting pointedly at Beatty and Perry, the *Journal* continued:

> It has been suggested that these matters were discussed in portions of the engineers' reports that were omitted, but that is improbable, because no engineer who values his reputation would permit such a misuse of his report and be silent about it.

As if to justify Tom Lawson's perfervid verbiage, Sol Guggenheim painted his own word picture of Yukon's prospects in his report to stockholders in 1909. "In 1910," he promised, "the net profit should be from $2,000,000 to $2,500,000 and in 1911 and thereafter, $2,500,000 net per annum should be the minimum." Lawson's ads had promised total net profits of $36,000,000; Sol generously threw in another $4,000,000. In 1910 Yukon Gold was placed on an 8 percent dividend basis. The giant dredges were sucking 66 cents in gold out of each cubic yard of gravel at a cost of 31 cents.

Nevertheless Yukon Gold sank to 2-3 and remained there stubbornly forevermore. The curtain was rung down in 1916 on the stock that was as "safe as a Government bond" and especially recommended for women investors. Yukon Gold was tossed into the Yukon-Alaska Trust. It had paid, by then, $7,583,000 in dividends. Operations were discontinued in 1915 when war prices for supplies and labor kited costs and cut profits to nil. Efforts to resume in the twenties were defeated by yearly deficits of a half million dollars. The giant dredges and other machinery were transferred to Malay to work on newer and more promising Guggenheim properties.

Casting up the balance sheet in 1916 on Tom Lawson's venture into Fair Finance, one could read:

Approximate cost of stock to buyers at $6 ...... $4,200,000
Dividends they received 1,500,000
Return on principal ....
Dividends paid to Guggenheim Exploration 6,000,000
Profit split by Lawson and Thompson 270,000

14. ENGINEERS AND CAPITALISTS

WHEN YUKON GOLD blew up, the celebrated alliance between John Hays Hammond and Daniel Guggenheim ended. There were two stories as to what happened when Hammond's "million-dollar" contract expired in February, 1908. Hammond's own version was given, obliquely but with great clarity none the less, in an article several months later in the *Engineering and Mining Journal* entitled, "Professional Ethics for the Mining Engineer." "If one cannot 'stand for' the policies or practices of one's employer," stated Hammond, "the straightforward course is to seek employment elsewhere." The scope of engineering, he explained, had widened in recent years from the strictly technical to include "financial and commercial aspects." While an engineer's duty was primarily to his employer, he assumed a "sacred trust, obligating him to safeguard the interests of a wider and more important clientele," the investing public.

Dan's version was different. Upon his return from his summer trip to Europe in 1908, he said:

"Before I left for Europe I set the ball rolling by reducing my own salary; and my brothers, who devote their entire time to the affairs of the company, also voluntarily reduced their salaries. Like all well managed companies, we cleaned out our Augean stables last spring, and the cleaning process has been completed. While our salary list alone is reduced by $750,000, I am confident that the efficiency of our labor has greatly improved."

This exchange of amenities, as between "not standing" for an employer's practices, and the cleaning of "Augean stables" proceeded no further. On quitting, Hammond as-

214

signed ill health as the reason and expressed his satisfaction with his five years of service, and the brothers in return expressed their regrets at his departure. Even had Hammond not been squeamish, his name could hardly have helped the temporarily discredited Guggenheims; and as for Dan, the luxury of Hammond's fame, for the nonce, was certainly not worth any $250,000 a year plus a quarter interest in new Guggenex properties, or indeed worth anything.

In any event the great engineer had found a more interesting kettle of fish than scouting mines for Exploration. He was growing old and stout and had become a capitalist in his own right. By now he was a big figure in Republican conclaves and had formed a lasting friendship with that fast-rising star of Republicanism, William Howard Taft. Fed by the flattery of his intimates, he felt that the Vice-Presidency was within his grasp. So enamored had he become of this idea by the spring of 1908, when his contract expired, that he definitely became a candidate and none other than William Boyce Thompson became his manager. Thompson spent thousands of his own, of Hammond's and other mining men's money on headquarters, traveling expenses, parties, and other political accessories. Hammond passed many a blissful hour contemplating his future Vice-Presidential grandeur, his intimate access to the White House, his pontifical sway over the august Senate. Alas for dreams! It was not to be.

Whether Hammond heightened his stature as a mining engineer during his Guggenheim years was open to question. Undoubtedly he brought many valuable properties into the fold. But the days of the great gold-silver-lead discoveries seemed over for the present and interest had shifted to the huge porphyry copper mines. Given a suitable grade of ore scattered on the earth's surface and easily explored, it was more a problem of excavating than mining engineering.

The great secret in mine exploration was to divine the whither-wending of veins, the pinching-out of lodes deep down in the earth's vitals. It was tricky enough even when shafts and stopes had been opened: beyond that one had to depend on analogies and calculate probabilities. But in the open-cut porphyry copper mines, there was little guess-work on that score. Drill-tests established with certainty the amount and the richness of the ore. After that it was a matter of working steam shovels fast enough to make low-grade ores profitable. In this Hammond had no prior experience and younger men arose in the West who were his undoubted superiors. The porphyries rich enough to warrant exploitation were few and far between and when the Guggenheims had gained control of them, Hammond was no longer needed.

Alfred Chester Beatty was the man on whom Hammond's toga was to fall when he left Guggenheim Exploration. Thoughtfully, his chief had given him praise and scope to assume that rôle. Yukon Gold rudely shook all those plans. Young Beatty was forced to decide whether to accept the jibes of the oracle of his craft, the *Engineering and Mining Journal,* that "no engineer who values his reputation would permit such a misuse of his report and be silent about it."

The Guggenheims solved his quandary for him. In a case celebrated in mining annals, they pronounced imprecations on the head of their assistant general manager. "Low cunning and lubricity," thundered the eloquent Louis Marshall, Guggenheim counsel. "It is clear that he is a man consumed by greed . . . unscrupulous manner . . . acts of a sordid character . . . possessed of a most grasping and avaricious nature." When Beatty's lawyers responded in kind, Marshall rose to high flights of indignation in assailing the "unworthy slings, innuendoes and insinuations" against the Guggenheims' honor and protested that they were being treated "as if they were highwaymen."

"Grasping . . . avaricious." Mining engineers, in the cozy fastnesses of the Rocky Mountain Club in New York or in shacks on mountain sides in Mexico, Alaska and Chile, roared with laughter as they read the Guggenheim attorney's choice of adjectives. The Guggenheims "highwaymen"! Mine owners from Montana to Arizona smiled bitterly as they looked over the batches of smelter statements they received monthly from Guggenheim smelters.

The issue between Beatty and his employers, compressed into a few words from the volumes it occupied in the law books, was: Did Beatty save Yukon Gold in the summer of 1905 for the Guggenheims after Dan had turned it down? And when he advanced $27,300 cash to his fellow-engineer, O. B. Perry, to hold together the claims on lower Bonanza Creek, was it merely a low trick by which he could get his foot in the door when the Guggenheims formed Yukon Gold, and claim an inordinate interest, despite his "princely salary"? In all, the engineer asked $54,000 to cover his outlay in cash with interest, which held together the nucleus of the Bonanza claims, plus 23,000 shares in Yukon Gold, an option of 40,000 more at $2 a share, and $225,000 in damages.

Learned counsel fought over the great principle of *uberrima fides*—the utmost confidence—as it applied to Beatty, expert adviser to the mine-ignorant capitalists who hired him.

"If Beatty had not come to the front and put up his money and credit to save the whole thing," contended his counsel, "the millions in profits which the Guggenheims subsequently made out of the properties would never have been realized."

Nothing of the kind, retorted Louis Marshall. If he did advance money to hold together the claims, it was merely a loan for which the Guggenheims had reimbursed him with options on Guggenex. Marshall summed up his argument against Beatty's "lubricity" thus:

This trusted engineer had egged on Perry to demand a 4 per cent free interest in Yukon Gold and an option on 4 per cent more in part payment for his services. Of this Perry agreed to turn over 1½ per cent in the free interest and 3 per cent in the option to his confederate, Beatty. Clearly Perry had asked more than he would have been content with, had it not been for the secret split with Beatty.

Dan and Hammond both testified they did not know the exact terms of the Beatty-Perry agreement. Hammond had heard Beatty's interest discussed by the brothers "but I think they were afraid to tell me anything about it because they thought probably I would want some myself."

Dan himself was a remarkable witness. On fifty-five occasions he said: "I can't remember," "I don't recollect," "I have forgotten." "I eliminate details from my mind," he explained.

Tom Lawson testified, beaming alternately upon the Guggenheims, biggest mine-floaters in America, and on Beatty, with whom he also had promotional relations. He was sure Dan knew of Beatty's interest in Yukon because they had discussed it at length when Lawson was assuring himself that there would be no extra Yukon stock dumped on the market during his flotation. "I must know before I stated to the public what I was going to do, whether I was selling stock for a company or making a market for other people to sell on." He had not discussed Beatty's interest with him because "we thought it best that we do not come together. The essence of this whole trade was secrecy."

Marshall was sarcastic. "When one considers the extended and the distracted character of the business in which he has been engaged in recent years, the imaginative powers which he possesses, his mastery of fiction stimulated

218

by a soaring poetic temperament, I can readily see how his testimony may have been shaped by hypnotic suggestions."

Justice James W. Gerard, later to be Ambassador to Germany, decided June 4, 1913, that the $27,300 which Beatty had advanced should be paid him, but the 21,710 shares of stock which he claimed should be turned over to Exploration. Beatty appealed.

The appellate division of the New York Supreme Court reversed Gerard, 3-2. Their decision gave Beatty $39,312 for his advance and interest thereon, 21,710 shares of Yukon Gold and their dividends, and an option on 39,000 shares at $2.30, the current price. Realizing that the option was an empty victory, the court awarded him $174,845 damages.

On such a decision, recourse to the Court of Appeals was inevitable. In 1918, seven years after the beginning of the trial, the higher court reversed the appellate decision, 5-1, and ordered a new trial. Appalled by that prospect with all its delays and expenses, Beatty's counsel begged for reargument, especially on the point of the good faith of the Perry loan.

Miracles happen—even in law courts. The motion for reargument was granted and Justice Cardozo, now member of the U. S. Supreme Court, delivered the revised opinion, 5-2. It stuck to the original opinion that Beatty was guilty of breach of faith in egging on Perry to ask for a bigger percentage of interest, but held him guiltless as to the advance of $27,300. He was awarded this sum with interest and 5,460 shares of Yukon Gold, worth $27,300 with dividends of $10,920 declared since 1908. Damages were stricken out.

Beatty became a foremost authority on the porphyry coppers and lived to see the day when he represented the Bwana M'Kubwa and Roan Antelope properties of South Africa in the struggle with the Guggenheims for domination of the world copper market.

15. SILVER PRINCE IN THE SENATE

IN those cozy days when the United States Senate was dubbed the choicest millionaires' club in America and when its seats were auctioned off in the more venal legislatures like hams at a county fair, it was not presumptuous that Simon Guggenheim, western viceroy for the great mining and smelting family, should aspire to be a senator.

Some said he sought the toga for crass reasons, to mold the federal mining laws and their administrators nearer the Smelter Trust's desire. But to the sad-eyed little man who sat in the Trust's Denver office, political advancement was precious in itself. The Guggenheims had won wealth; now they wanted prestige. They ruled the economic life of the mountain states; was it unreasonable for them to seek to sit among the political rulers? In the West men used harsh words to describe the family's climb to power; the respect due a senator would soften those words and gild the Guggenheims' reputation.

Simon coveted the senatorship not only for the family's sake, but for his own. It would end his voluntary exile in the West. To Dan, Murry and Sol, he was still a youngster, more level-headed than Ben and Will, but still a junior member of M. Guggenheim's Sons. He had been sympathetic to Ben and Will in their fight against forming Guggenheim Exploration and going into the Smelters Trust. At times he looked askance at Dan's more daring financial ventures. By success in the political field, he could salve a wounded ego and be the first to polish the rude but puissant name of Guggenheim with the luster of senatorial dignity.

Fortunately for him, aspirants for that high position were not obliged in those days to pass a public review at the polls. Everyone in Colorado, friend and foe alike, admitted that Simon Guggenheim was no match for the spellbinders who flapped their strident tongues in public on the great issue of the day—silver. In the hurly-burly of Colorado politics, whose tone was set by that peerless champion of the common people, Senator Patterson, with the battle cry, "Let there be trouble," the tongue-tied Smelters viceroy was a helpless tyro. Fortunately for him, the great silver mine owners of the Rockies had set a style which he could follow. It was to their ample moneybags that the Great Commoner had access in his "cross of gold" campaign. The mark of the Silver Dollar was writ large across the politics of all the Rocky Mountain states from Idaho to Arizona, reinforced by the Copper Collar which decorated the necks of many a Montana solon.

Two types of political magnates shuffled across the stage of Colorado politics: the millionaire mine owner from Leadville, Cripple Creek or Central City, and the apostle of Populism and radical democracy. The silver magnates were accustomed to buy their politicians along with their engineers, lawyers and palaces. In alliance with the Denver and Rio Grande, the Colorado Fuel and Iron Company, the Colorado Southern, and the open-handed Denver light, gas, and water companies, they nurtured the legislature, the governor, and the judiciary, except for the brief period of Populist insurrection in the nineties.

In that troubled decade, marked by the silver collapse of 1893, regular Republicanism of the Mark Hanna type got short shrift. Embarrassed regulars who itched for office disguised themselves as Silver Republicans and Democrats impatient of Grover Cleveland's gold treason joined the ruined farmers in shouting for Populism.

Adroit hands pushed the eager, affable Simon straight into the maelstrom of the 1896 campaign. Otto Mears, famed over the Rockies for the solid silver passes he gave his friends to ride his railroad; Dick Broad, Jr., the rising young politico from Boulder; and Horton Pope, boss of Pueblo Republicanism, attached themselves eagerly to the Guggenheim "barrel." Without opening his mouth, the young man found the nomination for lieutenant-governor on the Silver Republican ticket tossed in his lap. The honor having been thrown his way, it was as speedily snatched back on the ground that Simon was only twenty-nine and therefore ineligible.

The *Denver News* suggested that his supporters' main interest was in the "capacity of his barrel" and remarked that his ineligibility "may be sad news to the Philadelphia citizen but it is hardly a circumstance to what will strike him next November should be have the misfortune to run up against the people of Colorado as the pet of the corporations."

Guggenheim thanked Broad in a letter which assured the citizenry:

My sole motive in permitting my name to go before the convention was to devote myself unselfishly to the cause of the people, to the service of the state, and to the unfolding of the great possibilities of our Commonwealth. . . . Extended business relations and the experience of previous years lead me to believe that I might have rendered my state good service had the people of Colorado reposed in me their confidence.

Despite his withdrawal he was heart and soul for "the triumph of silver on which rests the hopes of humanity."

The *Pueblo Chieftain,* loyal to its leading smelter man, denounced the "gratuitous insult" of Guggenheim's forced withdrawal as a "mere technicality which should not have been allowed to cut any figure."

Ike Stevens of the *Denver Republican* was credited with the political stroke of 1898 which shoved young Guggen-

heim, then thirty-one, into the contest for governor. All
three parties were badly split. Senator Wolcott, the regular
Republican, believed the time had come to admit that the
Silver Calf had been overthrown. Senator Teller led the
faction that worshiped silver. Ike Stevens believed that he
could confute the Teller Silverites by packing their convention, nominating Guggenheim, and then manipulating
him into another withdrawal, leaving the field in the possession of the Wolcott stalwarts. Reported the hostile *Denver
News* on the eve of the Silver Republican conclave in Colorado Springs:

The sublime is mingled with the ridiculous and the *haut
ton* with the rabble at Colorado Springs' swell hotel tonight. The spacious halls and corridors that are usually
haunted by the wealthy and cultured beauties of the land
are tonight occupied by a surging, jostling horde of politicians and others. The ward-heeler elbows the capitalist
and railway promoter, and the hirelings of the gang of
ballot box wreckers, whose greatest incomes are during
such times as these, mingle and hobnob with men whose
avocations are honest.

Beer was what was wanted and beer the mob had and
will continue to have so long as Simon Guggenheim's
barrel contains a dollar that he is willing to sacrifice on
the bid for also-ran in the race for the mahogany chair
in the pile on Capitol Hill. . . . The energetic Simon is
everywhere, almost hidden behind this tall lady or that,
but on hand just the same and with the curtsies and bows
of a Chesterfield and the warm grasp of an old-time friend
he does the act of welcoming. But, poor things, they think
they are not in the swim unless they elbow their way
through the grand crush of men filling the corridors and
then step into the Holy of Holies for one grasp of the
hand that can write a signature that possibly few can

read but for which the cashier will gladly hand out money in rolls large enough to wad Dewey's guns.

The Guggenheim managers hired the Opera House for the convention and grinned at the indignation of the Teller-ites, who were for the most part hard-bitten victims of the silver depression and desperate in their devotion to Senator Teller and Silver Republicanism. Determined to repel the Guggenheimites, they crept into the Opera House early on the convention morning, posted armed guards at all doors and set themselves for a siege. The Guggenheim faction, somewhat the worse for drink, trooped innocently into the ambush. Teller shotguns blazed and one Guggenheimite bit the dust for eternity in best Wild West fashion. Simon's cohorts beat a hasty retreat, bearing their wounded with them, while the wires to the east sizzled with flashes on this latest episode in Colorado's fevered political life. Both sides, abashed at the bloodshed, abandoned their claims to the Opera House.

Some of the Guggenheim crowd, badly shaken in morale, were all for peace with the Tellerites by now. In baldly apocryphal style, the *Denver News* reported Simon's speech:

I want you men who are opposing me to understand that you are down here on my money. I am supporting you and paying your board, paying you cash. I want you to understand that I must be nominated for governor. I want you to understand that I have preserved a list showing the name of every person to whom I have paid a dollar and what it was paid for. If I am not nominated I will publish the list and I want you to understand that if you nominate another man, I will spend $300,000 to defeat him.

These remarkable sentiments may well have been uttered by an overwrought lieutenant but they were alien to the

"CLIMBIN' UP DE GOLDEN STAIR."

suave young Guggenheim who shrank from the platform, spoke with the greatest difficulty, and never bluntly.

The Tellerites abandoned Silver Republicanism to Simon and joined the Populists and Democrats in a Fusion ticket. Cried the venerable Teller, long-time spokesman for Colorado in the Senate and Secretary of the Interior in Chester A. Arthur's cabinet:

> Who ever heard of this man [Guggenheim] for governor, except for his bank account? I will say that if he hadn't any more money than Mr. Thomas [the Democratic nominee] or myself, he would never have been heard of even for justice of the peace. They say he can be beaten. By the living God he shall be beaten! On election day you will find him and his barrel or barrels snowed under by the votes cast for Charles S. Thomas.

The *News* commented: "Guggenheim got what he paid for." The price, the *News* announced in its usual well informed style, was $70,000. Its editor, Thomas Patterson, predicted cheerfully that the Silverites would "cut his throat" and that the regulars would bleed him. "It is not every day that a very rich and ambitious man falls into the hands of the experienced gangsters who compose Mr. Wolcott's entourage."

A neat trick which brought no little amusement to the Guggenheim camp was a maneuvered split in Populist ranks by the overnight creation of the Middle-of-the-Road Populist party. A bought-and-paid-for crowd of delegates was assembled in Denver to adopt a platform for labor legislation, the initiative and referendum, and opposition to monopoly. "We have as a true body of the National People's Party," wrote politicians Mears-Broad-Stevens, "accepted the declaration of the Hon. Simon Guggenheim as good doctrine, especially his position on direct legislation." They adopted a party emblem, the Log Cabin, and the slogan, West and South.

226

Editor Patterson snorted:

The campaign conducted by the millionaire barrels is reaching depths of depravity unsounded in Colorado politics. The employment of money to debauch individuals has not been uncommon, but this year there is presented the spectacle of parties springing into existence at the touch of the wizards of boodle.

Presented as "the business man's candidate, the working man's candidate, everybody's candidate," Simon assured his constituents, in a statement:

I feel that in me as your candidate these elements [in the Silver Republican party] can be united and place party above individual. I shall not permit any selfish ambition of mine to stand in the way of the triumph of the principles which I have always advocated. . . . The triumph of Democracy means unrest and injury to the business interests of the state. The triumph of the Silver Republican party means unparalleled prosperity as well as placing the great and all-absorbing silver question in the hands of a party which is sincere in the advocacy of silver for silver's sake alone.

In the midst of his campaigning Simon received a summons from 71 Broadway. His political ambitions were getting in the way of business. The regular Republicans let the older brothers know that Simon's flirting with Silverism was gnawing at the roots of sound national Republican principles.

Over the wire from New York came announcement of Simon's withdrawal from the race. *GUGGENHEIM GOES GLIMMERING*, headlined Editor Patterson, who jibed at Dick Broad for assuring an audience a few days before that Simon "would stick until the last horn blew on the morn of Resurrection."

Returning briefly from New York, Guggenheim gave the lie to Patterson's story that his candidacy had been a blind all the time for the Wolcott Republicans. "I want the world to know," he said, "that I am a silver man and that I will not assist in the election of state senators who will send any but an out-and-out silver man to the U. S. Senate from Colorado." He came out flatly for Thomas, the Democrat-Fusion candidate, who was elected a few weeks later. As he boarded the train for the East again, Editor Patterson shouted after him that he had "ruthlessly and heartlessly left Colorado politicians with financial ambitions in the yawning lurch."

But Simon had more interesting matters to contemplate. His marriage to beautiful Olga Hirsh was in the offing, to be followed by a honeymoon in Japan. On his wedding day, November 24, Simon ordered largess distributed in Denver in feudal style, with Parson Uzzell as almoner. Turkey was fed to a thousand poor boys. "The wealthy, generous philanthropist," said the *Denver Republican,* "is idolized by the poor boys of the city who remember also the gift of five hundred suits of new clothes which made them happy one Christmas day a few years ago."

Even Editor Patterson's caustic pen was stilled after Simon's return from his honeymoon, for the American Smelting and Refining Company had been organized in New York; and the Guggenheims' Pueblo smelter, as the sole non-Trust plant in Colorado, was the star of hope for the mining interests. During this political honeymoon, which lifted Simon to the role of Colorado's smelting hero, Editor Patterson achieved his dearest aim, election to the U. S. Senate. For him it was the culmination of a political career that began as territorial delegate when he helped gain Colorado's admission to the Union in 1876 as the Centennial State.

Simon, basking in public acclaim from mine owner and

CLEAR THE TRACK!

miner alike in the brief interlude from the Trust's organization in 1899 to its absorption by the Guggenheims in 1901, enjoyed to the full this sudden reversal in popular esteem. The Guggenheim suite at the Brown Palace, center of Denver's social and political life, was the rendezvous for politicians and mine owners high and low. Later, when the newlyweds moved into Otto Mears's mansion, a good slice of the social life of the city gravitated toward them. Simon, suave, charming in manner, cultured in Continental fashion, was matched by his beautiful and gracious wife, who busied herself, a Lady Bountiful, in personal and public charities. Only the highest reaches of Denver society were closed to them—that tight little group which owed their millions to the silver riches of Central City, Leadville, and other camps of the sixties and seventies. Nor would the Denver Club, their fortress, admit Simon to membership. The club's starched anti-Semitism drove another distinguished Denver Jew, Sam Newhouse, into exile to Salt Lake City. There he invested in realty and copper mines and became a valuable ally of the Guggenheims in later years.

The millions dumped into the family's lap by the American Smelting and Refining coup in 1901 kept Simon busy. As western representative for the Smelters Trust and Guggenheim Exploration, he was in charge of field forces that roamed the Rockies for suitable outlets for the Guggenheim surplus. The cry of anger that arose at the family's treason to the mining interests once more reversed the tide of public favor and robbed him of the halo that had descended briefly over his head.

The 1902 election witnessed the end of Populism and the election as governor of Jim Peabody, the first out-and-out corporation man to sit in the Capitol since the Great Depression of the nineties. Senator Teller's senatorial term had expired, and so close was the division in the State Senate over his re-election that Colorado was treated to another of those Wild West displays that periodically reminded the nation of the state's early mining camp traditions. Democratic State Senators stood armed guard over the Chamber by day and by night to prevent the rascally Republicans from slipping over their candidate. The Republicans appealed to city and state for police protection. Meals were served on the Senate floor in this early exhibition of the sit-down technique. The forces of righteousness triumphed after all, and Senator Teller was sent back to Washington to begin his sixth term.

Simon Guggenheim watched with eager eye the slow ebbing of the forces of Populism and Democracy. A senatorial seat became his consuming desire and he set out, in the methodical Guggenheim manner, to attain his objective when Senator Patterson's seat would be vacated in 1906.

Across his path lay the implacable hatred of the Western Federation of Miners, that turbulent, powerful union of hard-fisted, hard-rock blasters who wandered through the Rockies, working in every camp, indifferent to danger, imbued with a hardy pioneer distrust of Eastern monopolists and fat capitalists. With the hard-bitten farmers of Colorado's parched plains, they had been the backbone of Populism. Many of them now followed the fast-growing Socialist Party and were soon to be the nucleus of the Industrial Workers of the World.

For years the Western Federation had worked for a law to end the twelve-hour shift in mine and smelter. When they gained their coveted eight-hour law, the three-man Colorado Supreme Court contemptuously cast it on the legal scrap heap with the word "unconstitutional." The smelter strike of 1900 followed. Simon, cashing in on anti-Trust sentiment, granted the eight-hour demand in his Pueblo plant, contingent on the strike's success in Trust smelters. The strike lost, the Guggenheim smelter went back to the twelve-hour shift, with all the credit of having tried to help labor.

By 1902 the people of Colorado had enacted, by 46,000 majority, a constitutional amendment to validate an eight-hour law. The Guggenheims, allied with mine owners and railroad bosses, were able in 1903 to thwart the passage of the now constitutional bill. Enraged, Charles Moyer, the bitter, relentless president of the Western Federation, and Big Bill Haywood, its secretary, declared that labor must fall back on direct action. Another of those fierce smelter strikes which periodically convulsed Colorado was on. The fat resources of the Smelters Trust outbalanced the lean pockets of their smeltermen, and the strike was lost. The bitter controversy flared again in the rich Cripple Creek gold camp, where mine owner and miner fought each other in the most savage industrial war yet recorded in Colorado's bloody labor annals. Governor Peabody poured troops into Cripple Creek and appealed to President Roosevelt for federal reinforcements. After the miners' union had been drowned in an unparalleled blood bath, Governor Peabody was banqueted by the corporations. Simon Guggenheim toasted him for his "bold and vigorous stand for those rights the Constitution guarantees to even the humblest citizen," namely, the imported strikebreakers.

Editor O'Neill of the *Miners Magazine* declared that Guggenheim had entered a pool with Denver Tramways and Colorado Fuel & Iron to offer $2,500 to $5,000 for legislators' votes.

If a brazen steal is consummated, there is liable to be an uprising in Colorado composed of men who will march to the State Capitol with blood in their eyes and vengeance in their hearts. The citizenship of this state are not yet ready to be disfranchised by corporation combinations.

The anti-Guggenheim press played the arrest of W. E. Singer, charged with beating a board bill. Police found in his letters one signed by Governor Peabody stating that he was "pleased to recommend you most heartily to Mr. Simon Guggenheim or his representative, Mr. Richard Broad, for any position you may apply for either in connection with his numerous enterprises in this state or in the political field as you may prefer."

Tom Walsh, magnifico of the famed Camp Bird mine and father of the possessor of the Hope diamond, was also angling for a U. S. senatorship. The *Miners Magazine* explained the opposition of conservatives to the Walsh candidacy:

Guggenheim is admired for his cold-blooded methods of doing business and because he is loyal to the class that exploits labor. Walsh is condemned because he manifests a semblance of generosity toward the class that wears cotton and eats hoof-steaks. . . . The despotism of a Guggenheim will hasten the crisis in our civilization. The charity of a Walsh will delay the sunburst of economic liberty.

Nevertheless the Guggenheim political Juggernaut progressed toward its goal with a Republican victory in 1904. Senator Patterson tried desperately to upset the machine in a sensational charge that the Supreme Court had been packed with corporation lackeys. Haled before the court on contempt, Patterson, represented by Senator Teller and Governor-Elect Alva Adams, pleaded the truth as self-defense. The fiery old warhorse asserted flatly that Guggenheim, the railroads, the Denver utilities and the Cripple Creek mine owners had put up $40,000 to renominate Peabody and $200,000 for his election, pro-rated according to their tax assessments. The prize they sought, he declared, was the naming of two additional Supreme Court justices, by Governor Peabody. But Peabody had been nosed out by 9,000 votes. The court obligingly tossed out the required number of Denver Democratic votes, but even so there were not enough Republican legislators willing to award the contested governorship to Peabody. In a remarkable compromise they re-elected him on the condition that he would resign immediately after naming the two new Supreme Court judges.

Under Dick Broad's alert management, the Guggenheim machine moved on toward the crucial 1906 election. To many a politician it would have seemed impossible to elevate so unlikely a candidate as the Smelter Trust's western representative. He had no public personality. Colorado liked vituperative political leaders who stood in the public forum slugging with two fists, and a horseshoe in the glove was not barred. Wolcott, the arrogant, irascible Republican leader, and Patterson, the Democratic leader who knew no fear of the libel laws, were like that. But Guggenheim was shy, retiring, ill at ease with the rough gladiators of the Colorado arena, equipped with no verbal pyrotechnics or love of battle for itself. Fortunately his election was to require no appeal to the prejudices of voters. Candidates for the legislature were quietly buttonholed and informed of the condition on which their campaign would be financed. A press barrage was laid for Guggenheim, the philanthropist. He financed parties for the newsboys of the redoubtable *Denver Post*, then under the management of Tammen and Bonfils, two of the slickest go-getters in American journalism. He gave a much-needed building to the starved Colorado School of Mines. This he followed with similar gifts for buildings at the State University and the State Agricultural College.

The Republican press lauded so eminent and generous a patron of education and even the Democrats gave grudging admission that Guggenheim had stepped in handsomely

234

Incommunicado

where the Legislature had been niggardly. Only the unregenerate *Miners Magazine* caviled:

> For the past week or more the press of Colorado has teemed with praise of Simon Guggenheim. Plain, simple English in prose failed to do justice to this lauded philanthropist, and the genius of the poet was called upon to rhyme stanzas in adulation of the magnanimous gift that was tendered to the state by this Kingpin of the Smelters Trust, being heralded for a seat in the millionaires' club in Washington. It matters not that the victims who produced his dividends live in hovels. The $50,000 donation makes fawning sycophants forget the lawless methods by which this Caesar has become a monarch in our industrial realm and makes them forget that his gold is but the minted product that came from the misery of over-worked human beings. . . . Simon could not be convicted of murder yet every smelter of the trust in which he is interested has populated cemeteries with the remains of men who have gone down to premature graves because Simon and his brethren placed more value upon profit than upon human flesh.

The operation of machine politics was revealed later by Morton Alexander, successful Republican senatorial nominee in the 1906 election.

"We're going to put you on the ticket in this district for Senate, Morton," he was informed by John F. Vivian, Guggenheim manager.

"But what about the people?" asked the abashed Arvada farmer. "I'm not well known around here."

"To hell with the people," replied the imperturbable Vivian.

A few weeks later Alexander met Vivian on the street in Denver. "Well, we nominated you today," hailed Vivian. "You're as good as elected."

"But I haven't any money for a campaign," said the new designee.

"Don't worry about that. We'll take care of the money."

It was an adage in Colorado that thousand dollar bills sprouted on the sagebrush at election time. Alexander found himself elected almost without effort.

The Republican caucus was called in Denver. Nominations was open for United States Senator, and Simon's name was put forward. Almost unanimously it was approved.

Alexander, rather naïve in political ways, was astounded. "The people don't want Guggenheim," he broke in. "Nobody mentioned Guggenheim's name in the campaign."

It was Vivian's turn to be astounded. "What's the matter with you, Morton? I've been your friend. I helped elect you. Are you going back on me?"

The legislature was about to meet. Alexander set himself up as the leader of the Republican anti-Guggenheim forces. He buttonholed Senator after Senator and gained their assurance that they would not support the Smelter man. "The people up in Boulder would hang me to a telegraph pole," exclaimed Senator Millard. Twenty Senators met and vowed death to Guggenheim's political ambitions. The machine got busy and the next time Alexander's private caucus met, there were only sixteen Senators present. That dwindled to seven on the third meeting, and finally only Alexander and De La Vergne of Colorado Springs were left.

"I'll never support Guggenheim," swore De La Vergne. "It would be the ruination of the mining industry."

The two met later at the Brown Palace. De La Vergne called the eighth floor—Republican headquarters—to inform them of his decision. He was summoned upstairs.

An hour later he returned and the two men walked down the street together. De La Vergne was broken in spirit. "They'll set me out a pauper tomorrow if I don't vote right.

237

I'm getting to be an old man. I've got to think of my wife," he said, and broke down and cried.

"Fortunately God made me a poor man," said Alexander, consoling his friend, "and I've never interfered with Him. All I've got is a cabbage farm."

The Guggenheim cohorts were insistent on a solid Republican vote for their man. Railery from the Democrats was to be expected, but the Republicans must present a united front. News of Alexander's stand was made public and the day before caucus delegations from far and wide laid siege to his "cabbage farm," a few miles north of Denver, wheedling, cajoling, threatening him, breaking down his fence, trampling down his lawn. "For God's sake," they asked, one and all, "what's the matter with you?" Vivian, blue with rage, declared Alexander should be sent to the pen for receiving money under false pretenses.

Senator Stevens of Colorado Springs went to the recalcitrant Republican.

"This is awful, the money they're spending," said Stevens, wiping his brow. "What would you do if I laid $5,000 down here?" he said suddenly turning on his fellow-Senator.

"Why, I'd take it to Senator Patterson and send Guggenheim to the pen," answered Alexander, too rashly. Later he bewailed his hasty answer and wished he had taken the money, for evidence.

Vivian, smarting under criticism that "his man" had bolted, made a last-minute appeal to Alexander to reconsider. "What *is* it that you want?" he implored. "Do you want the governorship, the senatorship, is there *anything* you want?" Alexander shook his head.

About this time big advertisements appeared in all Colorado dailies concerning the state's marvellous mineral resources and the great future that lay ahead. Signed by Simon Guggenheim as western Representative of American Smelting and Refining, they were an innovation in the West,

238

the first sample of "institutional advertising" in that part of the country.

On December 31, 1906, the Republican caucus met at the Brown Palace to nominate Guggenheim. He made a short speech:

> I stand for a greater Colorado. I want to see the state get more government money for its irrigation canals. . . . I want to see the smaller towns of the state get recognition in federal appropriations. Other states have government postoffice buildings in towns of 5,000 people. Why should not we have them?

Senator Patterson congratulated Senator-Designate Guggenheim.

> On Sunday Simon Guggenheim was thirty-nine years of age. Within a few months he will occupy a seat in the distinguished body of lawmakers and multimillionaires, some of whom labored twice as many years and spent twice as much money for their party before they were draped with the senatorial toga.

The smelter man, said Senator Patterson, had "ignored the people utterly."

> He has dealt only with a cabal of party managers. He has gone after the senatorship as he would go about the purchase of a desirable piece of property. . . . Practically the first authorized announcement of Mr. Guggenheim's candidacy was made at the caucus. The *News* ventures the assertion that this is a record without parallel in the history of senator-making in the United States. We believe Colorado has reached the nadir of her political life.

An Eastern journalist, Frederick Lawrence, interviewed Guggenheim and claimed he defended his purchase. "It is

239

merely conducting political campaigns as they are conducted these days," Guggenheim was quoted. "The money I have contributed has helped to elect these man and naturally they feel under obligation to vote for me. It is done all over the United States today. I do not consider that it is wrong and neither do I think that it can in any sense be called bribery."

The University Club had an evening of merriment and a skit which featured the Senator-to-be. Souvenirs were given guests: "In $ I trust. Vote for Guggenheim."

William Jennings Bryan from the *Commoner's* editorial sanctum in neighboring Nebraska, declared:

> While Guggenheim may not intend to represent the smelters and other corporations, he is so accustomed to look at the interests of the people through corporation spectacles that he will be quite sure that what is good for the corporations is good for the people. . . . As a horrible example, Mr. Guggenheim may prove a useful member of the U. S. Senate; as a representative of the people of Colorado he will be a failure from the beginning.

The open Guggenheim checkbook was reinforced, Charles Edward Russell stated, by tips to legislators on American Smelting and Refining stock, which was then booming on the Exchange. John J. McCarthy, editor of a Jefferson County paper, told in later years how he had conscientiously, as a good Republican, put in a plug, free of charge, for Guggenheim. He received a letter from the Senator praising his honesty. Later he discovered that his lack of business acumen had cost him $1,000. Other editors were paid for such puffs.

January 15 dawned bright in Denver's clear mountain air and by ten the House and Senate had assembled. The House chaplain, thoroughly in spirit with the occasion and mindful of the colorful history of Colorado's Assembly, intoned: "We thank thee, O Lord, that we are this morning alive, sober, and out of jail."

Guggenheim's nominator spoke to the House:

> The time has gone by in Colorado when by merely scratching the ground you can take hold of our stores of wealth and resources. . . . The time has come when politics must be business and industry. . . . You say my candidate is wealthy; but I say to you [aiming at Senator Patterson's *News*] that he does not make it by advertising those death-dealing agencies, Peruna, Liquozone and Pennyroyal pills.

Senator A. V. Bohn, Leadville pioneer, sponsored the smelter magnate's name in the Upper House.

Merle Vincent, sole Republican Senator to speak in opposition, declared Guggenheim could not support the Republican platform which called for direct election of United States Senators, a railroad commission law, and an effective anti-trust act. "You have bargained off this senatorship for so many dollars. I don't qualify this, and I don't get the information secondhand."

Senator Tully Scott urged that a coin be struck in honor of the event showing:

> Simon Guggenheim sitting a la Lawrence interview with foot firmly placed upon the neck of a prostrate miner with pick in hand and with an appropriate background of smokeless mills and abandoned mines; the whole relieved by a broad border of dollar marks done in seal brown.

Ignoring these strictures, the Republican steam roller elected Guggenheim by 68 votes to 27 for Charles S. Thomas, the Democrat, and 4 for an anti-Guggenheim Republican.

Senator Guggenheim, waiting in the Governor's office, was

brought before the joint assembly. His deep-set, weary eyes seemed to belie the smile that played on his features. Punctiliously the little man shook hands with the speakers of the two Houses and advanced nervously to the rostrum to make his speech of acceptance:

Sincerely do I thank you for the great honor and for the confidence you have reposed in me in electing me to the highest office in the gift of our state. I appreciate my responsibilities and in order to give my entire time to the people of our nation and state during the sessions of Congress and also during the recesses, I have withdrawn from all active business. . . . Gladly do I give up a commercial career for the purpose of assuming the responsibility of senatorship and of devoting myself entirely to the obligations of high office. . . . At this time I wish to state clearly that I am going to Washington to represent all the people; that I am free and untrammeled and under obligations to no interest, company, railroad, or corporation. I am in hearty sympathy with the progress and achievements of our party and of President Roosevelt. I favor all legislation adopted by Congress to correct industrial evils and abuses and will support and suggest further measures that experience and wisdom may demonstrate as necessary. Anyone occupying a public position must expect to be the target of criticism. Just criticism is beneficial; malicious misrepresentation digs its own grave.

A public reception was held later in the day at Guggenheim campaign headquarters in the Brown Palace, with punch bowls "big as bathtubs" and cigars for all. Under the vocal leadership of the triumphant Dick Broad and John Vivian, the boys sang till the rafters rang, to the tune of "The Good Old Summertime":

What Shall We Do With Our Retiring Captains of Industry?

The good old Guggenheim,
The good old Guggenheim,
He'll make the prince of Senators, Simon Guggenheim.
Just watch his smoke, there's lots of it
And that's a very good sign,
It means he's always doing things,
Is Simon Guggenheim.

"Put the Flag at halfmast and raise the auctioneer's flag," editorialized embittered Senator Patterson, as he left political life.

We like Mr. Guggenheim personally. We admire his persistence. We appreciate his liberal appraisement of the merchandise which he set out to purchase. But none the less we think his elevation to the Senate a disgrace to the state and a thing which could only be accomplished by dark and devious methods. Mr. Guggenheim has taken no notable part in the life of the state save by his distribution of money. He has been a liberal giver to various charities. He has enriched our state schools. But aside from these activities which are hardly senatorial in their importance, he is known only as the representative of the Smelters Trust, the combination which has stifled competition by commercial piracy, flooded the state with cheap labor, established truck stores and script systems to win back the pittance it could not avoid paying, corrupted legislatures, levied toll on the mines, and made the railroads do its unlawful will. He has said he will resign all active part in the business which has made him rich but men cannot resign habits and customs ingrained by years and by interest. Mr. Guggenheim knows this; he knows the people know it; and in this mutual knowledge must be found the explanation of this campaign in the dark.

In reply, the new Senator said:

In going to the Senate, it will not be to represent the Smelter Company or any other company or interest. I will go as Simon Guggenheim, plain citizen, and representative of the people of Colorado. An honorable ambition is permitted to every man, even to the wealthiest, and it is my ambition to serve my country. When I was a younger man I had the ambition to make myself independent. I have done this. I wanted independence that I might go into politics with free hands. Why shouldn't an independent man serve his country with all his wealth and his heart, as well?

The *Pueblo Chieftain*, erstwhile supporter and Roosevelt Republican organ, commented:

The fact remains that the system by which Mr. Guggenheim secured his election is undemocratic, dangerous and contrary to the principle of popular self-government. Senator Guggenheim might prove to be the best senator Colorado ever sent to Washington without altering the fact that the people of Colorado and not corporation attorneys or political bosses ought to determine the selection of U. S. senators and all other public officials.

The *Colorado Springs Gazette*, another Roosevelt Republican paper, asserted:

Simon Guggenheim in the U. S. Senate will be a joke, but a most discreditable joke on Colorado. He will be to this state what William A. Clark is to Montana and what J. Edward Addicks tried to be to Delaware—simply a dollar mark placed there to show that another state has sold out.

The *Denver Post* was complaisant. The *Pueblo Chieftain*, in a front-page, red-ink captioned, three-column editorial, appealed to the new Senator:

With the glowing example of the people of Colorado before his eyes, breaking down and obliterating all trace of race preference or prejudice in bestowing of public honors, will not Mr. Guggenheim with all the power of his great office, insist that all of those other barriers should be broken by which public service corporations and wealthy men are preventing honorable men who have the courage to refuse to wear a tyrannical yoke from holding public office because of their courage, their independence and their honor?

On January 25 a special Pullman car took Simon Guggenheim and his family over the Rock Island to New York and Washington, ending forever his position as western representative of the Smelters Trust and beginning his service as Senator from Colorado. One unsympathetic observer cried: "New York now has four Senators, Platt, Depew, Clark of Montana and Guggenheim."

Hardly had the Legislature elected Simon to the Senate than its lower House adopted a memorial to Congress asking for the direct election of United States Senators. In this it echoed the platforms of all Colorado parties and of several Colorado legislatures. Indeed so notorious was the outright domination of the United States Senate by millionaires who bought their seats from corrupt legislatures that the United States House of Representatives as early as 1893 had passed a direct-election amendment, promptly vetoed by the offended Senate. The reform was damned as an effort to "undermine the Constitution," to cater to the rabble and to elevate demagogues to mingle in the Senate with the guardians of the nation's property interests.

No fewer than eighteen millionaires sat in the Senate beside Simon Guggenheim, and of all these, Simon represented the most wealth. His family's fortune was set down at $50,000,000. The others were: Elkins, West Virginia, $25,000,000; Stephenson, Wisconsin, $20,000,000; War-

ren, Wyoming, $15,000,000; Depew, New York, $15,000,-
000; Oliver, Pennsylvania, $15,000,000; Crane, Massachu-
setts, $10,000,000; Aldrich, Rhode Island, $10,000,000;
Wetmore, Rhode Island, $10,000,000; Du Pont, Delaware,
$8,000,000; Kean, New Jersey, $5,000,000; Newlands,
Nevada, $5,000,000; Lodge, Massachusetts, $5,000,000;
Scott, West Virginia, $5,000,000; Bourne, Oregon, $5,-
000,000; Smoot, Utah, $5,000,000; Hale, Maine, $3,000,-
000; Root, New York, $3,000,000; and Brandegee,
Connecticut, $3,000,000.

These were the men who headed the all-important Senate
committees which dealt with federal finance, taxation, and
tariffs—all of major concern to the propertied interests.
Courteously, they arranged tariffs to suit the convenience
of their confreres, and the doughty Joe Cannon, czar of the
less wealthy House, whipped their measures through by
simple gag rule.

Senator Bristow objected to the senatorial courtesy rule
that raised the duty on lead in 1910. "A duty was imposed
on lead not measuring the difference in the cost of smelting
at home and abroad, as promised in the Republican platform, but from $2.50 to $6 higher than the entire cost of
smelting in the country," he declaimed. "This was done, not
in the interest of protecting a struggling American industry
but in the interest of a monopoly controlled by the Guggenheims. Because I presume to object to this sort of thing,
Mr. Cannon calls me a Democrat demagogue, a lunatic and
a pickpocket."

Simon objected, in a brief speech in the Senate. It is
"of importance," he said, "to keep out the cheap Spanish
lead and also the Australian lead." He went down the line
with the Republican leaders, voting ninety-six times for the
schedules of the Payne-Aldrich tariff.

With a member of the family in the Senate, interviews
were sought from the other brothers on weighty public prob-

lems. Isaac, interviewed in Denver when the Knickerbocker panic broke in 1907, was sure the Wall Street panic would not affect the rest of the country. He declared:

Wall Street is no longer dominating the commercial business of the country. The frenzied flurries of the past week in Stock Exchange prices have not had the slightest effect upon the prosperity of the United States. On the contrary, the present conditions and the outlook for the future in all kinds of industry are better than ever before.

Judge Gary's remark about the business world divorcing itself from Wall Street is correct. Whether Union Pacific stock sells at 120 or 150 makes not the slightest difference to a country engaged in producing enormous crops and dealing in products of farm, factory and mine.

I had a talk on Saturday with Mr. Cortelyou, Secretary of the Treasury. He said to me: "Mr. Guggenheim, I am here to do and I am doing all I can for the business interests of the country."

While I believe President Roosevelt to be an able, energetic, and conscientious man, convinced that what he is doing is for the best interests of the country, I cannot agree with the methods he is employing. He is going at the corporations too brusquely, with a strangle hold on their necks, and smashing with a big stick. The treatment is too harsh, too severe, for not all corporations are bad and not all trusts are thieves and robbers.

A great combination of capital like the Steel Trust, magnificently managed, is a positive benefit to the country, both for labor and the consumer. I may be pardoned for citing our own smelter company. It has raised the wages of the workmen and cheapened the cost of smelting to the miner.

The tendency for many of the states is to go too far in

the radical attack upon corporations of all kinds. Some of our political leaders who have started out with bright prospects backed by general confidence of the people may find themselves buried under a reaction that follows any extreme.

A few months later, Dan, also interviewed in Denver, admitted that the Wall Street panic had some organic relation to the country. But it was caused, he said, because "the people have been too extravagant and the country has been too prosperous." Now is the psychological time, he urged, for silver advocates to get together for legislation to rehabilitate silver.

Both interviews revealed the Guggenheims as staunchly conservative Republicans—save for the silver heresy which was pardonable in men with big silver mines. One and all they had sopped up Republicanism in their early Philadelphia days as part of the atmosphere in high-tariff, low-wage Pennsylvania.

Guggenheim never rose to important position in the Senate. He had never been interested in practical politics, held no burning convictions, apparently sought mainly the honor and prestige of the senatorship. He was not a hard-shell Tory and his vote occasionally favored liberal projects such as the creation of the Children's Bureau, as bitterly fought then as the child labor amendment was in later years. On the spot, he voted favorably on the amendment for the direct election of United States Senators. Privately, he expressed the conviction that it made not much difference. He held the direct primary to be the rich man's friend because of the heavy expenditure needed to conduct a campaign among the entire electorate instead of merely among legislators. He believed the election of Senator Lorimer of Illinois to be valid despite the bald corruption involved.

A prepared funeral oration over his colleague, Senator Charles J. Hughes, Jr., was his only extended speech in six years in the Senate. Otherwise his remarks were limited to a few minutes.

Mrs. Guggenheim loved the social life of Washington and entertained frequently. With the 1912 Presidential campaign in the offing, she hoped for Taft's re-election because his wife "has done more to create an atmosphere of social permanency and stability such as prevails in the courts of Europe than the wife of any preceding executive." "There is no doubt," Mrs. Guggenheim added, "that Mrs. Taft, given time, will do for the society of this country what no other woman, however accomplished or impregnable in social prestige through birth or fortune has succeeded in doing." Washington, she believed, was "very rapidly becoming a city of leisured people and magnificent homes." New York was "too rushingly busy" to please her.

But the Rooseveltian insurgent rebellion against Taft was rising across the country. The Republican state committee in Colorado reined in the bit to halt the rebellion. The insurgents wanted a pledge from Guggenheim that he would not seek re-election in 1912, but the resolution was smothered in the committee. A former Congressman announced his candidacy. "We had a 'dark-lantern' campaign four years ago," he proclaimed, "and it is for the voters to determine whether the same methods should be pursued again."

"It is too soon," said Simon, "to be talking about who will be the next Senator from Colorado. I may or may not be a candidate." But by December 3, 1911, he had made up his mind. It would be unkind to suggest that the impending rupture in the Republican party helped him decide. More probably he felt that the dignity and prestige compressed into one senatorial term would hardly be doubled by serving another six years. The six years had been none too exciting. He was no roaring lion to delight the Senate galleries, no crafty schemer to warm the hearts of the Old Guard, indeed it could hardly be said he was a senator in anything but name. At the end of his term he was chairman of the committees on the Philippines and the University of the United States and could claim, for his six years' tenure, only increased appropriations for post-offices and such like. No important piece of legislation was linked with his name; no great public cause had enlisted his active support. His particular strength lay in his secretary, who darted industriously among the bureaus, forwarding the claims of Colorado clients. The quiet efficiency of the Guggenheim office and its knack of getting things done around Washington raised the Senator's prestige among the folks back home who wanted something in the National Capital.

The *Denver Times* proclaimed:

Senator Guggenheim was a vigilant Agent-General of this state in Washington; no citizen of Colorado was too poor or too obscure to receive from the Senator the same courtesy and the same promptitude that were accorded the most influential of our people; and there are thousands of men and women who count those qualities as virtues and remember them with good will and gratitude.

"My only ambition," added Simon, "is to get as much as possible for Colorado."

President Taft expressed his regrets over Guggenheim's refusal to run again. Simon explained:

I simply felt that it was now time that I again devote myself strictly to business. I have for six years almost neglected the interests that should have had my attention. My brothers want me to return to the firm and want me to give up politics. . . . I shall be interested in politics

251

just the same but I shall not be a candidate for office again. I shall always keep in close touch with the Republican party in Colorado and shall do my part toward bringing the state back into the Republican column.

As he was about to leave the Senate he took part in a filibuster February 25, 1913, against the bill creating the Department of Labor. Senator Borah asked unanimous consent to consider the measure. Senator Guggenheim suggested the absence of a quorum, and failing to halt discussion, asked that the lengthy bill be read. Failing again, he offered an amendment by Senator Lodge abolishing the Department of Commerce. Then followed one of those parliamentary snarls which delight obstructionists. Only two Senators favored the Guggenheim-Lodge amendment, 34 opposed. No quorum, a wait, and then the roll call. Vote 0-37. No quorum, roll call, vote Aye 1 (Guggenheim), No, 46. No quorum, roll call, Vote 0-44, Guggenheim not voting. Senator Smith of Georgia asked unanimous consent to dispense with further roll calls. Guggenheim objected. Smith demanded that Guggenheim then answer the roll call. He asked to be excused from answering. Several Senators objected, so he answered, "Present," to the next roll call. Senator Gronna thereupon took over the leadership of the filibuster.

The Senator's last official act was to resign March 1, 1913, as chairman of the joint committee on governmental purchase of pneumatic tubes. With the inauguration of Woodrow Wilson, Simon withdrew to New York. He severed his last tie with political life when he resigned April 11, 1914, as Republican national committeeman.

His brothers, cognizant of the honors that Senator Guggenheim had brought to the family, created the positions of chairman of the board of American Smelting, American

252

Smelters Securities, and Guggenheim Exploration, and named him to all of them. As chairman, nominally he took precedence even over Dan, who was merely president of these firms. To distinguish him from his brothers, he was thereafter called "Senator," the form of address in use twenty-five years after he had abandoned Washington.

16. GUGGENMORGAN OVER ALASKA

DAN GUGGENHEIM'S dream of empire, as he stood upon the barren ridge overlooking the desolate Klondike country in the summer of 1906, rapidly swelled beyond the Yukon to include all the country north of 54° 40″. When his dream became too big for his own pocketbook, he incorporated it as the Alaska Syndicate and invited J. P. Morgan and Company to share the wealth.

The Alaska Syndicate perched its banner on 6,000-foot crags in the god-forsaken Wrangel Mountains. There gleamed, in the rare sunshine, coppery lodes so wondrous rich that mining men refused to believe the tales that came from the Far North. Of ore that ran 20 to 70 percent in copper, and millions of tons of such ore! Nowhere in all the world were there deposits so rich and so extensive; and Pope Yeatman, successor to John Hays Hammond in Guggenheim Exploration, estimated that this ore could be delivered to the Guggenheim smelter in Tacoma for less than 5 cents a pound. Copper sold anywhere from 12 to 20 cents a pound.

So great was the prize that to reach it Dan Guggenheim, Jacob Schiff, and George Perkins of the Morgan firm, approved the construction of a $20,000,000 railroad bridged across glaciers, hung along towering canyons, thrust two hundred miles into the bleakest wilderness in all America. To link its terminus with the Tacoma smelter, they bought control of steamship companies. Seeing wealth in the cold waters that laved Alaska's shores, the Syndicate acquired fisheries. Needing fuel for its mines, railroad, steamships and canneries, the Syndicate sought to buy the choicest of Alaska's coal lands. Syndicate agents combed every sec-

WILLIAM GUGGENHEIM

GRACE BROWN HERBERT
GUGGENHEIM

AIMÉE LILLIAN STEIN-
BERGER GUGGENHEIM

Photos by Bain News Service and International.

tion of Alaska and the Yukon, and northern British Columbia, until it was said that the "Morganheims" had raped Alaska, had seized her every virgin resource that promised profit, had gained control of her government, and doomed the Far North to the evils of predatory exploitation.

This power, a happy dream to Dan Guggenheim, was viewed by the public through a glass darkly, as a nightmare of dread monopoly seeking to bind a continent in chains and exhaust natural resources with greedy haste. It broke the friendship between President Taft and his creator, Theodore Roosevelt, rent the Republican party, and was an essential cause for the election, in 1912, of the second Democratic President since the Civil War.

Hardly had Simon Guggenheim's election to a seat in the United States Senate been ratified in Denver than the alarum was sounded in a battle which was to make the name of Guggenheim the bugaboo of American politics. The cry arose first in Alaska when the *Juneau Daily Dispatch*, on February 22, 1907, exclaimed:

The Guggenheims, having taken the State of Colorado into camp, are now preparing to annex Alaska so far as its mineral output is concerned. They have begun by buying up most of the land available for gold dredging and are now moving on the immense copper and coal deposits of the Copper River Country.

The Alaska Syndicate had bought Northwestern Steamship, Northwestern Commercial, Northwestern Fisheries, and then the Alaska Steamship Company.

"Nothing has escaped the Guggenheim trust," mourned the *Dispatch*. "In short, it *owns Alaska*." The territory, wailed the *Fairbanks News-Miner*, has become "the prize package of the corporations."

The harbingers of doom heard by Alaskan editors were the crackling rifles of Guggenheim agents in Keystone Can-

yon. On September 25, 1907, a gang of laborers tearing a
roadbed through the canyon for the Alaska Home Railway
found themselves looking into the muzzles of Guggenheim
guns, guarding the approach to the Copper River country.
The Home Railway men claimed they had run into an ambush; the Guggenheim men said that while they were protecting an abandoned right-of-way—key to the Copper
River—which belonged to the Alaska Syndicate, their rivals
attacked them with pickaxes. The Home Railway crew
retreated to their base at Valdez, carrying one corpse and
six wounded men. Valdez was wild with anger but Governor
Brady was nonchalant. "I expected it all the time," he
commented. And indeed he needed no clairvoyance to sus-
pect that hell would break loose somewhere along the desolate coast from Valdez to Katalla, for no fewer than five
railroads were building or surveying toward what Rex
Beach called the "richest copper district in the world." The
drama of that chase toward Kennecott he recorded in a best-
seller, *The Iron Trail.* There were the Alaska, Copper River
and Yukon, the Valdez and Copper River, the Alaska and
Pacific, the Copper River and Northwestern, and most fantastic of all, Henry D. Reynolds' Alaska Home Railway.
The Reynolds-Alaska Development Company carried in its
portfolio all the dreams of Dan Guggenheim, but none of
his money. Reynolds, scheming erratic, the incarnation of
the fevered boom-booming that raced across the vast Territory, had devised a company with $1,000,000 in founders'
shares and $2,000,000 in "deferred" shares. He had induced
Governor Brady to become treasurer of his company, had
opened a copper mine on Prince William Sound, and was
projecting his railway to the interior.

While one crew guarded Keystone Canyon from Reynolds, another Guggenheim crew was battling along the
Katalla Flats against the Alaska and Pacific in a mock-
heroic war which crashed and dynamited pile drivers and
256

Another Triumph in the Far North
The great American Trust has discovered Alaska
From the Minneapolis Minn. "Journal"

steam locomotives. Guggenheim engineers were throwing a million-dollar breakwater across exposed Katalla Bay, but the first of the dreaded winter gales crumpled the breakwater as if it had been made of sand. The storm wrecked Katalla's hopes too. The Syndicate promptly abandoned the town to its fate and moved laborers and machinery over to Cordova. The Guggenheim desertion stung proud Katalla's boomers, who mourned her deserted oil fields and her promising railroad (aimed at the rich anthracite deposits of the

Bering River) now turning into two lines of rust ending down on the Flats.

That left two towns stranded; for Reynolds' promotion at Valdez crashed soon after the Keystone Canyon incident, and the promoter went crazy. His men, abandoned, payless and foodless, threatened to wreck the town. The Syndicate sent a boat up to forlorn Valdez to collect as many laborers as it needed, and the new governor, Hoggatt, had the rest of the men shipped back to Seattle at a nominal charge. Within a few months Valdez was decimated and the snows swept off the mountains to bury the almost deserted town up to its cold chimney tops.

Ed Hasey, the gunman identified as the leader of the Guggenheim men in Keystone Canyon, was removed from lynch-mad Valdez to Juneau. Guggenheim lawyers, marshaled by the astute Captain David H. Jarvis, the Syndicate's chief trouble-shooter, obtained his acquittal of murder, but when he was tried, on substantially the same evidence, for wounding a man so critically that he was incapacitated for life, another jury sent him away to McNeil's Island Penitentiary in Puget Sound for eighteen months. Governor Hoggatt obligingly worked for Hasey's pardon while he remained on the Syndicate payroll in prison.

The volley fired in Keystone Canyon re-echoed across Alaska from Nome to Ketchikan, tolling the end of the individual pioneer who had been the hero of the gold rushes, and the coming of the corporation. From the Klondike days of '97, Alaska had been the last frontier, the beacon that attracted rugged individualists with no capital but their hands, their courage, and a winter's grubstake, to wring an independent fortune from the Territory's gravels. Thousands came, a few won, nearly all returned to the States. Those who lingered on loved in an inarticulate way the vast ruggedness and grandeur of the country, the intoxicating spirit of freedom, the simplicity of a rough life which had no luxuries and few commercial needs. It was over these, and their vision of Alaska as the last outpost of freedom from the Money Power, that the shadow of the Alaska Syndicate fell.

Cheated in their hopes of fortune, these little men became sullen wage-workers for the Syndicate and other corporations, formed turbulent Miners' Unions which dominated Nome and Fairbanks, gravitated toward the Socialist party which for a time eclipsed the Republican party, and unfailingly sent their tribune, James W. (It Makes My Blood Boil) Wickersham to Congress as a delegate, voteless but voiceful. Aligned with them in irregular bonds were boomers of towns passed up by the Syndicate, promoters of railroads not acceptable to the Guggenheims, little business men who clung by their finger nails to a slim livelihood, and most of the editors of the four-page dailies and weeklies that sprang up wherever a few hundred persons collected.

Two battlecries rang over the land in those years between 1906 and 1912—Down With the Guggenheims, and Down With Monopoly. The little men and their champions waged a bitter, raucous, losing struggle against the Syndicate and its allies: complaisant federal "carpetbaggers" who filled the choice patronage jobs, the Seattle Chamber of Commerce, acting the benevolent patron for the development of Alaska along business lines, and lobbyists who worked assiduously in Washington for their masters.

Alaskans dreaded, of all things, Monopoly. The first of the monopolies, the fur seal fisheries, threatened within one generation to wipe out the industry and leave only barren rookeries in the Bering Sea. The government itself stepped in to stop the wanton slaughter.

Then came the effort to form the Salmon Trust—the Alaska Packers Association, out of San Francisco, and the Northwestern Fisheries, under the Syndicate. Their floating canneries, manned by Hindus, Filipinos and Chinese, anchored in Alaskan harbors and brought home to residents the lesson that corporation control meant Asiatic labor. The cannery taxes went for a time to roads and schools but when it became apparent that the salmon were headed for the same fate as the seals, a paternalistic Government stepped in to divert the proceeds to establish fish hatcheries. Alaskans cried in rage that the Salmon Trust's taxes were practically returned to their own coffers to the detriment of the Territory's pressing needs.

So impressed was President Roosevelt with the facts on the exhaustion of America's natural resources, as presented to him by ascetic, evangelic Gifford Pinchot, his Chief Forester, that Conservation became his creed and hobby, the plundering "land-grabbers" his phobia. Western Congressmen, disdainful of the Roosevelt-Pinchot efforts to put the Pacific Slope into an "economic ice-box," tacked a rider on the Agricultural Bill prohibiting further withdrawal of public lands from entry. Pinchot, under Presidential instructions, labored night and day for a week between the bill's passage and its signature, withdrawing into public forest reserves every acre of public land in the West and Alaska that boasted a sagebrush. His enemies "turned handsprings," Roosevelt said, when they discovered the trick.

Roosevelt hoped to reserve Alaska's coal and oil fields to the little man under entry laws which set 160 acres as the limit for individual working. But the Alaska Syndicate, needing coal for its steamships, its railroads and mines, as well as for profitable sale along the coal-hungry Pacific Coast, laughed at the President's efforts. Syndicate agents organized the holders of thirty-three adjacent coal claims in the rich Bering River field near Katalla. In the summer of 1907 Dan Guggenheim met Clarence Cunningham, former Governor Miles C. Moore of Washington, and A. B. Campbell, representing the Katalla claimants, and signed an option to pay $250,000 for a half interest in the Cunningham claims, covering Alaska's most prized anthracite and semi-anthracite coal field.

Louis R. Glavis, a young man who combined the instincts of a ferret and the holy zeal of Gifford Pinchot, was a western field agent for the Government Land Office through which the Cunningham claims must be cleared before title was granted. When he found that the Alaska Syndicate had pounced upon the valuable Bering River deposits in violation of Rooseveltian edict, he protested to his chief, Richard Achilles Ballinger, Land Office commissioner, former mayor of Seattle, and a firm believer that only men with millions could unlock Alaska's treasure store.

Three big dates stood out in the public life of "Slippery Dick" Ballinger. On March 4, 1907, he became commissioner. On March 4, 1908, having failed to lobby a bill through Congress validating the Cunningham claims, he resigned in order to represent the Alaska Syndicate (in violation of federal statute). On March 4, 1909, Ballinger became Secretary of the Interior in easy-going William Howard Taft's cabinet.

Senator Simon, angry at Pinchot's intransigence, introduced a joint resolution for an inquiry into his Forestry Service and moved to cut $500,000 from Pinchot's budget. Young Glavis was fired out of government service for insubordination when he appealed above Ballinger's head, and Pinchot followed him. Roosevelt's protégé headed for the Nile to meet his chief emerging from his great hunting trip and informing him of Taft's betrayal of "my policies."

The prize at issue, said Pinchot, was a field estimated to yield 60,000,000 tons of coal and a profit of $25,000,000. *Collier's Magazine*, scenting the story, entered the fray with a series of snorting exposés by that paragon of Muckrakers, Mark Sullivan. "Are the Guggenheims," inquired Sullivan, "in charge of the Interior Department?" Norman Hapgood, editor of *Collier's*, retained Louis D. Brandeis of Boston, the renowned people's counsel, for a fee of $25,000 to press Pinchot's fight. The House shook off the shackles of Speaker Joe Cannon's czarism to name its own committee to probe the Alaska business—the beginning of the end of "Cannonism."

The Brandeis-Pinchot brief argued:

> Industries of Alaska have been for years largely in the hands of a great and oppressive monopoly, the Guggenheim syndicate, which has kept out other capital and held Alaska at a standstill in spite of its enormous wealth in minerals, forests, water power and fisheries. . . . Coal development in the shape of monopoly by the Morgan-Guggenheim interests would merely strengthen the power which today holds Alaska in its paralyzing grip.

Stephen Birch, tall, brusque spokesman for the Syndicate, and its managing director, testifying before the Senate Committee on Territories, minimized the Brandeis-Pinchot tale as a tall story out of the North. The Syndicate had but one railroad and one copper mine in all that far country. Quizzed more carefully by the special Congressional committee, whose insurgent members were primed by Brandeis, Birch was embarrassed as the long roll of Syndicate activities was rehearsed. He excused himself by saying that he had not been under oath before the Committee on Territories. "Had I realized at the time," he apologized, "that I was talking to a press gallery, I might have been a little more careful in what I said." He conceded that the Syndicate was engaged in practically all the industries of Alaska.

The Congressional committee's majority report acquitted the Syndicate and Secretary Ballinger of all blame; the minority upheld Pinchot. President Taft in a resounding state paper declared his Secretary of the Interior fully vindicated, but Ballinger soon after crept from the unwelcome spotlight and retired to Seattle.

Alaska was stirred to its core by the Congressional Inquiry. In Cordova, dubbed Guggenheimburg, the Boston tea party was emulated when a crowd threw overboard a cargo of British Columbia coal to give point to their demand that Alaska's coal be unlocked from the Government's "economic ice-box." A figure of Pinchot was burned in effigy. The editor of the loyal *Cordova Alaskan* exclaimed:

Hail! Guggenheims! We are with you heart and soul, in all your efforts for the development and upbuilding of Alaska; we have no use for demagogues and cheap politicians who, for selfish purposes, are decrying your enterprises and attempting to besmirch your good name; we are for the Square deal, all around, and because of your past record, we believe in you.

The rival *Cordova North Star* retorted:

Rot! Such agonies must give clear minded, independent, self-reliant people a pain. The Guggenheims are doing a great work in Alaska, and for this and every other enterprise that will assist in the legitimate development of the Northland, the *North Star* is willing to aid and praise them, but when it comes to setting them on a pedestal and worshiping them, and treating them as benefactors, and not daring to draw our breath except to shout praises for them—when it comes to such sickening toadyism as that, we pass. No one will deny that the *Alaskan* is with the Guggenheims "heart and soul," and the editor might have added, "pocketbook," too.

In the backwash of the Keystone Canyon case, U. S. Attorney John J. Boyce and U. S. Marshal Dan Sutherland, later Alaska's delegate to Congress, were removed, reportedly because they had obtained the conviction of Ed Hasey, the Guggenheim gunman. "And yet," cried the *Daily Alaskan* of Juneau, the Territory's most important paper, "some will argue that the Guggenheims have not got the Taft administration body and breeches. To the ashheap with such arguments against the facts." Declaring that Juneau gold mines were being squeezed by the Tacoma smelter, the *Alaskan* nevertheless rejoiced that "the end is in sight. . . . The prison doors stand ajar awaiting the arrival of the organized cabal of looters."

Appointment of the successors to the dismissed U. S. attorney and marshal [Delegate Wickersham stated] has been secured by the Alaska Syndicate for the purpose of protecting the great monopoly and its high officials from indictment for corruption of witnesses and jurors in the Hasey case [the original murder trial which ended in acquittal]; their appointment has been secured by the Alaska Syndicate in aid of its preparations to control the great litigation which is soon to result from an effort to secure patents to the Cunningham and other coal claims held by the Alaska Syndicate.

The *Washington Post* asserted:

If there is an investigation it will be directed at the broad proposition of whether the Morgan-Guggenheim interests and other great corporate interests are in reality trying to gobble up Alaska, and not content with grabbing its great natural resources, are trying to control the government by getting their creatures named to federal offices.

A Senator was quoted as declaring there was only one parallel—that of the East India Company. He overlooked the Russian-American Company which ruled Alaska before the Stars and Stripes waved over Sitka.

Elections for delegate to Congress provided Alaska's only opportunity to vote on her one great issue—monopoly. Invariably she sent her anti-monopoly, anti-Guggenheim favorite, Jim Wickersham, to Washington. Gladly accepting the epithet of "roughnecks" hurled by the Republican "carpetbaggers" who held the Territory's choice political jobs, the Wickersham Democrats disregarded the indisputable proof that the Syndicate had offered their favorite a $25,000 job to represent them, and that he had considered accepting it. So faint became Republicanism that its man polled fewer votes than the Socialist candidate. Elections were hilarious affairs, with wild charges that the Guggenheims intended to vote hordes of "Barbary Coast scum" working on their cannery boats, and appeals to Guggenheim employees worded: "Be a man or a mouse. If you are a man, vote for Wickersham and if you are a mouse, hide behind your bunk and don't let the Guggenheim straw bosses vote you for Orr."

Opposition to the Syndicate developed to the point where suspicion ate into every phase of political life. The *Seattle Post-Intelligencer*, one of whose writers, on the Guggenheim payroll for three years, was transferred to the governor's chair at Juneau, published an editorial famous in Alaskan history, captioned: "Wickersham Has Bug on Guggies." It read:

James insists that if you do not agree with him as to the time of day or other more or less important topics, you are a secret agent, emissary, or hireling of the Guggies, alias the band of high financiers, trust operators, and associate smelting and mining operators commonly known as the Guggenheims. The honest James believes or said he believed that the Guggies were after him in Alaska and consequently he is agin the Guggies, and his bug is that everyone in the United State from President Taft to the the humble *P.-I.*, if they do not agree with all his ideas, is owned by or is the poor tool of the Guggies.

It was said that Editor Brainard resigned in protest against the editorial, and the rival *Seattle Star* jeered at the Guggenheim "organ" for glorying in its shame. "Are the Guggs bogies? Well rather," commented the brisk *Nome Gold Digger*.

A happy interlude in the 1910 campaign was the pompous visit of Banker Jacob Schiff to Alaskan shores. Dan Guggenheim's European financial agent decided to look over their joint interests in the Yukon and Copper River and arrived in high state on a chartered steamer at Skagway, accompanied by a retinue of flunkeys and a "bunch of French and Eyetalian cooks." This confirmed the sturdy Alaskans' worst fears of the effete nature of their capitalists. It all ended in high comedy when Schiff indignantly returned to Skagway from White Horse upon the refusal of the cook on the Yukon steamer to yield his galley to the foreign chefs. Schiff, in ill humor at the personal affront from the uncouth Northerners, ordered his retinue about face and he left Skagway in high dudgeon for Seattle without ever seeing a single one of the mines he had come 3,500 miles to inspect.

The discontent that gnawed Alaska grew out of frustration. The pioneers and sturdy men who loved the Alaskan way of life, simple and free, declared there was no reason why the Territory should not boast a population, industry, and culture comparable to the Scandinavian peninsula. The climate of southeastern Alaska was milder than most of the States; in southwestern Alaska along the coast it was certainly no more rigorous. Long summer days gave promise of agricultural abundance; the forests could never be exhausted; the mines would last a century, the fisheries forever; hydro-electric power could fill every need of a thriving, populous country of several millions.

One writer in the *Alaska-Yukon Magazine* gave way to a fantasy in 1910. Thirty years from then, he predicted, three million people would inhabit America's fastest-growing state. Two Alaskans would occupy Cabinet posts and another would be headed for the White House. Fast ocean liners would race from Cordova, center of the smelting industry, to Seattle in two days. A day's ride by train would take the Alaskan to the eastern edge of the Rockies, which the "aeros" could not surmount, and another day would land him in Washington. The newspapers in Cordova and at Fairbanks, the capital, would rival Seattle's and San Francisco's. It all recalled a similiar post-Civil War dream of a railroad from Montana to Siberia and Japan with a branch to the southern Alaska coast.

Against the magnificent vision of the Alaska-that-might-be was the bitter actuality that the territory was losing people, losing hope. Deserted towns crumbled to ruin; docks fell into the sea; rails rusted. Alaska's ores were hauled to the States to be smelted; Asiatic and transient labor manned its canneries; its forests and coal fields remained untouched. The people themselves held no power, and all political life gravitated around lame-ducks and lobbyists mantled with Federal power.

To many Alaskans it seemed that the Rooseveltian conservation policy was the bane; others blamed the high rates charged by the Syndicate's steamship lines, which were interested mainly in hauling Syndicate cargoes. It was said that it cost four times as much to ship from Seattle to Alaska as to China. The legislature memorialized Washington for government steamship service and finally did obtain a Government railroad which lacked initiative or energy to bring tourists and settlers into the land.

The uncompromising hostility of the underlying populace to the Syndicate eventually produced a stalemate. President Taft was reluctant to furnish more ammunition to frowning Theodore Roosevelt and so the clamp fastened on natural resources by the Conservationists prevented ready exploitation by big capital. Stephen Birch, the Syndicate's managing director, said that inasmuch as the Government had seen fit to stop the development of the Copper River valley, the Syndicate could do nothing. Isaac Guggenheim, on a swing through the Pacific Northwest, declared the Copper River and Northwestern would not be extended to the Bering River coal fields until the Government reversed its policy. This President Wilson was unwilling to do, and the coming of the World War postponed all idea of Alaska's development.

Finally in 1919 a lease was granted on Bering River's coal fields but the profit of $2,500,000 that Pinchot had predicted on 60,000,000 tons of coal never materialized. There was no profit at all; instead, $400,000 was lost in the effort to develop coal in commercial quantities. As for Northwestern Commercial and Northwestern Fisheries, the Alaska Syndicate had disposed of them years before. The "rape" of Alaska, which pioneers had feared in the first decade of the century, turned into desertion.

Historians may speculate on the economic and social forces that dried up Alaska. Had the pioneer urge of America spent itself? Had the pressure of population ceased? Could not a million Swedes and Norwegians have settled Alaska as readily as they did the northern plains of the States and Canada? The Socialist party of Alaska railed at monopoly as the curse and called for government development, with public ownership of coal mines, smelters, fisheries, canneries, and transportation. It called for federal assistance to plant tens of thousands of families on Alaskan soil, deriving their living from the soil, the sea, the mines, and attendant industries.

Such speculations concerned Pope Yeatman and Stephen Birch not at all. As head men for the Syndicate, it was their job to tap Kennecott's treasures as speedily as possible. That called for all the resources of engineering skill. Kennecott lay 195 miles from tidewater on the top of a range of the Wrangel Mountains. For centuries men had known of southwestern Alaska's copper riches. Thlinkit Indians used sheets of copper covered with heraldic designs which they carried before their chiefs. Manager Baranof of the Russian-American Company collected the stuff from the Indians, and pious Russians cast a 203-pound bell for an Orthodox Church. Machinery on the gunboat Politofsky was fashioned of copper. Later when she touched at San Francisco to be refitted, her machinery more than paid the entire cost of her original construction.

When intrepid Lieutenant Henry T. Allen and his companions ventured up the Copper River in the eighties, he was told by old Chief Nicolai of the source of his copper bullets. Allen went up the headwaters of the Nizina and was shown ledges on the mountain tops that looked for all the world like green pastures. His reports were bound in the arid tomes of the Geodetic Survey. But when the Klondike Gold Rush pulled tens of thousands of men from Canada and the States, many ventured into the Yukon country by way of the Copper River. Along that treacherous route of rapids, gorges, glaciers, they panned out some five million dollars in gold, but none stopped by the greenstone ledges. Copper was not a poor man's metal. A prospector could easily carry out ten thousand dollars in gold in a convenient pouch; fifty pounds of copper, even if pure, was worth only five dollars or so.

Stephen Birch, just out of Columbia School of Mines, was scouting the Alaska coast for adventure and profit when he chanced, in the fall of 1900, upon Jack Smith and Clarence Warner, prospectors, just down from the Copper River country. Over a glass of whiskey, they told the young engineer of their Bonanza claim high on a mountain alongside Kennecott glacier. They were two of a company of eleven prospectors who worked together covering the headwaters of the Chitina. They had divided into groups, each combing a section, under an agreement to share and share alike. Tired and disgusted, Warner and Smith had stopped along the milky glacial water of Kennecott Creek to rest. Smith's eye caught the gleam of green grass near the mountain top, four thousand feet above the narrow valley. They were speculating on the Alpine pasturage when Warner kicked the gravel and noticed a green-stone float. The two men examined the rock—true copper and perhaps three-quarters pure metal. They found more copper float strewn along the valley floor. Next morning they were up with the sun to climb to the "alpine pasture." Thus the Bonanza mine was staked.

Birch took an option on the claim and hurried back to New York, to the lodestone of all engineers and prospectors, the Guggenheims. Always interested in likely properties, they encouraged him. He formed the Chitina Exploration Company and was about to take over the claim when he discovered that some thirty-two men were involved, the eleven partners, and their various grubstakers. Suit was started in federal court and dragged along until 1906, holding up development because the Guggenheims declined to spend a penny on properties whose title was not clear. In 1906 Pope Yeatman, John Hays Hammond's understudy and specialist in copper, marched up that toilsome route from Valdez to Kennecott to verify Birch's account. With the suit settled, Yeatman flashed the Go signal. The Alaska Syndicate was ready. The brothers had decided that Bonanza's riches were too dazzling to be passed up, despite the $20,000,000 required for a railroad to tap the upper Nizina country. Thousands of tons of ore, ranging from 20 to 70 percent copper, the richest deposit known in the history of copper mining, promised profits in the tens of millions to the organization that could invest the tremendous sums required. Dan Guggenheim, Jacob Schiff of Kuhn-Loeb and

George W. Perkins of J. P. Morgan formed the Alaska Syndicate as a closed corporation, with shares distributed among insiders of the three groups. The Guggenheims personally kept a quarter or more and J. P. Morgan held a respectable block for himself.

Already $1,500,000 had been spent, wasted, in the Syndicate's abortive starts from Valdez and Katalla before Mike Heney's gangs of railway laborers and his machinery were dumped into Cordova, to the delirious and profitable joy of the few hundred boomers who had insisted all along that their town was the key to the Copper River country. Men by the hundreds poured into Cordova from Seattle, slept in saloons, on floors, or were tickled to fall into beds still warm from occupancy under the three-shift system. There were hard times in the States in the winter of 1907, and men worked for $3 a day on the Copper River and Northwestern, paying 50 cents apiece for meals and $1 a night for lodging.

As soon as Mike Heney got his roadbed over the hill from Cordova, he was on the marshy Copper River delta, as treacherous a bog as man ever tried to cross. In the winter it was ice, slush and muck; in the spring and summer there were floods and muck; at all times muck, muck, muck, everywhere, so deep that tens of thousands of piles and millions of cubic yards of moraine had to be placed across the thirty miles of delta until the road confronted the twin glaciers, Miles and Childs. One presented a solid face of ice four miles wide and three hundred feet high. A bridge 1,150 feet long, costing $1,500,000, was needed between the two glaciers. Who shall calculate the cost in human misery that winter when gangs of men, their faces stung by winds roaring down from the Chugach Mountains, their hands and feet numbed by cold that descended to sixty below zero, drove thousands of piles through seven feet of ice and forty feet of moraine for temporary supports for the bridge spans. Two spans had been swung on to permanent supports by the end of April. These piers were sunk sixty feet into the river bed, solid concrete eighty-six feet around and sheathed with heavy steel rails to withstand the glacier bergs that would hurtle against them in the Copper River's twelve-mile current.

From sunrise till midnight the crews worked completing the third and last span in a race with the ice which would begin to move almost any day. Suddenly the flood came, heaving up the seven-foot crust of ice and forcing it against the wooden falsework which supported the third span. By dusk the falsework had been moved fifteen inches out of place. All night long men worked with steam lines thawing the ice around the piles while other crews rigged tackle which moved the four hundred and fifty feet of falsework back to its normal position. An hour after the span had been moved from the falsework and attached to the permanent piers, the ice broke. Great masses were hurled against the falsework which swayed and fell. Even the pile drivers were lost in the river's wild rush, but the engineers and crew were happy—the great glacier bridge was in place. A year had been gained by the margin of one hour!

Followed the terrors of narrow Abercrombie Canyon where the roadbed had to be blasted out of solid rock. The wind blew down the canyon in a steady roar of forty-five to seventy miles an hour. Men worked for short spells and then raced for shelter to regain their breath and life itself. "Coyotes" containing as much as seventeen tons of powder blew out walls of the canyon for a roadbed. The rails were laid up the Canyon. Great drifts of snow blocked the way. One trainload of one hundred and sixty men ran into one such drift, and the rotary plow stalled. Within three minutes the train was buried and remained snowbound for twenty-one days. In the spring the snow thawed to ice and the rails were covered with a sheath of ice six inches to two feet deep. The rotary was derailed one thousand five hundred times in the course of fifty miles!

Out of the canyon in the spring, the gangs advanced up the Copper River to its junction with the Chitina (Indian word for copper-water), then up the Chitina to the Nizina, and thence to Kennecott Creek whose waters dribbled from the glacier named for Lieutenant Kennicott, U. S. A. The last spike, driven early in 1911, was made, appropriately, of copper from Kennecott.

Standing there on the banks of the creek, one looked almost straight up some four thousand feet to the portals of Bonanza. Men and horses climbed the face of Kennecott by zigzag trail, established a camp on a narrow ledge at the base of cliffs fantastically sculptured by the erosion of an eon. Cables were dragged up and within a few months an aerial tramway four miles long connected the upper face of the mountain with the valley below. Stout bunkhouses were built up there, set on rollers because the sliding talus which served as a foundation was constantly moving down the steep declivity to the valley. The buildings were made fast to the mountain side with cables anchored into the cliffs above, while the real estate kept shuffling down under them.

Working in from the portals, miners blasted tunnels into the rock and frozen earth. The tunnels promptly coated their sides with hoarfrost that shone radiantly to the feeble light of miners' lamps.

As soon as the final copper spike was driven into the railroad, the first trainload of ore was ready. It had been mined by wind, rain and frost on the face of Kennecott, torn down from copper rock into rubble. The only mining needed after dynamite had loosened the ice-bound pieces of chalcocite copper and limestone, was to lead the talus into buckets and shoot the buckets down that four-mile tramway to the waiting gondolas in the valley. The first trainload bore ore assaying 75 percent copper, compared with 2-3 percent ore in the great porphyry copper mines of Utah and Nevada. Each gondola carried $12,000—$15,000 worth of copper, all contained in sacks for easy shipment in the Syndicate's boats at Cordova. The first cargo to leave for the Guggenheim smelter at Tacoma was valued at $500,000.

Although $20,000,000 had been thrown into the railroad, and although the ore had to be carried 2,500 miles to the smelter, Kennecott's copper was the cheapest in all the world. Of the production cost of 4½ cents a pound delivered to the smelter, half went into transportation. That left 2¼ cents mining cost. Copper men in New York and London clucked with astonishment, and Bostonians feared that their deep Michigan mines must close from the flood of Kennecott cheap metal.

With development work hardly under way in 1911, the Alaska Syndicate counted a profit of $1,658,000 from the Bonanza mine. By the end of 1912 Kennecott had paid dividends of $3,000,000. But that was merely an appetizer for the main feast. The World War was in the offing, and the Bonanza and its companion mines, the Jumbo and Erie, were to pour such floods into the treasury of M. Guggenheim's Sons that the price of the Alaska Purchase in 1867, when the United States paid Russia $7,200,000 for Seward's Folly, would seem small change.

17. COPPER CANYON

BEN GUGGENHEIM, on a swing around the West in 1900, was offered an interest in the sere brown mountainside at the head of Bingham Canyon for a song. Ben asked how high the copper content ran, and lost interest when told it was only two per cent. His engineer assured him that the refuse tailings of the Butte mines ran higher than that. Ben's older brothers had occasion to rue his light-hearted gesture of contempt because that hill high up in the picturesque Oquirrh Mountains was to become one of the richest pieces of real estate in all America and as such the object of prayerful concern to designing men in lower Manhattan.

To the early Mormons Bingham Canyon was useful as a timber source in that treeless Paradise that they aimed to make into the Republic of Deseret. If the Oquirrh range bore precious minerals, Brigham Young would have none of them. "The true use of gold," he declared scornfully, "is for paving streets, covering houses and making culinary dishes." He forbade the Latter-Day Saints to prospect for gold or silver, although he encouraged the search for coal and iron. During the California gold rush, some of his Saints begged him for permission to leave for the Coast. "If you elders of Israel want to go to the gold mines, go and be damned," he said.

Into the green heaven of the Mormons came the Unionist General Connor during the Civil War. The General itched for military action and nearly provoked the laborious, peace-loving inhabitants of Deseret into armed rebellion in order to satisfy his ambitions. The Church, he informed Washington, was "disloyal and traitorous to the core." The way to tame its rebellious spirit was to flood the Territory with Gentiles to exploit the minerals which the Mormons disdained. To this end he granted furloughs to his idle soldiers to scout the hills.

One story is that the General with his officers and their wives were picnicking in Bingham Canyon one fine Sunday afternoon when a lady tripped over gleaming rock. Gold there was in the Canyon and a million dollars was panned and dug from crude shafts. But that wasn't much of a strike and history merely put it in a footnote.

It was Enos A. Wall whose curious eye discovered the Oquirrhs' true wealth. Stalking about the head of the Canyon in July of 1887 he noticed a discoloration in the gulch where waters seeped from the old drifts and inclines, already long abandoned. Quietly, he relocated old claims and tied up his cash in ground. After a while it was noised about Salt Lake City that Wall had struck something up the Canyon, but other prospectors reported nothing but some extremely low-grade copper ore, not worth the trouble of looking at. When Wall claimed he had a copper mountain, practical miners winked at each other significantly. Of what earthly use were millions of cubic yards of mountain flecked ever so lightly with porphyry copper?

But what caused them to regard Colonel Wall as "touched" was his claim that this dirt should be "mined." How was it possible to mine without digging shafts and drifts, dynamiting the hard rock and hauling it to the top? Who ever heard of a mine on the surface? Anyone knew that copper occurred in veins and fissures deep down in the earth and that it must run rich to reward the effort of disemboweling it thousands of feet under Butte's Big Hill.

His copper mountain and its wealth became an obsession with Colonel Wall, a religion and a vision that haunted him by day and night. No newcomer was he, but one of the pioneers of western mining. He had prospected the Rockies

276

in the early sixties and had been a state senator in Idaho. Since 1885 he had been poking around Utah's painted hills, developing and selling mines. He sold the Brickyard mine in 1894 to Captain Joseph R. De Lamar, Amsterdam-born and a world-adventurer who had gained his title on the quarter-deck.

Wall enticed the sea captain into taking an option on a three-quarter interest in his Bingham Canyon claims at $375,000, but De Lamar threw it up when the assays showed only two per cent ore. When the price of copper went up in 1898, he changed his mind and took a quarter interest from Wall for $50,000, with an option on a second quarter for $250,000 and a third for $1,250,000. He hired a young giant who had learned his engineering in the Missouri School of Mines to run mill tests. The young fellow was Daniel C. Jackling, six foot three and untrammeled by the traditions of copper mining. He examined his tests of Bingham Canyon ore, running lean and thin, and then spent the rest of his time experimenting and figuring.

The floor around his desk was littered with papers full of hieroglyphics. Why couldn't copper be mined like soft lead in Missouri? Wasn't it after all a matter of tearing down the copper mountain cheaply enough to make a profit? His figures showed profits, fantastic profits that made him doubt his arithmetic. A small-scale mill must be built. Captain De Lamar laughed and refused to put up more than the $50,-000 which had been used for tests and development work.

Copper mountain and its options and quarter interests became a joke around Salt Lake City. Young Jackling went off to the new lead mines in northeast Washington. Colonel Wall, ever hopeful, resented De Lamar's scorn and tried to pry him out of his quarter interest. He had no intention of letting go of a quarter interest so cheaply to anyone who lacked faith in the Canyon and money to back it.

Jackling, no less than Wall, had faith. A few years later

he was working for the Colorado Springs capitalists, the Penroses and Charles W. MacNeill, in their Cripple Creek mines. He told them of the tantalizing copper mountain, worth a hundred million by one reckoning, nothing at all by another. The key to it all, he maintained, was mass excavation, the way the Steel Trust mined Mesabi's Iron Range. The whole mountain would have to be shoveled unceremoniously into a concentrating mill and the enriched ore then turned into the furnaces. Spencer Penrose, brother of the Pennsylvania Senator, could see the possibilities. He commissioned Jackling to go over to Salt Lake and see Colonel Wall. Wall was in no mood to talk with anyone who reminded him of De Lamar. Jackling got an associate to deal with the old man. The story was that big New York interests able to put millions into the Canyon wanted an option. This meant business. Colonel Wall yielded the option on a half interest, the price to be $350,000 cash.

Jackling now ventured into the open, bringing the Penroses and MacNeill over from Colorado Springs. They closed with Wall at $385,000 for a 55 per cent interest, plus $35,000 for the option, and agreed to buy the De Lamar interest. That left 20 per cent still in Wall's hands. The De Lamar quarter interest had an illuminating history. John Hays Hammond has confessed that he once had it; Ben Guggenheim turned it down disdainfully. It was offered to Charles A. Coffin of General Electric, who wanted a copper supply for his manufacturing. When General Electric engineers reported 5,000,000 tons of 1.98 per cent ore in sight, Coffin snorted that he did "not believe the damned figures." The De Lamar interest passed into Penrose-MacNeill hands for $125,000.

The formation of Utah Copper in 1903 did not pass unobserved in New York. Those smart Jewish jacks-of-all-trades, Samuel Untermyer and Bernard Baruch, had heard the tall stories from the West and had conferred at length with Sam Newhouse, the ex-Denverite who had picked up home and capital and moved to Salt Lake in protest against the anti-Semitism of Denver's élite. On the hill next to Colonel Wall's, Newhouse had staked out a first-class promotion. Names were important for stock market operators, and so the name of the mother-city of copper speculation, Boston, was coupled with a synonym for celebrated Amalgamated Copper and the result was Boston Consolidated. These goings-on reached the ear of Dan Guggenheim, for whom the Boston Consolidated's promoters did legal and broker jobs.

By 1905 enough work had been done in developing Utah Copper to confirm the ideas of Dan Jackling and his production man, Bob Gemmell. They had begun mass excavation along the lines planned by U. S. Army engineers for the proposed Panama Canal. John Hays Hammond, now chief supervisor for Guggenheim Exploration, was sent out to Salt Lake City to take a look into this newfangled mining which defied all the rules by using steam shovels to scrape the surface. The great engineer, flanked by his understudies, Alfred Chester Beatty and Seeley W. Mudd, reported that it was possible to make millions out of lean 2 per cent copper ore if the operations were conducted on a grandiose scale.

Dan Guggenheim discovered that Utah Copper's capitalization at least had been taken care of on a grandiose scale. There were some 450,000 shares of $10 par value. He also discovered that Utah Copper was achingly in need of more capital. He proposed that John Hays Hammond be made managing director and that the glamor of the Hammond name be backed by the Guggenheim prestige. Guggenheim Exploration would take a quarter interest for $1,500,000, retire $750,000 of the three-year 7 per cent notes the Penrose-MacNeill management had floated in 1904, and put $750,000 in a great concentrating mill which would permit mass excavation on a scale worthy of Jackling's ambitions.

279

The distraught Utah Copper interests accepted eagerly. Capitalization was boosted in 1906 from $4,500,000 to $6,000,000.

The Magma concentrating mill was conceived on a scale fitting the Guggenheim-Jackling ideas, the lordly dimensions of the copper mountain, and the public's purse. The steam shovels gnawing away at the gray-green flanks of the mountainside dumped the earth into gondolas which ran down almost by gravity through the narrow, twisting canyon to the concentrating mill. A special railroad was to be built, on money supplied by the public through another bond issue, along the brown flanks of the Oquirrhs down to the shores of Great Salt Lake where the Guggenheims were building the Garfield copper smelter.

The contract negotiated by the Guggenheims between American Smelting and Refining and Utah Copper was in itself the crowning glory of the Guggenheim control of Bingham Canyon. For twenty years Utah Copper bound itself to ship its ores to the Garfield smelter, to pay a minimum base charge of $6 a ton for reduction (later boosted to $7) and $30 a ton for refining. Utah was to be paid for 95 per cent of the copper extracted from its ore, 90 per cent of the silver and 67 per cent of the gold. It was the biggest contract ever signed by American Smelting and Refining and was valued by hostile critics at $5,000,000. Old Colonel Wall, wizened and embittered, declared Utah Copper was being milked by the Guggenheims to the tune of $3 a ton on smelting charges, in comparison with other copper smelters. For twenty years, American Smelting and Refining, he said, would collect a toll of $\frac{8}{10}$ of a cent on every pound of copper wrested from the great mine at the head of Bingham Canyon, plus a commission of $\frac{1}{2}$ cent a pound on its sale.

Although the Guggenheims held only a minority interest in Utah Copper, by virtue of the smelting contract they became in fact the directors of its destinies. To make doubly sure that their smelter ladles skimmed the cream from the world's greatest open-cut copper mine, they provided that the management of Utah Copper should be reserved to Guggenheim Exploration, through their chief engineer, Hammond, and, later, Pope Yeatman.

The Utah Copper coup placed the firm of M. Guggenheim's Sons squarely in the ranks of the Copper Kings. Hitherto they had been known in the press as Silver Princes and Lead Barons. Now they controlled Mexico's copper output, were preparing to tap Bonanza's lodes in Alaska, were planted squarely astride Utah Copper and were on the *qui vive* for other porphyry developments on the American continents.

That brought the brothers smack up against the Cole-Ryan Amalgamated-Anaconda interests and their selling agency, the Lewisohns' United Metals, and at a most critical time, in 1907-8, when the Guggenheims were stripped to the bone. Luckily Amalgamated Copper, with a loss of $7,500,000 on operations for 1908, was in no position to strike hard. Nevertheless it threatened to invade Salt Lake territory with a copper smelter and to wean away an important Canyon producer, Utah Consolidated. Rumors floated about, in the artfully aimless way such maneuvers were carried on, that the Cole-Ryan group would build a Salt Lake smelter for custom ores, thus carrying the war to American Smelting and Refining's own monopoly over lead and silver. In the meantime the bear raids on American Smelting and Refining stock were in full force. The situation was serious enough for Dan Guggenheim to make one of his rare formal announcements to the press:

Quite some years ago the speculating public were kept in a ferment by the cry of "Wolf!" in connection with sugar refining stocks, due to competition between the Havemeyers and the Arbuckles. It is now the Smelting

Company with other large financial interests. As American Sugar Refining stocks are now so largely absorbed and put away in the boxes, the American Smelting and Refining common stock is being speculated with in its stead. This will continue until it is absorbed and put away in the boxes. . . .

The group of gentlemen known as the Ryan-Cole and their following have been for many years in the copper mining and copper smelting business. They are great believers undoubtedly in copper as a metal. So am I. They can see that a great deal of money can be made in this business—as it can be when intelligently prosecuted.

Dan announced that American Smelting and Refining had no intention of going into custom smelting of other people's coppers, that it would confine itself to ores which it controlled, such as Utah Copper.

Despite this proffer of peace, war continued and the *Engineering and Mining Journal* observed:

Cole & Ryan are known to be ambitious. The weakness in the stock of A S and R indicates knowledge of what is impending. It will be interesting to discover to what extent the new scheme [of invading A S and R territory] will be financed from the proceeds of bear operations in the stock market.

It was reported that the new smelting company would invade Colorado, fortress of the Guggenheims.

In the meantime a feverish search had been waged all over the West for more porphyry mines on Utah's scale. Two per cent ores had never before challenged the attention of the prospector; now they were the cynosure of all inquiring eyes. Strikes were reported here, there, and elsewhere, and the gullible speculating public became a sucker for the magic word—porphyry.

Porphyry copper was struck in a desert valley in eastern Nevada whose underground waters ranchers used to transform the desolate country into a delightful oasis. Only two miles from the frontier settlement of Ely in the Steptoe Valley copper of "nearly unlimited tonnage" was discovered, but William Boyce Thompson, who was a strange combination of desert rat and Wall Street promoter, passed it up. Young Mark Requa, later a political force in coast Republicanism, stayed and collected enough claims to build Nevada Consolidated Copper Company. A few years later Thompson was glad to take an option on 40 per cent of the stock at $12 a share. He reported to his associate, Dan Guggenheim, who sent Henry Crumb, an engineer reputedly as "impersonal as a plumb line" to check up Thompson's glowing story about a second Utah Copper. Guggenheim Exploration took up Thompson's option at $12.50 a share and the promoter counted a neat profit of $200,000, in addition to the shares he had bought for his own account. Later he combined nearby properties under Cumberland-Ely Copper Company and waited for the propitious moment when the Guggenheims would want it, too.

The Guggenheims marched in to the tune of millions to tear up the desert by the acre. A 130-mile railroad was built from the desolate spot up to the Southern Pacific. By 1906 Guggenex held a clear 54 per cent of Nevada Consolidated's proliferous 1,200,000 shares which were valued, on the eve of the 1907 panic, at $24,000,000 on the basis of quotations which had been built up on the market, thanks to Thompson, Baruch, and other copper specialists. Cumberland-Ely was likewise built up into a darling of the market operators, and the Guggenheims, as expected, took over the majority interest, on the recommendation of Hammond and Beatty. "If it is good enough for you, why, I think we will go ahead with the business," said Dan.

Dan and his astute helpers merged the two companies,

much to the distressful cries of minority stockholders of each company, who haggled for better terms. The *Engineering and Mining Journal* sided with the Consolidated minority in terming the deal "jugglery." At any rate, there were sound economic reasons for the merger, which was more than could be said for later combinations in which Nevada Consolidated was to figure. The two companies, lying cheek by jowl in the middle of a howling wilderness, more than 150 miles from Salt Lake City, the nearest sizable town, had need of joint railroad, mill, and smelter facilities. The smaller Cumberland-Ely company was invited into fifty-fifty participation in the Nevada Northern Railroad and the Steptoe smelter, much to the disgust of President James Phillips, Jr., of Nevada Consolidated who became an avowed enemy of the Guggenheims.

Development work for both companies called for millions and perhaps the Guggenheims could hardly be blamed for permitting an eager public to subscribe the funds needed. Stock and bond issues were showered obligingly on the market and copper specialists gratefully buried their arms elbow-deep in the securities. The risks of capital, it became apparent, were to be assumed by the bond-buying public, while the Guggenheims, holding stock control, reaped the harvest. *The Engineering and Mining Journal,* alarmed by the flood of securities based on the porphyries, cautioned the Guggenheims to go easy if they were "to preserve some of the esteem among investors that they once had so richly."

The Steptoe Valley became one of America's great mining centers. Steam shovels worked by day and night stripping the cupriferous earth, dumping it into patient little gondolas which were carted away in scores by little humpbacked engines running on narrow-gauge tracks. Each trainload bore a mite of the tens of millions of tons of desert sand to the concentrating mills and thence to the smelter. The Nevada Northern's locomotives hauled long trains of bullion to the Southern Pacific junction, whence they were hustled on to San Francisco Bay or across country to Perth Amboy, site of the great Guggenheim copper refinery.

Dan, Murry, and Sol, the triumvirate who were now M. Guggenheim's Sons, sat on the board of the consolidated Nevada Consolidated, along with their allies and satellites. Most important of these was Charles Hayden, of Hayden, Stone and Company, brokers, who was to rise to financial pre-eminence on the porphyry coppers, give a $150,000 planetarium in his name to New York and leave $50,000,000 as a foundation for American boys. It was to Hayden in 1907-8 that the hard-pressed Guggenheims turned for money for Utah Copper. His firm floated bond issues which permitted the work to go on in Bingham Canyon, and Hayden became quite a connoisseur of porphyries and an associate in Nevada Consolidated. MacNeill and the Penroses, the Colorado Springs operators who had been the original financers of Utah Copper, went into Nevada on the coat-tails of their engineer, Dan Jackling. The great Jackling, to whom went most of the glory for the technique of mass excavation and concentration of the low-grade porphyries, became the biggest figure in the top ranks of Western engineers. Shortly before the San Francisco Exposition of 1915, he is said to have entered a newly built hotel and asked for the entire top floor of a wing, to entertain his guests. The astonished proprietor summoned the architect and within an hour Jackling's signature was cold on a $24,000 a year lease plus an authorized expenditure of $100,000 for furnishings. It was the same Jackling who at nineteen, planned to teach school for $30 a month until he could get a job clerking at $75, of which he would save $60. Within three years he would have enough saved to buy 108 acres of good farming land on which he could live in comfortable independence for the rest of his life.

The merger fever hit Bingham Canyon, too, and brought

that winding avenue to riches under unified control of the Guggenheims and their allies. Old Colonel Wall, crabbed with infirmities and jealousy, regarded scornfully the maneuvers of the New York copper financiers as they played with Bingham Canyon stocks and bonds. He was an enemy, too, of Dan Jackling who had garnered all the glory of the Canyon while Wall, the man whose faith had brought it to fame, was neglected and forgotten. To the public Jackling might be the hero but to the old colonel he was a bungler whose methods were costing Utah Copper stockholders millions. He fulminated and he sued and in 1908 quit the board in a series of explosions which were aired in the magazine he subsidized, *Mines and Methods*. The old fellow who had nursed his despised "Wall-rock" to glittering fame among the coppers, had the sympathy of Salt Lake mining men. To them it seemed that the riches of the state were being squeezed into the fists of the Guggenheims, Baruchs, Untermyers and other members of the *"haute Juiverie"* who tossed stocks and bonds back and forth, gouging the public's pockets for their own aggrandizement, engineering bull and bear raids alternately for their added profit. The munificently paid engineers for these promoters—the Hammonds, Beattys, Yeatmans and Jacklings—it seemed to their humbler confreres in the West, were more promoters and tipsters than engineers.

If such rancor was entertained for the Guggenheims and their engineers, what would leather-necked Western mining men have been able to say about that ace of all mining promoters—Tom Lawson and his Consolidated Copper Company which was to outrival H. H. Rogers' Amalgamated Copper? Lawson, the apostle of Fair Finance in the Yukon Gold promotion, held options with William Boyce Thompson on the Guggenheims' holdings in both Utah and Nevada porphyries. It will be remembered that the soaring prospectus for Yukon Gold held out to the public as an added inducement the prospect "later on" of a $60,000,000 copper flotation as part of the campaign to let the people in on Wall Street's good things. Consolidated Copper died in the dream stage when Yukon Gold flopped. Its heir was Copper Mines, Inc., which also carried in its hypothetical portfolio Tom Lawson's latest brain child, the historic Chino mines at Santa Rita, New Mexico. Thus the three great porphyry properties on the North American continent were to be bundled together and given to the "great people" at a mere fraction of their sure worth. That fraction was $60,000,000, which in 1908 was about double what Dan Guggenheim thought the Utah and Nevada properties could stand in the way of flotations.

The copper expert of the *Engineering and Mining Journal* shook his head sadly at such dreams and predicted a dim future for Copper Mines, Inc. Its plans resulted from what was "apparently an unholy alliance brought about by Samuel Untermyer and the Guggenheims. The latter are beginning to see the effect of the Lawsonian connection and it is not a very pleasant situation for them." Copper Mines fell to pieces in 1908, Thompson resigning from Hayden, Stone and Company and the indefatigable Lawson piped his energy into the Chino property.

More in the realm of practicality was the merger of Utah Copper and Boston Consolidated. Utah offered Untermyer and his associates one share of Utah for three of Boston and settled at two and one-half to one. Minority stockholders on both sides insisted they were being gypped and the papers reverberated with charges, countercharges, injunctions, and whatnot. Colonel Wall poured his bile on Untermyer's head. The sage New York lawyer-promoter was indeed in an equivocal position; he was head man in Guggenheims' legal battery and he was counsel for the rival Boston Consolidated. Deterred not in the least, he boldly plunged ahead with the plans for consolidation and used his undoubted arts of persuasion on other important Boston Consolidated interests. Untermyer profited handsomely from his legal work. An assessment of 25 cents on the multitudinous Boston shares for legal expenses incident to consolidation brought him in $193,750, while from Utah he had realized $581,250 in cash and 3,250 shares. Colonel Wall charged that Untermyer's harvest was $777,250—"the price of treachery . . . merciless rape . . . bloated incompetence." He forgot that most of Boston's shareholders were Europeans and that it was a complicated business to make the English understand the beauties of amalgamation.

Dan Guggenheim and William Boyce Thompson planned also to bring Nevada Consolidated into Utah's orbit, along with Boston. This was an even more difficult job, for President Phillips of Nevada could see no point to a merger between two widely separated properties which had nothing in common save that they mined the same kind of copper. He complained that mining costs of the Utah companies were 10 cents a pound against 6½ cents for Nevada, that the proposed exchange of two and one-half shares of Nevada for one of Utah was sheer robbery, that Utah deliberately "fixed" its quarterly statements and refused to reveal the amount of tonnage run through the mill. The *Engineering and Mining Journal* ventured that "one more trick is being played on that distinguished enterprise"—Nevada Consolidated. "Why the Guggenheims should want to perpetrate this deal may remain a mystery for a while."

The vastly swollen Utah Copper Company emerged in 1910 with 2,500,000 shares of $10 par value of which 310,000 had been given Boston Consolidated shareholders and over 400,000 to Nevada. A little under a third of Utah's stock was listed in the names of Guggenheim Exploration and members of the Guggenheim family.

If carpers among the economists complained that the new Utah company was vastly overcapitalized, the Guggenheims had but to point to 1910 earnings of $5,401,000 and dividends of $4,648,000. Utah claimed that cost of production, including smelting and refining, in its great al fresco mines was a trifle over 8 cents a pound, against a market price of 12½. It cost but 25 cents to tear a ton of ore out of the mountainside and dump it in a waiting ore car. It was said that even those who paid the highest price for Utah stock before 1910 made anywhere from 500 to 1,000 per cent on their investment.

"It's the greatest industrial sight in the whole world," declared John D. Rockefeller, Jr., as he viewed Utah Copper shovels at work on the two dozen terraces that lined the copper mountain from the gulch up to the very top. There must have been a terrific din, what with charges of powder tearing off chunks of mountain, a score of steam shovels whining and groaning over their loads, a dozen locomotives shuttling back and forth up and down the switchbacks. But the thunder was swallowed up by the Oquirrhs, so large was the scale of operations. Standing on a shoulder of the opposite hill, one heard the shrill blasts of a whistle which warned of an impending explosion. Tiny figures which were undoubtedly men clambered to safe positions. A miniature section of the mountain would heave and subside. The little men would come a-running, a tiny locomotive shoved toy cars ahead, the steam shovel swung gravely into its job of filling the cars. All over the face of the great hill these operations went on simultaneously. Down in the narrow valley, straddled by miners' shacks and spanned by iron trestles of the Bingham and Garfield Railroad, the only noise was the rumbling of the ore trains over the bridges.

Superimposed on the great works in Bingham Canyon and Steptoe Valley by 1910 were flotations of securities which caused the *Engineering and Mining Journal* to ask:

289

Why this never-ending financing? Why is it that the promoters of these enterprises do not provide sufficient money in the first place? Is it because the engineers are incapable of estimating accurately the requirements? Or are the promoters afraid to ask at once for the huge sum that they know will be required? Or is the gradual expansion of capacity really due to progressive enlargement of plans?

T. A. Rickard, the mining engineer and journalist, asserted in the *Mining Magazine* of London:

No better illustration can be afforded of the muddle created by the merger of the duties of the engineer with those of the promoter than the vagaries of the Nevada-Utah amalgamation. When the legal engineering advisers of mining companies take a hand in the unlimited game of finance . . . when engineers express opinions like brokers . . . then the business of mining assumes an aspect that makes faro look respectable and gives to poker the status of a Sunday school pastime.

Dan Guggenheim chuckled as he read the criticisms. The trouble with his critics was that they were nineteenth century-minded. He believed Utah and Nevada held greater dividends in their low-grade ore than Kennecott's precious lodes in Alaska or the far-famed gold in the sands along the Klondike. If Utah Copper seemed to stagger under the burden of $25,000,000 capitalization, that was as nothing to the plans that Dan Guggenheim tucked away in the back of his head. If prices could be stabilized . . .

Dan and his brothers spent their summers in German watering places and often sandwiched in a winter trip to Europe. They watched the cartel movement that was sweeping Germany. Integration was the order of the day in that neatly regulated land. Eventually it must come to sprawling disorderly America. Take the disgraceful brawl under way between their American Smelting and Refining and United Metals Selling Company. Dan objected to United Metals taking a cut on every pound of American Smelting and Refining ore it sold in Europe. There was a million-dollar lawsuit pending in New York courts over the long-standing quarrel between the two companies. United Metals represented the Amalgamated Copper crowd, which in the initial, stumbling days of the Smelters Trust had been able to force upon it a ten-year contract to handle all its copper output, at a commission of 1 percent.

The Amalgamated crowd had of course offered to take all of the Guggenheims' copper properties off their hands—mines, smelters, and refineries—in order to achieve a functioning monopoly. Dan didn't care for that idea and the Cole-Ryan interests were never able to offer enough to induce him to part with the fast-growing copper end of the Guggenheim mining and smelting enterprise. But he held there should be a true community of interests among copper producers. On the eve of his European departure in the summer of 1911, Dan viewed with alarm (the idea caused some amusement in mining circles) the rapidly ascending price of copper. This was his statement:

> Nothing can be done to prevent a runaway price unless the various copper interests get together, study conditions, and discuss their affairs. But this the copper people are not willing to do because they fear the annoyance of persecution. It is quite true they have had several dinners and discussed matters, but beyond this and being entertained by their charming hosts, nothing was accomplished.

In reply, the *Engineering and Mining Journal* observed:

> Mr. Guggenheim is well known as an advocate of governmental regulation of prices, he being in fact a species of Socialist, although he might fail to recognize himself in

291

that guise. He says that America is now the laughing-stock of all European economists, because it is unwilling to allow its trusts a free hand, which, of course, means the ultimate regulation of prices by them. "In Germany," says Mr. Guggenheim, "everything is done to permit the stabilizing of prices."

Dan's argument had an uncanny prescience. The day would come in his own lifetime when Copper Exporters, Inc., would regulate the export price of American copper, and, a few years later, when the copper producers would be permitted to regulate the domestic price, as well, with the approval of a Blue Eagle. But in 1911 such ideas were un-American and shredded the fibers of rugged individualists for whom the editor of the country's leading mining magazine spoke when he declared:

Daniel is the latest exponent of the idea that prices can and ought to be regulated. His own word is "stabilized." Having had some unsuccessful experience, antedating that of the U. S. Steel Corporation, as to the ability of a great industrial combination to do this, he goes a step further and holds up the cartels and conventions of Germany, some of which have the aid and abettal of the government, as examples that are worthy of emulation, showing how the producers of commodities may by combination and restriction of production obtain in the markets of the world the very highest price for their product. As a new argument in favor of this policy, Mr. Guggenheim blows the trumpet of conservation of resources. Thus do our captains of industry hike on toward paternalism. This is the logical outcome, although for the moment the entrepreneurs think only how lovely a thing would it be to have the world working to pay interest on their watered investments in the natural resources that they have gobbled.

Harsh opinions rarely brought forth a retort from Daniel Guggenheim. Perhaps it was instilled in him that success, particularly for Jews, was bound to be accompanied by Christian curses. To him many of the criticisms that were leveled at Guggenheim financing seemed particularly pointless. The family had never pioneered in these practices but had picked up the tools at hand. Watered investments? Well, American Smelting and Refining had built up a pretty solid business despite its faith, hope, and charity common stock of 1899-1901. Price stabilization ridiculous? And what sense was there in copper producers beating down each others' prices? His ideas were yet to become sanctified and codified, the accepted rule of business practice.

Perhaps what struck Dan as strangest in some of these criticisms was the provincial American note. To many, German practices were quite outlandish, a foreign growth that had no meaning for America. Dan, who was more at home in European capitals than in the western mining centers whence his money came, believed that Germany had merely reached a desirable stage in business evolution earlier than America. To him it was obvious that the process of concentration should proceed until all industry was co-ordinated into a neat meshwork.

Sage observer of the European scene, he saw the shadow of war extending across that continent. He knew that the greatly increased war preparations were not to be in vain. On the coming battlefields copper would be as important as blood and steel.

So Dan Guggenheim chuckled at the petty-minded critics who objected to his operations in the porphyry coppers and his preaching the doctrine of stabilization. He could not understand why a concern which reported $5,000,000 dividends should be considered top-heavy with $25,000,000 capitalization. The trouble was that anti-Wall Street ignored Morgan's wise observation, "Don't sell America short." American economy could absorb, not tens of millions, but billions in securities. In years to come the productive capacity of the American people and the country's natural resources could be used to underwrite all the debts that Dan Guggenheim and a thousand other bold promoters could imagine.

18. THE LADY AND THE CHINAMAN

ON THE RIM of a mountain range near Silver City, New Mexico, stands an isolated column of rock which suggests a woman kneeling. Legend relates that the Spaniards had a mission or cloister in the valley from which Sister Rita fled after she had broken her vows. Turned to rock, she kneels forever in supplication for forgiveness, the Santa Rita of the countryside.

In her shadow lies the most famous mine of the Southwest, known to Indians of old as a source of virgin copper and revealed to a Spanish lieutenant in 1800. The American explorer, Lieutenant Zebulon Pike, prisoner of the Spaniards, saw Santa Rita and noted that it produced "20,000 mule-loads of copper annually." Patient burros were flogged all the way to Mexico City and thence to the coast, bearing their precious burdens for shipment to Spain.

After Mexico had won her independence, the Patties, father and son, first leased Santa Rita in 1825 for $1,000 a year and later bought it for $30,000 gold, paid to a "Spanish agent." The Patties achieved the difficult feat of making peace with the Indians. The Apaches had been on the warpath ever since Spaniards and white Mexicans trapped a peace party in the confines of a walled town and massacred them. The tribe had vowed never to make peace with the treacherous whites but relented when the elder Pattie assured the chiefs that he was of a different breed. In the crudely walled mine settlement of Santa Rita, the chiefs dug holes in the ground, spat therein and then covered them up with rocks to signify that spite and revenge had been cast out and anger buried. There was a great feast and the Apaches generously gave the Patties a plot of corn-land which their Indians could work in peace. Unfortunately for the prestige the Patties built up, American hunters in the Gila Valley, finding little to reward them, adopted the suggestion of the Mexican government that they accept bounties on Apache scalps. A band of friendly Indians were enticed into the encampment and massacred. Thereafter the Apache nation set out to build up a reputation for ferocity that became world-wide.

By 1870 Santa Rita's copper was being freighted hundreds of miles overland to the Western terminus of the Kansas Pacific Railway. Silver City had sprung up nearby as the biggest of New Mexico's mining camps. Following the Leadville discoveries, prospectors spied everywhere for silver as they had a few years before for gold. Thousands poured into Silver City, so many that the Red Onion and Blue Goose saloons used three shifts of barkeeps, imported orchestras from San Francisco, and kept armed men on guard as miners gambled with stacks of gold and silver on the gaming tables. Santa Rita was all but forgotten although Mexican laborers still delved in its black interior, climbing hundreds of feet up "chicken ladders"—logs set on end and notched to provide a foothold. Each miner carried 150 to 200 pounds of ore in a sack, supported on his back by a leather thong passed across the forehead to leave hands free for the tricky "chicken ladder." Convicts had been used in earlier days and their skeletons were often uncovered by latter-day miners exploring old drifts.

Santa Rita was an immense bed of porphyry copper, the grains of the metal disseminated through the ground. Water had seeped through, collecting a sulphate which came to rest in fissures. As ages passed, pure sheet copper was formed, and it was for this that Santa Rita was famous. Senator George Hearst of California bought the mine and left it to his widow, Mrs. Phoebe Hearst, mother of the publisher. In 1899 the Amalgamated Copper Syndicate swept Santa Rita into its grab bag, paying Mrs. Hearst $1,400,000 for her mine. But its low-grade ore discouraged exploitation and a decade passed before the roving eye of Tom Lawson, the Yukon Gold promoter, lit on Santa Rita. By then Dan Jackling's porphyry process had turned aggregations such as Santa Rita's into the world's most valuable copper deposits. Some 80,000,000 pounds of the metal had been extracted from Santa Rita since the first Spaniard laid eyes on the valley; now experts estimated there were billions of pounds of copper disseminated through at least fifty times as much earth.

With flair and color worthy of his erratic genius, Lawson launched the Santa Rita Mining Company. He knew that the public was by now pretty well fed up with porphyry promotions concocted solely to precipitate the scattered gold deposits to be found in the pockets of the gullible. He therefore produced out of his fertile imagination a new gadget to tickle the investor's fancy—a "wet-chemical" process for treating copper ore. This discovery was hitched to the name of Charles S. Bradley, a pioneer in the electrometallurgy of aluminum. It was similar, said the florid Lawson, to the cyanide process which had revolutionized the recovery of gold.

The Bostonian explained it all in a unique promotion stunt, a book of 300 pages sent to a list of 62,000 prospective customers the length and breadth of the country. Once more the selfishness of Wall Street was attacked; especially its practice of letting the public finance mine promotion. "One million of our ninety million people," cried Lawson, "have more than one-half the wealth." If wealth were equitably distributed, he propounded, the cost of living could be cut in half; or looking at it from another angle, interest on savings could be doubled from 4 per cent to 8. He proposed to take the first modest step in the better distribution of wealth by letting the public in on Santa Rita.

297

It was rather complicated. First, there was the Santa Rita Mining Company, 85 per cent of whose stock, along with the right to use the Bradley process, was to be handed over to the Process Copper Company for $3,000,000 in 8 per cent bonds convertible into 8 per cent stock, $9,000,000 in common stock and $3,000,000 in preferred. Lawson and his associates might be prepared to share with the public $30,000,000 in 8 per cent bonds of the Process Company, which controlled the patents. And beyond that there was the assurance that the bold, bad reign of Wall Street would be curtailed further by offering the public $90,000,000 in Process Company preferred, another $90,000,000 in common remaining in the hands of Lawson and his associates. That however was for the future, when other copper companies came to Process Company, begging for licenses to use the Bradley patents.

Of the $3,000,000 bonds of Process Copper Company the public was assured that each $1,000 unit would be worth $1,500-$2,000 as soon as purchased because of the very limited nature of the offering. Its ultimate worth would be $5,000. "In all the history of finance there has never been a parallel proposition to the one before you," Lawson concluded. Women investors were especially urged to take advantage of the new era.

The *Engineering and Mining Journal*, long-time enemy of Lawson and his promotions, was first to turn its sarcasm loose on his "latest philanthropy to the public, which he wants to see get rich quick." His book, "profuse with italics and black letter type," was a disappointment to the editor. "Let not the reader expect 300 pages of unalloyed pleasure, or anything like another 'Story of Amalgamated' distributed gratis." Some 150 pages were given over to the results of 8,094 samples of Santa Rita ore, "which far outdoes old Homer's catalogue of the ships, and would hold the record for aridity were it not for Vega's tables of logarithms."

The editor's complaint continued:

Alas, Mr. Lawson, that you should be uninteresting! . . .

We have looked through these 300 pages with a microscope to discover something of the nature of the Bradley process, but although we used an instrument of 100 diameters magnifying power, we failed to find more than a trace, the latter a remark that the process is being applied on a practical scale within gunshot of New York.

Never was failure written more promptly or completely than on Tom Lawson's Process promotion. His book-prospectus appeared in the middle of May, 1909, with a bond subscription, handsomely engraved, inserted and perforated for easy use. Three weeks later, the copper financiers, Hayden, Stone and Company had stepped into the picture and taken over Santa Rita.

The oracle of mining journalism sounded taps for Lawson in an editorial headed "A Lady Saint and a Chinaman":

In the natural course of events, the materialization of this publication [Lawson's prospectus] should have been followed by a loud blowing of the bazoo. Strange to say there was silence, and stranger still, the Santa Rita mine was brought out a few days later, under the name of Chino Copper Company, without mention of Mr. Lawson.

Dan Jackling came down from Salt Lake to survey Chino; Beatty was installed as chief engineer, and a board was appointed by Charles Hayden, six of whose members also adorned Utah Copper's board. It was apparent that the Wall Streeters, as Lawson had feared, were up to their old tricks: Chino had 750,000 shares, of which the promoters kept 375,000. The inevitable bond issue followed, for $2,500,000, and 100,000 more shares of stock were offered two years later.

The mass excavation of the disseminated copper in Santa

Rita's valley started at two widely separated points, but as the years passed, the two great holes, hundreds of feet deep, approached each other, leaving the mine buildings on an ever narrowing tongue of land between the deepest and widest pits man ever dug in the West. For a quarter century Chino produced copper and dividends before it was closed down, the pumps taken out, and the machinery moved away. As water gathered slowly in the bottom of the pits, the traveler by air saw two deep green eyes staring out of sockets blue and green, eternal reminder of Lawson's dream on which he had hoped to float a $250,000,000 promotion.

The management of Chino rested in the hands of Dan Jackling, Charles Hayden, and the Colorado Springs capitalists. The Guggenheims contented themselves with a stake, held in the name of their Exploration Company, which by 1916 was to be valued at $2,500,000, and another of those long-term smelting contracts that brought Chino's concentrates rolling down the Rio Grande, in hundred-car trains, to American Smelting and Refining's plant at El Paso, the bullion then speeding east to the Guggenheim refinery in Perth Amboy.

About 150 miles west of Santa Rita, the last of the great porphyry coppers was developed from the failure of the English Ray Copper Company, Limited. So tumultuous were the mountains in Pinal County, Arizona, that the Londoners had to build a narrow-gauge railroad seven miles from the mine to the nearest level patch. Having done that, they appropriated the ideal location for their yards to build a tennis court. Shareholders' sons, sent out to the American wilderness for experience and tempering, scandalized Arizona's mining community by knocking off promptly at four every day for afternoon tea. And indeed at almost any time of day young Englishmen could be seen, outfitted in the best Bond Street riding-habits, prancing along mountain trails, riding pad saddles on dock-tailed ponies.

The English company tried out a pet idea to compensate for the lack of a railroad to the nearest point on the Southern Pacific—steam motor engines which hauled long trains of wagons over a dirt road. Ore which ran considerably under 6 per cent exhausted all the money Ray Copper cared to risk. In 1907, ten years after the English company had started development, Dan Jackling's eye fell on abandoned Ray. He interested Charles Hayden and the Colorado Springs crowd—the Penrose family, MacNeill, and the Springs' leading brokerage house, Shove, Aldrich and Company. Ray Consolidated was the result, with an original capitalization of $6,000,000, which was boosted every year until 1911, when the underground mine began operating with two main shafts and thirty miles of drifts.

The Guggenheims waited expectantly. To their surprise Ray Consolidated began to construct its own smelter down in the Gila Valley at a spot named for Hayden. Dan Guggenheim couldn't see the need for an independent smelter in a property run by people associated with him in so many other copper mines. So American Smelting and Refining took over the Hayden smelter, signed the usual long term contract to handle Ray Consolidated's ore and to market its copper, and put $2,500,000 of Guggenheim Exploration money into it.

Dan Guggenheim had more plans for both Chino and Ray Consolidated in the back of his busy brain, but they waited on other events.

19. BIRTH OF THE I. W. W.

MEYER GUGGENHEIM, the Philadelphia merchant, wasted no more sentiment over a piece of labor than over a piece of lace. If it was good labor, he paid the market price, worked it intensively ten to twelve hours a day, and calculated his profit. It was before the era of profit-sharing, organized welfare, bloody conflicts between capitalist and proletarian, and the near-socialistic utterances of his son, Daniel, on labor's place in the sun.

In his fierce individualism, the elder Guggenheim had scant regard for theories which expressed sympathy with people content to remain laborers. He, too, had been a laborer, and a most lowly one, a peddler. Unaided he had worked himself up in his lifetime to be a millionaire and he believed any young man, given a good body and a good head, could do as much if he would use the push that God gave him. Nearly all his employees agreed that if they, too, did not become employers and millionaires, it was their fault. Few of them started with the handicaps that in Philadelphia in 1848 faced young Meyer, penniless, friendless, speaking no English, set down in a strange world. So for his men and women Meyer had contempt, pity, mercy for the few long in his employ who met unforeseen adversity.

When Meyer ventured into mining, he found the Leadville of 1881 as strange as Philadelphia had been in 1848. Here were no patient, docile clerks and warehouse employees, but restive miners, the flower of America's pioneer stock; pushful men who had abandoned the servility and tameness of the East. Typically, they were young, single, and unafraid. Some carried vaunting ambition under grimy clothes; they hoped to strike it rich for themselves some fine

ISAAC

MURRY

SOLOMON R.

BENJAMIN

THE GUGGENHEIM BROTHERS. *Photos by Bain News Service and International.*

day in a mountain canyon. So they bound themselves out, as it were, to gain a stake to tide them over hard months to be spent in lean prospecting. But mostly miners spent their money as they made it and when restlessness overcame them, moved on to the next camp.

It took a heavy hand to hold down such men when they found that life in a Western mining camp was a succession of twelve-hour work shifts alternated with sodden rest and intermittently punctuated by wild splurges of emotional release. Drudgery with pick and shovel was overhung by the terrible chance that a roof might collapse or a chunk of rock come tumbling down, breaking skulls like eggshells. That bred a certain devil-may-care attitude to life. Death struck swiftly and often, and none knew who was to be next.

Mine-operators themselves were men without mercy. Driven on by the lash of dividend-hungry owners, they reined in the bridle till the bit gashed, and the men rose in the fury of a sudden, wild, and tumultous strike. In Leadville the operators kept themselves in readiness for such outbursts. They organized their own militia to hold the fort until the Governor, himself usually a mine owner, could dash state troops up to the hills from the flat country below.

During the great depression of 1893, hordes of hungry men turned avidly to the Populistic doctrines which swept the state, and when Populism ebbed, the more rebellious turned to socialism, then in the springtime of its growth in America. Socialism as it was preached in the West played upon the glaring contrasts of wealth and poverty, and none could see this more clearly than the mine worker. It was almost an axiom that a mine must pay as much in dividends as in wages. Mine owners knew that they possessed a wasting asset, that the faster the ore was dug the nearer came the day when the mine must close, exhausted and valueless. That was small comfort, though, for miners confronted by the extravagant living costs of the camps, and the probability that a slump in silver prices or the exhaustion of a vein would send them out on the tramp for a job, competing with other thousands who had left the cramped, overcrowded East.

Meyer Guggenheim paid the same scale at the A. Y. and Minnie that prevailed in other Leadville mines. It was almost compulsory. All mine owners and managers belonged to the Leadville Mine-Operators Association, which devoted itself with concentrated fury to the war on three fronts: to fight labor costs, to fight smelter owners and to fight the railroads. The Association posted the wage scale and the men were free, in the manner of rugged individualism, to accept or reject. If they didn't want to work for $2 a day, they could go elsewhere, there being no other employment in Leadville.

By the turn of the century, the Western Federation of Miners had impinged on the rule of the operators' association in many mining camps, particularly those more remote from the ordinary sources of labor supply. In Leadville, the association weeded out the "agitators" with the card system, known contemptuously among miners as the "rustling card." To obtain employment now, the newcomer had to go to the operators' joint employment office, which enjoyed the advantages of a black list naming active members of the Western Federation. A forerunner of the refined Bertillon system, the rustling card was content to list name, age, color of hair and eyes, complexion, scars, previous employers and record. The man on the blacklist had to avoid "card camps."

Hardly had Meyer and his sons shifted into the smelter business in Pueblo in 1888 than they were fronted with a strike. The usual stratagem to defeat such uprisings was to switch ore to other smelters. Rife as competition was, smelter owners knew that the twelve-hour shift would be downed if the Western Federation ever stuck its foot in the

304

door. In the face of such a threat, they hung out the slogan of the miners' union, "An injury to one is an injury to all," and cheerfully opened their works to ore from embarrassed rivals.

In the Guggenheim refinery at Perth Amboy good old doctrine was upheld in a bitterly contested case fought through the New Jersey courts after Edward Flanigan, father of four children, had fallen off a faulty ladder in 1895. Guggenheim lawyers did not contest his total incapacitation. But, they argued, he had failed to establish negligence on the part of M. Guggenheim's Sons. He could have used a good ladder had he gone and got it. If there was any negligence, it was on the part of fellow-servants in leaving a bad ladder in position. The trial judge had ruled that if the ladder was on the property, Flanigan had a right to assume it was in good condition, but the Court of Appeals held this an error. Unfortunately, the ladder had been destroyed after the accident, so there was no way for the court to test its condition. The higher court held the award of $2,000 damages unreasonable for a man earning only $1.10 a day, and ordered it scaled down.

When the brothers took the Smelters Trust into camp in 1901, the Western Federation howled with fear that the power of such a monopoly could never be broken short of revolution. The *New York Commercial Advertiser*, recounting the gains of combination, declared: "Should the unions and smelter management come into conflict again, every smelter of any size can be closed down for an indefinite period without serious loss to the owners but bringing widespread disaster and distress to thousands of wage-earners." Union men, smarting under the black list in Guggenheim mines and faced with a stone wall in the smelters, began to veer from the mild forms of political socialism that held sway currently among the Americans and Germans in the East. A native type of direct action that grew straight out of

305

the labor policies evolved by the Guggenheims and the mine-operators associations began to spread among the hardier unionists. The great strikes at Leadville, Cripple Creek, and in the Coeur d'Alenes increased their distrust of the slogan of the American Federation of Labor, "A fair day's wage for a fair day's work." Instead, they raised the cry, "Abolition of the wage system!"

Inevitably, when they struck against the twelve-hour shift, they found themselves with empty bellies, looking down the barrels of loaded army rifles. The long battle of the Colorado miners and smeltermen for the eight-hour day confirmed their suspicions that the State was an instrument of force in the enemy's hands, from which nothing could be hoped in the way of gradual progress. The unions won the eight-hour law in the legislature only to lose it in the state Supreme Court. They fought on to push a constitutional amendment through to electoral victory by a vote of 70,000 to 30,000, only to find that the Guggenheims and the mine owners had switched the votes of enough legislators early in 1903 to balk the enactment of the now-constitutional law.

The defeat of the eight-hour bill provoked the general strike of the Western Federation in all Guggenheim smelters in the summer of 1903. Every plant was closed down in the first general strike in Colorado smelter history: labor's answer to the monopoly which made individual strikes seem foolish.

Simon Guggenheim, western regent of the Smelters Trust, stayed discreetly in the background, nursing his senatorial ambitions. Franklin Guiterman, his understudy, counterattacked with the assistance of the Citizens' Alliance, the general employers' organization which took care of union labor in the cities. Judge Nixon obligingly granted an injunction against the strikers, including not only the Western Federation, but the defunct American Labor Union, the Denver Trades and Labor Assembly, and the

306

Colorado Federation of Labor. He not only prohibited strikers from "interfering in any way with the business of the American Smelting and Refining Company" and from picketing, but forbade their officers to "publish any order, statements, rules, or directions." That effectively shut the strikers out of the newspapers. When some had the impunity to violate the court order, Judge Dixon tucked them away in jail for two months to consider the enormity of their contempt.

The Legislature was called into extraordinary session to pass an eight-hour law to remove the strikers' main complaint against the twelve-hour shift, but John Vivian and Dick Broad, faithful shepherds of Simon's political fortunes, allied with the mine-operators' lobby, got the legislators tangled up in conflicting bills. Half confused, half corrupted, they adjourned. By that time the smeltermen had been starved out, and as if to underline that fact, Guiterman announced that one of the Denver smelters would never reopen.

Editor O'Neill of the *Miners' Magazine* retorted:

Manager Guiterman is aware of the fact that the men employed in and around the smelters are the poorest paid and most overworked of any department of labor in America. He knows that in a few years the physique of the smelter employee is wrecked and that the victim who has succumbed to long hours and poisonous fumes becomes the object of charity, whose health and strength has been coined into dividends for the Trust. The shacks and hovels that are called homes in which the serfs of the smelters dwell are mute evidence of the soulless cupidity that has characterized the management of this association of philanthropists. Men who have labored years swelling the profits of this heartless combination are confronted with the poorhouse. The corpse-like faces of men haunted

307

with premature death, the twisted limbs of broken down vassals of smelter servitude are pleading for justice and for an eight-hour day that will plant in the pathway between the cradle and the grave a few roses among the many thorns of life.

In the wake of the broken smelter strike, the miners of Cripple Creek went on strike, the bloodiest in all the turbulent annals of Colorado's dark strife. Force met force as men battled for their jobs. Strikers and strikebreakers were killed in open battle on the hills about Cripple Creek and Victor; dynamite ripped down shaft houses and twisted bridges; hundreds of miners were herded into trains and set down in the desert across the Kansas and New Mexico state lines with orders, reinforced by buckshot, never to return.

From 1903 on the philosophy and the tactic of revolutionary unionism permeated the western miners and seeped into the east. The Federation, staggering under the blows administered to a union seeking the ends of pure-and-simple trade unionism, joined forces with Eugene V. Debs, who had learned his Socialism in a jail cell after the Pullman strike of 1894, and Dan DeLeon, stormy leader of the still influential Socialist Labor Party, to found the Industrial Workers of the World. Tearing its philosophy in reverse from the pages of the Guggenheims' American Smelting and Refining Company and the mine-operators associations, it preached the solidarity of labor in industrial unions, the bitter truth of the class war, and it hoisted high the Red Flag.

The Western Federation of Miners joined the I. W. W., providing a majority of the new organization's membership. From the Western Federation, too, came one-eyed, two-fisted Bill Haywood, to be secretary-treasurer of the I. W. W., and with him many another leader. Eventually the I. W. W. split, the Western Federation going its own way alone and the DeLeonites forming a new industrial union.

Such was the power of monopoly however that neither conservative nor radical union could win a strike in a Guggenheim smelter. In 1907 the El Paso scale men struck for $1.50; a week later they were en route to other camps in the West. Six years afterward, another strike was on, for $1.65 for the twelve-hour day for laborers, the discharge of the company doctor, the abolition of fines, and a rule forbidding foremen from running stores at which employees were obliged to trade to hold their jobs. It was lost. "Like all Guggenheim properties," said the Western Federation organizer, "this smelter is run on a basis of huge dividends and starvation wages. Mexican workers pit their empty stomachs and their moneyless hands against the might of the Guggenheims." In Tacoma in 1907 smeltermen struck under the I. W. W. In 1910 the Globe smeltermen in Denver were out again, the third strike in a dozen years. The police were sent out "as a courtesy to the Smelters Trust and to Senator Guggenheim," as the *Miners Magazine* phrased it. In 1913 the Leadville smeltermen threatened to join the International Union of Mine, Mill, and Smeltermen, the reconstructed A. F. of L. union which had succeeded the Western Federation. But it mattered not a whit to the smelter manager what colors the union flew; he posted a notice that the smelter would shut down for good if the men joined the union. Those who had were invited to deposit their union cards in the office or lose their jobs.

It was about that time that Sol Guggenheim was quoted as saying: "I believe the wage earner is more extravagant in proportion to his earnings than the millionaire." The statement aroused wide comment in the press, both conservative and radical. The *Seattle Star*, youngster in lusty Scripps's growing chain, waxed sarcastic.

309

The crowning extravagance in which the poor indulge Mr. Guggenheim never refers to. The poor give up a large—very large—part of their incomes to make Guggenheims, Morgans and Rockefellers. When they come to real economy here's where they will begin to cut down expenses. When they have reformed in the matter of supporting millionaires, maybe they will be better able to stand the strain of more chuck steak and codfish.

In 1912 a fierce strike broke out in the Guggenheim refinery at Perth Amboy, New Jersey. Laborers, mostly Hungarian and Slav, struggled to rid themselves of the twelve-hour shift. Guggenheim managers, irritated by an outbreak so near the firm's head offices at 120 Broadway, called in the Waddell-Mahon strikebreaking agency in New York. "Nobles"—armed guards—and strikebreakers were shipped across the river, and savage battles raged in the streets of Perth Amboy. Four strikers were killed. Liberal and labor opinion in New York glowed white-hot at this demonstration of Guggenheim labor policies in the metropolitan backyard.

Out in Utah, big-fisted Dan Jackling tackled the "labor problem" in his own way, and in a manner that did credit to the vision of the young engineer who had pioneered in the porphyries. His innovation startled western mine operators; it was to short-circuit labor trouble by avoiding the use of the troublesome native Americans as much as possible. He imported six hundred Japanese laborers from the West Coast to muck along the serried terraces that switchbacked up the face of the copper mountain. The Japanese were strong, industrious, fed themselves on rice and a shred of meat, and understood discipline and loyalty. To balance them, Labor Agent Leonidas G. Skliris scoured the boats from the Balkans for healthy young recruits. To them $2 a day was fabulous money. The Western Federation found itself up against a blank wall in Bingham Canyon. None of its organizers could speak Japanese, Greek, South Slav, or Magyar, and if they had been able to, their message probably would not have been intelligible to the newcomers, so different were the backgrounds of the Western American miners and the "hunkies."

Yet the worm of discontent eventually bit into Jackling's Utah Copper apple. A faint signal was the visit of some Greek laborers to the office of the Salt Lake prosecutor to complain that they were held in virtual peonage in the Canyon. The prosecutor did nothing. In January, 1912, a Greek laborer was shot stealing coal. "The Greek deserved to be shot," observed the *Bingham Press-Bulletin*. "The foreign element is getting too quarrelsome and arbitrary for the good of the camp. The deluge of foreign riffraff is sweeping over us. These outlaws should be taught their place."

Editor O'Neill of the *Miners Magazine* wrote one of his wrathier editorials in response. "Who brought the Greeks to the sacred precincts of Bingham Canyon," he demanded, "and who gave them employment at such miserable wages that they must steal in order to keep warm? The Guggenheims!" He charged that Utah Copper killed more steam shovel men each year than the entire Southern Pacific system, and that the men were working every day of the month and had asked in vain for two days a month off.

A Federation executive board member reported:

The Guggenheims through their puppet Jackling control Utah and the agency through which this control is held absolute is the Mormon Church. The church heads are interested in practically all the industries in Utah. Therefore, the Guggenheims find Utah an ideal place to force upon the workers the most intolerable conditions existing anywhere in the country.

311

Even the *Engineering and Mining Journal*, cautious in its labor comments, declared:

Even at equal terms, we do not wonder that anybody would rather go to anywhere than stay in Bingham, which is the most repulsive mining camp that we know of in the United States. We do not deprecate its unfortunate inhabitants, but refer rather to its physical conditions, which are uncomfortable, forbidding, and unsanitary. Bingham has been most fittingly described as "a sewer four miles long."

Storm clouds lowered over the Canyon, but Jackling, the great engineer, knew nothing of them. Confident that his "Japs" and "hunkies" were toiling as ever, he had gone to Los Angeles where, on the morning of September 17, 1912, he was informed that his 6,000 employees had shut down the copper mountain. Jackling wired Governor Spry to declare martial law and instructed his assistant, Bob Gemmell, to deputize as many men in Salt Lake as possible until the Waddell-Mahon people in New York could rush expert "nobles" to the scene. Thousands of miners mounted the terraces, armed with guns and dynamite. "We are going up the hill and drive them down," announced Governor Spry, surveying the scene from a safe distance. But nobody volunteered to accompany him and so he went back to the Capitol.

"I will not discuss the labor situation," said Jackling, curtly, as he stepped off the train at Salt Lake. Questioned about the Waddell-Mahon gunmen, he retorted:

I'd rather do what I am going to do and talk about it afterwards. If it should be necessary to throw out all the union men and replace them with non-union men to keep the mines in operation, I should most certainly do that. This strike was caused by a few agitators—not workers— who were imported for the very purpose. They have been

312

mixing with the men for some time and ought to be run off the place. We know who they are and will take care that their kind never again get a foothold in our properties.

Slowly the facts about Leonidas G. Skliris and his padrone system at Utah Copper leaked out. He had been getting $5 to $20 for every man brought into camp. To avoid being fired, "his" men were required to pay $1 a month and to trade at the store run by his brother. Federal labor men declared Skliris' control ranged over the state of Utah into other mines. The *Deseret Evening News* deplored such bald traffic in labor. Skliris "resigned."

Sol Guggenheim came west to see what all the shooting was about, made a carefully guarded survey of the turbulent camp, and departed for his hunting lodge in Idaho, his lips sealed.

The Canyon had become the seat of guerrilla warfare. Three hundred armed men patrolled the winding road that led up the gulch; the miners held possession of the terraces, the steep slopes of the canyon where their shacks perched, and the gulches that led off from the main Canyon road. Strikebreakers were being brought in and housed within a barricade, awaiting the day when work could be resumed.

Utah mine owners watched the uprising with bated breath. The president of the operators' association encouraged Jackling to stick it out. "His determination not to recognize the union is likely to make the strikers hungry unless they get back to work," he observed. "I hope he does not give in, or in a short time we will all be in the hands of the employees. The result of the present strike will write a prescription for the future of Utah mine-operating." Spencer Penrose, brother of the Senator and a director of Utah Copper, reassured operators. "Utah Copper will never recognize the union at Bingham even if the mine is closed forever. I am receiving telegrams every hour from stock-holders telling us to stand pat."

The International Union spread the strike to Nevada Consolidated, where 3,500 men downed tools. The Garfield smeltermen voted not to touch Bingham ore. Waddell-Mahon gunmen killed two Greeks at the Steptoe smelter in Nevada and Governor Oddie proclaimed martial law to prevent the serving of warrants on the killers. The Salt Lake and the Utah labor federations arranged a parade down the main streets of Salt Lake to protest Waddell-Mahon rule in the Canyon. "Must we go to Russia for free-dom?" asked one placard. "No holdups now," announced another. "The thugs are all employed as deputies."

By the end of October, six weeks after the strike had started, hunger was winning in the Canyon. American miners were beginning to move on to some other camps—too proud, in the tradition of Western miners, to admit defeat. The Japanese, corralled, were willing to go to work and impatient because they were not being paid. The be-wildered Greeks, assured that Skliris was out, were divided. Bands of deputies, emboldened, now made sorties up the gulches, cleaning out recalcitrant miners, breaking down doors, grabbing men and sending them down the Canyon at double-quick time. Drunken deputies wounded each other; eighteen Waddell-Mahon men introduced a comic note by striking for higher pay; one was arrested for stealing a grip with $275 in it; two Greeks were killed in a café because they spoke up for the union.

Toward the end of November the strike was over and Jackling was wrangling with the county commissioners over who should pay for the deputies. At the beginning the com-missioners had announced they would deputize a thousand men even if it broke the county; now public opinion had swung over toward the strikers' side.

Jackling magnanimously announced a wage increase of

22-25 cents a day, because, he said, the price of copper had advanced. To his stockholders he confessed that the cost of producing copper had doubled during the last quarter of 1912, "partly because of the extraordinary expenses incurred during the strike period."

The savage outbursts in Perth Amboy and Bingham Canyon disturbed Dan Guggenheim. The blame was being unloaded on the Guggenheim family, and Dan was touchy. He had special reasons for avoiding the Guggenheims being made the whipping boys of gathering progressive forces which had just placed Woodrow Wilson in the White House for the "New Freedom." The shocking living conditions among his "hunkies" in Perth Amboy were still the subject of scandalous comment in the New York popular press; in Pueblo there was the abominable junk heap section dubbed "Colo-russia" by unionists, where Mexican laborers in the Guggenheim smelters stretched their $1.50 a day to cover bare necessities. El Paso had nothing better to show. It was a pitiable exhibit for a corporation which in 1914 could report $11,603,000 in profits against $10,212,000 paid in wages and salaries.

Mining and smelting had the reputation of being man-killers. In the mine at Ray, death struck in these ways in one year: squeezed against the side wall by an ore car, run over by an ore car, gassed in a blocked man-way, caught in a premature powder explosion, crushed by falling rock, suffocated in a muck pile, felled in a motor train wreck, men died. Dozens of men were sent out maimed each year by any fair-sized mine. Those who weren't crippled ran the chance of contracting miners' consumption, a ghastly disease to which air drill miners, muckers, chute tenders and carmen were subject. In the smelters, men dropped dead from arsenate of lead poisoning; the fumes ate into the bodies of others until they dragged themselves about more dead than alive. As late as 1913, one man out of four in American Smelting plants suffered a disabling accident each year.

Dan conferred with his brothers and with those shrewd observers of public opinion, Baruch, Untermyer, and Marshall. All felt that the political exigencies of the moment called for a grand gesture by the country's leading Jewish employer and industrialist. Simon, fresh from Washington, his term having expired, probably thought up the bright idea of hiring Dr. Charles P. Neill, retiring U. S. Commissioner of Labor as supervisor of Guggenheim labor relations. Simon had some first-hand acquaintance with Neill's job as he had been one of the Senators who tried to block the plan to elevate the position of commissioner to that of Secretary of Labor with full Cabinet rank. With the change in Administrations, Neill was out of a job and gladly accepted the tempting financial offer from ex-Senator Guggenheim. It was an astute stroke, worthy of the family, and paid richly in publicity value among the business papers which had been obliged reluctantly to print the recent inescapable news about Guggenheim labor troubles. Adolph Ochs, proprietor of the *New York Times* and a friend of the family, cried: "They treat their men as humans and not as machines. They have devised means of amusing them during their leisure hours. . . . The Guggenheims hold the affection of thousands, even hundreds of thousands."

Dr. Neill recommended a pension plan for aged employees, housing projects in the company's own towns in the West, hospital facilities, accident compensation, and the range of welfare work made familiar by the U. S. Steel Corporation's recently set up bureau of welfare and sanitation.

Dr. Neill's bureau came not a moment too soon, for President Wilson had set up the Industrial Relations Commission under the chairmanship of Frank P. Walsh. The inquisitive Irishman was holding hearings all over the country, probing captains of industry on their ideas about labor, and labor leaders on their ambitions, airing the much discussed "labor problem" from all angles. He pried into the burning to death of nineteen wives and children of strikers in an unprotected tent colony by the Colorado Fuel and Iron Company, headed by those eminent Baptists and church-goers, the Rockefellers. (This accomplishment, incidentally, was never approached by the Guggenheims in all their wars on organized labor.) In due course Walsh got around to American Smelting and Refining and asked Dan Guggenheim to submit to inspection.

It was a gala day for capital-baiters, and a crowd turned out to hear the great Guggenheim defend his labor policies. Labor people, Socialists, social workers made up the bigger part of the audience which came to see a capitalist writhe on the witness stand under the unflinching questioning of a champion of the underdog. Some remembered his statement, during the hard times of 1907-8 about the efficiency of labor. "Whenever a thousand men are needed," said Dan, "1,200 apply. The result is that the thousand best men are picked; the others of necessity must be turned away. But the thousand work more conscientiously, knowing that two hundred are waiting to take the places of the incompetents." Few recognized the short, thickset figure of Guggenheim as he advanced up the aisle. Jovial, florid of face, full of his characteristic brimming vitality, he greeted Walsh and other members of the commission. Determined not to be put on the defensive in this crucial test of his family's name, Dan launched into a description of American Smelting's new labor program.

"Do you oppose the policy of organized labor?" Walsh interrupted.

"Employees," responded the unruffled capitalist, "are fully justified in organizing." The audience gasped. "Often the capitalist is arbitrary," Dan continued, "just as the

317

laborer is, at times. I have no objection to what our employees do outside the plant. They are human."

Walsh was puzzled and shifted to a more general question. "Do you think discontent is increasing?"

"I think it is on the increase," replied the imperturbable Guggenheim, "and I fear it will continue to increase unless something is done to prevent it. The high cost of living is partly responsible for that, but the greatest canker in the world is envy. A man these days sees so many things to invite his envy. But envy is a pretty well distributed trait. I think we are getting to a higher standard in dealing with labor, just as I think the world today believes it is no longer necessary to kill off your competitor to get along; or grind down your fellow man."

The audience looked incredulously at the man who was to sizzle on the pan heated by Frank Walsh. Instead he was turning the commission hearing into a sounding board to undo the mischief of a generation of unfavorable publicity.

"There is not enough legislation," he said, with a half-smile. "I am not one of those who complain that our statute books are cluttered up with useless laws for changing this and that. We are many years behind England and Germany in legislation which helps the workingman—the poor man."

The head of the House of Guggenheim expounded his theory. "There is today too great a difference between the rich man and the poor man. To remedy this is too big a job for the state or the employer to tackle single-handed. There should be a combination in this work between the Federal Government, the state, the employer and the employee. The men want more comforts—more of the luxuries of life. They are entitled to them. I say this because humanity owes it to them."

Walsh listened attentively and wondered at the contrast between the man's words and the Guggenheim record. He

318

decided to probe nearer the nerve. "Do you think, Mr. Guggenheim, that the workingman should have a voice in the arrangement of the conditions under which he labors?"

Dan, on guard, rose beautifully to the question. "The workingman should have not only a voice—he should have a compelling voice. The Workmen's Compensation Act was won by the workingman. He will win more legislative victories. And legislation that will benefit the many is desirable, no matter what that legislation is."

Dan peered into the future. "I think the State should furnish work for the men who lack employment. You may call me socialistic, if you like, but it is a job of the United States to look after its people. Were it not for philanthropic work, there would be a revolution here. But sufficient is not given in this case. People won't give up the money they make easily, even though they have more than they need. So the Government must raise the money—raise it by taxing the estates of the rich, if you will—but the United States must raise it some way."

Did Mr. Guggenheim have any practical suggestions about the division of the fruits of industry? He did.

In the scheme of uplift in which we are all interested, I think, I believe the workers are entitled to share in the profits of all industries. This should be so arranged that the money could be taken in bulk at the end of the year and deposited to their account in a banking institution. If that were done, it would change conditions in thousands of homes. Workers, in the mass, do not understand how to save. My method would teach them. It would be the same as teaching a child to read and write. The people in this country who have built up fortunes in the last ten or fifteen years have done it because they have been thrifty. Many are poor because they did not save. Sometimes, of course, fortunes come without thrift, as in the

319

case of the son of a worthy or unworthy sire. The sons of the rich, in many cases, are entitled to sympathy, though I would not say as much sympathy as the poor.

How would Mr. Guggenheim end the strikes which were convulsing industry? Did he approve of compulsory arbitration?

"I prefer conciliation instead of arbitration," he countered. "Labor and capital will never get together when there is trouble if both sides are equally strong. I have always felt that conciliation can do more than compulsory arbitration, but legislation would do away with both. The laborers must organize to accomplish this object."

And when the laborer organized in a Guggenheim plant, what happened to him, Walsh was curious to know. The question was too direct to allow Dan much latitude. At last he was on the defensive, where he least wished to be. "We have in our plants the so-called 'open shop,'" he admitted. "Every man has a right to be heard as an individual or as the representative of an organization. We do not discriminate. A man may belong to a union or not as he pleases. Of course, we will not let any union organizer walk into our plants and tell us what we shall do. We have to use reason. We have the interests of our shareholders to consider. We do not think we have a right to control a man any more than we have a right to say what he shall eat or drink."

Anxious to avoid further direct questions, Dan told how American Smelting conducted its labor relations. "Up to a year and a half ago we did what we could to remedy conditions and make improvements. I told the members of the executive committee and the board of directors that we should do more than we had done—we should see to housing the men better, relieve the conditions under which they worked, establish a pension fund, try to throw a helpful, encouraging light into their lives. It meant better business—

320

higher efficiency." He related the hiring of Dr. Neill, the acceptance of workmen's compensation, the insuring of men in the event of death in the Perth Amboy plant. Perth Amboy! Walsh wondered what Guggenheim would say to a question about that plant.

"Do you recall what your men in the Perth Amboy plant were paid when they went on strike in 1912?" he asked.

"I do not," Dan replied. "It may have been $1.60 a day or $1.80. As soon as the trouble arose, I directed Willard S. Morse, a director, to go to Perth Amboy and study conditions and try to remedy them and do all he could. Our efforts in that were rewarded. Mr. Wilson, the Governor of New Jersey, sent a member of his staff to Perth Amboy, who telephoned me when our difficulty was settled that he was highly pleased, not only with Mr. Morse's work, but with the spirit of the company. Mr. Morse discussed the questions with many of the men. Some of them were unable to make clear what they wanted, as they didn't seem to know."

How did Mr. Guggenheim explain the prevalence of strikes in his plants?

"I would not say we have frequent strikes. You must consider that the men are restless over the high cost of living. I sympathize with them and I do what I can to help them."

Pressed for details on his philanthropies, Dan modestly shrugged his shoulders. "Oh, I do not want to advertise," he answered.

He left the witness chair as jovial as he had entered it, shaking hands with his inquisitors, exchanging compliments, and bowing his way out, followed by newspaper men. His testimony hit the front page of the morning newspapers and made curious reading in Rocky Mountain journals, whose readers clucked in astonishment. It was not recorded that either the Socialist party or the Mine, Mill and Smelter Workers Union offered honorary memberships to the sponsor of ideas so advanced that it took the country twenty years to catch up to them. But Ida Tarbell, who had pilloried the Rockefellers, added Daniel Guggenheim to her growing list of good captains of industry. "He was earnest in his sympathy for the laboring men and radical in his ideas of what should be done to improve their lot," she commented. In fact, the head of the Smelters Trust was somewhat to the left of Miss Tarbell. "Mr. Guggenheim," she felt, "was not so sound in his economics when he preached the reduction of great fortunes by inheritance taxes." Otherwise she upheld his doctrine as "sound sense and sound economics."

Daniel had emerged from his trial before the Industrial Relations Commission with flying colors. He had blurred the public image of the Guggenheims as heartless, soulless exploiters. If some of his statements bordered on demagogy, their exaggeration was needed to whitewash that picture of the Guggenheims as sordid money-grubbers grinding the face of labor. His brothers, not appreciative fully of the effect he was striving for, turned somewhat sour eyes on him for his extravagance of words, but Sam Untermyer and Bernard Baruch, masters of the art of manipulation, congratulated him on a day's work well done.

Indeed, stripped of the generalities, little could be discovered in Dan's testimony to give much heart to an employee of American Smelting and Refining who believed that the principles of organization would work for him as well as for his employers. There was, after all, the bald declaration for the "so-called 'open-shop' "—the very negation of organization in any fruitful meaning of the word. "A man may belong to a union or not as he pleases." But if he did belong, ran the implication of Dan's next sentence, it would be useless waste of money, for American Smelting did not intend to tolerate having a "union organizer walk into our plants and tell us what we shall do." But, in a way, that was the essence of organization, that a union would have the strength to tell the employer what he should do in regard to his employees, within the limitations imposed by collective bargaining.

Despite all the brave words on that fine day before Frank Walsh's commission, Dan Guggenheim had not solved the labor question, as he was to discover.

20. REVOLUCIÓN!

DAN GUGGENHEIM, in his single-minded pursuit of the greatest profit, assisted unwittingly in the birth of the Mexican Revolution of 1910-20. His western mines and smelters bred the apostles of his own country's first native revolutionary movement, the Industrial Workers of the World; from his Mexican mines and smelters arose issues and men which were instrumental in forcing Don Porfirio Díaz, after a third of a century of dictatorship, to flee ignominiously from Chapultepec to Vera Cruz and exile. And to Don Porfirio's presidential throne ascended Dan Guggenheim's chief rival in the Mexican smelting industry, Francisco Madero, a little man no taller than Dan.

During Díaz' golden years no firm wielded greater power than American Smelting and Refining—"Asarco" south of the Rio Grande. Asarco was lord of the mining industry of the Sierras, owner of the choicest properties the Guggenheims could desire. If one great silver mine—Real del Monte—escaped Guggenheim suzerainty, it was because the peerless John Hays Hammond made a bad mistake in rejecting it.

As the Silver Prince, Dan Guggenheim held in his hand the biggest economic factor in Mexico—the price of silver. It was officials of Asarco who represented the Mexican government in international silver conferences, it was Asarco that solved the Government's minting problems, and was rewarded by friendly laws and vigilant police surveillance over its thousands of laborers.

The only people who counted in Mexico were Díaz and his retinue, generals, landowners, and the foreign capitalists —mainly mining, smelting, and railroad magnates. Beneath

324

them lay the Mexican people, illiterate, undernourished, soaked in their misery with alcohol, vice, and disease. Between the overlords and the underlying population were the efficient governors and *Jefes de Operaciones*—the military authorities. In return for the tax revenues that replenished their treasuries, Bernardo Reyes and Luis Terrazas maintained the iron peace under which foreign capital flourished.

When Dan Guggenheim first went to Mexico in 1890 he found a labor problem unique to him. Industrialism was new to the Indian and the *mestizo*. To them it seemed an inhuman and outlandish custom that they should be expected to rise early in the morning and work until nightfall. For centuries they had lived by tilling their corn patches on the mountainside, by fishing and hunting. They loved to lie in the sun, to sing, to watch their women grind the maize and cook the tortillas and frijoles that sustained life. The mines and smelters tore them away from their beloved hillsides, forced them to live in swine-like huts, to work twelve hours a day. A money economy bedeviled them, and the liquor dealer and the gambler had easy answers for them when they went to dispose of their daily wage. American Smelting experimented with Chinese coolies, but these, too, were unsatisfactory.

The mine manager dreaded, year after year, the approach of the rainy season when half or more of his working force might decamp to plant corn. Useless it was to point out to them that they could earn enough money to buy all the corn they needed. To the Mexican it was part of his ritual of life to plant the kernels, to watch the stalks grow, the tassels emerge, to harvest the ripened ears. Buying corn was an empty substitute for growing it.

Gradually the Guggenheims and other mine and smelter owners developed a proletariat divorced from the soil. It was a restive labor force which tried desperately on rare occasions to break through the repression clamped down by mine manager, governor, and the dreaded *rurales*. Strikes were forbidden and unions banned. Despite everything, laborers struck Asarco's Aguascalientes smelter. The strike took the smelter manager by surprise; he laid it to agitators from El Paso, the hated "Tex-mexes" who had learned libertarian ideas in the States.

"The men really didn't know what they wanted," he related years later. "Their leaders came in and when we asked them what they wanted, all they could answer was: '*Mas dinero, menos trabajo*'—more money, less work. I phoned the Governor and when I didn't get action right away, I phoned Mexico City. Next morning a troop of thirty *rurales* came riding up the road. The *Jefe* came into my office and asked me what was wrong. I told him. He clicked his heels, saluted, and strode out.

"Two hours later I saw five men, among them the damned Tex-mexes, marching down the road. Their arms were stretched out, one hand chained to the pommel of a *rurale's* saddle to the right of him, the other to the pommel on the left side.

"A little later the *Jefe* came into my office, saluted, and said: 'Everything's all right now, Señor! Your men are ready to go to work.'

"Well, that evening I walked down the road by the adobe wall that surrounds the smelter, and there was a fresh-dug grave. The five agitators had been lined up against the wall and shot, and their bodies thrown into the grave.

"I asked the *Jefe* next day if he had had a trial for the five fellows.

"'Ah, no, Señor,' he answered. 'We don't bother with trials. It is necessary to keep the courts from becoming congested.'

"That's the way to handle the labor problem," commented the manager. "It's simple and direct and it gets results."

Another mine manager—non-Guggenheim—elucidated

why he had to use the *rurales* to shoot down his striking workmen. "President Díaz," he explained, "ordered me not to raise wages, and I did not dare to disobey him."

Given the *rurales*, there was no labor problem in Mexico that the Guggenheims need worry about in their offices on lower Broadway. So long as the countryside was patrolled by these picked hussars, clad in their gray embroidered ranchero jackets and gray pantaloons, skin tight and adorned with silver buttons, both Díaz and the Guggenheims were safe. Their revolvers ended the uprising at the Guggenheims'. Velardeña smelter in 1909. Their plumed felt hats bobbing among the cactus were the signal that law and order was on the way. Each man was an accomplished horseman, and to each his most precious possession was his saddle, ornately carved and covered with hammered silver.

Sometimes local authorities tried avariciously to tax mining enterprises beyond their due. For these and other local annoyances, John Hays Hammond evolved a technique. He merely announced in the papers that he was going to Mexico City to see Don Porfirio. The effect was instantaneous. The Guggenheims' chief representative insisted that "under existing conditions in Mexico, despotic rule is the only kind possible." Díaz in turn graciously complimented him as a "collaborator in the development of Mexico."

Foreign enterprises such as Asarco sometimes found themselves at a disadvantage in local courts in cases involving native land- and mine-owners. Díaz himself confessed that "innumerable judges have come to tell me that owing to their intense patriotism they find it impossible to pass sentence against Mexican interests." His own system was to appoint lawyers to follow such cases in the local and appeal courts, which were allowed to decide as they chose. But if the verdict, in the view of Díaz' lawyers, was unjustified, "I empower my friends in the Supreme Court to use my name in ordering that justice may be done if they see that the Supreme Court is going to give an unjust verdict."

The Guggenheims kept jealous guard over their provinces. San Luis Potosí was such. In 1906 the *Compañía Metalúrgica Nacional* was organized to build a smelter in Matehuala, whose copper wealth Asarco considered in its chosen territory. The Mexican Mines Department charged that the Guggenheims impeded the efforts to raise capital in Chicago and Pittsburgh. Embarrassed in the 1907-8 panic, the independent smelter company was taken over by Asarco.

A more dangerous enemy was Charles M. Schwab, who saw an outlet for some of his Carnegie millions in the mines of Chihuahua and Tonopah, Nevada. He bought the rich Santoy mines and wanted to build a smelter in Chihuahua City, capital of a state which in 1905 was on the eve of great development. Asarco agents worked swiftly to tie up mines with essential fluxing ores. While Schwab dickered with Enrique C. Creel, the State's banking and industrial boss, for a smelter site, Asarco quietly bought a choice piece of land from Don Luis Terrazas, the governor, right where the two new railroads had their junction. Schwab finally tossed up the sponge and signed long-term contracts with the Guggenheim smelters to take both his Nevada and Chihuahua ores.

Different names would have rung out over the later history of Mexico had the Guggenheims acted decisively when the Madero family, big landowners, decided to open a smelter in Torreón. In 1905 the *Engineering and Mining Journal* reported:

> Had the Trust gone after the Torreón people at the start with the wisdom with which it is usually credited, it could easily have driven them to the wall; but now they have enough mines to be independent and can laugh at the Trust's efforts and can hold out for a stiff figure in the present deal.

Asarco was bargaining for the holdings of the *Compañía Metalúrgica de Torreón,* and negotiations had proceeded far enough for Ernesto Madero to go to New York to talk terms with Dan Guggenheim. Dan offered 4,200,000 pesos but Don Ernesto held out for 5,000,000. Anton Eilers, Dan's crack metallurgist, was sent down to appraise the Torreón properties. Eilers was impressed and Dan boosted the offer to 4,500,000 pesos but the Maderos refused. Another 500,000 pesos and the history of Mexico might have been altered.

Pedro Alvarado, the peon Silver King of Mexico, on the other hand, offered to buy out Asarco, lock, stock and barrel. In 1903 he calmly suggested to John Hays Hammond that he would pay $25,000,000 for the Guggenheim holdings south of the Rio Grande, and Hammond was at a loss to know how seriously to consider the offer. Nine years before Alvarado had been a laborer working for thirty centavos a day. He struck it rich, like Meyer Guggenheim. It was said that a compelling reason for his eagerness to buy out the Guggenheims was to get Hammond's palatial private car in which the great engineer entertained him. When Hammond turned down the $25,000,000 offer, Alvarado promptly added another $10,000,000. Hammond smiled and turned the conversation into other channels.

Besides the Maderos and Alvarado, there were scores of Mexican silver-mine owners who complained as bitterly against the Smelters Trust as did their fellows in Colorado. The government obligingly made a survey which proved that the Trust had a capacity of only 4,000 tons of ore daily against 14,000 for the independents. The independents scorned the implications. Almost all the fifty independent smelters were small plants handling their own ores and remote from railroads. Their finished product, nevertheless, was sold to the Trust at prices set by the Trust, and in quantities desired by the Trust. The independents insisted stubbornly, for all the *Científicos'* figures, that Asarco held unchallenged sway over Mexican mines.

Their discontent mounted as the dictator neared his eightieth year and senility. Powerful figures jockeyed for position in the race to take over Don Porfirio's swaying power in the 1910 elections. Bernardo Reyes, overlord of Nuevo León, coveted the parlous job. Díaz groomed the hated Ramón Corral, his Vice-President. Behind Reyes rallied the discontented, the progressives, and the intellectuals hopeful for an end to reaction. For Reyes they compounded a platform of Mexico for the Mexicans. One plank read:

[The government] has permitted the Guggenheims to monopolize almost completely the important metallurgical industry upon which the progress of mining in the country depended. The Guggenheims controlled the smelter plants of Monterrey, San Luis Potosí, Aguascalientes, and Velardeña and were trying to get a foothold in Pachuca and Real del Monte, thereby forcing the retirement of all the companies that have sunk a great amount of capital in smelters and mining ventures.

Miners, said the Reyistas, were "treated like slaves." The Government was accused of having changed the mining code to assign coal rights to the owners of surface lands, to the enrichment of the Guggenheims who had acquired the valuable Sabinas coal fields in Coahuila for "an insignificant sum."

A leading Mexican savant wailed:

Mexico during the last years of the Porfirian government had been transformed into an enormous market to which the people of all nationalities flocked to make their fortunes until it became a land of adventurers without country, religion, or family, whose God was gold and who, like the gypsies, pitched their tents on the spot which

330

HOW ABSURD! HE WANTS HIS OWN COUNTRY

From "The Best of Art Young." (Courtesy of The Vanguard Press.)

331

Mercury designated as propitious. . . . The monopolization of mines and lands was so wanton that it was no longer possible to find a piece of land as big as the palm of one's hand that did not belong to some American, German, or Spanish capitalist. Everything was auctioned or sold, and the sons of the soil begged at the doors of the palaces of the foreign Croesuses.

Díaz was unimpressed by the criticism, and turned thumbs down on Reyes' candidacy. The governor of Nuevo León was divested of his power and sent abroad on a "mission." His faint-heartedness lost him a prize which, as events were about to prove, was ready to fall to the first one who shook the bough.

All the elements of discontent behind Reyes turned, at his defection, to Francisco Madero, of the smelting family of Torreón. Unlike Reyes, his professed principles did not clash with his record. His simplicity and honesty were essential qualities in a crusade against the pompous, rotten Díaz false-front. And because he was a member of a pre-eminent family of domestic capitalists, bourgeois elements inclined to his banners to ward off the radicals to whom revolt meant social revolution. All the more they were attracted to him as the symbol of another upsurge—that of native capitalists against the paralyzing grip of foreign imperialism.

The revolt of May, 1911, was a pushover. The Díaz régime, challenged by a handful of Maderistas at a frontier city, collapsed like a house of cards and Don Porfirio fled into exile. Madero entered the capital city a shining knight, without fear and without reproach, whose starry-eyed idealism obscured an understanding of the sinister forces which waited to overthrow him.

In the wake of his revolution, strikes broke out in Asarco properties. The men quit "after making unreasonable demands" at the Chihuahua smelter for a 25 per cent wage increase, lower house rents, and the abolition of the Asarco private police and smelter store. Unions proliferated and a state federation of labor was set up in Chihuahua, the first in history. But Madero was no labor agitator. As a smelter owner, he thought twice about permitting labor unrest to overwhelm operators, even though they be the hated Guggenheims. Federal police, as of old, were sent in to break strikes, although with a gentler hand.

Agents of Asarco, losing little love for the rival smelter man who had succeeded Díaz, watched *zopilote*-like, as the forces of disintegration gathered way. Sitting in the American Embassy was their friend, Henry Lane Wilson, who owed his position to Richard A. Ballinger, the villain of the celebrated Pinchot controversy over those Alaska coal lands the Guggenheims coveted. Encouraged by Wilson, dean of the diplomatic corps, Victoriano Huerta and a junta of army officers overthrew the Madero government early in 1913 and assassinated Don Francisco. Huerta was a disciple of the Díaz method. *Poner al rojo el acero* (thrust steel to the red) was his motto.

To the dismay of the mining and oil interests, Huerta's cold steel was unable to halt the march of the Mexican revolution. Standards of revolt were raised in both north and south. With the change in administrations in Washington, the Taft-Ballinger ambassador was withdrawn and Woodrow Wilson, outraged by the assassination of a fellow-President, vowed to overthrow Huerta by diplomatic pressure. Venustiano Carranza and Francisco Villa added their arms and soon all the country was a bloody battlefield. Mines and smelters led an uneasy life, operating as they might when supplies, transport and labor were available. Railroads were commandeered by the generals, bridges blown up with dynamite intended for use in the mines, and workers quit unceremoniously for the brave life of marauding. "What are you fighting for?" John Reed, the journa-

333

list, asked a corporal. "Why, it is good fighting. You don't have to work in the mines."

More royalist than the king, Guggenheim mine and smelter managers were all for intervention. It infuriated them to see their plants crippled while only a few hundred miles away rested thousands of American troops whose generals itched for action. Complained one engineer: "The time is ripe for a concentrated move to induce intervention so we can go on with our work in this country. The Mexican people will never again agree on the organization of a central government." He and other Americans called for annexation of northern Mexico. "This is simply a case," cried one, "where 86 or 87 per cent of the total inhabitants are illiterates, depraved and armed to the teeth, possessing nothing but the blanket on their backs, fighting against a class who are educated, enlightened, and the class who should rule." One and all, the Americans in Monterrey and Chihuahua railed against the Wilson Administration and its anti-Huerta policy.

Dan Guggenheim was more discreet. While he yearned as much as his hired men for stability and believed as firmly as they in Mexico's need of an iron man, he could not overlook the fact that 1912, Madero's year, had been the most profitable in Asarco's history and that in 1913, under Huerta and his rule of frightfulness, Asarco was losing $2,000,000 on its Mexican properties. Leaving for Carlsbad in the summer of 1913, Dan said: "I am going away confident that whatever the administration of Woodrow Wilson does will be for the best interests of all concerned."

It did not pay, Dan concluded, for Asarco to express its preferences when contending forces were still battling for supremacy. Generals of both sides were content to leave smelter and mine property undamaged, realizing full well that taxes and forced levies could not issue from ruined properties. From smelter pots and furnaces, too, came the gold and silver bullion needed to buy guns and ammunition, and consequently they enjoyed a high respect.

But even the smelters closed and American employees of Asarco were evacuated while Carranza-Villa forces locked with Huerta's early in 1914. The Trust, it was said, had to pay $250,000 in bullion to extricate its American employees from Aguascalientes. By midsummer Carranza was in Mexico City. That left the genial, bloody Villa supreme in northern Mexico. Dan Guggenheim's men struck an alliance with Villa. The general was willing, because he needed money. Asarco was pleased, because Carranza had expressed anti-Guggenheim sentiments and it was desirable to drive a wedge between the two leaders of the Constitutionalist forces. In a short time Villa was detached from his lightly held allegiance to the First Chief, and Mexico was once more engulfed in civil war.

"We are on the most friendly terms with Villa and his men," announced an Asarco official. "On several occasions they have gone out of their way to extend assistance to our company." One was the time the Industrial Workers of the World appeared in Chihuahua to organize Guggenheim smeltermen. Villa curtly told the organizers to get out or he would shoot them. "That ended the matter," curtly summed up the *Engineering and Mining Journal*. Asarco denied that it paid tribute to Villa; but the truth was that Villa operated in Guggenheim mining and smelting territory only through the financial assistance given him by friendly Asarco managers.

General Carranza, trying desperately to extend his rule, complained to President Wilson against the activities of George C. Carothers, American agent with the Villa forces. In a personal appeal, Carranza declared:

The special interests that have played such an important part in American politics and sustained the corrupt

335

administrations of the past are in league with this same Doroteo Arango [Francisco Villa] to put him in power in Mexico and enjoy rare concessions in the country and exploit the nation as heretofore. I would call attention to the significant fact that the Hearst chain of papers— Mr. Wilson's mortal enemies—are lending their columns to the aid of Arango [Villa] in every move he makes; Harrison Gray Otis's *Los Angeles Times* is taking the same attitude; and the Guggenheim interests, with all their powers of corruption, wish to make of Mexico a field of exploitation like Alaska and Colorado, and to that end are, we sincerely believe, lending not only moral support but also financial aid to the Arango [Villa] revolt, hoping to seat Arango in the Dictator's chair and thus gain the field of exploitation sought.

The Trust replied that "this company's representatives have been particularly careful not to interfere in the politics of Mexico and to refuse all requests for financial support of any faction."

This was undoubtedly the correct policy, but too many engineers testified that the Guggenheim interests were openly allied with Villa against Carranza for the company's statement to obtain much credence. Undoubtedly Carranza was mistaken in thinking that so shrewd a capitalist as Dan Guggenheim wished to see an unreliable cutthroat like Villa elevated to the Presidency; the alliance was a temporary one in which Asarco bent to the fact that Villa controlled most of the territory in which it operated. As the company announced in 1915, five of its plants in Villa territory in Durango and Chihuahua were operating whereas none worked in Carranza territory. Carranza had levied a tax on smelters eight times as great as that imposed under the Díaz régime.

While other American capitalists lost heart, Dan Guggenheim was confident that sooner or later exhaustion would end the civil war and that profits as rich as ever lay in store for the forehanded. So during the worst year—1915—when Constitutionalists and Villa troops fought across northern Mexico, Asarco cagily invested some $2,700,000 in Mexican mines owned by the skittish who were glad to sell out for a song. By 1916 Villa was reduced to guerrilla tactics. Asarco swung to the winner and now Pancho turned fiercely against the Smelters Trust. A party of sixteen mining men, negotiating with him for a truce to permit their mines to operate, were murdered in cold blood. Chihuahua and Durango smelters closed. Villa took over the Chihuahua plant to extract silver, but he succeeded only in ruining some of the equipment. Slowly the Constitutionalists circled Villa while Asarco advanced gold to Carranza through an understanding with the Federal Reserve Board.

In the wake of civil war came typhus. The Guggenheims, out of their own pockets, equipped a medical expedition to stamp the plague out of Aguascalientes, where five thousand cases were reported, so they could reopen their smelter. Their ranks reinforced by men who had gained their experience in war-torn Serbia, the expedition, clad in rubber and silk, fought the dread disease.

When Alvaro Obregón, the *buen ranchero* of Sonora, came to power in 1920, the bloody decade of the Mexican revolution ended. American Smelting and Refining rejoiced in the return of a strong man to rule the country and gave evidence of its confidence by investing millions in a by-product coke plant in Coahuila which, unlike other Asarco communities, boasted a model village for laborers. The fierce controversy which raged between Obregón and the oil companies passed Asarco by. All its concessions and mining properties had been acquired before 1917, the date of the new Constitution. When Obregón was in a tight place in the

1924 rebellion, Asarco advanced taxes to help him quell the uprising.

One result of the turbulent decade was a more enlightened labor policy. The *rurales* existed no more and strike leaders were not summarily shot. Asarco gained the reputation of being the best employer in all Mexico. It established welfare practices introduced in its United States plants in 1911. The eight-hour day became general and children under sixteen were barred from employment.

Asarco nevertheless refused to deal with the new miners' union. It closed the Chihuahua smelter rather than sign a contract. The state legislature thereupon passed laws giving workers a percentage of their employer's net income and providing for the union's right to audit books. Asarco used its newer techniques. It closed the mines and smelter, negotiated with Obregón, and reopened on its own terms. Asarco representatives knew how to massage local courts and humor the military commanders, nourished from Asarco taxes. In case a controversy became serious, the company held the whip hand, the threat to close the plant, throw thousands out of work, and dry up the public revenues. No matter how much a leader might hate the Guggenheims and their monopoly, the ties that bound the great mines and smelter company to Mexico's economic life were too intimate to admit of sudden, drastic action.

It was not until the Obregón-Calles régimes had passed and General Lazaro Cárdenas, the Socialist leader of Michoacán, was inaugurated, that the Union of Miners and Metal Workers made much headway in Asarco plants. In 1931, under a Calles administration, the Monterrey smelter workers struck suddenly, allowing the lead to "freeze" in the pots and causing damage claimed at $100,000. Asarco appealed to Mexico City, the police were sent out and the picket line smashed and the agitators fired. Under the Cárdenas régime, on the other hand, Secretary A. Guzmán of the miners union organized the smelter workers and negotiated an agreement that included the company check-off of union dues, a 36 per cent wage increase, the establishment of union offices on company property, and a grievance set-up. Wages ranged upward from a three-peso bottom; the compensation laws were strictly enforced. Asarco professed its satisfaction, the more so as labor costs were but a small item in the running of a smelter.

Union and management snarled however at its San Luis Potosí smelter. The men went out in 1936 and Asarco stolidly refused to negotiate or listen to federal arbitration. In the face of a general strike in all Asarco properties, the company yielded, signing an agreement, paying 10 per cent of the wages lost during the strike—320,000 pesos—plus 10,000 pesos for strike expenses. The minimum wage was boosted from 2 to 2.70 pesos a day with smaller increases for higher-paid men.

American mining people, vexed by the enforcement of the laws under Cárdenas and the activities of union organizers, yearned for the good old days of Díaz when the *rurales* took care of economic discontent. Many accused Asarco of selfishly abandoning the united front of American mining interests in order to make peace with the government. In the Foreign Club at Monterrey, sipping Doctor Peppers, mining men alternately cursed the Mexican and American governments the while they related horrendous stories of their sufferings under spiny Cárdenas and spineless Josephus Daniels. The operator of a new gold mine recounted the appearance on his property of a union officer who organized his men and demanded a 90 per cent wage increase. That refused, the organizer gave the needed legal notice, ten days' warning of an impending strike. The operator called in a squad of troops, furnished obligingly by the *Jefe de Operaciones*, and obtained an *amparo* (injunction) from the district judge. The union contested the injunction. The operator had a friend in Mexico who knew a Supreme Court justice. He inquired about the chances for having the *amparo* upheld. "Under the Cárdenas administration," he was informed, "we have instructions to decide all labor cases in favor of the union." It sounded like the Díaz technique, in reverse. The operator, declaring that he could not run his mine on the new wage scale, settled with the union for 23,-000 pesos strike pay, as provided by law, paid three months' discharge pay, also required by law, and an allowance to older employees in accordance with the number of years of their employment, all at a cost of 90,000 pesos. "Then I shut her down and down she'll stay so long as Cárdenas is running things."

The smaller American interests still sang the old intervention song, speculating on the great development northern Mexico would enjoy under the Stars and Stripes. But American Smelting and Refining, in the spirit of Daniel Guggenheim, was more realistic. It realized that "the good old days" of Díaz had gone, never to return. Its plants operated profitably even under Cárdenas. Let others dream of the united front—the simultaneous closure of all properties—by which they hoped to paralyze the government and stir up local forces of reaction to rise in revolt. Happy in the profits wrung through monopoly, Asarco sat contentedly on top of the heap.

21. COPPER LORDS AND THE WAR

IN the summer of 1914 Daniel Guggenheim was at Carlsbad, as was his custom, mending an ailing body and posting himself on those phases of European politics of interest to America's most important merchant of metals. Dan had planned carefully for the war which he knew was brewing, but so suddenly did the armies begin to march and so quickly did he flee Germany that he arrived in London penniless and had to cable for funds as his overseas account was tangled up in the war's first frenzy. "Now you know how. it feels to be broke," said his son, Harry, as he sent money.

Dan enjoyed the joke, the more so as he believed M. Guggenheim's Sons stood on the threshold of the greatest prosperity the partnership had ever known. He cabled his brothers to disregard the gloomy panic talk in Wall Street. Within a month he was back at 120 Broadway, preparing for the golden harvest and marveling at the blindness of his fellow-captains of industry and finance who saw only ruined trade and vanished markets. He announced:

We are in the presence of the greatest opportunity in the history of this country. It is up to the press and public-spirited men to emphasize this. It is a public duty. Ordinarily, I do not advocate paternalism in the central government, but I believe this the exception that proves the rule. Let everyone push and pull to get started. Washington should pass laws, and speedily, to develop our finance and commerce, ship subsidies, special bills, anything necessary to get going.

Almost breathlessly, the head of the House of Guggenheim shouted his message:

For the first time the world's marts lie at our feet uncontested. Our European competitors are hopelessly crippled for the time being, and it is up to us to reap the benefits.

There must be financing and plenty of it, but we can do it. The new currency act gives us power to finance a thousand millions of trade. The machinery to set this country humming is at hand—it only remains to see whether we are energetic and enterprising enough to set it in motion. The outlook? In six months, even less, I expect this country to be fairly boiling with activity.

It was apparent that war meant only one thing to Dan—business, more business, business, world without end. Whatever compassion he harbored in his heart for the young men of Europe, he found no time now to utter it or to lift a voice against the lucrative trade that was eventually to drag his own sons into the mêlée.

War could not have come at a more propitious time for the Guggenheims. They, at least, were ready, with the world's greatest copper mines awaiting a lusty market. The wondrous Bonanza lode on Kennecott Creek was swinging into full production; down at the other end of the Pacific, development work was being rushed on Chile's fabulous Chuquicamata porphyry copper field. Utah Copper, Nevada Consolidated, Ray and Chino, the porphyries of the West, awaited the war industries which were to call for ever more copper to feed the maws of cannon and machine guns.

With foresight that seemed uncanny to observers after the event, the Guggenheims had read the writing in the skies as Europe staggered along under ever mounting war budgets in the years before 1914, and had thrown their energy into the coppers. They knew the war budgets and the Anglo-German naval race were not to be in vain. Observers declared the Guggenheims were intent on their own business suicide, developing so many great copper properties that the world could not absorb their products; the market would break and all copper men would go down to common ruin. The brothers smiled. In the deepest gloom of the fall of 1914, when it seemed the world had crashed, Sol was buoyant. "We shall not stop development work on any of our [copper] properties," he announced. "Contracts for our Chile Copper Company development, placed in Germany, will be transferred to America."

Dan had only one fear to plead to. The Department of Justice was still snooping about in the affairs of his Smelters Trust. The roar against monopoly which thundered across the land after the panic of 1893 and echoed in 1908, was renewed as the metal markets hit the doldrums in 1913-14. Mine operators recited their old woes: the Trust made excessive deductions for moisture and objectionable elements in the ore; fixed an arbitrary valuation on metals, exacted exorbitant charges for treating ore; cheated on sampling and assaying; made an extra profit on selling the refined metal. In Montana, Colorado and Utah, mine owners tried in vain to coax financial interests into the smelting field and when this failed, talked of starting their own smelters. Always they were snagged on the long-term contracts which the Trust had providentially exacted. Few big ore-shippers were free at any one time to throw enough business to justify the erection of a competing smelter.

State legislative action was futile, so the operators' associations and the American Mining Congress asked Taft, and later, Wilson to act to enforce the law. Emboldened by the seeming success of the Standard Oil dissolution and the Government's suit against the U. S. Steel Corporation, western mining interests demanded that American Smelting and Refining be haled on the carpet. Attorney General Wickersham said he would look into it, and Smelters shares broke badly on Wall Street. When nothing happened, Congressman Martin of Colorado introduced a resolution to prod the Department of Justice and Victor Berger, the Milwaukee Socialist, asked an inquiry into the Trust's plan to take over minting from the U. S. Treasury. Wickersham finally reported there was no Trust. Martin demanded that Congress hold its own investigation of the "most audacious of all illegal combines." Such an inquiry, said the doughty Martin, would throw "some light on the financial and political relations of the Guggenheims. Not only," he predicted, "will the Guggenheim 'barrel' run like slag from a furnace in lining up Taft delegates in Colorado, but in the event of his nomination, the same barrel will be used to debauch the electorate of the state."

With Woodrow Wilson in the White House, Department of Justice agents percolated through Colorado, listening to the stories of the independent smelters at Golden and Florence and their untimely demise, and the plaints of those mine owners with enough courage to mount the witness stand against the Trust. Attorney General McReynolds, later to be Supreme Court justice, was cautious and conservative. Dan, for his own part, was acting resolutely. He hired the retiring U. S. Labor Commissioner to take charge of the Trust's welfare bureau and gained kudos for his progressive attitude on the labor question. And he retained former President Roosevelt's private secretary, William Loeb, Jr., to represent the Trust in Washington. Publicly Dan deplored the small-minded attitude of some people there. With the war's clarion call to American business to step in and take the world's trade, such opportunities were open that "the Government should now stop baiting the trusts." Two years earlier Dan had been gloomy over the U. S. Steel investigation; he feared that "pre-natal prosperity" might never get born because of the way in which capital, the sire of prosperity, was being antagonized.

Lead interests in the Idaho Coeur D'Alenes charged.

There is no doubt that American Smelting and Refining has so manipulated matters as to secure to itself practically undisputed sway. Combination with its erstwhile victims has killed competition and when outside contracts expire, the entire district [the Idaho silver-lead region] will pass under the domination of the most unscrupulous and rapacious combination that has ever squeezed life out of legitimate business.

The Department's investigation dragged on until the rising metal market of 1915 once again stilled the clamor of mine operators in the flood of profits that began to roll in on all—both Trust and independent.

Presently arose matters of much more concern. The British Navy was seizing copper shipments to Italy, fearful that their ultimate destination was Germany. The Guggenheims and the Lewisohns were believed in London to be tainted with pro-Germanism. They were notified that if they wanted Allied business, they would have to play the game straight from the Allied point of view. By March, 1915, this had been arranged. Secretary Bryan had put his O.K. on direct negotiations between the Guggenheims and the British embassy in Washington and thenceforward copper was shipped to Europe with the consent of the British Government. It was an ominous portent, in view of President Wilson's repeated assurances of America's neutrality.

The last shred of neutrality was thrown away October 1, 1915, when the firm of M. Guggenheim's Sons was among the first to subscribe to Morgan's $500,000,000 Anglo-French war loan. Proceeds were to be spent for American goods and it was understood that subscribers would be favored. Leading American industrialists who hoped to profit from Allied orders absorbed large blocks of the loan. M. Guggenheim's Sons took $2,500,000 and Kennecott Copper, $2,000,000.

The Allies showered upon the Guggenheims demands for all the copper their mines and smelters could produce. A thrill ran along the keel of Isaac Guggenheim, oldest and most phlegmatic of the brothers. He expressed it thus:

> I will say that the longer the war continues in Europe the better it will be for us. In a short time the trouble abroad will make the United States the money center of the world and we are certain to become a creditor instead of a debtor nation.

To meet Europe's needs, Dan rushed the development of a great ore deposit down on the Chilean desert, known as Chuquicamata. He had not gotten into Chuqui a moment too soon. True, one of his own engineers, scouting Antofagasta as far back as 1900, had written his employer about a wonderful copper deposit midway between the ocean and the Andes on Chile's narrow littoral. The Guggenheims could have it for £45,000, but Dan wouldn't waste a postage stamp on the lean copper ore on a hillside ten thousand miles away. In that he joined his brother Ben, who tossed away a chance in the same year to take an interest in old Colonel Wall's copper mountain in Bingham Canyon. Ten years later Dan was glad to hand over $25,000,000 in stock for control of Chuqui.

Perhaps Dan was sour about Chile in those early days. He had contracted to smelt Huanchaco's silver ores under a contract, penny-wise and pound-foolish, that provided no payment to the mine for lead if it ran less than 15 per cent, and a return for only the percentage above 15 on richer ore. It turned out to be a hard ore to treat and the Guggenheim smelter needed lead. Rather than revise the contract, the Guggenheims imported lead from Australia and found the shipping charges too high. Then they turned to British Columbia and later began shipping lead to far-away Chile from their Perth Amboy refinery. Finally they closed their Antofagasta smelter—stiffnecked to the end.

346

After Dan Jackling and his crew proved that 2 per cent porphyry coppers were really the richest mines in the world, Albert C. Burrage, a Boston engineer, one of the two original owners, of seven, who had stuck to his investment in Chino in New Mexico, had his agents poking around London looking for reports of likely properties. He learned of Chuqui, rushed engineers to Chile, and instructed them to tie up all the claims within miles. He brought that property, thus integrated, to Dan, and in due time Guggenheim Exploration's ace engineer, Pope Yeatman, inspected Chuqui after looking over the Braden copper mines, already owned by the House of Guggenheim.

Chuqui was almost as tough a proposition to handle as Kennecott. Fortunately, the little narrow-gauge railroad that panted from Antofagasta up to Bolivia's 16,000-foot elevations, passed reasonably near. But the ore lay in one of the driest spots in the whole world, a vast waterless wilderness, 9,000 feet high, a waste of sand and rock, avoided even by high-flying birds. The first drilling crews got their water from the port 150 miles away by train and horse cart. The tests in 1912 revealed ore even richer than Burrage had claimed, richer than Utah Copper's. In comparison, Kennecott, despite ore that ran ten times as rich in lodes and veins deep under the earth, was a mere flash in the pan. For here at Chuqui, reported Burrage, were 300,000,000 tons of 2.23 per cent ore, readily accessible on the surface of a gently sloping hill, 8,000 feet long and 1,000 feet wide. Quite appropriately the Guggenheims' newly organized Chile Exploration Company bought the machinery that Army engineers were beginning to discard on the nearly finished Panama Canal for an excavation that would be even greater than Panama's.

Chile Exploration built a 53,000 horsepower oil electric plant costing $3,500,000, at a poor little port called Tocopilla, 89 miles away by beeline on the Coast, to bring power and light to the desert. For water Chilex obtained a concession from the Government—which carefully rationed the Andes' water—for 2,160 tons of fresh water daily, and 30,000 tons for industrial use from a salt river only 40 miles away toward the mountains.

All in all, Chilex had to put $12,000,000 into the construction and equipment of a property to handle 10,000 tons of ore and produce 360,000 pounds of copper daily. Bernard Baruch and his partner, Eugene Meyer, Jr., were lost in admiration for a concern that could handle ore complete through to the market for $2.10 a ton, or 5.853 cents a pound for the refined copper, delivered in America or Europe, and continue doing it for eighty-three years. Gladly they consented to act as midwives for the new Chile Copper Company which they felt was not overvalued at $110,000,000. They invited the investing public to compensate the Guggenheims for their $12,000,000 outlay by subscribing to a $15,000,000 bond issue. Of the 3,800,000 shares of $25 par value stock, Engineer-Promoter Burrage received 1,000,000 shares in handsome remuneration for his trouble, and M. Guggenheim's Sons salted away the remainder in their vaults. It was to prove the richest of all their investments although it had cost them only the bill for engraving—and perhaps even that was taken care of by the bond-buying public.

Dan was, of course, president of Chile Copper, while Burrage and Murry Guggenheim shared the vice presidencies, Yeatman became consulting engineer and a new name, that of E. A. Cappelen Smith, appeared as chief metallurgist. He was the engineer whose experiments, on a commercial scale, had proved up the $2.10 a ton figure which satisfied Baruch and Meyer, and justified them in selling $15,000,000 in bonds to the public. Before Cappelen Smith was the staggering task of seeing that his process—which for the first time sidetracked smelting and refining, and turned the copper concentrates into electrolytic copper right at the mine—would work as well on 10,000 tons a day as in his smaller plant. He had to prove that, day in and day out, $2.10 really could cover the cost of treating a ton of Chile desert and extracting 36 pounds of marketable copper which, by 1916, was to fetch $9.

A city had to be built out there in the desert at the base of Chuqui hill, altitude nine thousand feet, to house the American staff and the Chilean laborers. Fortunately it was a model city and not a duplicate of the slums of Perth Amboy, El Paso and Pueblo. Two bright and shining developments arose, one for Americans, the other for Chileans, with Catholic and Protestant churches, schools, recreation halls, liquor banned, and barracks for a picked troop of Carbineros to handle whatever problems of law and order might arise from the "proud, independent, and improvident" Chilean laborers.

The Chilean Government was delighted to have a taxable industry arise where no life had hitherto existed, and cooperated gladly with the Guggenheims. It in turn was praised by Chile Copper as stable, progressive and sympathetic to mining enterprises. Both sides were happy, and the Guggenheims especially, because they paid for labor and supplies bought in Chile in terms of a depreciated currency, and sold their copper on a gold basis only.

Chile Copper was to be ready March 1, 1915, to pour its wealth into war markets. Braden Copper, the Guggenheims' smaller development at Rancagua, Chile, was already in full swing. It was of this promotion, and its repeated appeals to the public purse through bond issues, of which Garet Garrett wrote indignantly in *Collier's* in 1912:

There is a particular brand of finance hardly any more popular in Wall Street than elsewhere, which may be called Guggenheim finance. A Guggenheim prospectus appealing to private capital, in the first instance, is a marvel of typographical beauty. It is done on heavy calendared paper, expensive to the touch and suggestive to the imagination . . . a perfect document treating of history, climate, geology, society, costs, capitalization, profits.

For all that, Braden Copper was far from being one of Wall Street's worst promotions. Its capitalization was pegged at $14,000,000 in $5 par value stock, held by the Guggenheims, and $9,000,000 in bonds. Bill Braden, who knew the mines of Chile at least as well as those of the Rockies, had picked up the old Rancagua mines in 1904, had used 2,500 oxen to drag in machinery over a dirt road and had sold the property to the waiting Guggenheims. By 1915 it was producing 50,000,000 pounds of copper yearly at a cost of 7.75 cents a pound—not so cheap as Chuqui or Kennecott but good enough as copper bounded up from 15 cents to 25.

The *New York Times* looked over the millions the Guggenheims were investing in Chile and philosophized:

> The Guggenheims were willing to spend millions for the development of our distant and much-neglected province of Alaska but the government would not have it. It would not permit them to carry on large-scale coal mining or to build railroads. . . . The Guggenheims were forbidden to do business in Alaska but they have an open-handed welcome in Chile where they will carry on one of the world's largest copper mining industries. . . . If Washington continues to turn out bills and laws according to its present policy and its present temper, American capital will presently shun industrial investments. The policy if adhered to will undoubtedly be vastly helpful to China and to Chile. The consequences to ourselves are too obvious to require pointing out.

A notable result of the Guggenheim invasion of Chile with the first big-scale investment in the country's history at a time of demoralization of the pound sterling was the conquest of the west coast of South America by the United States dollar. Dollar exchange became current for the first time, thanks to Chile Copper and the growing interests of American Smelting and Refining in Chilean and Bolivian copper, lead, and tin ore. Even British mining companies found it difficult to finance their needs with drafts on London. Chile and Braden obliged mine owners and industrialists with dollar drafts on New York, through the co-operation of the Chilean Government, and this was extended to the nitrate industry. The innovation swung up through Bolivia and Peru to Ecuador, and the reign of London over the west coast ended.

Dan Guggenheim was not the man to sit idly by, complacent in the ownership and control of the majority of the copper output of the two Americas while the European nations clamored frantically for more and more copper. His was not a production mind but rather one that looked at all things from the point of view of the promoter and financier. Chile, Braden, Kennecott, Utah, Nevada, Ray and Chino were pouring out millions in dividends? Good, but not good enough. There was always the public to be considered. It clamored for admittance to the new speculative field of the coppers and Dan and his confreres hastened to oblige.

Why not hitch all the coppers together and pour out millions more in stock and bond certificates? In that way income from these mines could be doubled and the troublesome loss that loomed on the $20,000,000 Copper River and Northwestern Railroad up in the Alaskan wilderness could be spread among the many. The Morgan firm was worried when its partner, George W. Perkins, reported that Kennecott, rich as it was, could not pay off the expense of the railroad built to tap it. The Guggenheims had made a mistake. Senator Simon, in his last year at Washington, tried to get the government to buy the road for use as a link in the projected line to the interior. Simon got Vice-President Sherman to introduce him and his brother Dan to President Taft. Commented the *Engineering and Mining Journal:* "If the Government should buy the Copper River for $20,000,000 and should saddle the charge upon Alaska, it would be a staggering blow to the mining industry of that territory."

But Taft remembered his sad experience with Secretary Ballinger and the Guggenheim coal lands, and did not wish in a Presidential election year to toss in a $20,000,000 argument to his opponents. In 1914 J. P. Morgan himself made a special trip to Washington to see Secretary Lane about selling the road. The great man waited his turn in the Secretary's anteroom. His sales talk apparently did not take. It became urgent to pass on Kennecott's liability, and what better time than now, when the great investing public was greedy for copper stocks?

Dan and his brothers, Sol and Murry, conferred with the brightest minds in lower Manhattan on this problem: with Baruch, Charles Hayden, Sam Untermyer and Dwight Morrow. They decided it was best to throw all the Guggenheim coppers into one bag, and as a first step, to dismantle Guggenheim Exploration. By May 17, 1916, Dan was able to inform Guggenex stockholders that on an investment of $27,650,000, they had realized $97,171,000 in sixteen short years. Dividends of $24,152,000 had been paid and assets of $73,018,000 had been distributed. And what assets! A whole row of war-babies, whose stocks were booming on the Exchange! Typical were Utah Copper shares with a par value of $4,000,000 and a market value of $30,000,000. On such securities, Guggenex had been a steady player, with dividends averaging $3,000,000 a year, or 10 to 16 per cent.

Dan advised his stockholders, who comprised, in addition to his brothers, principally the Whitneys and Thomas Fortune Ryan, that it would be impracticable to distribute Guggenex's holdings in copper stocks and unwise to dump them on the market. They proposed an exchange which involved the creation of the Kennecott Copper Corporation. This ambitious scheme would start out modestly with 720,000 no par value shares and take over the Morgan-Guggenheim Alaska Syndicate holdings in Kennecott. The Morgan firm would lend $10,000,000 to the new firm in mortgage bonds convertible into stock at $25 a share.

This accomplished, Kennecott would promptly enlarge its capitalization to 3,000,000 shares. Of the 2,280,000 new shares, apportionment would be made this way:

(1.) 606,756 shares to buy Guggenex's investment in Utah Copper.

(2.) 800,000 shares to buy Guggenex's investment in Braden Copper.

(3.) 200,000 shares to buy the Alaska Syndicate's interest in Copper River and Northwestern and Alaska Steamship.

(4.) 400,000 shares to retire the Morgan $10,000,000 bond issue on Kennecott.

(5.) 65,000 shares to compensate the underwriters.

To accommodate the leftovers, the Yukon-Alaska Trust was organized to assume Guggenex's interest in the Guggenheim-Ryan Congo Company, some Smelters Securities stock, and Yukon Gold's 2,800,000 shares, for which there was no market because gold operations were being closed in the North. To cover Yukon Gold's obligations, the Trust was given $1,000,000 in cash.

The Guggenheims went cheerfully about the creation of the new Kennecott Corporation. When the public appetite for its shares had been whetted by encouraging dispatches from the North by Henry Crumb, chief metallurgist: "Kennecott a world beater . . . ore showing is the greatest in the history of mining and has wonderful possibilities," and the no par value shares had risen from $25 to $50, it was decided that the time had come to unload more of the new issue. William Boyce Thompson was cut in as manager of the Kennecott syndicate. The underwriters, it was said, had obligated themselves to put up $65,000,000 in case the holders of the various stocks in Guggenheim Exploration demanded cash instead of new Kennecott shares. As three-fourths of Guggenex stock was held by the Guggenheims, the Whitneys and Ryan, this prospect seemed remote and as a matter of fact less than 1 per cent asked cash. The syndicate nevertheless received $3,400,000 for the "risk" they had assumed, to be split up with the Guggenheims and the Morgan firm. Some called it barefaced robbery of Kennecott shareholders and the business conduct committee of the Stock Exchange was called upon to do justice. It was charged that the syndicate had "churned" the stock and turned the market into a "washboard." The Guggenheims, it was said, were in the business of manufacturing stocks rather than copper. To the practical men on the business conduct committee, there was nothing extraordinary in that. Some members of the syndicate, it was explained, had tired of the slow process of doling out the new stock through the syndicate managers and had acted for themselves. The Guggenheims, however, sold none of theirs. The Treasury Department showed great interest in Kennecott's new "no par value" stock. Its agents believed that this was a dodge to avoid payment of the new tax of 5 cents a share on new stocks issued in denominations of $100 or less.

Perhaps the critics were a little too insistent on the amount of "churning" needed for a war-baby. All copper stocks were shooting up. Chile Copper's $25 par value stock —none of which represented any actual investment—was quoted in August, 1916, at 39, which gave that promotion a market valuation of $148,000,000. As for new Kennecott,

354

this reconstruction of Guggenheim Exploration Company now had a market value of $195,000,000.

That part of southwestern Alaska which depended on Guggenheim copper entered its greatest boom. Every boat in the Alaska trade, whether on the Nome or the southeastern Alaska runs, was pulled hundreds of miles out of its route to stop at Cordova, port of the Kennecott mines. More cargo left that one harbor outbound, than came into all Alaska. In one week, shipments to the value of $1,000,000 made Cordova the world's biggest copper port. The Tacoma smelter was overwhelmed, and long trains crawled over the Cascades and up the Snake River, bound for the smelter on the shores of Great Salt Lake.

It was during this period that the firm which stood at the center of this network of hundred million dollar properties, reorganized itself. The partnership of M. Guggenheim's Sons provided for dissolution or reorganization after the death of a partner. The *Titanic* took Ben with it to the bottom of the ocean on April 15, 1912, and reorganization was imperative, the more so as the five older brothers wished to take in new blood. It was as old Meyer would have had it, the firm perpetuating itself from the third generation. But whereas Meyer had seven sons, all those seven could muster only two eligibles to the new partnership of Guggenheim Brothers. Let geneticists ponder the problem of the evaporation of hardy old Meyer Guggenheim's stock in the male line: three of his sons had three daughters each and no sons; Daniel had two sons, only one of whom showed business aptitude; Murry had one; Simon's oldest died and the other was not in good health; and William's lone son was still too young to count even had his father been an active member of the firm.

The new partnership of Guggenheim Brothers (Will objected to the continued title of M. Guggenheim's Sons if he was not included) announced to the world on March 7, 1916, that it was composed of Meyer's five oldest sons, and Harry F., Dan's second son, Edmond A., son of Murry, and in contravention of Meyer's earnest injunctions, an outsider, William C. Potter. Potter had grown up with American Smelting and Refining, had been in charge of their Mexican operations, and had switched over to Guaranty Trust to become first vice-president. Now he returned to Guggenheim Brothers to take charge of their Chilean business because of his wide acquaintance with Latin American methods. Harry and Edmond were made his assistants, and to this triumvirate was entrusted the supervision of the family's Chilean affairs. Potter remained on Guaranty's board and executive committee—a useful link. But to the older Guggenheims, his admittance to their own partnership, welcome as it was, must have seemed a portent of the distant doom they saw overhanging the House of Guggenheim, waning at its center at the very moment when it was expanding to unprecedented heights of power and wealth.

The reorganization of M. Guggenheim's Sons would have been a routine affair had it not been for Will, youngest brother and family black sheep. Will, with his brother, Ben, had disagreed sharply with his older brothers when they took the family's smelting interests into the Smelters Trust in exchange for control of that combine. Will believed the family should stick to its own business; publicly he announced that he was skeptical of the Wall Street promotional flavor of the Trust and would have nothing to do with it. So with an income of $250,000 Will "retired" in 1900 at the age of 31, after seven years of partnership, to devote himself, as he said, to philanthropy and good works. But by the time that M. Guggenheim's Sons was being reorganized in 1913, Will's income had dwindled far below $250,000. Hungrily he looked at the Chile Copper promotion. He announced that he wanted "in." Dan refused.

Will struck back with fury. He entered suit in New York

court for a division of the Chile spoils, claiming that he had been fraudulently hoodwinked out of $10,000,000, one-sixth interest in the company. The complaint harked back to that old legal principle on which other Guggenheim cases had been fought—that of *uberrima fides*, or utmost faith, as among partners and business associates.

Their own brothers, he said, had tricked Ben and him into signing away their rights in Chile Copper by concealing the real nature of the wealth of the project. To him it had been represented as a venture into which millions must be sunk. Indeed, many copper men themselves had said that when Chile went into full production, the world market could never stand such a flood of the metal, prices would break and stark ruin would involve all the copper companies.

The brothers stood arrayed in court—five stocky figures bereft of their usual expansive good nature, staring sullenly across the room or at papers; and separated by a space, the embittered Will, full of hatred and intent on the $10,-000,000 he claimed was his. His wife was at his side. Shielding the five older brothers was an array of New York's most expensive legal talent—Sam Untermyer, Louis Marshall, William D. Guthrie, John B. Stanchfield, Francis Lynde Stetson. The judge refused to dismiss Will's complaint. They appealed. The appellate court likewise turned down their motion for a judgment on the pleadings and ordered the case to trial.

The action hinged on the waivers Will and Ben signed January 4, 1912, permitting their older brothers to form the Chile Copper Company. Will repudiated the waiver, saying it was signed in ignorance as a result of fraudulent concealment.

Sam Untermyer replied in an address that ran the emotional gamut from indignation to contempt. From the day he had been taken into the partnership in 1893, Will had added no assets to the firm, Untermyer said. After his retirement he had shown no interest whatever in the business. He had repeatedly signed waivers as the brothers went into new ventures. And now, after hearing the favorable engineering reports on Chuqui, he came crying "Fraud!" According to Untermyer, Big Brother Dan had told wayward Will that he could come back into the partnership if he would stop his "idleness and speculation." "I will give you an interest and lend you the money," said Dan. "But you can't come into this one [Chile Copper]; it is closed, but you can come into all ventures hereafter." Will was quoted as replying: "No, if you won't give me an interest in the Chuquicamata venture, I won't come back."

Untermyer then swung into the legal technicalities: Will had signed the waiver so he was barred from bringing this action. The Chuqui deal was not a partnership venture but undertaken by the five brothers individually. They had no duty to divulge secrets to non-members of the firm. They were under no obligation to supply detailed facts on Chuqui to Will, especially as he had been signing waivers for twelve years without question. If the brothers felt that Chuqui was to be profitable, nevertheless they were not called upon to express this opinion to Will, and certainly not without specific inquiry on his part. They had put him "on inquiry" by informing him of the venture and if he had no further curiosity to ask questions, they were not bound to enter into the minutiae of the project. And even if there were fraud, Will would have to show he was damaged, which he had failed to do. As for the $60,000,000 profits the brothers were alleged to have garnered, so far there wasn't a penny as the mine was still being developed. Millions had been dumped into Chuqui with no return.

Will's attorneys returned to the fray with exhibits of the partnership agreement of 1893 which forbade any of the brothers to enter any mining deal individually. His retirement in 1900 was only temporary and in 1911 he had been accepted back in active partnership and made chairman of the board of International Steam Pump, one of brother Ben's less fortunate promotions. They however had continued to refuse him access to business secrets, violating the "implicit confidence" which they should have exercised toward all members of the firm. Certainly had he known the real nature of the Chuqui venture, he would have entered it.

The trial had proceeded one week and Will's attorneys were on the point of forcing into the record the accounts of M. Guggenheim's Sons when the brothers ran up the white flag. They had no taste for airing the business secrets of the firm in public where all the world might stare curiously at the goings-on in this powerful family, and snicker. Will had played his trump card . . . and won.

Untermyer denied that they had settled for $5,000,000 but he refused to reveal what terms had been reached. Beyond saying that Will would settle for not a penny less than $5,000,000 his attorney likewise declined to make public the settlement. The *Brooklyn Eagle* reported that $5,000,-000 was the figure, of which Will's attorney was to get $500,000. "Preposterous," said Untermyer. And with that the curtain was rung down on another celebrated Guggenheim vs. Guggenheim case.

By August 1, 1916, even $5,000,000 had ceased to be a staggering figure for the five brothers. Never in all the history of the country had there been such a year as 1916; the dividends came rolling in as the Allied nations extended their credit to dangerous tension to provide supplies for war. Copper and the other metals of which the brothers were the largest American suppliers were essential.

Dan was in frequent conference at the corner of Broad and Wall with the Morgan partners, chief purchasing agents for the Allies, and Tom Cochran, a Morgan partner, sat in on the Guggenheim boards. Two big figures loomed in the American metals market, Dan Guggenheim and John D. Ryan, the head of the Anaconda interests which controlled Butte's copper production, and of these Dan was by far the more important. For he controlled the output of all the great porphyries—Utah, Nevada, Chino, Ray, Chile —and of Kennecott. The profits of these companies mounted to astounding sums in 1916:

	PROFIT	PER SHARE	DIVIDENDS	PER SHARE
Utah Copper ..	$39,738,000	$24.46	$19,493,000	$12
Kennecott	22,460,000	7.48	15,320,000	5.10
Ray	12,084,000	7.66	4,337,000	2.75
Chino	12,843,000	14.76	7,177,000	8.25
Nevada	15,435,000	7.71	7,497,000	3.75

Of Nevada's dividends, $3,751,000 was paid to Utah; and of Utah's $4,854,000 went to Kennecott.

Behind them all stood American Smelting and Refining, coining a second profit which totalled $25,242,000, or 32 per cent on the common stock so despised a scant fifteen years before. The Smelters Trust, originally concerned almost wholly with silver and lead, refined 1,300,000,000 pounds of copper and entered directly into the munitions business with the manufacture of 15,000,000 loaded cartridges. As with all the companies, the profits far exceeded payments for wages and salaries; Trust stockholders counted $7,000,000 more in profits than did their 22,000 employees in wages.

At a conservative estimate, at least a quarter of the dividends declared by Utah and Kennecott found their way into the pockets of the five Guggenheim brothers. Small wonder that Will wanted to share! Each of his older brothers very likely realized in that one year a sum greater than Will's entire fortune, excluding whatever sum he extracted in the Chile Copper suit.

22. PATRIOTS OR PROFITEERS?

WHATEVER fondness the Guggenheim brothers may have had for *Mittel Europa* was suppressed April 6, 1917, the fateful day when Congress and the President formally acknowledged the state of war which had been existing between America and Germany on the economic plane from the day the House of Morgan extended credits to the Allies and orders to American industry.

Germany and nearby Switzerland were the brothers' fosterland; in youth they had gone to school there, and ever since they had been making sentimental journeys to the pleasant summer country in the German uplands. To Germany Dan had repeatedly paid the sincerest flattery, urging America to imitate her governmental co-operation with industry. But the day after war was declared all Dan could think of to tell the reporters was a reminiscence of how he had had to register in Paris hotels as a Swiss rather than a German in the revengeful days after the Franco-Prussian war. If reporters considered this a strange expedient upon the part of an American, they forgot that the second generation of the Guggenheim dynasty was still more Continental than American, more at home in Frankfort than Chicago, and acclimated only to the rootless, cosmopolitan upper crust of New York, who came from everywhere and belonged nowhere.

Nevertheless Dan did not give way to graceless hate of Germany. While many Americans were crying hoarsely for the march on Berlin and for hanging the Kaiser, Dan, in a two-column interview in the *New York Times*, shrewdly forecast that the war would end with revolt in Germany and Austria. He deprecated the jingo demand that harsh indemnities be squeezed out of Germany. Peace, he said, as had Wilson a year before, should be arranged fraternally among the democracies of both sides. He agreed heartily with the President that this must be a war to end autocracies and thereby war, because there could be no war among democracies.

On April 6 there was no special commotion in the offices of the Guggenheim corporations. The stately quiet of Guggenheim Brothers was as unruffled as ever. The New York offices of American Smelting and the big copper companies hummed as usual. They had been shifted into high gear early in 1915 and it would have been quite impossible to push them faster now. For two years the steam shovels had been gnawing day and night along the sides of the copper mountain in Bingham Canyon, into Steptoe Valley in Nevada, into the two big sockets of Santa Rita and the desert sands of Chuquicamata. The underground shafts and tunnels of Kennecott in the frozen Alaskan mountains and of Braden in the Chilean Andes echoed to the blasts of powder; by night all the Smelter Trust's plants blazed with light as they worked to capacity turning out essential metals for Mars' insatiable maw. Not only was copper indispensable, but lead, too. From the Omaha refinery in one day ten trains left loaded with 6,000 tons of pig lead from which British munitions factories were to make 600,000,000 rifle bullets. Never had the metal industries worked at such white heat as in those feverish years, 1915-18.

Dan, who had thought of retiring and had taken the preliminary steps of breaking third generation scions into harness, summoned back that boundless vitality of his which bounced over the approaching infirmities of age, and bustled about New York in the hot summer of 1917, dividing his time between long conferences with executives, legal and brokerage staffs in his offices at 120 Broadway, working

362

for the Victory loan and the Red Cross drive, and frequent visits to Washington.

His enterprises would yield the palm to none in patriotism. American Smelting offered full pay and sure jobs on their return to all who would volunteer. Eventually its service flag, under the spur of the draft, boasted 1,147 stars. All his companies subscribed heavily to the various war loans, both American and Allied. Money was pouring in so fast from extra dividends that Governmental loans were the one sure depositary for excess profits. Having been among the first to subscribe to the Anglo-French loan in 1915, Guggenheim Brothers cheerfully dropped millions into succeeding loans. In August, 1916, Kennecott alone bought $3,000,000 in United Kingdom 5s, being surpassed only by Bethlehem Steel and J. P. Morgan and Company. In this loan Guggenheim Brothers invested $1,000,000. In October, 1916, Guggenheim Brothers joined the syndicate marketing the United Kingdom's 5½ per cent loan, subscribing another million. Guggenheim Brothers were members also of the French 5½ per cent loan syndicate of March, 1917, with $300,000 invested.

These investments in the world's most solid securities might properly have been gifts from Guggenheim Brothers in return for the juicy contracts they enjoyed from the Allies. In eight months of 1916 alone their American Smelting sold $234,000,000 of metal—mostly copper—to the British and French Governments through J. P. Morgan and Company.

To his fellows, Dan cried exuberantly the merits of American Victory bonds: "For millionaires they are an exceptional opportunity, saving taxes as well as affording an absolutely sure return on the money put into them." His wife became an ardent saleswoman. "What pleases me more than anything else in connection with the work," she said, "is to secure subscriptions from the real poor people

363

who have not sufficient means for buying bonds outright. I refer especially to the people who do household work." Her chauffeur developed into a good salesman, she reported, and was lining up other chauffeurs for Victory bonds.

"I am an optimist and thank God for it!" proclaimed Mrs. Guggenheim. "My experience has been that pessimists are not good salesmen." She added that there was no need to sell to men of means, as they understood the issues involved, but many of their wives must have been on her list, for she sold $4,000,000 in American war loans.

Mrs. Guggenheim distinguished herself even before America's entry into the war by giving to Miss Anne Morgan, head of a French war relief committee, $12,000 for five light ambulance cars to service French soldiers in advance trenches where heavier ambulances could not penetrate. One car was a portable operating room; the second carried electric light and heat installations; the third was equipped to launder six hundred pounds of linen at a time; the fourth was a laundry drier; and the fifth, a disinfectant car, could, it was said, douche eighty men at a time.

For similar work among American troops, the Guggenheim coppers donated special 1 per cent dividends, amounting to $565,000 from Kennecott; $812,000 from Utah Copper; $299,000 from Nevada Consolidated; $500,000 from American Smelting. Guggenheim Brothers chipped in $250,000. To meet the needs of afflicted Jews in hate-torn eastern Europe, the Guggenheim brothers, Jacob Schiff, Nathan Straus and Julius Rosenwald each gave $100,000 at a Carnegie Hall meeting unparalleled for its outpouring of sympathy. Women gave jewels and earrings and men emptied their pockets as Louis Marshall and Judah L. Magnes pleaded for the war-plagued race.

Dan's sons volunteered for war service. Bob, the older, who had rattled around in the Guggenheim organization for several years and then dropped out, became a lieutenant in the 69th Regiment and found at last, among military men, an agreeable outlet for his energies and the kind of companionship he yearned for. Harry, the younger, enlisted in the Navy aviation service as a lieutenant and began cutting out a career that was to figure in later Guggenheim history. He served a year in aviation forces in France and Italy. Dan's son-in-law, Roger W. Straus, likewise became a lieutenant.

Isaac had no sons, but two sons-in-law were in service, Louis M. Josephthal, a broker, becoming captain in the Navy and Edmund L. Haas a captain of ordnance in the Army. Sol contributed by volunteering, before war was proclaimed, to underwrite the expenses of a great patriotic parade by 50,000 New York school children. At a dinner of the Public School Athletic League of which he was treasurer, Sol was given a statuette of Victory in recognition of his financial aid.

Will's son was too young for service but his father stood guard against the insidious forces of pacifism and defeatism. Prominent in the American Defense Society and the American Rights League, he sponsored a postal card barrage on Wilson calling for "war to the bitter end." In a statement he blistered pacifists as "treacherous foes" and demanded "uncompromising prosecution of the war" and "opposition to all peace negotiations." "That the wages of sin is death is the truth that the German people must learn," he warned.

Responding to a Government appeal as chairman of the Army and Navy committee of the American Defense Society, Will urged all patriot landowners to give black walnut trees for plane propellors and gunstocks. After making a motor inspection of Long Island, he charged flatly that German agents had tried to buy up all the black walnut before we entered the war. Fortunately many trees had eluded them, and were at the service of their country.

In a second appeal to patriots, William summoned from them all the Baedekers of Germany, Austria, France, Russia, Italy and Greece they might possess to guide American army officers. He was able to send five hundred overseas. When it seemed the German nation was cracking in 1918, Will warned that it was a maneuver aimed to hinder our own war preparations and to menace the success of the Fourth Liberty Loan. He called for a "peace based on unmistakable victory which means unconditional surrender."

The older brothers never joined the hymn of hate with Will's ferocity, but of their loyalty there was no doubt. Some people looked askance at the international Jewish circle in New York—bankers, importers, manufacturers—who seemed to have deep ideological roots in imperial Germany. To them German was as natural as English, and German regimentation seemed an ideal pattern. That curious official blend of absolutism and parliamentarism, at any rate, outlawed such disgraceful squabbles as took place in America between Big Business and the Government. In Germany, the Guggenheims' great smelting and mining combinations would have been hailed as a natural evolution rather than as a furtive conspiracy against the commonweal.

The admiration the Guggenheims expressed for the German system was hushed abruptly when the British Navy shut off the North Sea and J. P. Morgan and Company began handing out fat contracts for war supplies for the Allies. So involved had the Guggenheims become in 1917 in the mesh of Allied business and credits that a German victory or a stalemate would have sent them plunging to ruin. America's entry into the war came as a godsend.

Dan's prediction of an end to the war in 1917 by revolt in Germany having proved premature, he joined other mining magnates in forming the Rainbow Division of the Third Liberty Loan drive in the spring of 1918, and cried to all:

M. ROBERT GUGGENHEIM AND HIS THIRD WIFE, ELIZA-
BETH EATON GUGGENHEIM. *Photos by Bain News
Service and Wide World.*

COUNTESS CASTLE STEWART (ELEANOR GUGGEN-
HEIM), THE EARL, AND THEIR OLDEST CHIL-
DREN, DAVID ANDREW NOEL, THE VISCOUNT
STUART, AND ROBERT OCHILTREE.

Citizens in time of peace, patriots in time of war—what else can we be? Patriotism means sacrifice, of body, of service, of wealth. In making our sacrifice—we whose lot it is to remain at home—we must not fail, as we value our country, our honor, the respect of our fellows and our posterity. Our sons and brothers—the youth and young manhood of all our families—have gone forth, cheerfully offering their future and themselves in this war for the security of our common country. But they, for all their bravery and sacrifice, cannot win the war alone. To us, their comrades in the rear, they shall not look in vain for the support they need. It is our part to put the weapons in their hands, and all the costly engines and implements of war; to feed and clothe their bodies, and to justify their faith. As society is organized, except by the loyal performance of our daily tasks, each in his own occupation, in keeping industries alive and increasing their output, our only means of giving the aid required of us is with our money, freely placed at the disposal of our Government.

Napoleon declared that three things are essential to success in war—money, money, money. . . . That the might of this nation should be baffled, and our cause be defeated, for lack of money is unthinkable. Only two ways are open to the Government for obtaining the money so indispensably required: by taxes or by borrowing from its people; the way of compulsion and the way of voluntary offering. Let us be volunteers. Both means are of necessity employed. What the Government does not get by borrowing, it will have to get by taxes. In lending to our country, we are lending to ourselves. The acknowledgment we receive is a promissory note, drawn in our favor, signed and sealed by the United States of America, the greatest democracy known to history, composed of a hundred million freemen.

Let us not be daunted by the greatness of the sums required. Our task is to finance our Allies as well as ourselves. And let us not doubt the necessity which confronts us. The fate of Russia is our warning. Her defeat was the inevitable result of her lack of money, and of the arms and munitions and supplies which money would have furnished.

Such arguments infuriated the muzzled Progressives on Capitol Hill who had fought entry into a war which they termed a financial-industrial plot to coin money out of American blood. What was "sacrifice" in the first paragraph, they pointed out, revealed itself in the second as a tax-dodging technique and a gilt-edge securities' investment for those who hardly knew what to do with the rush of extra dividends, and in the third as an insurance policy covering popular uprisings against war-bent Governments.

Dan rejected pleas that war costs be paid by those who profited most. "I believe," he declared, "that a great deal of our obligations should not be paid off by the present generation, but should be borne and paid to quite an extent by future generations whose safety as well as our own was at stake."

The main business at hand, as Dan said, was to furnish weapons and supplies for the armed forces. The Council of National Defense had been formed weeks before the formal declaration of war, and one of its most important committees was that on mines and metals. The Administration looked about for a likely chief for this division, which was to be much concerned with copper, second only to steel in importance. Its choice fell on Bernard M. Baruch, copper promoter and broker, and one of the few Democrats privy to the interior workings of Wall Street and its captains. For fifteen years Baruch had been associated with the Guggenheims in various copper deals. He had ever worked with

368

the quiet intensity of an expert manipulator who felt that the spotlight interfered with his effectiveness. Suddenly he was shot into the public eye and progressive Democrats clucked in astonishment as he ingratiated himself with the White House, was elevated to head the War Industries Board, and became Wilson's chief liaison with Wall Street. Eugene Meyer, Jr., Baruch's partner as a copper promoter, was named chief of the non-ferrous metals section of the War Industries Board, to be succeeded by Pope Yeatman, manager of the Guggenheim Chile coppers, when Meyer assumed control of the War Finance Corporation. Dan Jackling took over the Government's explosives problems.

Charged with mobilizing copper on a war basis, Baruch asked Dan Guggenheim and John D. Ryan, head of Anaconda, to summon the copper men to a conference on the price for needed supplies. In Baruch's words, both men answered promptly:

That is not necessary. The matter is settled. We will see to it that you get your metal at the average price for which it sold before the war boosted prices. Our duty is preparing the nation for war with no profit more than we received from our regular production in normal times.

Baruch was impressed. He said:

That was the extent of the persuasion it was necessary to use to get Big Business back of the Government in preparation for war. Those two men deserve all the credit. Anyone who tries to squeeze the United States to make easy profits is going to have trouble. The Big Business men are going to help the country, and they are going to do it as a patriotic duty, not to make money.

Baruch announced that Dan and Ryan had agreed to sell 45,000,000 pounds of copper to the Army and Navy for 16⅔ cents a pound. The press shook with plaudits for the

369

Copper Kings and for Baruch, and people assumed that the country's war needs were cared for. Acually the 45,000,000 pounds, only a tenth of what the Allies ordered in the spring of 1917, was a small consignment in those days. The price represented a saving of about $5,000,000 under the market, but it was hardly fair to assume that the average price for 1907-16 represented a sacrifice for the copper producers. The average was tilted upward by including the war years. And recently the big porphyries had come into production, cutting costs enormously in comparison with underground mining. The Baruch price was, in fact, above twice the cost for producing copper in the new porphyries. This special price on a small part of the output enabled the copper men to stave off for several months the imposition of a fixed price on all their metal sold to manufacturers and the Allies. This, it was computed, netted the industry an extra $53,000,000 in profits.

The copper honeymoon lasted only a month. The Government needed more copper and neither Guggenheim nor Ryan volunteered more at 16⅔ cents. The *Engineering and Mining Journal* summed up the situation:

The ideas that have prevailed in many quarters that the naming of 16⅔ cents by the producers would constitute a precedent and would establish the future market price for copper, both to the United States and the Allies, were too foolish to merit any consideration except in a passing mood of pessimism. As we said at the time, the 16⅔-cents transaction was in the nature of a gift of the producers, an exhibition of patriotism. . . . The essential thing for both the Government and the public to bear in mind is that production must be maintained at the highest possible rate, and that no idea of cheese-paring should be allowed to jeopardize the incentive to produce, to reduce the wages of miners or to upset industrial conditions.

And why should it? Neither Baruch nor Wilson himself had been able to browbeat U. S. Steel into giving the Government a price which represented an average peace-time profit. Shipbuilders and others were taking fat Government contracts on a cost-plus basis. The argument was that the country needed 100 per cent production; a good bit of this came from high-cost marginal producers; ergo, prices must be fixed to encourage the small producer. Solicitude was paid small producers in steel and copper who never before had known the hidden affection that the big corporations bore them. The Baruch-Guggenheim-Ryan bargain caused sparks to fly in the House with Congressman J. Hampton Moore leading a savage attack on Baruch and the power given him by the White House. Congressman Lunn of New York rushed to Baruch's defense, and even Speaker Champ Clark joined the fray.

"Mr. Baruch," said Lunn, "has secured for the Government a price for copper around 16 cents instead of the 34 or 35 cents which it was bringing in the open market at the time. That was a saving for us of millions of dollars."

"You say," broke in Champ Clark, "that Mr. Baruch got 16 cents for copper, but do you know that the Utah Copper Company, in its report to its stockholders, declared it could put copper free on board cars at 5⅛ cents a pound?"

"If that is a fact," said Lunn, "we have made a tremendous mistake in our revenue bill that we did not put on an excess profits tax that would take care of that."

"I think so, too," retorted Speaker Clark, "but the Utah Copper Company says it can deliver the copper at 5⅛ cents at the cars, and Mr. Baruch thinks we have brought it down to 16 cents. Why does not the Attorney-General hop into these fellows that put copper up to 30 cents? I am willing to give Baruch credit for pulling it down from 30 cents to

371

16, but he did not pull it down far enough. The Attorney-General should put every one of those fellows in jail between now and Saturday night who keep the price up."

The *Engineering and Mining Journal* was aghast at the Congressional attack and while it did not dare impugn Speaker Clark, it declared flatly that Congressman Moore —later Mayor of Philadelphia—was an "enemy of the Republic" and ought to be interned. President Wilson, concerned with the fusillade directed at his fair-haired Wall Street boy, issued a statement defending not only him but Guggenheim and Ryan.

The higgling and haggling of the market, about which economists speak, ensued between the War Industries Board and the copper men. They emerged with 23½ cents set as the price for domestic copper. The Guggenheims' Chilean copper still sold at the higher market price. As costs for the Guggenheim porphyries hardly averaged out to 10 cents, it was considered a good bargain, but early in 1918 the copper industry was back in Washington. Anxious to maintain production at full pitch, the producers pleaded for a rise, but the Administration held firm. The controversy over copper prices and profits now ascended to the Senate, and that body ordered the Federal Trade Commission to look into the situation. The Commission reported a few months later that the profits of 21 copper companies averaged 24.4 per cent in 1917. "These same companies," the Commission explained, "showed an average profit of 11.7 per cent in 1913, which may be considered a normal year. Thus the average profit of the industry has more than doubled." These profits, the Commission hastened to add, did not include Federal income or excess-profits taxes, and "therefore represent sums actually retained by the companies for addition to surplus or dividends."

The Commission's report continued:

In the case of basic metals, as in steel, when the Government announced a fixed price it was made so high that it would insure and stimulate production. This has resulted in giving a wide range of profit; these profits are necessarily great in the case of the low-cost mills. Thus while the market was prevented from running away, as it would have done undoubtedly if it had not been regulated by a fixed price, the stronger factors in the industry was further strengthened in their position and enriched by profits which are without precedent.

As a measure of profits, the Commission cited the margin between average copper costs of 13.7 cents a pound in 1917 and 14.1 cents in 1918, and the fixed price of 23.5 cents and later of 26 cents.

Swinging its attention from the copper companies to American Smelting and Refining, the Commission reported:

There are certain strong interests among the producers and marketers which predominate in certain stages of production, and these appear to have taken steps to maintain prices at unnecessarily high levels. In the first place, the smelters, and notably American Smelting and Refining, have continued to hold in force certain deductions for risk of carrying copper bought from the mines, which risks have ceased to exist. These deductions were put in force during the early period of the war, before the price was fixed by agreement with the War Industries Board. Their present maintenance amounts to profiteering at the expense of the miners, especially the small producers.

The Commission noted, on the other hand, that some of the bigger mines had advantageous long-term contracts which forced some smelters and refineries to operate at a loss.

Brushing aside the Commission's report, the magnates

demanded that the price be increased. In compensation, they offered gallantly not to cut wages (which they could not do anyway in view of the labor shortage) or production. To everybody's surprise, and especially to the Federal Trade Commission's, the price was upped to 26 cents. Even the copper men were gratified: they had not expected more than 24½ cents.

It was the theory that high prices which enabled the small marginal producer to stay in business and favored the low-cost mines with great profits would be balanced by the excess-profits tax. This tax bore with a wicked weight, the Guggenheim coppers complained. The tax was calculated on the proportion of profits to capitalization, and all their companies stood revealed as meagerly-capitalized orphans of the storm and thereby subjected to inordinately high levies. They filed a statement with Congress protesting that the law imposed "upon them grossly unjust and inequitable taxes. By this is meant that in comparison with other companies engaged in the same or other businesses whose organizers have been less conservative in the matter of capitalization, these companies would suffer." They showed their plight in a table:

TABLE II

COMPANY	STOCK PAR VALUE	MARKET VALUE, JAN. 1, 1914
Utah	$16,000,000	$81,000,000
Nevada Consolidated .	10,000,000	30,000,000
Chino	4,300,000	30,000,000
Ray Consolidated ...	15,750,000	28,500,000

From another view, the modest share capital was a monument to the Guggenheims' desire to let it stand merely as the symbol of ownership while the bond issues, subscribed to by the public, represented actual invested capital. Congressional critics also maintained that if actual share capi-

374

tal was an unfair basis, so too were the bloated market valuations of war-babies.

All the Guggenheim enterprises functioned with notable success during 1917. American Smelting showed a profit of $25,035,000, which equaled a return of 22½ per cent on common, after all bonds and preferred stock had been cared for. Dan brushed that aside however. What concerned him was the decline in net earnings of $206,000 under 1916 and a further prospective decline. He complained:

> The company is now suffering from an entire lack of economic law and is operating under the direction of governmental commissions whereby the value of the metal products of the company is fixed. But the cost of labor and supplies is not fixed. The company's ability to pay a fair return to its stockholders is seriously jeopardized.

His fears were given melancholy confirmation in the 1918 report which showed profits of only $14,137,000, or nearly $11,000,000 less than in 1917, and wage payments of $27,335,000, a jump of some two million dollars.

Utah Copper showed the same downturn. Its 1917 earnings of $23,555,000 provided dividends of $14.50, but in 1918 the profits were down to $18,945,000, which permitted only a $10 dividend.

Dan's own pride and joy, Kennecott, turned in $15,320,000 in 1916, or far more than the fabulous mines and their development had cost the Morgan-Guggenheim Syndicate. In 1917, profits were $15,887,000, which came within a few millions of paying the entire cost of the Copper River and Northwestern railway. So fast were the dividends, regular and extra, pouring money into the Guggenheim pockets that Dan decided to increase Kennecott's holdings in Utah. Nearly two hundred thousand shares were bought for $20,000,000, giving Kennecott a total of 600,000 shares of Utah, or three-eighths of its total share capital. Utah itself helped finance its increasing absorption by Kennecott, for it was paying that corporation some $8,400,000 a year on the 400,000 shares already owned. The day was drawing nearer when Dan could achieve his intention of making Kennecott the mother-corporation of all the coppers in which his family was interested.

Directors were exchanged between Utah and Kennecott, and the two rising scions of the Guggenheim family, Edmond and Harry, joined the Utah board. These two had also been placed on Chile Copper's board. It was the brothers' plan to work their sons into this new enterprise so they could take over the reins when their fathers retired. Chile Copper swung into production May 18, 1915, reported a small deficit for its first year, and a balance of $1,936,000 for 1916 operations, which the brothers, the major stockholders, left in the kitty as a sweetener. So promising did Chile Copper seem that Dan decided that the capacity of the plant—a mere 10,000 tons of ore daily—should be stepped up immediately to 27,000. That called for a $35,000,000 bond issue convertible to common stock at $35. Guggenheim Brothers, Baruch's firm of Eugene Meyer, Jr., and W. C. Potter's Guaranty Trust underwrote the issue for a fee of $2,100,000. Dan's son, Harry, joined his Uncle Murry and Engineer A. C. Burrage as vice-presidents of Chile, and became chairman of the executive committee. The other three members of the committee in charge of Chile's fortunes were Cousin Edmond (son of Murry), Burrage, and Potter.

All too soon for Chile Copper and the other Guggenheim enterprises, the war was over. In October, 1918, the death rattle could be heard as Dan's predicted revolt at last removed Austria-Hungary from the conflict and began to cripple Germany. Agitated, the copper men implored the War Industries Board to continue price-fixing for November and December, come what might, to save them from the terrors of a tumbling world market. It obliged, with a price of 23½ cents a pound for copper.

The war over, the flood of criticism which had been impounded by patriotic restraint and the sedition laws began to pour over the Guggenheims and their fellows. Even the Republicans joined the anvil chorus. Representative Mason of Illinois declared that Baruch, "the closest man to the President of the United States . . . stole $50,000,000 in copper alone." The ex-copper speculator turned war-time administrator objected to being made the whipping boy of Wilson's administration and demanded that Mason post his proof with Congress and the Attorney-General or shut up. Mason amended his charge to read: "You and your associates stole $200,000,000 in copper alone." Belligerently he added that he would not trouble to give his evidence to a Democratic Attorney-General but would submit it to the Department of Justice after March 4, 1921. Baruch retorted that "it is about time that these Borgia-like assassins of character cease their work or accept the responsibility of their actions."

W. Jett Lauck, economist for the railroad brotherhoods and the United Mine Workers, passed up the Baruch-Mason personalities and confined himself to figures on the record, in a report to the Railway Labor Board. Profiteering in copper during the war, he said, had cost the people no less than $350,000,000. "Profits in various forms," his report stated, "constituted more than half the price of copper. In fact the profit received by capital was larger than the entire cost of producing the copper, including production, transportation, marketing, and charges for depletion and depreciation."

Fourteen leading companies, said Lauck, showed profits three times as large in the war years as in 1912-14. Their average annual net return for 1912-14 was $46,557,000 and in 1916-18, $137,000,000. The return jumped from

19.7 per cent on capital stock to 54 per cent. In the four years, 1915-18, their net earnings had amounted to $485,-000,000, or twice the amount of their capital stock.

"This is an index of merciless profiteering of these companies. And if it is recognized that the face value of their capitalizations is probably considerably above the actual investment, their profiteering is far greater." Capital, Lauck deduced, got proportionately two and a half times as much as labor in the copper industry during the war years.

To Lauck's analysis there was no reply, either by Baruch, or by Dan Guggenheim, or by any other copper man. The figures had been taken from the reports of the copper companies themselves, and there seemed no appeal. It could only be said that Lauck's figures applied to profits, not to dividends.

By the end of 1918, the Guggenheim coppers had paid more than $200,000,000 in dividends and had accumulated lordly surpluses. Such profits from the world's misery naturally attracted the darts of radicals. Meanwhile Henry Ford, himself to be America's premier millionaire, raised a philosophic objection. "Why," he asked, "should such men as the Guggenheims be paid for ore in the ground in the state of nature?" He admitted that as employers and suppliers of tools, they were entitled to a part of the world's wealth, "but by what right could they claim the ore that lies in the bosom of the earth?"

Nevertheless Baruch, on December 1, 1918, paid a handsome compliment to the copper magnates. He "wished to place on record the Government's appreciation of the patriotic spirit in which the copper producers had accepted maximum prices suggested by the price-fixing committee."

Eighteen years served to cool his enthusiasm. Appearing before the Senate committee investigating the munitions industries to relate his experiences with the copper industry, he conceded that the War Industries Board had been so vexed that it had considered commandeering some of the big copper companies. In this the Board was backed by President Wilson who had threatened to exercise his powers to place the entire copper industry under direct Governmental supervision if the Guggenheims and Ryan would not agree to the price of 23½ cents. The only thing that deterred Wilson was the fear that such action would be challenged as unconstitutional by the copper men themselves, and the whole case catapulted into the Court of Claims, with the probability that the Government would find itself paying an even higher price for needed war supplies. Baruch admitted that although the price offered the copper men by the War Industries Board assured them a fair profit, it wasn't enough to satisfy war-whetted appetites.

By one of history's curious quirks, it was the son of Speaker Champ Clark, critic of the copper magnates during the war, who appeared in 1935 as one of Baruch's inquisitors. Senator Bennett Champ Clark asked him if the copper industry had not "held a gun to Uncle Sam."

"Do not put me down," pleaded Baruch, "in the position of defending these companies."

And so it was that a business associate of the Guggenheims themselves answered the question: "Were they patriots or profiteers?" Or, perhaps, both?

23. WAR CAPITAL AND WAR LABOR

WAR'S crowning achievement for domestic peace was the dramatic meeting of the captains of industry and the lieutenants of labor in the council room of the American Federation of Labor Building in Washington on May 15, 1917. To represent capital, the Administration picked two genial money-masters known both for their championship of the new era of social pacification and for the bloody labor wars which had involved their names and fortunes. They were John D. Rockefeller, Jr., whose armed guards had but a few years before machine-gunned women and children in the strikers' tent colony in bloody Ludlow, Colorado; and Daniel Guggenheim, whose wars with the Western Federation of Miners had crimsoned the annals of mining history.

Samuel Gompers, president of the labor federation and chairman of the committee on labor of the advisory commission of the Council of National Defense, summoned Rockefeller, Guggenheim and a score of other capitalist plenipotentiaries to sit with an equal number of chieftains of labor. They all spoke on the united cause of labor and capital in wiping war from the face of the globe and spreading the tenets of democracy over the accursed lands of Central Europe. After the set speeches, the industrialists and union leaders were called upon for testimonials.

Dan Guggenheim sprang to his feet, his round, florid face beaming with delight. "This is a great revelation to me," he exclaimed. "Yes, it is a revelation and it has inspired me. I have felt for some years that my work was near its end; that I might be allowed to take things a little easier. You see, I have worked for forty-five years and I was thinking of turning over my work to my two sons and to my son-in-law. But recently I arranged things so they could all go to the front when the call came, and I could go back into harness and do the work they were going to do for me. When the call came from Mr. Gompers, perhaps I felt that I had enough on my shoulders. But I came here and I want to say that I am prepared to do anything I can do—just so long as I am able to carry it out.

"You're on the right track. You're doing the right thing."

Turning to Gompers, Dan added: "I am prepared to offer my services, Mr. President. My services are at your disposal and at the disposal of the entire organization."

And with that the plump little capitalist grasped the hands of the gnarled, gnome-like Gompers and they embraced as brother-capitalist and brother-labor leader.

"I congratulate Mr. Guggenheim," said Gompers, beaming with joy. "He has simply taken on a new lease of life."

That scene was chronicled in the Seattle papers that eventually straggled into the wind-beaten Alaskan mining camp at Kennecott. The fraternal union between Guggenheim and the American Federation of Labor must have seemed to the miners a benediction cast over their new union which was asking a wage increase of 50 cents a day, to $4.50 with board.

The same papers reported Kennecott's dividends of $15,-320,000 for 1916, with a labor cost considerably under $1,000,000. Everywhere Kennecott was hailed as the world's lowest-cost copper mine, able to produce a pound of copper for 5.1 cents, against a selling price of 23½ cents. But the Kennecott management was unimpressed, either by the doings in far-off Washington or the miners' demand for a bigger slice of the fabulous earnings. It declined to negotiate with the union. A month after the conference in the A. F. of L. Building, Kennecott's miners struck, and were evicted from their bunkhouses in that remote region. They moved down the river to the first piece of non-Guggenheim land, at McCarthy, and set up strike headquarters and shelter.

The nation was informed by Kennecott officials that pro-German elements had instigated the strike against the nation's military resources, the Government was asked to post guards over the Copper River and Northwestern Railroad, and the facts were laid before federal officials in charge of enforcing the sedition laws.

Kennecott labor agents combed Valdez and Anchorage for strikebreakers. As the weeks wore on, the strikers straggled out of their hunger-bound shacks, heading for other camps. By midsummer the mines were operating again. Wages were raised 25 cents and more bunkhouses built.

Nevertheless the message of unionism managed to seep into Kennecott again in 1918. The management decided, once and for all, to end the threat by having its employees sign a "yellow-dog" contract which bound the miner against joining a union, as a condition of employment. The Supreme Court had approved such a contract in a celebrated case brought by the Hitchman Coal and Coke Company against the United Mine Workers in West Virginia. Sam Gompers thundered against the decision as riveting the bonds of slavery around the necks of free American workers, but the Guggenheim legal department nevertheless recommended it to hard-pressed labor managers. The notice, as posted in the Kennecott mines, read:

To the end that the attitude of Kennecott Copper Corporation concerning labor unions may be made clear to employees and that misunderstandings as to such attitude may be avoided, the following statement is made to all employees:

1. This company does not recognize any union or unions or organized and active bodies of workmen at or in the vicinity of Kennecott. Any employee who at the present time belongs to any union which is now active at or in the vicinity of Kennecott or who is seeking membership among the employees of this company is requested promptly to sever his relations with either the union or the company.

2. The company has not the slightest objection to the retention of membership in any labor union or organized body of workmen which is not active at or in the vicinity of Kennecott or is not seeking membership among the employees of this company.

3. This position is taken by the company in order to protect those of its employees who do not care to join any union and who would be forced out of camp should any union get a foothold, as well as to preserve the friendly relationship between the company and its employees. It is believed that the relations between the Kennecott Copper Corporation and the union which is at present seeking membership among the employees could not and would not be cordial.

4. In order that every employee may understand that this company is fully within its rights in assuming the attitude expressed above, attention is called to the following excerpts quoted from a syllabus to the decision of the Supreme Court of the United States in the case of *Hitchman Coal and Coke Company* vs. *the United Mine Workers of America.*

5. It is assumed that all employees who shall not have severed their connections with the company by 6 p.m., March 5, 1918, pledge themselves to accept the terms of employment as outlined in the foregoing articles. As a matter of record such men are asked to call upon their respective foremen and to sign a statement to that effect.

What a distance between the brotherly embrace of Dan Guggenheim and Sam Gompers, and the yellow-dog contract at Kennecott! The International Union of Mine, Mill, and Smelter Workers accused Guggenheim of downright insincerity and treachery. It contrasted his statements before the Industrial Relations Commission ("employees are fully justified in organizing . . . the workman should not only have a voice but he should have the controlling voice") with the anti-union reality in his mining camps and smelters.

Such accusations never fazed Dan's serenity. The sincerity of that dichotomous soul was not to be doubted: when he embraced Sam Gompers, who had been, like his own father, a penniless Jewish immigrant boy, there was nothing in the gesture but the exuberance of Dan's sentimental soul. As for his utterances before Frank Walsh's industrial commission, well, he had meant every word he said, in his own manner, at the moment. That what he said might mean a number of things to the multitude was Dan's own way of fencing with the world. A product of Wall Street's devious wanderings in promotion and speculation, he was accustomed to the spectacle of one friend doing another out of a million one day and having dinner with him in the highest of spirits the next day. It was unsporting to bear a grudge, for on the very next day one might turn the tables and recoup the million. That was something that the simple-minded officers and members of the Mine, Mill, and Smelter Workers Union could never understand.

The Kennecott affair put the managers of other Guggenheim copper properties on their guard. These were troublous times, with living costs mounting sharply, with the messengers of unionism shouting their creed of organization throughout the West and pointing the finger of scorn particularly at the copper magnates, who were amassing millions and grudgingly doling out wage increases only as they felt the pulse of rebellion growing stronger among their employees.

An electric tension pervaded the air in Bingham Canyon. Even the Bingham *Press-Bulletin*, carefully self-censored, felt constrained to warn Utah Copper.

Few mining camps in the world really work their men as hard and as long as do some of the mining companies in this, the greatest copper camp in the world. Our mining companies are amassing millions of dollars and the profits during the past year or so have been enormous, and yet not one move has been made by some of these companies to lighten the burden of the men who come and go through the streets of our town looking more like sewer rats than like miners. Where is the trouble and who is to blame for these conditions? First, the ten-hour shift is too long when you consider the fact that the men have to spend at least one hour getting to the mine and another hour in getting home. This makes the shift equal to a twelve-hour working day, and the worst part about this trip is that the men have to walk home in their wet, muddy clothes and cannot help taking cold. Thus the health of the miner is endangered and his family does not get the care and attention from him that they should because his health is poor and he is overworked. In our opinion this is about the only camp where such conditions prevail.

Dan Jackling, big boss of Utah and all the other porphyry camps, redoubled his mine guards and felt confident in the loyalty of the strikebreakers he had imported in 1912, reinforced by numbers of his men who had little garden farms in Salt Lake Valley. The old hard-rock miners referred to them contemptuously as "valley cats." Into the Canyon, fortress of anti-unionism, went Ben Goggins, a mine union organizer. The chief of police told him to move on, but Goggins stood doggedly on his rights and called a meeting. Hundreds turned out, augmented by town police and company guards. The company became alarmed at Goggins' progress. He was summoned to a conference with the chief of Utah Copper's armed guards and representatives of the "Citizens Protective Alliance." Pointed reference was made to the hanging of Harry Little, the union organizer, under a trestle near Butte. This was no time for organizing and fomenting strikes. The country was at war, copper was a military necessity, and patriots in the Canyon would see that there was no interruption to its production. If Goggins wanted to organize after the war was over, that was another matter. But not now!

The alarmed mine organizer appealed to Sam Gompers to use his influence with his friend, Dan Guggenheim. Federal mediators responded to the clamor from the Canyon and held hearings in the Bingham Chamber of Commerce. The chief of Utah's armed guards admitted he had ordered Goggins out of town but denied any threat of lynching. The Protective Alliance spokesman was more blunt: "The committee has ordered the organizers to go and has no intention of permitting them to stay. And little technicalities of the law shall not be permitted to stand in the way." The former district attorney suggested that Goggins and his ilk be shipped off to a leper island.

Their meaning was unmistakable. Men with guns protruding from ill-concealed holsters established a day and night watch on the union headquarters in a little room overlooking the crooked, crowded road that wound up the Canyon. Goggins yielded to *force majeure* and left.

Armed guards protected other Guggenheim properties— the smelter at Garfield, near Bingham, the properties of Nevada Consolidated and the other porphyries. At Nevada Consolidated works, 150 miles from any sizable town, it was simple to keep agitators out. Deputies met each incoming train. A few years before the union had built a hall "on a small portion of this planet that does not belong to the Guggenheims," as one organizer put it, but this was closed.

To meet the labor shortage, the chief of police of Salt Lake City published a ukase that all able-bodied men must work. Unemployed men were picked up as "vagrants" and turned over to American Smelting's labor agent for duty at $2.50 a day.

In charge of the Ray Consolidated properties in Arizona, in which the Guggenheims held an important interest, was a man who ranked with Dan Jackling as engineer-boss-politician of the Western mining region. He was Louis Cates, tough, hard-fisted, burly and brainy, of the kind who delighted to stand at the bar of the Rocky Mountain Club in New York, whisky highball in hand, and relate how he handled labor agitators. Cates' will was law in Pinal County. His thousand Mexican laborers might strike in desperation and no word could seep out except that sent over his own telegraph. Where Kennecott officials saw pro-Germanism and sedition in their strike, Cates announced his was an uprising engineered by Mexican revolutionists. He sent to Phoenix for squads of two-fisted Americans who emptied the gun stores overnight. At Ray, they found hundreds of Mexicans and native Spanish-speaking Arizonans on strike for the eight-hour shift, a thirty-minute lunch period underground, the right to speak freely, and the wage scale in effect at the Miami mines.

The strike at Ray was one of a series that convulsed Arizona copper camps and caused Governor Hunt, beloved among miners, to denounce the "profiteering patriots" whom he blamed for the unrest that swept the state. He offered Cates the use of the state militia, but the Ray boss answered that his own men had the situation well in hand. The State Federation of Labor agent reported:

387

Within fifty feet of where I am writing this letter are four men with Winchesters. Further down the street are men and boys armed with different kinds of musketry. The approaches to the yards and tunnels, shafts, offices and bridges, as well as the different vantage points of the surrounding country, are patrolled by men continuously pacing up and down, armed and equipped to give battle to the defenseless $2.75 and $3 a day Spaniards and Mexicans.

After two weeks, the men's families began to get hungry. Cates traded permission for them to join any union they wanted in return for their disbanding the local at Ray; he conceded a sixty cents a day increase in return for the men yielding on the eight-hour issue. The union charter was returned to Phoenix and work was resumed.

Cates and his fellow-mine-managers in Arizona cried for more Mexican immigration to relieve the labor shortage which they held partly responsible for the unrest. When they demanded 20,000 be imported, the government official in charge declined, saying there were hundreds of American miners out of work. He was supplanted by a Guggenheim engineer fresh up from Chile, the State Federation of Labor charged, and thousands of Mexicans were invited into the mines.

Dan Guggenheim and his brothers were able to look with some detachment on the unrest which swept their properties . . . and the world. To salve their consciences, they had the welfare bureau in American Smelting and Refining, which supervised hospitals, accident prevention, pensions, and insurance. The rougher conflicts were screened from their gaze by the self-justifying reports of their managers. It was nearly impossible to bring men who moved in their own world of luxury into contact with the reality that gaped beneath them. Their interest was fastened on the major outlines of production, price and profit. So long as labor was available and would work for a reasonable price, there was no acute labor problem to alarm them.

Certainly it could not be said that the Guggenheims were more callous than their fellow-millionaires toward the misery which enveloped the world in the throes of war and post-war adjustment. But its details never concerned them intimately. Each moved in his own ambit of life in New York, the South and Europe.

That the European war had been a grand success Dan demonstrated when he moved from upper middle-class El-beron, New Jersey, where he maintained a large wooden summer house, to the multimillionaires' enclave at Sands Point, Long Island, in 1917. By cable he bought Castle-gould, copied after Kilkenny Castle in Ireland, from Howard Gould, then in Europe. Young Gould had projected the million-dollar mansion in 1901 after his marriage to Catherine Clemmons, the actress. Castlegould had 70 rooms, against the 60 in Kilkenny. It was a massive stone structure 228 feet long, 110 feet wide and 60 feet high, surrounded by a moat and approached in medieval style by a bridge. Between the house and the Sound a casino had been built with bowling alleys and a swimming pool. Standing out on the promontory of Sands Point, Castlegould's tower and turret were boldly visible across lower Long Island Sound, a reminder that America had developed its own nobility. North of Dan's estate Brother Will had another mansion; to the South Isaac established himself, and in the years to come other Guggenheims established their homes along the aristocratic Sands Point neck of land.

The news of the proletarian revolution in Russia, of the upheavals in Central Europe, of the turbulence which shook all the Old Countries and grew apace in the New World, seeped into Dan Guggenheim's rechristened Hempstead House. Forces were at large in the world which threatened the very foundations of the House of Guggenheim. Concessions were in order, and a tighter organization of the social body. The brothers Guggenheim, who perhaps more than any other American family had profited from the war, thanks to their prescience in appraising, years before, the vital role of copper, took counsel with themselves. Labor unions, they saw, were the root of the menace. Other employers, weaker than themselves, had yielded to labor at the key point of production. Emboldened, the unions had demanded more and more, and in the dim distance Dan saw the figure of Bolshevism, and the end of that system which had enriched the Silver Princes and the Copper Kings.

Dan decided to expound his views in the columns of his favorite newspaper, the *New York Times*. With his usual adroitness, he paid his compliments to organized labor which now was able to "combat the powerful employer on more nearly equal terms" (but not on Guggenheim property). Unfortunately labor was attempting to "use its power to the limit," he said reproachfully.

The radicals in the labor movement are demanding what is virtually the control of industry. The demand is in essence an attempt for a class autocracy of labor which is nothing more or less than Bolshevism. . . . I believe the American people who have before them the example of Russia will never permit Bolshevism, the control by the ignorant, nor control by an oligarchy of the rich to exist in this country either in government or industry.

The American people have seen within the last two years in Russia both these extremes; first the knout of the Cossack carrying out the orders of the small autocratic group and then the ravages of the "red" group

390

carrying out the orders of a small clique of the proletariat, more autocratic than the monarchists.

I have been told by unimpeachable authority that when the Bolsheviki took control of certain mines in Siberia, the workmen ordered the former foremen, superintendents, engineers and managers into the mines as laborers, and they then took over the management of the mines. The leader elected to become manager said his idea of the duties of a manager was to write out a lot of figures on pieces of paper and tear them up and smoke cigarets. The result of such management was just what could be expected and the mines were abandoned.

I have been told of ex-janitors of schools being made local heads of educational departments overnight. This state of affairs will never be sanctioned by the American people for they have too much sanity and common sense and will never permit any control of either government or industry by the ignorant.

How did he propose to avert such a calamity in America? Guggenheim sketched his plan. It was a compliment to Daniel's farsighted intelligence that the proposals he outlined in 1919 were the very ones being advanced some eighteen years later by the United States Chamber of Commerce and the National Association of Manufacturers as a solution to the labor problem which followed the Supreme Court's validation of the Wagner Labor Relations Act.

The Federal Government, under the Guggenheim plan, was to take charge of labor relations in interstate business. It was to charter unions, forbid strikes until an investigation had been made and a report rendered, establish the financial liability of unions for contracts and set up a Federal Labor Commission. This body was to be appointed by Congress from panels submitted by employers' and civic organizations (Dan did not mention the American Federation of Labor), and its members were to hold office for life, being placed on a non-political pedestal like the Supreme Court. This commission could revoke labor union charters and confiscate their funds, for disobedience. Under such rigid control, Dan felt that legislation outlawing strikes would be unneeded.

Dan then proposed to short-circuit the unions by instituting needed reforms through governmental initiative. These would include rules for health and safety in industry, inclusion of occupational diseases in workmen's compensation, provision for old age and unemployment insurance "that will not put a premium on laziness," restrictions around child labor and the working hours for women, and the establishment of proper living conditions.

Dan's own philosophy he called:

a middle of the road progressive policy [that would] stabilize industry, encourage initiative and enterprise and at the same time build up a self-respecting, healthy and happy class of employees, all of whom will feel that their rights are carefully safeguarded and that the avenues of opportunity for betterment of their financial condition are not closed but that everyone has an opportunity of reaching a level commensurate with his own ability and that at no time will anyone who is willing to do an honest day's work be unable to earn a decent living for himself and his family.

His own American Smelting and Refining had shown, said Dan, what the individual corporation could do. The twelve-hour shift was no more. Pensions and death benefits had been introduced. The employee was entitled to a part of unusual profits, but Dan was undecided whether this should be by profit-sharing or bonus. The employee must realize however that in the end wages depend on production. "The shirker deserves nothing."

Dan was tolerant about unions. "A man has a right to join any society he desires so long as that society is a lawful one and does not aim to overthrow the American government," he said. Or, he might have added, attempt to control wages, hours or working conditions.

It was evident that Dan believed that employers, if they be intelligent, could build insurmountable walls about their possessions. His plan envisioned modern industrial counterparts of medieval barons, surrounded by a faithful, well-fed and happy yeomanry. A firm but beneficent Government, aided by broad-minded employers, would give labor all it deserved, remove the patent abuses from industry, and provide for stability and order. Only two factors Dan had not considered. What if the laborers declined to yield the power that was theirs through organization? And what would happen to such well laid plans for assuring contentment if forces utterly beyond the control of a government run to please property-owners should smash the whole scheme?

Dan thought he had a ready answer to the first question. He would provide the laborers with an organization, ready-made. He grew enthusiastic over employee representative plans "to advise and consult with the management." These he introduced into his smelters and copper properties, where they co-operated with the welfare work in such a way that workmen understood that hospitals, visiting nurses and Y. M. C. A.'s had not been "given them either as a charity or imposed upon them as by a benevolent despot."

Such a company union was installed in Bingham Canyon, with separate divisions for the Japanese and Greeks, "with the object in view of maintaining the present pleasant relations existing between the management and the employees." A paper was established, the *Porphyry*, to install proper ideas in employees' heads and to counteract the Bolshevik propaganda that was seeping into the Canyon. It seemed that malcontents had spread word through the Canyon that

393

Utah Copper in its life had declared dividends of $131,-000,000, had tucked $42,000,000 away in surplus and paid only $65,000,000 in wages and salaries. "Labor can get only what it produces," announced the *Porphyry*. "If it wants more, it must produce more."

The *Porphyry* was incensed with the "plague of panaceas" which was sweeping the land. Everything was being proposed from "pap to dynamite." "This is the greatest era of pap, piffle and poison the world has ever seen," the editor cried in alarm. "If our Republican institutions are to survive, the Bolsheviki and the I. W. W.'s must go, and the quicker the fact becomes generally known, the less trouble there will be."

Dan saw even greater possibilities in company unions than he outlined publicly, for suddenly there appeared, mysteriously and to the surprise of smelter and mine workers, a conference in Washington early in 1919 of employers and employees of the copper industry, shepherded by the Secretary of Labor. An alarming surplus of copper now hung over the world markets and Dan and his confrères in the industry were trying to get the Government to finance its withdrawal for a period of years. The proposal might have seemed a bit bald, coming from magnates who had made a third of a billion in profits during the war. But from the lips of employee representatives, the demand for governmental credits for the copper industry came as the genuine cry of workmen pleading for help against the threat of wage cuts and unemployment. Congress, however, did not take kindly to the idea, and the wage cuts were thereupon imposed.

Returning from Europe on the eve of the 1921 depression, Dan was cheery. In fact, he reported, everybody was optimistic but Wall Street. True, there were some unemployed, but they were "roving, itinerant workers."

The good, steady, married American is holding his job and has saved much during the period of high wages. He has raised his standard of living, eats better food, dresses better and his children have better educational opportunities. . . . He realizes that wages must be cut and is not blindly fighting reduction so long as the cut does not go too far or is out of proportion to the cost of living. . . . The efficiency in industrial plants is increasing by leaps and bounds, principally because the shiftless itinerant laborer who is both inefficient and a trouble-maker, is left out, and the sober American worker is buckling down and getting results.

This proved small consolation to the sober American workman, for by 1921 many of the big Guggenheim mines and smelters were completely shut down and the others were working only part time. The native-born American and the imported Greek and Japanese suffered alike. To such an industrial catastrophe Dan had no ready-made answer, nor were the other Guggenheim brothers able to summon explanation, justification, or remedy.

The employee representation plans fell to pieces during this period. The menace of Bolshevism seemed less immediate; the Mine, Mill and Smelter Workers Union shriveled in the economic desert; and the workmen showed little enthusiasm for the device. They were not to be revived until the National Industrial Recovery Act in 1933 laid down a charter of labor's rights. By then, the miners' union had all but died in the West and was unable to profit by the advantages of famed Section 7A of NIRA or the succeeding Wagner Act. And by then the American copper mines were in a parlous state, what with the competition of the great mines of Chile which the Guggenheims had sponsored, and the new discoveries in south-central Africa. The flight of the years had not softened the brothers' enmity to labor's organization. When the miners at Santa Rita managed to organize, to appeal successfully for a National Labor Board election, and win it, the great porphyry property was closed, the machinery was shipped off, the miners evicted. The houses they had toiled to build for themselves stood on company property, and the company ordered them off. Travelers were often startled to see a truck with an enormous platform carrying a shack down the valley for one who could afford the fee. "Yes, all those little houses yonder came over from Santa Rita," the natives would explain to visitors unaccustomed to such restless real estate.

Kennecott Copper, which by that time owned all the American porphyries, asserted that the Santa Rita mine had closed, not because of the National Labor Board ruling that the union must be recognized, but because the property no longer paid. Neutral people in neighboring Central City observed, however, that the mine had operated throughout the depression when the price of copper was even lower than in 1935. The Labor Board itself concluded that Santa Rita had closed because of unprofitable operation.

The fact remained that the hostility of the Guggenheims toward independent labor organization, maintained over two generations, continued to the very end. Employees in the Perth Amboy refinery were able finally, in 1937, to hoist the banner of the International Union of Mine, Mill and Smelter Workers, an affiliate of John L. Lewis' Committee for Industrial Organization, over the great works. Although American Smelting and Refining refused to grant a union shop contract, it was obliged by the Wagner Labor Relations Act to recognize the union as the sole bargaining agency. Won only at the end of dramatic sit-down strike within the refinery, this victory seemed to signalize the ending of the old autocratic rule which the Guggenheims had wielded for fifty years, the beginning of a new era in labor relations which Dan could hardly have envisaged ten years before.

24. REVOLT IN THE RANKS

AFTER the war, the reckoning. The world copper market sagged under the burden of Guggenheim metal. The ruin that independent copper men had predicted years before from the threatening flood of porphyries seemed all too real. A million tons hung over the market.

When the Government declined to extend easy credits to relieve the market of excess stocks, consumers dreamed of the immense reserves being dumped at buyers' prices. Instead, the Guggenheims, Anaconda and other producers, by virtue of bank loans, segregated the surplus, formed the Copper Export Association, with Simon as chairman, and proceeded to dole out the metal at a fixed price of twenty-three cents. "We prefer operating at 50 per cent of capacity," it was explained, "to cutting the price under twenty-three cents." But Europe and America alike refused to buy at the fantastic war figure. Sol went overseas to examine the buyers' strike and returned, quite mournful. "Europe," he said, "is sick, very sick."

After the deceptive boom of 1920, the sensitive metal market went into a tailspin. In 1921 Ray and Chino were shut down, Utah and Kennecott operated at a fraction of capacity, the El Paso smelter's fires went out, and the Smelters Trust passed its common dividend for the first time since 1904. Hordes of miners and smelter workers were discharged, the rest saw their wartime wage scale tumble. Even the Guggenheims took a 20 per cent cut in salaries, with other Trust officials. Fortunately all their copper companies, as well as American Smelting, were well padded with wartime surpluses and the brothers merely sat back awaiting the inevitable comeback in demand, while smaller copper producers croaked of impending doom.

With the end of the war, Daniel achieved the ambition, held in 1916, of retiring from active business. He was sixty-three. In the last twenty turbulent years he had supervised the erection, on the modest base provided by his father in the Pueblo smelter, of the world's greatest mining and smelting enterprise. Shrewd business man that he was, he knew that in the next few years there would be little to do in a world saturated with metals. The business could well get along without him now, and would most certainly have to do without him within a few years.

In accordance with Smelting's curious custom by which the president outranked the chairman of the board, Daniel relinquished the presidency and Simon stepped up from the chairmanship to that position. "The Honorable Simon Guggenheim, formerly United States Senator," announced Dan, would succeed him. "He is a very capable merchant, experienced in the smelting business and by temperament will qualify to fill the position of president." Assisting Simon was Roger Straus, Dan's son-in-law. Simon's associate in the old Denver days, E. L. Newhouse, became chairman. Murry and Sol retired as chairmen of the finance and executive committees, Simon taking both assignments. Isaac had been in retirement several years, so that left but one of the brothers in harness.

Let none imagine however that the triumvirate which had piloted the Trust through eighteen years had suddenly surrendered their control. On the thirty-fifth floor at busy 120 Broadway, one flight above Smelters' headquarters, were the hushed, sumptuous offices of Guggenheim Brothers. There, in a great room, paneled in walnut, were the partners' desks. From the windows to the west, they could see, on a clear day, the smoke of their Perth Amboy refinery; to the south the other pinnacles of finance; to the north the midtown towers. In these offices Daniel, Solomon, and Murry considered the affairs of copper, gold, silver, and lead.

The visitor in the lobby had time to inspect cases of minerals, precious and base: gold quartz, spongy pure wire silver, the first copper bar from Chuquicamata's porphyry. In the great room reserved to the brothers, pictures of Meyer and themselves graced the walls. On a center table was an autographed picture of Andrew W. Mellon, whose monopoly in another metal—aluminum—outshone even the Guggenheims' in the perfection of its control. Mellon was Secretary of the Treasury, the greatest since Alexander Hamilton, and the brothers applauded his businesslike views on taxation. And with reason. Had not the Senate committee investigating Mellon's Bureau of Internal Revenue stated that the copper companies saved $50,000,000 in wartime taxes thanks to Secretary Mellon's post-war rulings? Dan had small patience with taxes on profits. "I am a great believer in the sales tax," he said. "It would not handicap business enterprises as taxes on profits do."

Adorning the wall in the board room of Guggenheim Brothers was the most famous of all Guggenheim pictures, that of old Meyer himself, smiling beneficently through his white side-whiskers, and flanked by all his seven sons in the days before schism had divided the House.

The board room of Guggenheim Brothers was a pardonable extravagance. Board meetings meant little to the brothers, whether they concerned their own partnership or the affairs of the Smelters Trust. Such meetings were mere formalities, to ratify a decision already formed by the brothers after consultation with whatever director-employees specialized in the problem under consideration. In the old days the triumvirate—Dan, Murry, and Sol—arrived at its conclusions, the secretary drew up the minutes, and they were circulated among the directors for *pro forma* signatures. Indeed American Smelting was as much a partnership, in its direction, as Guggenheim Brothers.

Few noted that in the reshuffling of offices attendant on Dan's retirement, Karl Eilers had "resigned" as director. Those in the know said that Eilers had been fired as an employee and defeated for re-election to the board of American Smelting. But few gave the matter any importance; the Guggenheims had run the Smelters Trust as their own family property since 1901, and in all those years none arose seriously to challenge their control. Behind scenes in the Trust a tussle had been going on between Karl Eilers, son of that genial old metallurgical wizard, Anton, and the new president. Simon and Karl had grown up together, as it were, in the smelting business. The Eilers' smelter was running in Pueblo when Meyer Guggenheim decided to build his own there. Their sons were trained in the business: Karl as an expert metallurgist under his father's personal attention; Simon as western representative of the Guggenheim interests. Before 1901 they had been rivals in Rocky Mountain smelting; in that year Simon became western representative for the Smelters Trust, and Karl just another employee. It rankled in the hearts of old western smelting men to have the smart Guggenheim brothers cracking the whip in the Trust, but so securely entrenched were they that no insurrection could succeed. Karl, sole representative of the old smelter men on the Trust's board, inherited his father's repugnance to control by financiers; now that Dan had retired, and the company's affairs were in a bad way, he felt the time had come when insurrection might succeed. Simon acted firmly. He wrote Karl, March 31, 1920:

Shortly after I became president of American Smelting and Refining, it became evident that you were not in sympathy with my administration. . . . Our views differ

400

so fundamentally and on so many questions that we cannot with advantage to the company or in justice to either of us, continue to be longer associated in the management. . . . This letter is written that you may have the opportunity of yourself taking the initiative and tendering your resignation before the coming annual election if you so desire.

Karl declined to resign, and was ousted.

When Lucifer rebelled, there could have been no greater consternation in Heaven than spread through the mining world when Karl Eilers filed suit in New York Supreme Court December 20, 1920, challenging the Guggenheims' right to control the Smelters Trust, accusing them of gutting the company for their own private profit, and demanding access to the list of stockholders so he could place his arguments before the stockholders—all 19,000 of them. Graying mine owners in the Rockies read greedily every word of Eilers' sensational petition and Wall Street looked on with astonishment as the world's most important metal kings were obliged to deny publicly that they had pocketed millions that rightfully belonged to their stockholders. All the dirty linen that had accumulated in the Trust since Dan Guggenheim executed his daring coup in 1901 was to be hung out in the public press.

The son of old Anton Eilers stoutly declared he had every right to press for redress. He and his family, he asserted, owned more stock than all the officers and directors of the Trust together. Indeed he was the only director financially able, he claimed, to stand up in public and speak out his own mind. In proof that the Guggenheims ran Smelters without check, he pointed to Simon's letter stating in so many words that nobody disagreeing with him could continue as a director.

Karl entered briskly into personalities. Everything in the

corporation had declined, he said, stock values, earnings, cash, morale, dividends and prospects. And "its directing head has declined from a Daniel Guggenheim to a Simon Guggenheim." The board of directors, he charged, had nothing to say about Simon's elevation to the presidency. Dan had merely sent a letter to the stockholders announcing the change and "the board had not been notified, much less consulted." Returning the personalities, Simon said Karl's attack was that of a "discharged employee." He had shown "poor judgment, extravagance, and disregard for the policies of the directors." Despite his proclaimed solicitude about the wasting of company money, he had asked a full year's pay although discharged in April, 1920. Solomon added that Eilers had wasted millions of the company's funds.

Eilers retaliated. In 1907 the Guggenheims, he related, were forced to sell most of their stock, because of financial reverses, and since then had held a negligible financial stake in American Smelting. Despite that, they retained control in order to use the company for their own enrichment. Salary control, for instance, had been vested in a special committee which permitted the brothers to pay themselves $25,-000 to $50,000 a year salaries—Eilers did not know how much exactly, as the information was kept from most of the directors. Under latter-day Securities and Exchange Commission rules, Simon's salary was revealed as $50,000 a year.

The brothers used company money to investigate Bolivian tin properties and then proceeded to buy them for Guggenheim Brothers instead of for the company. They opposed the company's acquiring an interest in the Premier gold and silver mine in British Columbia unless they were given a share. Worst of all, the Guggenheims had speculated in copper, Eilers stated, with the result that the Trust had lost a million a year. In 1919-20 they miscalculated on the falling market in selling for future deliveries, and lost the company fifteen million by holding copper.

Repeatedly, said Eilers, he and several other board members protested Guggenheim policies. Of them, Newhouse was silenced by being promoted to chairman, another was made vice-president, one continued despite a salary cut while three, including himself, resigned or were forced to quit.

"Libelous accusations," retorted American Smelting and Refining. Simon was elected president by "free and unanimous choice." The Guggenheims, if they dominated the board at all, did so because of their "great abilities and unusual knowledge of the business." Simon and his wife, far from holding a mere 100 shares, were the largest stockholders, with 28,000 shares worth $2,800,000 at par, plus $300,000 in bonds. Isaac and Dan held 8,000 shares rather than 223; Solomon had 8,000 even though none was listed under his name.

Guggenheim Brothers had bought none of the Bolivian tin properties investigated by American Smelting and Refining; the company invested in Premier only to assure itself the smelting and refining of Premier ores; the company had made $5,451,000 in eight years from copper sales and now that such sales showed a loss, the agency had been transferred to Guggenheim Brothers.

As for the company's losses in 1920, Simon regretted, on behalf of shareholders, that Eilers' attack had been made in "a period of drastic readjustment of all securities values, inevitably causing a needlessly severe and unjustified fall in the market price of the stock." American Smelting and Refining common touched a low of 29¼ while the preferred, still paying dividends, sank to 64½.

As for the firm being gutted by the Guggenheims, well, the figures themselves shouted to the contrary. In 1901 the company returned 3.83 per cent on its capital stock but since then net earnings of $250,000,000 had been realized, averaging more than 8 per cent from 1902 to 1914, over 15 per cent in the first three war years, 11 per cent in 1918 and 9 per cent in 1919.

On the basis of the firm's reply, the *Engineering and Mining Journal* estimated Guggenheim holdings in Smelters at $3,300,000 which "represents probably far less than 1 per cent of the family's total wealth." Actually their holdings, it developed, were more nearly $5,000,000—about 2 per cent of the Guggenheim fortune.

With Eilers permitted access to the list of stockholders, his court action ended and he transferred the field of battle to a series of statements mailed to the company's owners, each of which was answered in a war of words that exposed to public view every skeleton in the Trust's closet. With flat statements followed by denials just as emphatic, it became apparent to some that if the truth were to be known, an independent investigation must be started. The questions raised by Eilers which such an inquiry must sift were these:

1. Why had the Guggenheims disposed of $35,000,000 in Smelters stock by 1907 and not seen fit to re-invest?

2. Why did they keep Kennecott and the porphyry coppers for themselves instead of permitting A. S. and R. to finance them and enjoy the profits?

3. When they dismantled Guggenheim Exploration, why did they turn their immensely valuable Utah Copper stock into their own Kennecott Corporation while "dumping" $22,000,000 of their less desirable mines into A. S. and R.'s lap? "By a remarkable series of coincidences," said Eilers, "neither Chile, nor Braden, nor Utah, nor Nevada Consolidated ever found its way into Smelters." As for Utah, the company had been obliged to spend more for a smelter to treat its ores than the Guggenheims had invested in the mines themselves, "but the great profit has not come to A. S. and R."

4. Why did they make A. S. and R. assume responsibility

404

for $31,000,000 in first mortgage bonds in order to retire
the inferior stock of American Smelters Securities?

5. Why was the copper sales agency, which, Eilers said,
turned in $10,000,000 in profits in eight years, handed over
as a gift to Guggenheim Brothers?

6. Why have salaries believed to aggregate over $500,000
been paid to each of the Guggenheims?

7. Why have quick assets not increased in fourteen years,
common stock declined to 4½ per cent, and its market quo-
tation to the lowest figure in twenty years?

Alarmed by the criticism that welled up from hundreds of
stockholders in the wake of the Eilers letters, the Guggenheims decided that an investigation must be held under
independent auspices so distinguished that it could not be
assailed. They proposed that former President Taft undertake the job and he accepted, only to be appointed Chief
Justice of the Supreme Court. Elihu Root substituted.
Eilers was not satisfied. Root was "of counsel for Guggenheim Brothers" and anyway it was not proper for the de-
fendants to pick the judge and pay him.

In the meantime the regular annual stockholders' meeting
was held in Jersey City, with Eilers holding proxies for
202,000 votes, nearly a fourth of all cast. It fell to Sol,
more at ease on his feet than Simon, to make the family's
defense. He reminded the stockholders that only two years
ago Edward Brush, a director and original stockholder, had
spread on the company's minutes a eulogy of the Guggenheim brothers. The company's success, said the resolution,
was due to their "farseeing devotion, constructive imagination, great ability, and untiring industry." "And among
those voting for this unusual testimonial only two years
ago," announced Sol, "was Karl Eilers!" If the Guggenheims had sold most of their Smelters stock, where, asked
Sol, were the 70,000 shares given Anton Eilers for his
Pueblo smelters? His son admitted to having only 3,622.

Karl Eilers sailed into the board as mere creatures of the brothers. He quoted Vice-President Brownell, later to be chairman of the board, as saying: "I certainly do not approve of all the board but what are you going to do when you are working for a man?" This Brownell denied. "One of us is not telling the truth," commented Eilers. He denounced the board for having thrown him "bodily out." "I might remark," rejoined Simon, "that the best interests of the stockholders have been served by this action."

Nevertheless, in response to the pressure of Eilers' 200,000 votes, eight non-employees were elected to the board, against twenty employees. Only Dan and Simon remained of the Guggenheim clan.

Two investigations were under way, the one by Elihu Root and the other by a stockholders' committee which was independent both of the company and of Eilers. When it became apparent that Root's findings would be considered *ex parte*, A. S. and R asked the independent committee to name three more members from the board to its membership, and paid all the expenses of the investigation. The committee split, four to three, as might have been expected, with A. S. and R.'s three directors dissenting. George W. Wickersham, Taft's Attorney-General and counsel to the committee, concurred with the majority report.

In its pages were to be found perhaps as definitive a judgment as will ever be made on the role of the House of Guggenheim in American Smelting and Refining. At the very first, the committee declared that Guggenheim management had been efficient and successful. The record of earnings and dividend payments were patent proof of that, it was held. Indeed, dividend payments had been too generous during the war period, leaving the company without adequate reserves for the strain and stress of post-war adjustment. From that point, the report became critical. The committee delved into the very beginning of the Guggenheim connection and discovered that Dan's great coup was indeed accomplished, to the initial loss of the Smelters Trust. His statement that the pre-Trust Guggenheim smelting properties were earning $4,000,000 was held to be "very greatly exaggerated." It was partly on the basis of that glowing income statement that the Trust handed over stock worth $34,000,000 to the Guggenheims. But, said the committee, the Trust got only $14,000,000 in properties for its outlay. And the brothers realized $37,-000,000 on the Smelters stock—a neat profit of $23,000,000 and a corresponding loss to the Smelters stockholders.

The committee believed the entire American Smelters Securities episode was a piece of stockjobbing by which the Guggenheims created some $77,000,000 in stock certificates and cashed in handsomely on the solid value given the paper from the Smelting company's resources. Particularly reprehensible, said the investigators, was the sale of half of the Securities common, valued on Guggenheim Exploration books at $1, to the smelting company at par value.

The transfer, in 1920, of the copper sales agency for Kennecott and the porphyries from American Smelting to Guggenheim Brothers was condemned. The Trust had made millions by selling copper, but it had handed over this lucrative business to the Guggenheims free of charge.

To prevent repetition of these conflicts in interest between the brothers and the Smelting company, the committee recommended that a board of directors be elected completely independent of the family.

Elihu Root gave the other side of the picture. In glowing words he summed up A. S. and R.'s great dividend record. In twenty years the stockholders had realized their entire cash outlay, plus 6 per cent a year, plus $23,000,000, and still owned a company worth $128,000,000, equivalent to par on both common and preferred plus $17,000,000 extra.

In that period the Smelters Trust paid $118,000,000 in dividends on a cash investment of $47,000,000.

Root defended the American Smelters Securities deal. The Trust in 1904-5 was in no position to raise the money needed for expansion unless it took Jacob Schiff into virtual partnership. This had been avoided by offering an attractive guaranteed stock, and A. S. and R. had retained its independence. It was "for the best interests of all concerned" that Guggenheim Brothers had taken over the copper sales agency from the Trust. He reminded critics that the Trust had profited mightily from the fact that the Guggenheims were interested both in the porphyry coppers and in the Trust. As for the board of directors being mostly employees, it merely followed the precepts of Standard Oil of New Jersey, most of whose directors were "men in the business." Who else were better qualified to run a company, Root asked.

The rosy statements about the Smelters Trust's great dividend record provoked a howl in the West. In the depth of post-war depression, mine owners agreed thoroughly with Elihu Root's appraisal of the company's success and added that it came from "swindle-sheet" smelter statements which mulcted honest operators of their due on ore. The plaints became so vehement that A. S. and R. issued a formal statement assuring producers that it had their best interests at heart.

The criticism which played about the Smelters Securities deal led to that company's absorption by A. S. and R. By 1922 the Smelting company owned all the Securities' common and most of the preferred. A Kuhn, Loeb bond issue for $7,500,000 paid off outside investors and gave that banking house a final cut on an issue which it and Jacob Schiff had helped to float seventeen years before.

The Guggenheims held out the olive branch. Before the 1922 stockholders' meeting, a compromise was reached with the independent stockholders' committee by which it was agreed to elect eighteen outsiders to the board, to ten employees. Among the new directors were General George W. Goethals, Charles D. Hilles, Harvey D. Gibson, and Elihu Root. Eilers gave his assent and there was no contest.

He had gained all he could hope for on the basis of the support of one-fourth of Smelters stock. He had aired to the world once and for all the rankling grievances which he and other practical metallurgists held against the financiers in charge of the Trust. He had shown that the Guggenheims were no longer heavy owners in Smelters stock. He had obtained the election of a board most of whose members were not employees.

Guggenheim control remained. But it was a control which now had to be maintained by prestige and not by force of the stock held or the domination of men who owed their jobs to the president. With Dan's driving force removed, the board would no longer look to him as the genius who could get the company out of tight holes or lead it into ever greener pastures. Gradually American Smelting and Refining would become another of those anonymous corporations run by self-interested executives, untroubled by stockholders so long as dividends flowed out reasonably.

The truth, unpalatable as it must have been to Dan and Murry and Sol, was that the Guggenheim genius and drive were petering out. The twilight of the Guggenheims approached.

25. CHILEAN TRANSMUTATION

TO Chilean patriots it seemed, after the World War, that their proud land was becoming an economic province of the Guggenheims. The brothers owned Chile Copper, biggest corporation in the country, and were interesting themselves in Chile's greatest natural resource, nitrates. Thoughtful men saw the North American monopolists stretching their dreaded control to the very rim of the Andes and seizing an industry on which the government relied for 40 per cent of its revenues.

The government itself, hard-pressed for money when the post-war depression cut nitrate sales and export duties, found itself obliged to go hat in hand to Wall Street for a $24,000,000 loan, upon which Dan Guggenheim placed his benediction. The loan, said Dan, "is an event of considerable significance in that it affords a splendid opportunity not only for what I believe to be a sound and attractive investment, but even more important also, for cementing invaluable economic relations with one of the leading countries of South America." Dan was full of compliments for the government, the people, the natural resources. "The efforts to co-operate in the development of Chile's natural resources," he added, "have been fully understood and intelligently encouraged by the Chileans who are a nation with a high degree of culture, character, and business acumen, all of which qualities will play an important part in the future development of the country."

Chilean progressives and the militant labor movement alike looked with apprehension at the growing economic ties between New York financiers and their own government. They could not know at that time, of course, that the loan was to be all velvet, that the 7 per cent external bonds were to be selling within 10 years at 10 to 20 per cent of face value. What they did know was that those restless souls, Albert C. Burrage and E. A. Cappelen Smith, were seeking wider fields than Chuqui's porphyries to conquer. It was Burrage who had introduced Chuqui to the Guggenheims, in 1911, when it was a wasteland estimated to hold 134,000,-000,000 pounds of copper in its desert embrace. Cappelen Smith, engineer par excellence, evolved the method of treating Chuqui's ore. These two could not stop speculating on the nitrate wealth that surrounded them. In that desert, the driest expanse known to man, nature over the ages had precipitated nitrate of soda in incalculable quantities from the rocks and lava. English research in the early nineteenth century proved the value of this nitrate in stimulating farm production. Thus the sands of the uninhabited South Pacific desert doubled Europe's population and caused the fierce war that Chile waged against Bolivia and Peru for the conquest of the provinces of Tarapacá and Antofagasta.

To Cappelen Smith, inheritor and improver of the mass reduction processes evolved under Dan Jackling in Utah's copper canyon, it seemed a shame that the British interests in Chile should cling to the antiquated Shanks process which wasted nearly half the nitrate and doomed enormous deposits of caliche—the nitrate ore—to remain mere desert. He and Burrage convinced the Guggenheim brothers that in Chuqui's copper they had only just begun the exploitation of Chile's mineral wealth.

This was in the bonanza days of 1916, when money rolled in faster than Guggenheim Brothers could figure, and they were full of grand plans for their great Chuqui property. They talked over the prospect with Dwight Morrow, J. P. Morgan's expert on Latin American affairs. A nitrate account was opened, split evenly between Guggenheim Brothers and J. P. Morgan and Company, with Burrage

411

cut in for 10 per cent of the Guggenheim share. He scouted for nitrate lands but the prices were war-swollen. Then in 1919 desert owners, plagued by the shrinking market for natural nitrates, began offering their properties to the firm.

Harry Guggenheim, Dan's son, who had interested himself in the family's Chilean investments, declared that the revival of Chile's nitrate industry waited upon two factors:

1. A cheaper method must be found for nitrate reduction, along the lines on which Cappelen Smith was experimenting.

2. With that process, all of Chile's nitrate industry must be trustified; the old plants, with their tens of thousands of laborers, closed; the Government must waive its $12.50 a ton export tax.

His announcement sent cold shivers running up the spines of Chileans.

Harry was off for London late in 1919 to talk it over with the stiff-necked Anthony Gibbs interests, important Chilean producers. The Chilean Government, they rejoined, would never tolerate the formation of a monopoly or the sacrifice of the export tax.

By 1922 Cappelen Smith had perfected his laboratory process to the point that he needed a real plant to work with. He claimed that his method, now called the "Guggenheim process," would cut costs 40 per cent and scrap manual labor and antiquated "*oficinas*." Sol went down to Santiago to sell the Nitrate Producers Association on the new process, but they declined. As Don Agustín Edwards, Chilean minister to London and magnifico in the League of Nations, had told Harry, Cappelen Smith, and the Morgan, Grenfell people in London, they could hardly expect the producers to revolutionize the industry at great expense on the basis of a method not even tried out yet on a commercial scale. The Guggenheims were known to be a rich family who had put up millions to develop Chuqui. Why should they hesitate to

412

build, themselves, a $500,000 plant to test out their process? Vivian Smith of Morgan, Grenfell, writing to E. T. Stettinius of J. P. Morgan's, concurred. Foiled in his project of selling the Guggenheim process, Sol tried his hand at buying out a big producer, and failed again.

By the end of 1922, the Guggenheim-Morgan syndicate had spent $261,000 to develop the Guggenheim process, and there seemed no return in sight for the outlay. At that point negotiations of the most vital interest to Chile began in far-away New York. John D. Ryan, head of the Anaconda Copper Mining Company, was proposing to Guggenheim Brothers that they sell their Chuqui copper properties. To Anaconda it was no mere speculative venture but a matter of life and death. In all those years when the Guggenheims had been busy buying into porphyry coppers, Anaconda, heir to the H. H. Rogers-Tom Lawson Amalgamated Copper of 1899, had been content to burrow ever deeper into the Butte hills. But the deeper Anaconda burrowed, the higher mounted costs, already far out of line with the great porphyries. Now the great Butte company must assure itself other and cheaper sources of copper, or perish.

So Ryan finally offered Guggenheim Brothers $70,000,-000 for Chile Copper—and for a bare majority of its stock, at that. For a company encumbered with $50,000,000 of bonded debt, whose shares had sold as low as 7¾ and at the time of Ryan's offer were quoted at 28, the chance to sell at $35 a share seemed too good to resist. Chuqui, thanks to bond issues which had financed its development, had not cost the Guggenheims a red penny. And there it stood, a property which could produce 360,000 pounds of copper a day for nearly a century at a 1923 cost of less than 6 cents a pound, the lowest in the world.

The brothers thought it a nice deal, the more so as Chuqui had lost a million dollars in 1921 because the world

413

market was shot to pieces. Perhaps Ryan had come running all the quicker because Chuqui's copper had been dumped on the market for what it would bring, causing no little anguish to interests dependent solely on United States production.

Nevertheless Anaconda's offer opened up the second schism in the House of Guggenheim, the only one to disturb its unity since Ben and Will withdrew in 1901 over the American Smelting coup. As then, it was the younger members of the firm who objected—Harry, Dan's son, and Edmond, Murry's. They had grown up with Chile copper and believed it held the key to the future of world copper control. Not even the threatening flood of Katanga's slave-labor copper from Africa could faze the Guggenheims, the boys argued, if they were fortified with Chuqui's rich ores and matched their *"cholo"* laborers against the Congo's Negroes.

In reply the older members of the firm could say that actually Chuqui had returned little to the firm. It did not swing into production until 1916 and there had been trouble with the Cappelen Smith process that cut expected profits. Thereafter a $35,000,000 expansion program was ordered, just now completed. Next year a $15,000,000 bond issue would be due.

It was fathers against sons. The four Guggenheim brothers (Isaac had just died) voted down the two sons. On March 1, 1923, John D. Ryan handed to Murry Guggenheim a check for $70,000,000—the biggest written up to that date—in return for 2,000,000 of Chile's 3,800,-000 shares. Murry would have his joke, so he insisted that the check be certified. Anaconda then set another record, a $150,000,000 bond issue through Guaranty Trust and National City, to pay off the Guggenheims, finance other purchases, and provide working capital for Chile Copper.

Six weeks after Guggenheim Brothers received the record-breaking check, Harry and Ed resigned from the firm, so deep was the chasm opened by the sale of their favorite property, so bitter their resentment. Ed followed up by resigning his directorship in Kennecott Copper.

That ended the hopes of Meyer Guggenheim's sons that their partnership would continue as a family affair. It must needs be refreshed now by blood outside the family. All four brothers were advancing in years—Dan was sixty-seven and Simon, the youngest active in the firm, was fifty-six.

Only one outsider had ever been a member, William Chapman Potter, one-time manager of the Smelting Trust's Mexican properties, later vice-president of Guaranty Trust, who became a Guggenheim partner in charge of Chilean business with an 8⅓ per cent interest, the same as that held by Harry and Ed. On the day that Harding became President of the United States, Potter resigned to become president of Guaranty Trust, and his share was split between the two boys.

To replace Harry and Ed, the brothers admitted John K. MacGowan, long in their employ, and Cappelen Smith. In 1929 MacGowan was ousted over a disagreement on policy.

Increasingly the Guggenheims became dependent on hired help, not only to run their properties, but to run their own partnership. Simon's time was taken up with the Smelters Trust, Dan was in practical retirement, Isaac dead. It was not to be expected that Murry and Sol, on whom devolved the burden of responsibility, could become experts in a strange new enterprise—nitrates—in a land 5,500 miles away. And yet that was to be the main enterprise of Guggenheim Brothers.

Flush with $70,000,000, the Guggenheims were still the second biggest stockholders in Chile Copper, with an interest valued at $20,000,000 at going quotations. They were owners of Braden Copper, second largest of the Chilean copper companies. They were the most important stockholders in Kennecott Copper which set out in 1923, following the depression, to acquire complete control of Utah Copper. Kennecott, with assets of $268,000,000, became the biggest American copper enterprise. Its 1925 profits were recorded at $24,000,000; in 1929 at $52,000,000. When Kennecott stock climbed to 158, despite the flood of 5,000,000 shares, another 7,000,000 shares were added for the public.

Of Utah at the time of the merger it was said that the 2,156,000 pounds of copper it had produced would reach around the world sixty-four times in a wire the thickness of a lead pencil. Or it would string a telegraph wire to Mars. At that time Utah had extracted $374,000,000 in copper, returned $173,000,000 in profits, paid $131,000,000 in dividends and $65,000,000 in wages. To accomplish this as much earth had been removed as in the excavation of the Panama Canal. Another $50,000,000 in dividends were to be added by 1930.

As for Yukon Gold, its dredges were transferred to the Malay peninsula to scoop up tin. As the Guggenheims became more concerned with South America, they considered extending their holdings in Bolivia. Many an earnest conference was held. It was in the last of these conferences, after hours of talk, that Murry, turning to his brothers, remarked:

"We have heard the legal lights and the engineering lights, now what do the Israelites think of this proposition?"

All told, the brothers dumped some $16,000,000 of the Anaconda check into Caracoles Tin. If Guggenheim smelters could have reduced the ore at the price British smelters did, $36 a ton, Caracoles' might have been a happier story than Yukon Gold's. But the Perth Amboy plant, struggle as it would, could not get costs below $70 a ton. The British maintained their monopoly on tin smelting. The Guggenheims suffered their loss alone; no Caracoles stocks or bonds

416

were ever offered the public. This was in accord with the conservative policy they followed in later years.

After they had gobbled up Utah in Kennecott, the Guggenheims fixed their attention on Chile. The pioneering spirit that led Meyer Guggenheim on from one profitable venture to another, flitted like *ignis fatuus* before his sons in their declining years. They thought they saw on the Chilean desert a great nitrate monopoly built on the secret Guggenheim process and coining money faster than had the A.Y. and Minnie mines, the Pueblo smelter, or Kennecott and Chile Copper.

For seventy years the Guggenheims had been venturing and they had never failed in any major enterprise. The partnership Meyer Guggenheim founded led a charmed existence. Given their hired engineering brains, the best in the world, their money, their intimate connections in Santiago, and the great era of prosperity which was dawning, what could stop the four Guggenheim brothers from attaining the crowning victory of long and profitable years spent in exploitation? Granted that the House of Guggenheim was nearly spent in its vital reserves, why might not its final years prove the most brilliant of all?

Following Dwight Morrow's advice not to start from scratch in Chile, Guggenheim Brothers bought the Anglo-Chilean Nitrate and Railway Company; and following their own, they bought from the Chilean Government at auction the Coya Norte nitrate deposits for $3,185,000. They organized the Coya Norte syndicate early in 1924 and offered participation to J. P. Morgan and Company. The Morgan firm considered the Guggenheim offer, considered the ebbing price of nitrate, thanks to the boom in artificial nitrate, considered the exigencies of dealing with a Latin-American government over a long period of years, and declined.

Morgan, moreover, withdrew from the joint nitrate pros-

417

pect account which had been established to perfect the Guggenheim process. The Morgan share the four brothers divided among themselves, much to the astonishment of Harry and Ed, who demanded their percentages. One set of lawyers said "No," Elihu Root said, "Yes," and the boys were cut in.

Boldly Guggenheim Brothers plunged into their new enterprise without Morgan assistance. In December, 1924, they organized the Anglo-Chilean Consolidated Nitrate Company, which took over complete control of the Anglo-Chilean Nitrate and Railway Company for £3,600,000, payable in bonds, took over the Coya Norte lands from the Guggenheims at cost, and paid $550,000 for the license to use the Guggenheim process. The British firm felt highly flattered to receive £4 for each £1 share in the old Anglo-Chilean.

In consideration of the value of Coya Norte's land over and above its cost, the Guggenheims kept all of Anglo-Chilean's common stock. They agreed to advance $6,000,-000 in cash to build a 260,000-ton Guggenheim process plant, taking pay in preferred stock.

To relieve them of their cash outlay, the Guggenheims late in 1925 floated a $16,500,000 7 per cent bond issue through Lehman Brothers, and sat back to allow the profits to gush into their pockets. For an actual outlay of $149,000 in developing the Guggenheim process, they possessed Anglo-Chilean, valued at $36,000,000, and still held the patents.

Anglo's stock was distributed pro rata among the members of the Coya Norte syndicate. The four brothers held over half, the two sons about 11 per cent each, the estate of Isaac Guggenheim, about 6 per cent. Partner MacGowan got about 3 per cent; Engineer Burrage about 8 per cent; Morgan, Grenfell of London, 2½ per cent.

418

A 2½ per cent interest, worth $900,000, was given to Augustín Edwards, the Nestor of Chile. Edwards, for all his name, was Chile's most distinguished diplomat and man of affairs. Fourteen years minister to London, his country's highest diplomatic post, he had also been prime minister, minister of foreign affairs, president of the Third Assembly of the League of Nations in 1922, and president of the Fifth Pan-American Conference, held in Santiago in 1923. He founded four daily newspapers and five magazines and was the author of volumes highly regarded. All in all, Don Agustín was the most powerful figure in conservative Chile, so he received a 2½ per cent interest in Anglo-Chilean and was made chairman of its board. Cappelen Smith was named president.

If the brothers hoped to sit back and let the money roll in, as they had with so many a venture, they were mistaken in Anglo. It was quicksand in the desert, swallowing up all the Lehman Brothers millions. Cappelen Smith found he must have a 500,000-ton plant, enough to turn out a fourth of Chile's normal production, to get his costs down. So Guggenheim Brothers borrowed on securities of $5,-000,000 from L. F. Rothschild and Company early in 1927. It was a kind of inter-family loan for Rothschild was a brother-in-law, having married the Guggenheim sister, Cora; the original partner, Albert Loeb, now dead, had married another sister, Rose; still another partner married one of Isaac's daughters.

It was about this time that Chilean nitrates did a nose dive in world markets. The ridiculous efforts of the Nitrate Producers Association to hold up prices, despite growing competition by European manufacturers of synthetic nitrate, broke of their own weight. Prices descended to whatever depths the necessity of the producers and the exigencies of competition dictated. In the mêlée that rocked Chile,

Colonel Ibañez ousted the constitutional government and set up a dictatorship.

By now the Guggenheims had a bear by the tail. The Rothschild loan was not enough to finish the 500,000-ton plant. In June, 1927, Murry and Sol each lent $2,500,000; by the end of the year Anglo-Chilean's maw demanded $4,-000,000 more, which the brothers raised by pledging $5,000,000 in securities.

Cappelen Smith had solved Chuqui's technical problems but the nearer he got to the solution of Anglo's, the lower sank the price of nitrate. For each dollar he saved in production costs, he lost, tantalizingly, another in lower prices. Sol impatiently demanded results but his engineer told him that with the bigger capacity of the Guggenheim process plant, more nitrate lands must be bought.

The firm of Guggenheim Brothers was not used to this kind of business. When they took over the porphyries, they floated a bond issue, let the public pay the exploitation costs, and enjoyed the profits. But the Lehman bond issue for Anglo had long ago been exhausted and no more could be floated. Nor could they go to old reliable Guaranty Trust, presided over by their former partner, W. C. Potter. He read the newspaper dispatches about Chile and nitrates. Nor would National City take a chance on something marked "highly speculative."

The need of the moment was something which would entice millions out of these banks to recoup the Guggenheim expenditures. To prepare such a package, the brothers late in 1928 dug up out of their own pockets a $25,000,000 loan. This was to repay the Rothschild loan, to repay the brothers for their $4,000,000 advance and Murry and Solomon for their $5,000,000, and to provide $11,700,000 for expansion.

To round out their Chilean enterprise and make it attractive to the bankers, the brothers in 1929 bought the

Lautaro Nitrate Company through an exchange in stocks. This provided the extra lands needed for the big nitrate mill and boosted the production quota allotted Anglo by the Nitrate Producers Association. To cancel the juicy management contract held by Baburizza, Lukinovic and Company over Lautaro, Anglo-Chilean handed over notes for £1,-600,000, payable in four annual installments beginning in 1929. The brothers then guaranteed the notes and sold a third of them to Lehman Brothers and another third to National City.

Lautaro was acquired June 17, 1929, and the first payment of Guggenheim Brothers' $648,000 share on the Baburizza notes fell due October 15, 1929. That was just a few days before the bottom fell out of the Mellon-Coolidge ever-ascending plateau of prosperity. But the Guggenheims had not foreseen, any more than Irving Fisher and other economic pundits, the stock market panic, nor the four agonizing years that were to follow.

26. THE MUNIFICENT GUGGENHEIMS

THE wealth of the Guggenheims, after they received their $70,000,000 check for Chile Copper, rivaled that of the Rothschilds of Europe and placed them among America's four richest families, with the Fords, the Rockefellers and the Mellons. In an analysis of modern Midases, the *New York Times* credited the sons of Meyer Guggenheim with some two hundred million dollars, concentrated largely in Kennecott Copper, mother-corporation for the porphyries, and the proceeds of Chuquicamata's sale. The estimate seemed sober. Yet it meant that since Meyer's death in 1905, Daniel and his four brothers had quintupled the family fortune. In all the history of acquisitiveness, there was but one parallel to the amazing climb of the Guggenheims to the pinnacles of finance in the short span of twenty years, and that was achieved by their caustic critic, Henry Ford, who objected to men piling up wealth from mere ownership of natural resources.

From the back regions of the American continent criticism even bitterer than Ford's was hurled at this New York family who had levied toll on mineral resources all the way from Alaska's frozen mountains to Chile's torrid desert. The name of Guggenheim was Juggernaut to millions. Among them were owners of mines that paid tribute to the Smelters Trust; owners of mines whose ore the Smelters Trust would not touch; men whose mines suffered from the flood of low-cost metal which issued from the superior Guggenheim workings; the thousands who lived in sections of the Rockies suffering from the curse which they claimed the brothers laid upon development. Tens of thousands of

422

HARRY F. GUGGENHEIM AND CHARLES A. LINDBERGH. *Photos by International and Wide World.*

EDMOND A. GUGGENHEIM AND HIS GOLF INSTRUCTOR, JACK FORRESTER.

laborers in Guggenheim mines and smelters chafed under industrial serfdom which permitted them no effective voice in their jobs. Progressive-minded people all along the rocky backbone of the American continent were united in the opinion that it was unfair for any group of men to coin hundreds of millions from mere ownership of subsoil rights. Mostly, these men did not challenge the right of the five brothers, as developers and employers, to an honest return on the use of capital and machinery; they cried out against rules which permitted private individuals to lay claim to wealth they had not created but that had been stored by Mother Earth for the use of all her children. This opinion was expressed more vehemently south of the Rio Grande, where Latin concepts of ownership differed sharply from the Anglo-Saxon.

Sifting these plaints against Meyer Guggenheim's sons, one could detect the note of envy. Millions, however, objected to the *system* of making money by monopoly or by gutting the earth. Their answer centered on the Guggenheims, not for any personal quality in these genial, energetic men, but because they embodied a twisted set of values that glorified financial shrewdness and personal acquisitiveness. After the wealth of the Rockies, Alaska and Chile had been funneled into the vaults of Guggenheim Brothers, what resulted but five men sitting over an extraordinary accumulation of the world's goods?

It is not likely that philosophic speculation upset any of the brothers. Will, the youngest of the seven, detached for a quarter century from his brothers' enterprises, could sit in his big office-study at 3 Riverside Drive, gaze at the Hudson, and wonder about "cataclysmic changes" and "awakening socialism." To the rest, business was an exhilarating game in which the rewards went to the far-sighted and the forehanded. If the Guggenheims didn't grab, someone else would. And why should winners seek to change the rules of the game?

Dan's daring mind had seen the threat to the established order rising darkly, he thought, from Red Russia. But to the chorus of plaints from the back country, Dan was content to turn a soft answer. He reassured indignant mine owners that he had their best interests at heart, reproved anti-monopolists for attacking men who had opened up great stretches of waste land to civilization, ignored as visionaries those who claimed the Guggenheims had no right to all the gold, silver, lead, and copper they turned up from the earth.

When Dan, in 1923, resigned the last directorship he held (in American Smelting and Refining), it seemed that the name of Guggenheim would gradually disappear even from the mining world. No sons of the seven brothers thought it worth while to continue in their fathers' footsteps. Their corporations were headed toward anonymity. In another generation only historians would note that the Guggenheims had left their footprints on the sands of time. Nowhere but in the West and the mineral provinces of the Americas would men remember that name, and then think merely of money-grubbers who had grabbed ruthlessly and departed unceremoniously, leaving melancholy shack towns to crumble back into the wilderness.

To Daniel, sitting alone in his Hempstead House castle on Sands Point, it must have seemed a melancholy commentary that the sturdy name of Guggenheim appeared in the papers more often in connection with third-generation divorces than in any other way. Old Meyer's fierce spirit of acquisitiveness so soon had petered out into wastrelism: Guggenheims were more prominent in the world of dog shows, horse races, and divorce courts than in business.

It was his son, Harry, who led Dan up to a high mountain and opened great vistas for the name of Guggenheim. Harry's abundant energy, diverted from business, had returned to an old love—aviation. The dazzling rise of flying from a dare-devil avocation to a solid commercial enterprise serving millions of people was to be the theme of the twenties, and great honors would be heaped upon him who would stimulate that rise. Eagerly Harry sketched his plan: a fund that would serve as a central clearing house for aviation progress, subsidize the first faltering years of commercial flying, popularize man's conquest of the air. As a first step, Harry proposed that his father found the Daniel Guggenheim School of Aeronautics at New York University, the only institution in the country which offered a full undergraduate course in that branch. A building with wind tunnel, propeller laboratory and adjuncts could be erected for $225,000; the rest of the capital would endow three chairs, laboratory assistants, and maintenance. The plan touched the old pioneering spirit in Dan's heart, and gladly he gave the necessary $500,000. Turning the first spadeful of dirt October 22, 1925, he said:

As I am an old man whose active days of toil are passed, I shall dedicate the rest of my life with the active aid of my son, Harry, to the study and promotion of the science of aeronautics. I shall do this as a part of my duty to my country whose ample opportunities have ever been at my hand and whose bountiful blessings I have had the good fortune to enjoy. Were I a young man seeking a career in either science or commerce, I should unhesitatingly turn to aviation. I consider it the greatest road to opportunity which lies before the science and commerce of the civilized countries of the earth today.

Dan must have been amazed at the roar of acclaim that greeted his gift. The scientific world, the popular press which had just begun to feature aviation, the editorial writers of the dignified morning papers alike applauded this initial fillip to aeronautical research. For Harry it was no problem to draw his father into the next step of the plan, a $2,500,000 Daniel Guggenheim Fund for the Promotion of Aeronautics. It was to be no permanent endowment. To the contrary, Harry, a war-time naval aviator, passionately interested in the advance of flying, believed that the next five years would tell the tale in placing the air industry on its feet.

For the young man, the busiest, most joyful, most important years of his life opened. With the energy that his grandfather had thrown into opening a new line of embroidery, Harry established Fund offices in Pershing Square, hired a corps of publicity men and mobilized the aviation brains of the country. Through his office poured all the reports on aviation progress and from it, in a ceaseless stream, gushed press statements aiming to take the curse off aviation's record of fatalities, dispel fear of the plane as an engine of disaster, encourage safety, and interest even children in model plane contests. Loans were extended to commercial companies to establish weather reports, beacons, emergency landing fields and air markings. The Institutes of Technology of Massachusetts and California and the University of Washington were given Guggenheim schools comparable to New York University's. Grants for specific research jobs were showered on schools and individual pioneers. Whenever occasion offered, Harry himself was on hand with a speech to "sell" aviation to the public.

The scion of the House of Guggenheim associated with other dignitaries who patronized the fledgling industry— Harold S. Vanderbilt, Dwight Morrow, Otto H. Kahn, Jacob Schiff. He was on intimate terms with Harry Byrd,

Orville Wright, Glenn Curtiss and Glen Martin, the big names of aviation.

But it was left to a slender youth and his plane, the Spirit of St. Louis, to put aviation across. Lindbergh's flight to Paris, May 20-21, 1927, turned the country not merely air-conscious but air-delirious. For Harry Guggenheim it was the opportunity of a lifetime and eagerly he snatched it. No sooner had the young hero been released from the official embrace of Washington and New York on his triumphal return from Europe than Harry spirited the flier away to his new house at Sands Point, on his father's estate. There, as a guest of the Guggenheims, Lindbergh signed up for an air tour of the country under the auspices of the Fund and the Department of Commerce, to "stir the air-consciousness of the American people and give added impetus to commercial flying as a practical, safe, and useful means of transportation."

The Guggenheim Fund, expert in the ways of publicity, handled the tour that took Lindbergh into every state of the union on a 22,000-mile jaunt and soured him on the public. After the exhausting tour was over, Lindbergh accepted a position with the Fund, became a director, and flew with Harry down to Virginia for a vacation with Governor Byrd, brother of the Polar flier. A strong attachment grew between Lindbergh and Guggenheim. The pleasant, boyish but serious-minded idol of the nation liked Harry's frank, engaging personality, respected his sincere passion for aviation, and understood the importance of the job the Fund was trying to do.

To the nation, the name of Guggenheim became linked with aviation, the newest, most exciting of man's conquests. Easterners, to whom the name of the mining and smelting magnates had never meant much, regarded the Guggenheims as new-found benefactors; in the West many a mine owner sighed and remarked he was glad some of the money pried out of him by the Smelting Kings was at last being devoted to a good purpose. Harry Byrd, at Little America in the Antarctic, named his hangars and machine shop "Harry Guggenheim."

By 1928 Harry considered that the Fund's first job, to "sell" aviation and stimulate commercial interest, had been accomplished. The Fund switched to the less spectacular but vital problems of safety. It tackled the fog problem, encouraged the passion for flying fields that swept the country, and planned within the next few years to spend the rest of Dan's $2,500,000 gift. An extra $480,000 Dan gave, gratefully, to the Government of Chile for an aviation school.

The Fund had not only "made" aviation; it had made Harry Guggenheim. He was no longer just another rich man's son, but a public figure in his own right. He nursed ambitions not unlike those that animated his Uncle Simon twenty-five years before, and proceeded to attain them.

As for Dan, he had almost been lost sight of in the publicity that played about his son. But in 1929 he received the Spirit of St. Louis medal from the American Society of Mechanical Engineers. "We have heard a lot about Mr. Guggenheim's son, Harry, as president of the Fund," said the society's secretary, in presenting the medal. "But many seem to have forgotten 'the old man'."

Another gift, made jointly at the start, by Dan and Florence and Murry and Leonie Guggenheim, aroused the appreciation of music-loving people. For several years the Goldman band concerts in Central Park had been given indifferent financial support, despite their popularity with tens of thousands of people on summer evenings. Early in 1924 the Guggenheims announced they would defray all expenses for the three-month season, "the greatest gift ever made here for the cause of free music for all," as Bandmaster Edwin Franko Goldman said. Mayor Hylan ac-

428

cepted and, with his usual modesty, put his own name in black type across the programs. The Guggenheim names appeared below.

Next year a disgraceful row broke out. The Guggenheims objected to the concert program being made a political poster for Hylan. That patron of the arts thereupon barred Goldman from the Park, and Hylan henchmen recruited police, fire, biscuit company, and military bands to substitute. Hylan's chamberlain entered raucously into the hullabaloo. "Goldman thinks he owns Central Park," he barked. "The gentleman is wrong," countered Goldman. "Everyone knows that Hylan owns Central Park."

Groups of indignant ladies joined the mêlée by picketing Hylan's office at City Hall. Chased off, they returned laden with deflated toy balloons emblazoned, "We Want Goldman Concerts in the Park." These were given to hordes of small boys who appeared from everywhere. In a few minutes the rebuke to Mayor Hylan was ascending the sides of the tall Municipal Building, to the merriment of all New York. City Hall police dashed out to break up the nefarious plot against the city's rulers. The ladies retaliated by training children to sing in chorus:

> The Goldman band we kiddies all
> Want next summer on the Mall.

Chancellor Brown of New York University, mindful of Dan's munificent aeronautical school gift, threw open the Washington Heights campus; a bandstand and seats for 15,000 were built. The next year Jimmy Walker was mayor of New York and the Goldman concerts returned to Central Park. One to two million people heard the concerts yearly thereafter; as many as 45,000 at a time listened with delight to the spirited summer's eve programs given by the Guggenheims at a cost of nearly $100,000 a season. Radio enabled other millions across the country to listen. The gift

429

earned Dan an honorary membership in Musicians Local 802, one of the few such honors the union ever bestowed. Later on, the support of the Goldman Band was taken over wholly by the Daniel and Florence Guggenheim Foundation, a second charitable organization into which Dan poured his money in his declining years. This Foundation now has in its treasury some $4,000,000.

The two brothers also gave a $100,000 greenhouse to the New York Botanical Gardens to cultivate rare plants from the ends of the world. The four older brothers, on the solicitation of their friend and constant admirer, Adolph S. Ochs, gave $500,000 to Hebrew Union College at Cincinnati, matching the Schiff family's $500,000 and assuring the success of a $3,000,000 campaign. Gifts followed each other to Mt. Sinai Hospital, totaling a million dollars.

Honors flowed in on Dan in his declining years. New York University conferred the richly merited degree of Doctor of Commercial Science. "You are possessed of the rare ability to lift your eyes," said Chancellor Brown. "You are using your gathered gains for the peaceful conquest of the air and upon that subjugated element you are sending forth sweet music as a joy, a solace, and an inspiration to your fellow-men."

When James W. Gerard compiled his list of the fifty-nine Rulers of America, Dan ranked high. With him were named associates in the copper industry: John D. Ryan of Anaconda, who had bought the Guggenheims' Chile Copper Company; Charles Hayden, Dan's collaborator in financing the porphyry coppers; and William Loeb, Jr., the Guggenheim public relations and political counsellor.

It was left to Simon Guggenheim, one-time Senator and now head of American Smelting and Refining, to provide the magnificent gift which patronized both the arts and the sciences on a scale equalled financially only by the Rhodes scholarships and rivalled by none in the intelligence of its provisions. Simon, a man as broad in his culture as his older brothers, a good example of the best type of wealthy Jew—urban, catholic in tastes and eagerly appreciative of all branches of learning—watched his brother Dan's philanthropy, studied the Rhodes scholarships, and decided that he wanted to help men and women do creative work. He turned for advice to his legal associate, Carroll A. Wilson, himself a Rhodes scholar. Wilson called in President Frank Aydelotte of Swarthmore College, also a Rhodes scholar. The three shaped up the form of the celebrated Guggenheim fellowships. Simon felt the Rhodes conditions were too narrow: scholarship was but one of the four qualifications and actually Oxford complained that many scholars sent in from the Dominions and the States were below standard. Simon felt, too, that university training was by no means the indispensable mark of creative intelligence.

On February 21, 1925, Simon announced that he and his wife were giving $3,000,000 to endow fifty fellowships in memory of their second son, John Simon, whose tragic death in 1922, just as he was to enter Harvard, had saddened their lives. (At John's birth his father had given an $80,000 building to the Colorado School of Mines.) Simon Guggenheim declared:

> It is a matter of satisfaction to me that the income of the Foundation will be spent on men and not materials. I have noticed that it has always been an easy matter for educational enterprises to secure money for buildings; but money in the place where this Foundation proposes to use it is apparently hard to get.

The Guggenheim fellowships were open to men and women, preferably between twenty-five and thirty-five, regardless of race, creed, or color. The stipends were to average $2,500 a year, but Simon purposely refrained from hobbling his experiment with conditions. The sum might be larger or smaller, or for more than one year. The fellow could study what he chose and where he chose. Foreign travel was encouraged.

Results? Naturally the Foundation expected results, but it asked nothing specific. Conceivably a man might spend the year in travel that produced nothing immediately tangible but ripened his understanding. If so, the Foundation offered no complaint. No reports were expected, nor was any final product stipulated in the form of scientific discovery, scholarly paper, or work of art or literature.

In recognition of Latin America's aid in nourishing his fortune, Simon opened the fellowships to all the inhabitants of the Americas, and particularly to Mexico, Cuba, Chile, and Argentina.

Dr. Aydelotte was made chairman of the Educational Advisory Board, assisted by officials of universities and the learned societies, in charge of policy. Henry Allen Moe, his assistant, was made secretary, in charge of administration. The financial administration Simon kept in his own hands, naming a board made up of his associates in American Smelting and Refining.

The fellowships went to the great and the unknown alike, to writers, economists, scientists, artists, men and women in all branches of learning which are creative rather than interpretative. Among them were men and women of widely differing interests and bents—Arthur Compton, Stephen Benet, Bernadotte Schmidt, Herbert Feis, Nathaniel Peffer, Lionel Edie, Martha Graham, Angna Enters, Peter Blume, Alzada Comstock, and Katherine Anne Porter. Indeed, the roster of Guggenheim Fellows bade fair to become the *Who's Who* of American belles lettres and scientific advance.

Prejudice was not discernible in the Foundation's selection of fellows. Although a conservative millionaire and life-long Republican was the donor, progressive and left-wing writers and artists were encouraged with those of other

432

tendencies. Among these were Louis Adamic, James T. Farrell, Langston Hughes, Anita Brenner, Isidor Schneider, Granville Hicks, Lewis Mumford, and Tom Tippett.

To those who worried for fear they might not deliver a worthy product after accepting a fellowship, Secretary Moe suggested that probably the best thing they could do would be to take a good rest. Not even letters were required. "Don't write me unless you want something," were his parting words. "And why not," he exclaimed. "We can't make them do anything. Might as well give them their head. One man got a grant for some studies in Europe. At the last minute he wrote and asked if it would be all right if he studied cosmic rays in the Himalayas. I wrote back that it was not only all right, but I would try to get more money for him, because I knew his expenses would be greater."

The flood of applications soon indicated that many who were worthy would be turned away. Year by year Simon made up deficits caused by choosing added fellows, and gave new sums to the principal until the Foundation had $7,000,000 in its treasury in 1937.

In a way, the Guggenheim Foundation seemed to establish an all-time high in 1933 for the cost of giving away money. For $88,000 paid out in fellowships, $47,000 was spent on administration. It cost, roughly, fifty cents to give away a dollar. That year was extraordinary for its decrease in revenues from Foundation securities while overhead expenses remained constant. Usually the proportion allotted administration was about 33 per cent. In defense, Foundation officials said that the process of selecting forty to sixty fellows from a thousand applicants was bound to be expensive. To cut the administrative staff, it was feared, might waste more money on indifferent fellows than it would save in administration.

Granted the extraordinarily liberal policy of the Foundation, what would officials have to say about authors who

433

might find it necessary to criticize the Guggenheims in some aspect of their work? A review of American captains of industry written by an author subsidized by the Foundation failed to mention the Guggenheims. But the Foundation pointed to Carleton Beals' *The Crime of Cuba*, which minced no words about the responsibility of a Guggenheim for Cuban affairs under the dictator, Machado.

Murry Guggenheim surveyed his brothers' philanthropies and felt stirred to emulate them. He and his wife, Leonie, decided that Simon's help to some fifty scholars each year was too limited in its appeal. They wanted to help the masses. The Murry and Leonie Guggenheim Dental Clinic was the result. In a splendid six-story building at 422 East 72nd Street in New York City thousands of school children were treated each year. The only condition was that the parents be unable to pay. The building and equipment cost a million, and Murry and his wife added two million dollars for endowment and a considerable sum each year to make up the deficit in the $135,000 budget.

The inspirer of the clinic was Dr. Sigismund S. Goldwater of Mt. Sinai. It has pioneered in the problems of preventing dental decay and popularizing oral hygiene among children, as well as in remedial work. The task confronting the twenty-five dentists is a ticklish one. To still the fears of youngsters, Murry had the waiting rooms decorated with nursery rhymes, pied piper pictures and other distractions. In the dental rooms, canaries sing to keep the child's mind off its woes. One of Murry's favorite stories is of the children in the waiting room who noticed two dentists. "Which," asked one, "is Dr. Murry and which is Dr. Leonie?" They studied the faces of the men and decided that the chap with the mustache was Dr. Murry.

The benefactions of the Guggenheim brothers in aviation research, in encouraging the arts and letters and in caring for the needs of New York's children won them reams of praise in the nation's press and the kudos of the scientific world. The name of the Guggenheims was blazoned on the skies as patrons of the arts, and public benefactors. The younger generation of Americans, who had never heard of the family's enterprises in mining and smelting, knew them only as philanthropists.

Drowned in the chorus of praise were dissenting voices raised in places whence came the wealth that nourished these philanthropies. All but forgotten was the story of monopoly and exploitation by which the fortune had been accumulated; few paused to ask how the Guggenheims had acquired the millions that they showered on an appreciative world.

And yet, for a Lord's tithe of their fortune the Guggenheims had made a remarkable bargain in public esteem. John D. Rockefeller had to spend millions to wash away the blots on his escutcheon; Carnegie distributed practically everything to erase from public memory the picture of a shrewd, ruthless little steelmaster. The Guggenheim brothers had achieved the same result for much less, and they basked, in their declining years, in the warm glow of public praise.

27. AMBASSADOR GUGGENHEIM

"AN honorable ambition is permitted to every man, even to the wealthiest, and it is my ambition to serve my country." The words, spoken by Senator Simon Guggenheim in thanking the Colorado Legislature in 1907, suited his nephew, Harry Frank Guggenheim, some twenty years later. Having walked with the heroes and patrons across the fields of aviation, he now aspired to serve his country in a public post.

Election to office by the vote of his fellow-countrymen seemed as remote to Harry in the nineteen twenties as to Uncle Simon in the nineteen hundreds. State Legislatures no longer elected Senators. Fortunately one avenue of distinction was still open to men of honorable ambition, especially the wealthiest, and that was to serve as an Ambassador of the United States. Young Guggenheim could lay serious claim to the honor: his family had always been staunch Republicans; his Uncle Simon had been a liberal patron and reliable servitor of his party; his other uncles contributed generously to its needs. He himself had come under the approving eye of that rising star of Republicanism, Herbert Hoover, who by virtue of his office as Secretary of Commerce, supervised commercial aviation, which Harry had done so much to stimulate.

His father and Uncle Sol had been warm advocates of Secretary Mellon and his "tax plans." They approved heartily of Mellon's slashes in the higher income tax brackets. Said Sol in 1923:

A reduction of taxes is a necessary means to prosperity. Should we succeed in having a tax bill accepted

436

that will reduce the cost of living and bring the enormous sums of money that are going into tax-exempt securities back into the channels of industry, we should have excellent business for a long time. Otherwise I am not at all optimistic as to the future.

A week later he issued another statement.

If the Mellon tax plan goes through there will follow an unprecedented prosperity. It will help business generally more than anything else. . . . If business is stimulated generally, I look for an increased consumption of copper and with an increased consumption, copper prices will rise.

On behalf of Guggenheim Brothers, Dan wrote Secretary Mellon a few weeks later that high surtaxes were penalizing mining development.

Until recent years it was not uncommon for us directly through our firm or through corporations created for the purpose to spend fully $500,000 a year in the mere examination of mining properties. . . . If a reduction in the surtaxes is made in accordance with your proposals, there is no doubt that I personally will be relieved from certain taxation. But that fact will not add to my personal comfort or expenditures; it will merely give me additional funds to invest in profitable enterprise, the profit of which in turn will be subject to taxation.

He instanced the investment of $22,000,000 in Kennecott, before any dividends were returned. Its assets were now $150,000,000. The brothers invested $50,000,000, he said, in Chile Copper before dividends were drawn. Its assets likewise were now $150,000,000. Another $50,000,000 had been ventured in Braden Copper, he said, and $10,-000,000 in Bolivian tin.

The *New York Times*, faithful praiser of Guggenheim activities, commented editorially that an "ounce of fact is worth more than a ton of theory. Guesses in Congress must give way to actual experience in business." With the loyal support of the Guggenheims and other business enterprisers, the successive Mellon plans were enacted by whopping majorities despite Democratic caviling.

Sponsored by J. H. de Bragga, Sol was named a delegate to the Republican national convention which nominated Calvin Coolidge for the presidency. The victory at the polls in November, 1924, cheered Sol: "I rejoice over the election of President Coolidge. It means economical government, great industrial prosperity and progress in all our affairs, national and international." William Loeb, the Guggenheims' political adviser, echoed: "Radical nostrums do not appeal to our people as worthy of trial in the highly prosperous condition of our country." It seemed a curious shaft to aim at John W. Davis, the defeated Wall Street Democrat.

Harry Guggenheim was an original Hoover man. The Secretary's interest in aviation endeared him to the head of the Daniel Guggenheim Fund for the Promotion of Aeronautics. When mining engineers, loyal to their fellow engineer, formed a Hoover-for-President engineers' national committee, Harry rushed forward with a laudatory statement. Whenever possible he boomed the Secretary's stock over the opposition of many Old Guardists in Wall Street who regarded Hoover as too little a machine man and too much a personality in his own right. But the Old Guard had no candidate but Coolidge and the national convention could not be stampeded for a third-term gamble.

Shortly before the election, the Republican National Committee called on Dan Guggenheim, as a leader of Jewry, to offset the swing in New York to Al Smith, himself the representative of another religious minority and the object of savage attacks by Protestant bigots. Dan obliged with a formal statement.

When the campaign started, there were many in this state [New York] who seized upon two arguments as valid reasons for voting for Governor Smith. Both of them were protests: One was that a vote for Smith was a protest against religious intolerance. This latter argument was brought forward particularly by people of the Jewish faith whose race has suffered from religious persecution. However, as the campaign progresses, the vital issues are being considered by all classes and protests (no matter how strongly we may feel like protesting) are giving way to our more constructive thoughts.

The people, Dan summed up, could progress more with the Republicans than with the Democrats, and Hoover as a candidate was superior to Smith.

Hardly were the election returns in than Harry wired Hoover: "Your victory constitutes the greatest vindication of democracy in the history of the world. Its result will mark a new epoch in human progress."

If the praise seemed a bit extravagant, Harry could be pardoned. In Washington it was said that Hoover's election guaranteed the fulfillment of his dearest ambition—an ambassadorship. Instead, he was offered the post of Assistant Secretary of Commerce for Aeronautics, and when he declined that, President Hoover tried, unsuccessfully, to persuade him to change his mind. Young Guggenheim told the President that aeronautics, to him, was not an end, but merely a means to an end; namely, closer international relations through improved communication. Harry's real interest in life was international affairs, the President was informed, and he would be glad to accept an appointment in that service. He had already served as aeronautical expert for the United States, designated by the League of

439

Nations on a committee of aeronautic experts of the Preparatory Commission for the Disarmament Conference.

When the Cuban post became available, Guggenheim was eager to serve in it, the more so as President Hoover believed that 90 per cent of our diplomatic problems were in Latin America and the most difficult problem in Latin America was brewing in Cuba.

Both Harry and his Cuban hosts were pleased. His business training in Mexico, Chile, and Bolivia gave him an understanding of Latin temperament and problems; his own cultured background of Yale and Cambridge, his appreciation of the art of leisure, his gracious personality alike impressed genial, keen-minded Habaneros. Some thirty years before, his father had scored a personal triumph in his dealings with the court of Porfirio Díaz in Mexico City because of his ingratiating qualities. These had been passed on to his son. But whereas Dan looked every inch the Continental Jew, his son was tall—towering over his father—blue-eyed, athletic. He won the blue at Pembroke, third oldest of Cambridge's colleges, as captain of the tennis team. A farsighted young man, Harry had studied international law, backed that up with economics and balanced them both with chemistry.

The Senate held up confirmation of the new Ambassador to Cuba while western Senators scrutinized his record. But apart from his family connections, they could find no blemish, and his appointment was confirmed October 10, 1929. In Havana a month later, Harry took over the American embassy, leased an estate in Vedado, the fashionable seaside Havana suburb, entertained in each, formally and informally, established himself as the debonair host, became friends with President Gerardo Machado, and Dr. Clemente Vasquez Bello, president of the Senate, and proved himself a diplomat to the manner born.

The Cuban post was to be no mere social sinecure. Wall

Street crashed a few days after the Senate confirmed Guggenheim's appointment; in the wake of financial trouble in the United States came disaster to Cuba's rickety, one-industry economy. Sugar cloyed the world's markets; the sources of Cuban revenue dried up; the turbulent Cuban people became more restive than ever under General Machado's police rule.

All this was of most serious concern to the forty-year-old diplomat, suddenly transformed from a young Long Island country gentleman into the second most important political personage in a country riddled by economic distress and political rebellion. Thanks to the Platt Amendment to the Cuban-American treaty, the American Ambassador held power of life or death over the Cuban Government through threat of American intervention. Under a dictator such as Machado who allowed no free elections, the all-important question, discussed endlessly in the cafés and private homes of Havana, was: Will the United States intervene to rescue a tottering despot if the insurgents establish a state of war? The final power rested not in the hands of the Cuban people, nor even in the hands of Machado, but in the American State Department, itself a jealous guardian of Wall Street's heavy investments in the island. And the State Department depended on the judgment of Ambassador Guggenheim.

With characteristic energy, Guggenheim threw himself into the study of Cuban affairs. His friend and business associate in the Chilean nitrate venture, Dwight Morrow, had set a shining mark in diplomacy in Mexico, and Harry intended to emulate him. Like Morrow, he hired out of his own pocket personal financial and economic advisers, experts formerly with the State Department, to go over the Cuban sugar crisis, the Cuban governmental budget, and allied business. It was said that the Guggenheim staff knew more about Cuban finance and industry than the government itself.

All that was to help little. Dwight Morrow dealt with enlightened strong men in Obregón and Calles, men of broad social views coupled extraordinarily with military power; Guggenheim found himself up against an unintelligent, graft-ridden gangsterism headed by a cruel tyrant who worked hand in glove with the worst elements of Wall Street racketeering finance—the powers of the Chase National Bank. Goaded by the seething opposition of his own people, Machado maddened until his rule rested literally on the bayonets of his soldiers and the terror of his secret police and the allied Porra, toughs in mufti.

American liberal opinion wondered what Guggenheim could make of his difficult assignment. The comment of the Scripps' *Washington Daily News* was typical: "He will report and interpret the dictatorship for Washington. If he sees clearly and reports fearlessly, there should be a reversal of the Administration's policy toward Machado very soon."

Such hopefuls were doomed to disappointment. For all his intelligence and energy, Guggenheim was bounded by the business-like prejudices he had soaked up in his earlier relations in Mexico and South America. He had no sympathy with rebels who threatened law and order. He was all for postponing consideration of social and political evils until the business skies had cleared. To Cuban insurgents that was too long to wait and suffer.

Undoubtedly he had nothing but disgust and contempt for a government which had wasted $18,000,000 in graft on a Capitol more costly by far than Washington's, and which had put Cuba under an intolerable burden of debt with a $101,000,000 cement highway from Pinar del Rio to Santiago—a highway useful mainly to American tourists and Machado's janissaries. His job, however, was not to

442

reform Cuba but to secure stability. And the important task was to rehabilitate the sugar industry, Cuba's mainstay. Tom Chadbourne, partner in a New York law firm that represented the Guggenheims widely, was assigned to draw Cuba into an international sugar agreement which would segregate part of her unsold crop from the market and curtail production. Baited with an $80,000,000 loan from Chase National, Chadbourne and Guggenheim gained Machado's assent to a program which stirred domestic sugar producers to wrath, and added these conservative capitalists to the dictator's active enemies.

That completed the ring of popular opposition and stirred U. S. Senators to warn of an impending crisis. By the end of 1930 Machado was obliged to suspend constitutional guaranties, suppress hostile newspapers, and close not only the University of Havana but all the provincial high schools.

How far the actuality in gangster-ruled Cuba was from the dreams of ambassadorial position Guggenheim had held! He was to be the kindly, enlightened diplomat, helping Cuba to attain prosperity and stability. To him all respectable elements would turn for guidance; in his homeland he would be hailed as an enlightened proconsul, cementing economic, social and political ties between the United States and its most important economic possession. He had tasted these honors, before the Cuban crisis had descended into the abyss, in the luncheon tendered him in New York in the summer of 1930 by Karl A. Bickel, head of United Press. Luminaries in the newspaper, publishing, radio, and financial worlds were there to greet him, and Charles A. Lindbergh sat by his side as he was toasted. For his own part, he had patronized the sports in Havana. A Guggenheim cup had been given for the Island tennis tournament —his own favorite sport—one to the Country Club of Havana for golf, and another to the Havana Yacht Club

443

for star-boat races. But even the ultra-fashionable Yacht Club was to be raided by Machado as a center of intrigue!

The bewildered diplomat flew to Washington to confer with his chief, Secretary of State Stimson. It is not improbable that the young diplomat warned Secretary Stimson that Machado could not stay on his hate-ringed throne forever, that the United States must guide its policy in expectation of an overturn in Havana in the not distant future. Nevertheless, it was decided that Machado must be kept propped in power as long as possible. While Guggenheim observed punctiliously a correct formal aloofness from internal strife, leading oppositionists clamored that covertly he shored up the crumbling support for the dictator.

Upon his return to Havana, he appeared with Machado at social affairs, accompanied him on trips to provincial centers. "My Government," said the dictator, "is an honorable and just one, and here is the American Ambassador by my side to prove it." Explaining the crisis to correspondents, he declared the "snake of Russian Communism" had invaded the island. "On my word as an officer and a gentleman, on my word as President of this Republic, this is the truth," he said, "and your own ambassador, Señor Harry F. Guggenheim, knows this to be the truth."

Late in 1930 the Ambassador wrung a promise of free elections, together with constitutional reforms aimed to remove fears that Machado would perpetuate his rule. Guggenheim was jubilant. "It is time to work for the betterment of Cuba," he proclaimed, "not to talk." He asked united co-operation, at least "until the economic situation" grew "normal." But the Cuban House rejected Machado's constitutional reforms, 86 to 1, in a double cross the dictator worked on the Ambassador, and the elections were boycotted by the oppositionists. Talk of armed rebellion grew. Infuriated, Guggenheim warned them that "they would have small chance of success against President Machado's army."

444

He appealed to Mario Menocal, most conservative of the opposition leaders, and representative of domestic capitalists and landowners, to call off hostile demonstrations and work out a program of accord. But even Menocal's minimum demands were intolerable to Chase National and Machado.

A cry rose that Guggenheim was bolstering the tottering throne, and this was echoed in the American press and Congress. The State Department expressed complete confidence in its envoy and pointed out that naturally he was on friendly terms with a friendly government.

When the Menocalistas rose in revolt, with the help of a filibuster, and were easily crushed, Guggenheim charged that they had provoked the uprising for fear that "their chief arguments against Machado would be removed with the passage of Cuba's new constitutional reforms." To Machado the revolt was a good excuse to drop the proposed reforms, to maintain martial law and continue the suppression of newspapers.

It seemed to the American Ambassador that the Cubans insisted on all or nothing. The rebels had impatiently waved aside reforms in their eagerness to unseat Machado, and gained nothing. And now that Machado was victor, he too would yield nothing. Guggenheim wondered how long the dictator could hold out. He remembered Carlyle's advice from the French Revolution: "Most delicate is the mob-queller's vocation; wherein too much may be as bad as not enough." Early in 1932 the Ambassador informed the State Department that "the faith of the Cuban people in the ability and disposition of the President to restore moral peace has been wholly lost."

A black period of terroristic reprisal against the government followed. A guerrilla war was waged without mercy or pity. Professors, students, business and professional men were dumped by the scores in the prisons. The dread Secret Police invaded homes, seizing their victims without benefit

445

of warrants. The *ley de fuga* was invoked and the bodies of students were found in the suburbs, shot in the back while "escaping."

The Ambassador's help was asked repeatedly by socially prominent people of the capital for the rescue of members of their families. He interceded and in many cases secured the release of men and women accused of no overt act.

On the economic side, the Ambassador labored to balance the Cuban budget. When interest on foreign loans could no longer be paid, the banks kindly lent $2,500,000 more to provide interest payments. The wages of government employes were halved. But Machado was stubborn on one section of his budget: the appropriations for the 12,000 soldiers and 6,000 police could not be touched.

By 1932 not all the statesmanship of a Guggenheim availed aught. When even his patron, Herbert Hoover, floundered vainly in the White House for the solution of evils that beset an economy normally strong and sound, not much could be hoped from his disciple in Havana. At the time, indeed, there was nothing to be done except, by hook or crook to keep Machado in power until the worst of the storm had passed.

The fate of Machado depended on the tide of affairs in the United States and that tide began to rush rapidly from the business-like precepts of Herbert Hoover and his understudy, Harry Guggenheim. In November the tide swept Hoover and his values out of public life, and with him went Harry Guggenheim, with as bare a record of achievement as his uncle Simon when he quit the Senate in 1913.

In recognition of his services to the regime, President Machado awarded the former Ambassador the cross of the Order of Carlos Manuel de Cespedes, but he declined to accept it at that time. In August, 1933, Machado, too, was swept from power by a revolt in his own army. The rotten fabric of Cuban politics was rent. When Carlos Mendieta

446

became President, the Order of Carlos Manuel de Cespedes was again awarded the former diplomat, and accepted.

Reflecting on his difficult years in Havana, Guggenheim wrote a learned treatise, entitled *The United States and Cuba*. He recommended that the hated Platt Amendment, which stifled free political life by holding an ever present threat of military intervention over the Island, be abrogated. "I am in complete agreement," he wrote, "with the dictum that it is far better for Cuba to make her own mistakes than to have our government make mistakes for her." New political and commercial treaties should be drawn up between the two countries, rubbing out the Platt Amendment, allocating a fair quota for Cuban sugar in United States markets, and cutting the duty. The new treaty, said Guggenheim, should include "adequate and complete protection to American business interests."

The Roosevelt Administration in 1934 abrogated the Platt Amendment, concluded a new treaty and cut the sugar tariff, as Guggenheim recommended.

28. TWILIGHT OF THE
GUGGENHEIMS—I

DEATH came to Daniel, head of the House of Guggenheim, on September 28, 1930, in his seventy-fourth
year. Only a few weeks after he had been named by
James W. Gerard as one of America's fifty-nine rulers, heart
disease struck him down. With him in his last hours in his
great country home, Hempstead House—one-time Castle-
gould—were his wife, his son Harry, and his daughter
Gladys. His other son, Robert, hurried from Washington.

Leaders in finance and aviation laid their tributes at the
feet of the little giant of mining and smelting. President
Hoover sent his condolences. Thomas W. Lamont of Mor-
gan's mourned the loss of "an outstanding figure" in the
"American world of industry and finance." "No one," said
Lamont, "could be associated with him without realizing he
had a constructive mind of great penetration and force."
To Samuel Untermyer, his old associate in mining finance
and his most trusted legal adviser, Dan's death was a blow.
"I lost a dear friend," he said. "He was a fine type of
American citizen and had a positive genius for big construc-
tive business."

Ambassador Dávila of Chile paid his respects to the man
who had pioneered in Chilean copper and nitrates; all the
great lights in aviation extolled his contribution to the
science and business of flying. The press lavished its praise
on his memory, and none was more eloquent than Dan's old
friend, Adolph Ochs of the *New York Times:*

"There was always something about Mr. Guggenheim
greater in his personality than in any particular thing

448

which he did. He warmed both hands at the fire of life.
. . . His name was writ large in the romance of American mining, and his interests in the field of minerals were virtually world-wide. His career was a career of success upon success, but outstanding achievements failed to mar the man; they served to stimulate his humanity."

Edwin Franko Goldman, the bandmaster, recalled a conversation: "He said he wanted to relieve me of the financial burden so that I might devote myself solely to music. I thanked him for his generosity, but he said: 'No, it is I who owe you thanks; for you do the work and all I do is sign my name to a check.'"

On September 30, his body lay in magnificent Temple Emanu-el, of which he had long been a trustee. Named to serve as the honorary pallbearers were his associates in mining, finance, and philanthropy, John D. Ryan of Anaconda, Dwight Morrow, Bernard Baruch, Stephen Birch, Irving Lehman, John Hays Hammond, Colonel Lindbergh, Adolph Ochs, Samuel Untermyer, Elihu Root, Jr.

Those who crowded Emanu-el to its very doors constituted the Who's Who of New York in finance, mining, engineering. The respects of the metropolis itself were paid by Mayor Walker. A thousand men and women of lesser repute stood outside in Fifth Avenue to attend the last services for Jewry's greatest industrial leader. His body lay in a plain brown casket covered with a thick blanket of tea roses and orchids. Two Menorah lights burned at either side, and above was the perpetual light. Flowers were banked at the sides of the chancel.

The impressive service opened with an organ prelude, the Dead March from Saul. Rabbi Nathan Krass read from the Scriptures. But he pronounced no eulogy; there was no need of that for those who mourned Daniel Guggenheim. An invisible choir sang Mendelssohn's "Hear My Prayer."

Rabbi Krass read Elizabeth Barrett Browning's "He Giveth His Beloved Sleep." After the choir sang Handel's "Largo," there was a pause for meditation while the organ played softly, as if from a long distance. Then the body was borne from the Temple. The widow, veiled in deep mourning which hid the face completely, as is the Jewish custom, was led from Emanu-el on the arms of her sons. Dan's three brothers followed, their heads bent low. He was laid to rest in Salem Fields, beside Meyer and Barbara. And thus was closed the story of the most daring and dynamic figure that had ever walked across the stage of mining finance.

To his widow, Dan left the bulk of his estate, whose value was not recorded. Hempstead House, assessed at $1,323,000, stuffed with objects of art from all the world, all his personal effects, his pew in Emanu-el and $200,000 in cash, were hers, with an injunction—a sentimental last touch—that she should pay the tuition for any of the children of his employees at Hempstead House who wanted to learn to fly.

Harry and Gladys each got $2,000,000. Another $2,000,-000 was left in a trust fund for Robert, to revert to the estate if he died childless. His two sisters, Rose and Cora, each received $250,000, and his niece, Nettie, the same. To each of his widow's sisters was left $50,000. The Daniel Guggenheim Fund for the Promotion of Aeronautics was given $475,000 to complete the $2,500,000 sum; and $1,500,000 was given to the Daniel and Florence Guggenheim Foundation, whose income supported the Goldman band concerts and other charities.

The words in his will concerning his brothers Murry, Solomon, and Simon were touching:

I have named my said brothers to act as my executors or trustees because of the close and affectionate relationship which has ever existed between us, confident in the knowledge that whatever the burden involved, they will gladly undertake it in deference to my wish as well as for the sake of those for whom I would provide.

Dan's passing affected little the affairs of Guggenheim Brothers, of American Smelting and Refining, or of Kennecott. Seven years before, he had resigned his directorship in the Smelters Trust and maintained his only lively interest in the partnership. His heart had been a constant menace, forbidding active attention to business. He made few excursions except to Carlsbad for his usual summer retreat.

The driving force which had made the Guggenheim partnership the dominant firm in world mining had spent itself even before Dan's death. The three active brothers had summoned E. A. Cappelen Smith and Silas W. Howland, expert in corporation law in Elihu Root's firm, into their partnership. Both were concerned with the family's latest and last venture—Chilean nitrates—Cappelen Smith as technical manager, Howland, legal. More and more the firm became the conservator of assets rather than the pioneer in enterprises at the earth's ends.

Even so, Guggenheim Brothers was one of Wall Street's great financial reservoirs. Into it went the cream skimmed from the profits of all the great porphyry mines. It was a sincere compliment to the brothers' wealth that their firm was the only non-banking house which was asked to enter the $240,000,000 pool with which J. P. Morgan fought off panic in those dark October days of 1929 when the financial world seemed about to smash into utter ruin. On October 24, 20,000 shares of DuPont were dumped on the market—and there was no bid! Morgan summoned his associates and satellites—Charles E. Mitchell of National City, Albert H. Wiggin of Chase, William C. Potter of Guaranty, Seward Prosser of Bankers Trust, George F. Baker, Jr., of First National, and Murry Guggenheim. Each dup deep into the

liquid assets of his firm to produce a cushion of $240,000,-
000 between the Stock Exchange and disaster. The 20,000
shares of DuPont were bid in at 80. The appearance of support stopped the wild dumping of securities and on the next
day the Morgan syndicate was able to sell its DuPont at
100. Four months later the pool ended its account with a
slight margin of profit, Tom Lamont announced, and Guggenheim Brothers was reimbursed in full.

But all the great resources of Murry's firm were to be
taxed to the limit in the disaster which the pool had
cushioned but could not end. President Hoover remained
ever hopeful that the upturn was just around the corner;
Secretary Mellon served soothing syrup in regular doses to
market operators who early in October had hailed prosperity as endless. But month by month, in 1930, paralysis
advanced upon the body economic. Kennecott and American
Smelting paid dividends only by incurring deficits.

The financial community had not the slightest doubt that
the Guggenheims would ride out this panic as they had
those of 1907 and 1921. What with big chunks of that
$70,000,000 Anaconda check salted away in government
bonds, with the tens of millions held in the reserves of the
porphyry coppers and the Smelters Trust, no depression
could dent the resources of the firm which old Meyer Guggenheim had built on the rock of gold, silver, lead, and
copper.

Few realized in 1930 that the crisis would go on and on
and fewer knew that Guggenheim Brothers had entered
the period burdened with loans of $25,000,000 poured into
the gaping Anglo-Chilean and Lautaro nitrate properties.
Not even Murry himself, connoisseur of the metal market
that he was, could have known that of all the minerals, his
Chile nitrates were to be the worst hit. The sensitive coppers
were to be very paragons of stability in comparison. Even
in the lush years of endless prosperity in the twenties,

Chilean nitrates had been hammered unmercifully by the competition of the artificial product; in 1930, hard-pressed companies began dumping their stocks, and, by 1932, were accepting any price that represented cash and were even bartering the stuff for wheat. As depression deepened, the demand for farm products dropped and farmers found that they did not need to replenish the fertility of their soil, and indeed could not afford to, whatever nature's needs.

Not six months after the Wall Street crash, the Chilean government retreated from its long-held determination never to let a monopoly seize its nitrate fields. It soon became apparent that it must be a Nitrate Trust—or nothing. The Ibañez dictatorship worked anxiously with the Guggenheims to set stormsails. Cappelen Smith and Howland evolved the *Compañia de Salitre de Chile*—to be known to the world as Cosach—with the grandiose capitalization of 3,000,000,000 pesos (about $375,000,000) in 30,000,000 shares and with an expected bond issue of $200,000,000. Cosach was the biggest corporation in South America and the biggest that the Guggenheims themselves had ever evolved. Half of the stock went to the Government, along with four seats on the board of twelve, in exchange for the waiving of the export duty of $12.50 a ton. To compensate for the loss of its main source of revenue, the Government was guaranteed $22,500,000 in 1931 and lesser amounts in the next two years, plus half the dividends, plus a 6 per cent tax on dividends.

What could be more generous, cried President Ibañez in hailing the long-awaited "nationalization" of the nitrate industry. But he clapped a strict censorship over all details.

Murry and Solomon could congratulate themselves that at last they had sold the Guggenheim process for treating nitrate ore for $30,000,000 in Cosach stock. The process had cost them, net, something over $100,000. Cosach assumed the tremendous indebtedness of their Anglo-Chilean

453

and Lautaro companies and their common stock in exchange for 8,318,000 of its shares. And their man, Cappelen Smith, was named president of the giant trust.

Ignorant of the terms of the deal, Senator Huneeus, conservative business man, sounded the tocsin against the delivery of Chile's nitrates to the Guggenheims. The nitrate provinces of Tarapacá and Antofagasta, he said, had been sold, body and breeches, to foreigners. The Guggenheim process outlawed tens of thousands of laborers from industry. And even if the process could save a third in costs, the very weight of Cosach's $200,000,000 bond issue and its 30,000,000 shares of stock would drain Chile of its lifeblood.

Senator Huneeus did not know at the time what it had cost to form Cosach or he would have been even more indignant. A Chilean Government commission later found that organizing expenses totaled nearly $7,000,000; that of this some $878,000 went to the New York law firm of Root, Clark and Buckner, of which Guggenheim Partner Howland had been a member; that more thousands went to lawyers in London and Santiago.

To Murry, sitting disconsolately at his big desk on the 35th floor of 120 Broadway, Huneeus' cries seemed particularly unkind. For all those thirty million shares of Cosach weren't worth the paper they were engraved on; and as for the $200,000,000 in bonds, why, bankers in New York and London looked incredulously at Cappelen Smith when he suggested their merits. All the companies which had been dumped into Cosach were already mortgaged to the hilt. By the end of 1930 bankers asked Murry to put his firm's guarantee on all advances to Anglo and Lautaro; by April, 1931, Guggenheim Brothers had endorsed $12,225,000 in Anglo loans, to say nothing of the $25,000,000 they themselves had advanced, or the $16,500,000 dumped into their properties through the Lehman bond issue.

It was a solid testimonial to the prestige of Guggenheim

Brothers that Murry was able to scrape millions out of the tills of banks in 1931. Prices had descended to the distress level; Germany and Japan were selling nitrate for anything that promised cash; and Cosach must do likewise. It seemed that Murry, in his rounds, tapped every banking house of any note: J. P. Morgan and Company, Brown Brothers Harriman, French-American Banking Corporation, Bankers Trust, Guaranty Trust, Heidelbach Ickelheimer, Bank of the Manhattan Trust, International Acceptance Bank, Irving Trust, National City, Central Hanover, American Express Bank and Trust.

It was in the American Express bank that Murry and Solomon found the man they were looking for to handle the trouble-freighted affairs of Cosach. It had been evident for some time that the job of dealing with London bankers, the British owners of Cosach stock and the ever rising forces of discontent in Chile was too much for the distraught Cappelen Smith. He was an engineer primarily, not a financier. His brilliant success with Chile Copper was possible because the Guggenheims took care of financing. But the aging brothers could not be in London, Paris, Santiago, and New York to handle Cosach's tangled skein. So Cappelen Smith retired from Cosach's financial management.

To Medley Gordon Brittain Whelpley, thirty-eight-year-old president of American Express Bank and Trust, they turned. Tough and pushful, Whelpley had quit the University of Pennsylvania after one year to be a bond clerk in Wall Street. After winning a citation for distinguished service in the World War, the young man advanced quickly, from clerk to manager of a bond department, thence upward through a Chase National vice-presidency to head of the American Express bank.

Murry and Sol had to confess that they had reached the end of their rope. The entire Chilean business had turned out to be a frightful gamble. As bankers to Cosach, it was up to them to raise money from everywhere, by any device, to prevent the collapse of their monopoly. Chilean nitrates pressed upon the backs of the two sturdy, barrel-chested Guggenheims, and the weight was too much for them. They did not propose to venture their entire fortune, their hundreds of thousands of shares of Kennecott, to salvage an enterprise which had been fraught with expenditure from the very start. It was up to Whelpley to pull the nitrate enterprise out by brains rather than dollars.

The measure of the Britishers' confidence in Chilean nitrates—a subject they knew well—was to take only $15,000,000 of the projected $200,000,000 issue and then to pass it on as speedily as possible into the hands of hapless investors. So chilly was the public reception that American bankers, who had shown no qualms in selling Ivar Kreuger's stuff, refused point-blank to touch Cosach bonds. Not even the guaranty which the Chilean Government had slapped on the bonds served to convince them. President Ibañez had agreed to impose a tax of $7.30 a ton on nitrates for bond interest, but the bankers rightly interpreted that as just another burden put on natural nitrate to handicap it in competing with the cheaper artificial product.

Murry and Sol were obliged to accept $10,000,000 in the "prior secured" bonds and $17,000,000 in the junior issue, in return for the liquidation of the indebtedness of Anglo-Chilean to Cosach. But that provided no cash. The next desperate move was properly labelled Cosach's "salvage" bonds. Guggenheim Brothers took $10,000,000. Encouraged by that testimonial of faith, National City took $5,000,000 and a subsidiary of Anglo-South American took $4,000,000, at a 10 per cent discount.

That merely tided Cosach over until the end of 1931. Thereupon the resourceful Whelpley devised a "Whelpley plan" by which the Chilean Government, desperately in need of revenue as it was, agreed to postpone the payments guaranteed to it; Guggenheim Brothers agreed to continue the guaranty of some $9,000,000 of short term loans advanced by the banks, and to dig up $3,000,000 more. That was all they proposed to venture. Powerful Kennecott, on which Murry and Sol depended for their own current expenditures as well as to nourish the estates of Isaac and Daniel and their numerous descendants, kept slicing its dividends, from $5 in 1929 to $3.75 in 1930, to $1.50 in 1931. In 1932 it passed. The Smelters Trust passed its common dividend in 1931 and by the middle of 1932 omitted, for the first time payments on its preferred stock.

Financing Cosach descended in 1932 to a hand-to-mouth affair. As nitrate arrived in New York and London, the banks advanced funds based on warehouse receipts. National City and Central Hanover agreed to extend $20,000,-000 in all in this way, part of it guaranteed by Guggenheim Brothers. The continuation of a European credit of £5,000,000 was arranged, but when Cosach needed $4,500,-000 more, Bankers Trust and Guaranty cannily insisted on the Guggenheim guaranty. Finally Cosach had to hock its iodine, valued at $4,000 a ton, and when National City became panicky even on such a gilt-edge security, Murry was obliged to put his firm's name to the notes.

All this meant less than nothing to the majority of the Chilean nation. All they knew was that tens of thousands of laborers were unemployed, what with the Guggenheim process and the depression; that business in the northern provinces was at a standstill; that the Chilean Government had lost a rich source of revenue. The same explosive nitrates which had seated Colonel Ibañez in 1927 threw him out of office when the nation realized that its richest possession had been handed over to the Guggenheims.

None had a word to say in defense of the New Yorkers. The Press, with one voice, denounced the rape of the nitrate industry. Ibañez had no authority to lend governmental approval to a deal which had taken in foreigners as partners with the nation and placed fantastic valuations on their properties. Cosach, illegal, must be dissolved.

So menacing were the threats voiced in the press that Whelpley decided he must dash off on the next boat for Santiago. His arrival, at the beginning of 1932, was met with the threat of a general strike. He nevertheless found the government conciliatory. In truth the control of Chile's greatest industry lay with the Guggenheims; they had but to say the word and not a ton, not a pound of natural nitrate could be sold anywhere in the world. No banker would dream of financing its sale without the Guggenheim say-so, and Chile had not a penny to finance the marketing of nitrates. So President Montero assured him there was no thought of dissolving Cosach. Armed with that assurance, Whelpley hurried to London to arrange more credits, negotiate a reorganization, and stop the nitrogen price-war in Europe.

In the meantime Cosach had defaulted on all its bonds, including the $16,500,000 Lehman Brothers issue. The government did likewise, toppling its own excellent credit record. The Britishers were sour when Whelpley approached them for more money. Forget about Chile, they advised. Europe already had supplies sufficient for two years. Why not shut down the industry and quit worrying, they asked, pitilessly. Worse, they even questioned the superiority of the American Guggenheim process to the old English Shanks method of extracting nitrate from caliche.

Whelpley was off for New York to forestall the creation of an independent bondholders' protective committee. He induced Henry P. Fletcher, former Ambassador to Chile, to head Cosach's own committee. Solomon Guggenheim, Charles Mitchell of National City, Arthur Lehman and D. Stewart Iglehart of W. R. Grace and Company, important in nitrates as well as in South American shipping, completed the committee. A similar body was set up in England.

President Montero's glib assurances of Cosach's sanctity were torn to ribbons. Chilean laborites organized a "socialist republic" early in June, 1932, and announced that Cosach was no more, that the Shanks process would be instituted again to revive employment. But within a week Carlos Dávila, former ambassador and fervent admirer of the Guggenheims, overthrew the laborites, tucked five hundred of them into prison and proclaimed Cosach's inviolability. Nevertheless a revolutionary junta controlled Antofagasta. Whelpley closed the great Pedro de Valdivia plant, the world's largest. The liberals, massed around former President Alessandri, demanded Whelpley's expulsion. In the elections, Alessandri was returned to the Presidency from which Ibañez had forced him in 1927.

Cosach stockholders at a formal meeting in Santiago heard the doleful news that their company had lost $13,335,000 in 1932, and that it was to be dissolved by Government decree. Whelpley was pessimistic. He appealed tearfully to the Chilean people for sympathy and moral support. The Guggenheims, he said, were no devils seeking the ruin of Chile. They had ventured all their resources to save Cosach and stood to lose millions for their faith in the country. Except for this, the entire nitrate industry would have closed down, leaving Chile worse off than it was.

Alessandri and his Congress would not be moved. The formation of Cosach was decreed illegal and its existence a threat to the future of nitrates. Whelpley replied that Cosach would not resist the decree. He declared:

I will not comment on the abruptness of the procedure adopted, the pretended infractions advanced as reasons for the dissolution of the company, the disregard for those foreign interests which had been making prodigious efforts to assist Chile in its economic difficulties and the

459

international repercussions which a precipitous step of this nature may have on the delicate structure of future international credit.

The new American Secretary of State, Cordell Hull, was stern in his insistence that Chile abide by its Cosach agreement. The American Ambassador, arm in arm with the British, called on the foreign and finance ministers to protest the removal of the $7.30 export tax which guaranteed Cosach's bonds. American warships showed up on the northern coast and Chileans feared a new instance of dollar diplomacy. The Dutch and Germans joined their confreres in demanding justice for the holders of Cosach bonds. Trade reprisals were threatened. An agreement was patched up with Gustavo Ross, finance minister, by which Cosach's dissolution was cushioned through the formation of a sales corporation to handle all the Chilean product.

The job left to the Guggenheims and Whelpley was the salvage of Anglo-Chilean and Lautaro from the wreckage of Cosach. Lautaro emerged from the storm with a bonded indebtness of $40,000,000—valued at its lowest in 1935 at a trifle over $2,000,000—plus $40,000,000 in stock, value zero, and $15,000,000 due creditors. The indefatigable Whelpley managed to convert the staggering 6 per cent bond burden into income bonds, scarcely better than a common stock. The old stock was cut down and combined with a new issue totaling only $10,000,000, which was distributed to the bondholders, the Guggenheims and other former stockholders. The $15,000,000 due creditors was cut to $10,000,000 and placed on a low interest rate.

Anglo-Chilean staggered under $44,000,000 in bonds— worth a trifle over $1,000,000 at their lowest quotations— mostly promising a 7 per cent return. These were scaled down considerably, some bondholders took stock, and the debt burden was eased.

Struggle as they might, Solomon and Murry and Whelpley were unable, even by 1937, to get either Lautaro or Anglo-Chilean out of the red. Anglo's deficit in 1936, after payment of interest, was $2,500,000, and Lautaro's $1,250,- 000. Despite boards ornamented by former Chilean foreign ministers and a former U. S. Ambassador to Chile, despite the celebrated Guggenheim process, despite the great resources of Guggenheim Brothers and the undoubted energy of President Whelpley, neither company showed any sign of paying dividends in the visible future.

It was melancholy satisfaction for Harry and Edmond Guggenheim to contrast nitrates' unhappy record with the booming profits of Anaconda Copper, thanks to its great porphyry property at Chuquicamata, Chile. Of Anaconda's impressive sixteen millions of income in 1936, a third was from Chile Copper, which Harry and Ed had nourished from its infancy and which they had fought, unsuccessfully, to keep within the Guggenheim domain.

Had the estimate been made in the winter of 1934 when things looked worst for their nitrate companies, the Guggenheim brothers would probably have reckoned a loss of $50,- 000,000 on their Chilean venture. It was a sad comedown for a partnership which in its heyday had dealt only in bonanzas. Nevertheless, Murry and Solomon, with characteristic Guggenheim doggedness, were not crushed. They turned what threatened to be a débâcle into a minor catastrophe. They were hopeful that their Chilean companies, eased of some of their debt burden, could slowly be brought around to profitableness. Farmers preferred natural nitrates, and an aggressive sales organization operating out of 120 Broadway turned that preference into sales. Nevertheless, millions were gone, not to be recovered by any legerdemain. In addition the firm had lost the profitable sales agency for the American prophyry coppers at the end of 1933 to Kennecott. During the crisis the Morgans had advanced to undoubted control of Kennecott, with Henry S. Morgan, S. Parker Gilbert, George Whitney and other Morgan men

461

sitting on the boards of the mother corporation of Utah Copper.

By way of contrast, there were the Guggenheim laboratories in New York City, working on the problems of eliminating sulphur from smelter fumes and purifying sewage by an activated sludge process. Such discoveries, worthy as they were, seemed small potatoes for a firm which once had run the continent's copper and dominated the world's silver and lead markets. The sun had set on that brilliant chapter in mining history which linked the Guggenheim name with the development of the greatest copper mines in history.

Despite all reverses, the Guggenheims remained the largest of all American Jewish fortunes. They were still the largest single Jewish fortune. They were still the largest single owners of Kennecott, a corporation which measured its assets in 1937 at $335,000,000 and its profits at $25,-500,000, and of American Smelting and Refining, a $161,-000,000 firm with net income of $29,400,000. The Smelters Trust, with the three canny Guggenheim brothers still standing by the side of Chairman Brownell, had put funds from its surplus and fresh bond issues during the depression into new mining properties in Yugoslavia, Australia, Newfoundland and also Rhodesia, which promised to rival Chile as a source of low-cost copper. Its sway was extended into the field of fabricating copper, brass, and other metals.

The partnership of Guggenheim Brothers now consisted of the three brothers, Silas W. Howland, the legal expert, Medley Whelpley, the nitrate trouble-shooter par excellence, and Cappelen Smith, the technical wizard. If it was no longer the pioneering, venturing firm that Meyer Guggenheim meant it to be, it was in the hands of careful steady men who would stand guard over its main function, that of assuring an income to Meyer's numerous grandchildren, great-grandchildren, and their children for as many generations as possible.

29. TWILIGHT OF THE
GUGGENHEIMS—II

COULD old Meyer Guggenheim have risen from his grave at Salem Fields thirty years after his death, it is hard to say who would have been more amazed, his descendants as they viewed the apparition, or he himself as he surveyed their way of life.

A chuckle would have sounded through those white mutton-chop whiskers of his as he watched his oldest living son, Murry, dart out of 120 Broadway every noon to catch a subway home for luncheon with his ever charming wife, Leonie. But what could he have made of his son Solomon's passion for non-objective art? Or Simon's tossing $7,000,-000 into fellowships which might produce scathing left-wing verse or a slender story of a Mexican girl's love-life? Or of William's writing his own autobiography and setting up a cult of Franklinolatry?

And what could the one-time tailor of the Swiss ghetto at Lengnau have said about his daughters and his grandchildren and his great-grandchildren and the tortuous mazes of their marriages and divorces and remarriages? It is said, without benefit of mathematical scrutiny, that of all America's rich and wasting families, the Guggenheims had established an all-time high for divorces. Meyer certainly was no marital purist. He approved of monogamy mainly for social reasons. But it was not the fashion in his Victorian day for young folks to dash blithely and light-heartedly into both marriage and divorce. It could be said that the free and open attitude of the younger Guggenheims was much healthier, mentally, than the furtive mores of an older generation. But such harum-scarum goings-on the patriarch would certainly have regarded as ruinous to the continuity of the fortune he had founded.

Certainly Meyer would have been taken aback by the splendor of the offices of Guggenheim Brothers. He disliked ostentation as useless frippery which could add nothing to a man's innate worth. But as soon as his eye had become accustomed to the rich paneling, the heavy carpets, the great windows and luxurious furniture, he would certainly have peered about for signs of earnest young Guggenheims, mere striplings at the time of his death, industriously applying themselves to the problems of mining, metallurgy, and finance. Perhaps by good fortune he might have seen Edmond. For the rest, there would be his own sons Murry and Solomon, and two perfect strangers sitting at the partners' desks. He could have found his other son, Simon, a floor below, in the crowded little office of the President of American Smelting and Refining. But there would be no sign of William, estranged from his older brothers ever since the vitriolic suit over the Chile Copper in 1916.

Meyer, in his own will, had been generous to his sisters and his dependent niece, but the bulk of his fortune he bestowed on his own sons long before his death to assure the prosperity of the partnership. Most certainly he would sorrow to see great chunks of the Guggenheim patrimony, dynamic with future gain, immobilized in stocks and bonds which merely provided sumptuous incomes to female members of the family. Yet it was inevitable that nearly half of the family's money must pass into female hands, for three of the brothers, Isaac, Solomon, and Benjamin, had no sons.

"And not in such a way can a business prosper," Meyer would have muttered to himself and mournfully taken himself away to his resting place in Salem Fields.

After his death in 1922, Isaac's great house, Villa Carola, on Sands Point near his brothers' estates, was put under the auctioneer's hammer for $610,000. Villa Carola was built in the Italian Renaissance style on a knoll overlooking Hempstead Harbor and Long Island Sound. Replete with private golf links and clubhouse, private yacht landing and exquisite landscape gardening devised by the world's leading architects, the estate, it was estimated, would cost $2,000,000 to replace. The wealth of rugs, tapestries, porcelains, and other objets d'art from Villa Carola and Isaac's Park Avenue residence were sold for $75,000. The Metropolitan Museum was given its choice of treasures in his other town house on East Fifty-fifth Street.

After estate taxes of $2,300,000 had been paid, Isaac's fortune was put at $10,000,000, four-fifths of which, fortunately for his daughters, was in Chile Copper stocks and bonds. To each of the three girls he left $2,000,000; to three granddaughters, trust funds of $100,000 each, in addition to the $300,000 he had given another on her marriage. To his only grandson, who was known as Isaac Guggenheim II, perpetuated his name, he gave two-thirds of his interest in Caracoles Tin. But Isaac II tired of the title bequeathed him and reverted to his original name, William I. Spiegelberg, Jr.

Mrs. Isaac Guggenheim, in her will, split her fortune among relatives, stipulating that her executors care for "any and all dogs, fish and birds which may be owned by me." Her jewels she left her daughters; to numerous charities, $9,000 each; to her maid $10,000; and to her hairdresser, $2,000.

Daniel's three children were also favored with $2,000,000 bequests when their father died eight years after Isaac. But Daniel had little confidence in the business ability of his high-living, horse-loving, military-minded older son, Robert, and tied up his $2,000,000 in a trust fund. In vain he had tried to break Bob into the Smelters business and Guggenheim Brothers. Tedious details interfered with Bob's passion for dogs, horses, and high society. As a youngster

465

he ran $25,000 in the hole at the time of Seattle's hilarious Alaska-Yukon-Pacific exposition. By 1914 Bob was completely outside the Guggenheim business orbit and working for $125 a week for Thompson-Starrett, the construction firm. This fact was brought to light when Louis Sherry, the restaurateur, garnisheed his wages for a $135 bill. A year later his wife, Grace Bernheimer, was asking a divorce. This she obtained, with the custody of Daniel II and M. Robert, Jr., on condition that she remain in this country at least eight months of the year. Bob was given six hours in each month to see his boys. Hardly was the ink dry on the final decree than both Bob and Grace sprang into new marriages, she to a Philadelphia drygoods man, he to Margaret Weyher of Scranton, a well-known horsewoman. His second wife demanded that he renounce the Jewish faith for the Catholic, and that he did, nonchalantly, for religious formalities meant little or nothing to him. The quick remarriage unsettled eyebrows in the ranks of Holy Mother Church. Father Norris of St. Mary's hastened to explain, enigmatically, that "it is possible under the rules of the Catholic Church for persons who have been divorced by the courts to be married when certain provisions are applicable."

Bob and Margaret settled down to serious dog-raising and horse-riding at their Babylon, Long Island, estate, next to August Belmont's. He joined the Great Eastern Construction Company as vice-president and director. When America entered the World War, he enlisted in the 69th Infantry, became a major, loved it, and remained devoted to army ways thereafter. He served as major on Governor Nathan L. Miller's staff.

Bob made news briefly in 1922 with the arrest of a young man said to be poaching on his Babylon estate. Later in the year he was resisting what he called the inordinate demands of his father's law firm, Guggenheimer, Untermyer, and Marshall, for $3,000, said to be past due for legal services on his divorce. "I had discussed it with my father," said Bob, "and he said I would be a damned fool to pay any such amount." Guggenheimer, he said, had charged him $500 for a single interview. By this time he had shifted his business connection again, to serve as treasurer for the Guggenheim-O'Brien Company, Inc., another construction firm.

Margaret went the way of Grace, early in 1928, with a Paris divorce; and a week later Bob was married again, to Elizabeth Eaton of Babylon, and in a Lutheran rather than a Catholic church. Margaret later in the year married a Londoner, former captain of the Dragoon Guards.

Elizabeth was ensconced as mistress on the famed Firenze Farms at Babylon. She entered the life with high gusto and made a name for herself by riding horses over 230 fences in a single day. Tossed over a stone wall on one occasion, she showed up at the horse show luncheon an hour later with her collarbone in a steel brace. "I'm not so much hurt as I am damned mad," she exclaimed. It was not her first fall: in an Atlantic City horse show she was thrown, entered another event, was thrown again, and suffered concussion of the brain, which kept her off her mounts for several weeks. All the Guggenheim horses, as well as the prize dogs, carried the invariable first name of Firenze.

In winter, Bob and Elizabeth abandoned storm-swept Babylon for social life in Washington. As a lieutenant-colonel of the New York National Guard and an infantry reserve officer on duty with the War Department, Bob entertained extensively at his Woodland Drive home. Ambassadors, ministers, generals, and baronesses mixed amiably at his table.

Spirited Elizabeth drove fast automobiles in Washington. After one crash, she was summoned to court to explain why she did not stop to inquire after the health of the driver of the other. "I didn't know whether he was a gentleman," she replied, and paid her $75 fine.

Bob's first son, Daniel II, died suddenly while warming up for the forty-yard dash at a Phillips-Exeter track meet. His other, M. Robert, Jr., was married in 1934 to Helen Claire Allyn, daughter of a Montreal steel man. They left for Mexico, where young Bob looked in at the American Smelting and Refining office. After a year or so of that, he transferred to the Salt Lake City office, became a patron of the Little Theater and switched, at the age of twenty-five, from his learn-from-the-bottom-up job with the Smelters Trust to a similar job as call boy for Selznick International Pictures in Hollywood. "I am taking a modest position," he explained, "but I hope some day to be a director. My family realizes that I can be a success in the production of motion pictures as well as in any other field."

M. Robert, Sr., was one of the largest contributors to the Republican campaign fund, with a $25,000 gift, surpassed in the six-week pre-election period only by William Randolph Hearst's $30,000. His mother, Mrs. Daniel, and Brother Harry each gave $5,000. Bob in 1932 served as treasurer for the New York "Win with Donovan" committee and appealed for $1 contributions from the "mass of the voters" to put the Buffalo man across for the Republican nomination for governor.

Like his older brother, Harry Frank also began his active business years understudying for the day when he too would be a partner in Guggenheim Brothers. After three years in the Smelting company's Mexico City offices, he was transferred with his cousin Edmond to watch the Chilean copper venture, under the tutelage of William C. Potter, partner in Guggenheim Brothers. Both Harry and Ed in due time advanced to be partners. Harry and Potter together prospected the purchase of Caracoles Tin in 1920. Then next year Potter retired from partnership to become head of Guaranty Trust. It was said that he was so fascinated by his business affairs that he forgot his wife,

Caroline Morton. She obtained a Paris divorce while Harry's wife, Helen Rosenberg, got a New York decree. As soon as the decrees were final, Harry married Caroline and together they built a $225,000 Norman manor house on Dan's estate at Sands Point.

The years that followed his marriage to Caroline were full of public activity and honor. He was president of the Daniel Guggenheim Fund for the Promotion of Aeronautics and when its purpose was achieved, he became ambassador to Cuba. The aviator-diplomat wrote two books, *The Seven Skies* and *The United States and Cuba*. The depression struck while he was in the Havana embassy. The handsome young millionaire startled his audience at the American Club in 1932 with a speech in which he stated that "this order cannot survive and is not worthy of survival." Guggenheim pronounced:

> It may require some imagination to visualize a world-coordinated industry steering a steady course between overproduction and underproduction with its labor safeguarded through temporary slack periods by special reserves and by a judicious application of the so-called "stagger" system. This conception, as I say, may require some imagination, but none is needed to realize that the present order where millions are either unemployed or insecure in mind cannot survive and is not worthy of survival.

The diplomatic venture ended, Harry returned to his Port Washington estate and devoted himself to cultured loafing, reading the philosophers, flying his own planes, studying the birds and trees, playing tennis. He encouraged Dr. R. H. Goddard, the Clark University physicist whom many regarded as mad because he believed that rocket planes might attain a speed of seven hundred miles an hour. Responding to Jewish distress in Hitlerian Germany, Harry

469

gave to the $10,000,000 Refugee Economic Corporation and became a director.

Gone however were the good old days when his life was crowded with bustle and importance. He scrutinized the times for something which combined the daring of aviation and the prestige of diplomacy and thought he found it in New York's racketeering. When it was proposed that "civic vigilantes" aid Special Prosecutor Dewey, he agreed to head the Citizens Committee on the Control of Crime in New York which acted as a clearing house for news on the dark side of metropolitan life. His ferrets inspected racketeering on the spot; his envoys prodded city officials; his research force followed up quietly on the progress in the campaign to wipe out racketeering. His worst enemy, he found, were the business men themselves, many of whom profited by the racketeering which mulcted the consumer to the profit of all the conspirators. The name of Guggenheim returned to the pages of the New York press as Harry exhorted business groups to rally to the war on crime by contributing $200,000 to the Citizens Committee.

Harry's only sister, Gladys, lived quietly with her husband, Roger Williams Straus, scion of the celebrated Straus family. He served as lieutenant to Uncle Simon in American Smelting against the day when he would advance perhaps beyond his directorship after Simon would have retired from the presidency. Young Straus was an active Republican, eager in the aid of suffering Jews in Germany and Palestine, and a co-chairman of the National Conference of Jews and Christians. The couple had three children, Oscar S. II, Roger Williams, Jr., and Florence Guggenheim.

Head of the House of Guggenheim, after Dan's death, was Murry, "least modern" of the brothers but peerless for a generation in his knowledge of that fine point at which silver or lead or copper should be sold. Like his brothers,

Murry was the gallant, debonair gentleman, but in one respect he differed. He had never given an interview. He remarked, jokingly, that his brothers did enough talking.

His two children, Edmond A. and Lucille, promised to be the richest of the third generation Guggenheims when their father, in 1917, thriftily set aside trust funds of $8,000,000 for each of them. So sagely did he invest, that in 1932, at the depth of the depression, Edmond's fund earned $332,000 and Lucille's $327,000, and both had some $5,700,000 in undivided income. To the government it looked as if Murry had tried to outwit the gift taxes; otherwise why had he kept the power of revoking the trust funds until 1925? Murry lost his appeal to the Supreme Court and good-naturedly handed over the largest gift tax ever made by an individual, $3,449,000.

The Guggenheims were interlocked with other wealthy American Jewish families—the Loebs, Strauses, Gimbels, and Seligmans—but Murry picked his wife Leonie from the well-to-do Bernheims of Mulhouse, Alsace. His brother-in-law Alfred rose to head the powerful French *Comptoir de Textiles Artificiels* and pioneered in rayon and cellophane. The DuPonts became mightily interested in Bernheim's cellophane and bought exclusive American rights, much to their own and Bernheim's enrichment. In token of the esteem between the American Guggenheims and the French Bernheims, Alfred's picture occupied a place of honor in Guggenheims Brothers' offices, next to Andrew Mellon's.

Murry did not join his brothers in building great country houses near New York City. He preferred his yacht at St. Petersburg, Florida, where he golfed every day of the winter and kept up his business correspondence. He was no yachts-man but hated hotels. His boat, tied firmly and serenely in the sunny southern port, was home.

Murry's only son, Edmond, graduate of Columbia and

Yale, apprentice in the Smelters Trust, developer of Chile Copper, member of Guggenheim Brothers, blew up with his cousin Harry when Chile Copper was sold, and resigned. Edmond was one of Police Commissioner Enright's Millionaires, serving as Special Deputy Police Commissioner in charge of the Bronx. He lost that position when Mayor Walker abolished the position.

Perhaps little attention would have been paid to the annulment of the marriage of his daughter, Natalie, to Tom Gorman, son of the Manhasset, L. I., baggage-master, had not such extreme measures at concealment been taken to hush the affair. Supreme Court Justice Morshauser held the hearing in chambers at 5:30 P.M. after almost everyone had left, and no record appeared on the books. Guggenheim attorneys, when the case was uncovered, denied they had paid Gorman fifty to seventy-five thousand dollars to consent to the annulment. Natalie was given back her maiden name and three years later was married to Robert Michael Studin, son of Park Avenueites.

Ed's wife, Marron Price, became an airplane devotee, traveling days on end on long tours with youthful Russel W. Thaw, son of Harry K., at the controls. In 1934 she set out courageously to do the loop around South America, with Thaw as pilot, at a time when it was considered a daring exploit. In 1936 Marron got a divorce. That made it unanimous among Murry's children, for his daughter Lucille, had divorced a Gimbel.

Most magnificent of the Guggenheims was Solomon R., father of a viscountess, patron of non-objective art, worthy subject of Sir William Orpen and Edgardo Simone, equally at home in his shooting lodge in Scotland, his hunting preserve in Idaho, his winter house on the Battery in Charleston, South Carolina, his suite at the Plaza, his Long Island estate, Trillora Court, or his New Jersey summer house, the Towers, at Elberon.

472

Shooting was Solomon's passion and never had he bagged quail more surely, he boasted, than at the age of seventy-six. His love of game brought him and Tom Cochran of J. P. Morgan and Company to the attention of the Senate Public Lands Committee in 1925. The committee heard that the Guggenheim-Cochran Silver Tip Lodge on the rim of Yellowstone Park encroached on the park itself, and envious neighbors said that attendants even lured bear out of the park with bait of honey and meat. Such statements brought indignant denials. The property had been acquired at the solicitation of park authorities to keep it from being used as a poaching base, there were no firearms on the estate, and groups of children spent vacations there.

Five years later Solomon was under fire from Robert Moses, president of the Long Island State Park Commission, for holding up the building of a boulevard to Jones Beach in order to "prolong the life of a lame duck shooting preserve." "There have been a good many efforts on the part of selfish people of large wealth," said Moses, "to interrupt the park program but this attempt to maintain a private shooting ground on the finest ocean front on the Atlantic seaboard is the most impudent of all." Governor Roosevelt backed the park commissioner in the fight to break the $1 an acre Guggenheim leasehold.

In politics Solomon, like his brothers, was a rock-ribbed Republican who disliked change. He was frequently interviewed on the state of the nation on shipboard in New York harbor. "The wealth of America is so great," he said in 1927, "that there is no reason why the present prosperity should not continue for many years to come. The only thing that could effect a change would be political disturbances." But when prosperity declined despite Hoover, Solomon in 1932 urged rigid economy as the only antidote and warned that heavy taxation was "an important cause of the present trouble." Loyally he hoped for the best when

Roosevelt entered the White House but feared that excessive taxation would ruin the President's plans.

With pleasure he looked back upon his twenty-eight years as treasurer of the Public Schools Athletic League, which he helped to organize in 1903. The League had sold New York the idea that sports fought down the germs of vice to which the youth in the slums were exposed.

Like his older brother, Isaac, Solomon loved the graces of old England and educated his daughters there. Eleanor, first-born, studied art in Italy, served during the War as a "farmerette," and fell in love with Arthur Stuart, youngest son of the Earl of Castle Stewart of Stuart Hall, Stewartstown, County Tyrone, in Ulster. Only Arthur, of the heirs to the infirm Earl, emerged alive from the War, and he advanced to the rank of Viscount. For all his titles, Arthur was a serious-minded young fellow, a don at Cambridge, and prince charming to Eleanor Guggenheim. Their wedding in the winter of 1920 was a high-light of the London season, and the popular press dwelt effusively on this union of a poor but noble heir to an Irish earldom with an heiress to the great Guggenheim fortune. Canon David of Coventry, assisted by the rector of feudal Stewartstown, officiated. Eleanor was sheathed in a gown of hand-woven pearl white satin brocade embroidered with pearls and diamonds, topped by a rose point lace collar. Under all was a skirt of cloth of silver which trailed off in a gorgeous train. Sol gave his daughter $50,000 and this she distributed, Lady Bountiful-like, to charities in New York, to the King Edward Hospital Fund, and the County Tyrone Hospital.

The aged earl died a few years later and Arthur succeeded to his rank and pomp. The couple preferred a Sussex countryside dwelling in Nutley to the musty manor house in Ulster, and there Solomon loved to visit and to watch the growth of four fine sturdy grandsons. In the shooting season Solomon, the Earl, and Eleanor went to Glenkindie

Moor in Scotland. Sol's second daughter, Gertrude, also preferred England to her native land and lived in Coleman's Hatch, near Eleanor.

His third daughter, Barbara Josephine, likewise succumbed to the blandishments of the Old Country, studied there, and became engaged to John Robert, son of the Ormonde Lawson-Johnsons. Soon after John was named attaché to the British embassy in Washington and on January 29, 1924, a grand wedding was celebrated at the Hotel Plaza in New York with Sir Esme Howard, the Ambassador and his staff, the Earl of Castle Stewart and other notables present. Unlike the Earl, Lawson-Johnson was no sober scholar, the marriage broke; he married a former Albany, New York, cloak model; and Barbara returned to a childhood sweetheart, Fred Wettach, Jr., son of the owner of riding stables near her father's New Jersey summer home. They lived happily in New Jersey, minus titles, social honors, or high life.

Not to be outdone by his brothers Daniel, Murry and Simon, Solomon too established a Foundation, to bring to the world the rich beauties of the non-objective art which was his pride and joy. The Solomon R. Guggenheim Foundation took as its scope, the subsidizing of exhibitions, lectures, scholarships, publications, and a museum, "to the end that this country may become one of the great art centers of the world and may be accelerated in the process of developing its own great art works as the older nations have done."

Through his Foundation, Solomon enjoyed high distinction as the world's most opulent patron of a revolutionary school of painting that laughed at the cramped efforts of others to imitate nature through realism or distort it through surrealism. Eagerly he bought non-objective canvasses from painters all but unknown for sums ranging up to $10,000; and many a critic who believed the works freaks conceded that Guggenheim merited praise for supporting daring experimental artists rather than those embalmed in the sanctified air of the academies.

To the Baroness Hilla von Rebay von Ehrenwiesen, whom he named curator of the Foundation, Solomon owed his conversion to this strange new art form which used brilliantly-colored geometrical figures as its base. When he commissioned the Baroness to do his portrait, Solomon was collecting Dutch old masters and German and Italian primitives. She opened his eyes to the delights of Rudolph Bauer, Vasily Kandinsky, Ladislaus Moholy-Nagy and other young masters of non-objectivity who rigidly banned intellect and sought only form and color.

Mrs. Guggenheim was sick at the time and had been ordered not to talk. The Baroness, on one of her trips to paint Solomon, brought along a gay-colored Bauer to hang in her bedroom. Solomon came in, his eye was caught. "By Jove, that's beautiful," he exclaimed.

He had the corridor of his suite at the Plaza done over in a delicate blue to set off the somber pictures of his early collecting. But in his study the walls, ceiling and floor were of cork to display to best advantage the bright Kandinskys; the drawing room was done in brown for the Bauers.

"I like to sit here and feel the pictures," said Solomon. "I can't stay away from them for very long. You think you get to know them—then suddenly you are struck by an entirely new conception."

That was the rare beauty of non-objectivity: it meant nothing except what might be read into the squares, triangles, circles, and ectoplasmic forms that hung suspended against a dazzling background. It was "all spiritual," said the Baroness. "Home life," added Solomon, "is a constant pleasure and an elevating joy because of them."

The Guggenheim Foundation of Art prepared a beautiful catalogue of his treasured $500,000 collection for the Paris

Exposition of 1937. (Solomon was afraid to risk his pictures to the transatlantic trip despite the French Government's request for samples.) The proceeds from the sale of the catalogues were to go to a fund for artists. His native city, Philadelphia, was the second to hold an exhibition of the Guggenheim collection, his winter city, Charleston, having been favored first.

An irreverent critic described one painting as a "cross between a college pennant, a billiard table, London Bridge (falling down) and thirteen microbes, under a microscope." But to Baroness Rebay, the three principal non-objective objects—the circle "concentrated continuity in itself," the square, "a more spiritual form in relationship to space," and the triangle, "perhaps less spiritual"—were all "perfected absolute forms of purity and beauty." "Realistic painting," she snorted, " is relatively dull." Non-objectivity opened fields of divine rapture, of spiritual grace.

Not for Simon, most active business man in the House of Guggenheim, was Solomon's exquisite enjoyment of leisure. The President of American Smelting and Refining had his own modest collection of old masters, but lived in simple elegance in Park Avenue and boasted no lordly chain of country seats and lodges. Even his own crowded little office on the thirty-fourth floor at 120 Broadway, with its old-fashioned rolltop desk surmounted by pictures of his wife, his sons and the inevitable one of the five brothers in golfing togs, was in marked contrast to the spaciousness and funereal quiet of solemn Guggenheim Brothers on the floor above.

Nevertheless Simon was pre-eminent among his brothers for the munificence of his philanthropy—the John Simon Guggenheim Memorial Foundation for fellowships. By 1937 it was estimated that he had given away nearly half his fortune. In his own lifetime hundreds of creative practitioners of the arts and sciences were to remember him kindly for help given them—without strings. If he walked plainly and simply in his way of life, at least it could not be said that he had been unhonored. The University of Colorado conferred on him the degree of Doctor of Laws while remembering his gifts of some $230,000 to the state's colleges; and the press and learned leaders never ceased to praise his intelligently devised scholarships.

To Simon the blow of the world depression came with redoubled force, for he was not only a member of Guggenheim Brothers, encumbered with the weight of Chilean nitrate, but head of the Smelters Trust. "We created the basis of the crisis," he said (was it with some regret?) "when we entered the World War and increased the catastrophe of all powers, both human and financial. We must now repair the damage through years of toil and resignation." In 1931 he held out for continued payments on American Smelting dividends. "For what better purpose," he cried, "could surpluses built up in good years be used than in the maintenance of dividends, thereby creating good will and confidence among stockholders?" But his company passed, first its common, and then its preferred. Simon never lost courage. In the abject depth of the crisis he declared: "As I see it, all one needs is sound common sense and a willingness to work. Now is the time to build for the future and a better opportunity never existed."

If it seemed a somewhat callous statement to make when so many were plunged into misery, Simon was not conscious of that. Reminded, when prosperity returned, that millions were still unemployed, he replied: "Well, it's all a question of supply and demand. When people want our goods, we produce; otherwise we can't do it."

Such an explanation, or justification, of his firm's rôle in capitalist débâcle failed to satisfy his nephew, Harold A. Loeb. While the Guggenheim Brothers were congratulating themselves in 1934 that they had come through the

478

economic cyclone intact, Loeb, son of their sister, Rose, felt that there was something radically awry in the economic scheme of things. How was it that so much poverty existed when America stood in sight of plenty for all?

With all the energy and enthusiasm that his grandfather, Meyer, would have thrown into a new business enterprise, Harold gathered about him a dozen experts, gained support from the Federal Emergency Relief Administration and the patronage of Langdon Post, and set to work to determine, statistically, how rich America could be on the basis of her resources, manufacturing equipment and exchange apparatus.

The results he put into a small book which contained a formidable chart, known as *The Chart of Plenty*, which became the Bible of Technocracy. In an enthusiastic foreword, Stuart Chase hailed the work of Loeb and his associates as the first scholarly answer to the question, What could we produce? Loeb's answer was, in brief: "If the existing plant and man-power in the United States were fully employed in the production of honest goods and services for the consumer, the total output, valued in 1929 dollars, would be not less than 135 billions, or an average per family of approximately $4,400."

However revolutionary the implications of that statement, the Loebian approach to the problem of production and distribution was quite different from the Marxian. The lesson to be drawn from the *Survey of Potential Product Capacity* lay not so much in the mal-distribution of wealth as between the Guggenheims and the non-Guggenheims as in the generally woefully inadequate use of production facilities at hand. The answer, Loeb held, was to keep goods and services tumbling out of the Horn of Plenty to its full capacity.

Most tragic of the Guggenheims were Benjamin, fifth of the brothers, and his daughter, Barbara Hazel, pampered, strong-willed, purposeless. Benjamin joined William in revolt against the older brothers, retired from active partnership, launched an unfortunate business venture of his own and went to his death stoically on the *Titanic*. In troubled sleep, Barbara could see her father standing there on the deck of the ice-ripped liner while the cold waters of the Atlantic rose inexorably about him. Her nervous, distraught mother could do nothing to turn Barbara's morbid spirit into healthier channels. She married while still in college, was divorced next year and married again in 1923. They lived in England, where her husband wrote books.

Perhaps he was inattentive, perhaps she was selfish. At any rate after a few years he asked a divorce. In fury Barbara took the next boat for New York. She went to a relative's. No one was home in the penthouse apartment but a servant. Barbara took her two boys, one four, the other in arms, out on the roof. There were two gates between her and the parapet. Resolutely she went through both. A few minutes later the bodies of her boys lay dead on the street sixteen stories below.

Fortunately for Barbara, she was a Guggenheim. The police dealt gently with her, the chief medical examiner was sympathetic. The deaths, after two investigations, were pronounced accidental. Barbara went to a sanitarium for a while. A few years later she married an Englishman, had two more children and became an ardent fascist, unlike her older sister, Marguerite, who also married an Englishman but was markedly liberal in her viewpoints.

William Guggenheim, youngest of the brothers and allied with Benjamin, lived aloof from the great enterprises of the family and had time to ponder the world's problems with philosophic detachment. To William it seemed that the world had entered a "decade of shame" in 1926 from which it was just emerging into an "era of good feeling" in which the principles of Benjamin Franklin would guide mankind.

The third of a century in which the youngest of the Guggenheim brothers had been divorced from the firm's interests had mellowed his outlook and given him ample time for reflection. Coming out of the savagery of the World War and his participation in the American Defense Society's private crusade against the Kaiser, he urged an era of light, to be ushered in by "great carnivals of peace" to express the people's joy at the prospect of "creating a new earth." His gift for words, which seemed strange when practiced on the American employees of the Smelters Trust in Monterrey in the eighteen nineties, flowered in a series of speeches entitled, "The New World," "Is Jesus Here Today?" "Bolshevism and Its Cure," "The Crucial Need for Sound Money," and "What Price Government?" "Let us preach less the fear of Bolshevism," he counseled, "and preach more the fear of God."

Later he used the University of Pennsylvania Club of New York City and the Pennsylvania Society of New York City as the forum for his thoughts, which ranged along the whole train of philosophy and economics. He served as treasurer for these societies, introducing business methods into their slipshod finances and leaving them, on his resignation, with comfortable surpluses.

In his own business affairs he was not so fortunate. The Hudson Navigation Company, the U. S. Steamship Company, and the U. S. Transport Company all became involved in court suits. These reverses he brushed away in the social life which revolved about his $700,000 mansion at 833 Fifth Avenue, where he entertained Admiral Peary of Polar fame, distinguished Pennsylvania alumni and—annual affair—the cast of the Mask and Wig show. With advancing years, he sold his estate at Sands Point, left to his wife the Fifth Avenue house, and moved to 3 Riverside Drive, which became residence, office and seat of his publishing firm, The Lone Voice Publishing Company.

William pondered deeply the lessons of the great depression of the early thirties. His advice, given at one of his annual speeches to Pennsylvania alumni, in which he regularly reviewed the state of the nation and the world, was: don't produce commodities at a loss. He urged a return to the spirit of President McKinley and Senator Lodge. American greed, unrestricted competition, and governmental mismanagement were the evil trinity, he said, which threw us into the abyss. "We are fast drifting from capitalism into communism," he warned the alumni in 1933. The policy of "Soak the rich," was degenerating into "Swat the thrifty," in the Rooseveltian era, he held. Spending ourselves into prosperity was the height of absurdity.

William put it this way:

> With excessive welfare work animating the minds and actions of many of our good citizens, we are preparing our people for a state of anemia that may indeed become pernicious. Let us pray therefore for a return to the old condition of less government in business and more business in government and thereby turn our country back to our people.

His speech brought forth public protest as heartless in view of the "extreme tension and harrowing distress" in the winter of 1932-33.

In 1933 he found time to supervise the writing of his autobiography, *William Guggenheim*, under the pen-name of Gatenby Williams, in collaboration with Charles Monroe Heath. His own firm, the Lone Voice Publishing Company, brought out the volume and promised another, consisting of his writings and speeches. A third work, *Lover at Large*, awaited his further attention. In it he hoped to achieve a Boccaccio touch.

The crowning passion of the youngest of Meyer's sons, however, was his love of Benjamin Franklin. That great patriot, he believed, was the first and only American internationalist, a prime figure to lead a stumbling world forward into sanity and peace. To Governor Landon, while he was a candidate for the Presidency, Guggenheim sent a bust of Franklin. In his letter he quoted from the Founding Father: " 'No individual or no political body could spend more than they had and remain solvent.' You well typify his patriotism, thrift and economic sanity. May Franklin's spirit ever inspire you."

William worked feverishly through 1937 to consolidate the forces of good will around the International Benjamin Franklin Institute, of which he had been honorary president for years. He hoped to weld a united front composed of the Institute, the American Philosophical Society, other Franklin societies, and Pennsylvania alumni, which could guide humanity into happier days.

In Franklin he found that great-minded versatility which he himself strove to attain. Franklin had been printer, publisher, publicist, philosopher, patriot, and poet, and in each of these fields, except perhaps printing, Guggenheim too laid claim to distinction. He published little of his poetry, he admitted, because it was not becoming in this hard age for a man to show his inner feelings. Of his own poems he liked particularly:

MY ORCHID

I

I hold an orchid in my hand,
No gentle pressure can it withstand.
Its petals wafting in the breeze—
I long, and sigh—could I but seize
And press the flower to my breast,
What my wild nature forbids me do
To keep and hold a love so true.

II

But maddening thoughts surge in my brain;
Why should I stop? There's so much to gain
From all its Perils I must be freed,
For Nature sowed the lust and greed
That make men dare their prize to win
And share a Paradise so slim
That one false step may make us lose
The path reluctantly we choose.

III

I clench my fist and hold inside
The orchid's fate! but woe betide
The man who will not count the cost
And realize that all is lost
To quench life from a bleeding flower,
Minute by minute, hour by hour!
Fool that thou art, release your hold;
Exchange base metal for "Purest Gold!"

IV

Reeling, staggering, with excited brain,
I find at least composure again.
I have released the flower I held
'Ere it had been completely felled.
Thank Heaven its life was soon restored!
I breathe a prayer unto the Lord
And promise to care more tenderly
For the orchid that's in my hand—quite free.

So important was it to provide a solid base for the advancement of Franklin's ideas that Guggenheim considered turning his four-story Riverside Drive mansion, a block from Schwab's Renaissance palace, into the International Benjamin Franklin House, to serve as headquarters for the Institute. As his wife and son lived elsewhere, he had no need for so much space. His office overlooking the Hudson he contemplated naming the *Salon d'Or;* a small

484

room to the rear, used temporarily as a kitchen, the *Chambre de Cuivre;* his large bedroom, the *Chambre d'Argent;* and his secretary's office on the first floor, the *Bureau de Plombe* —all so named for the metals on which his fortune was based.

And so ends this story of the Guggenheims, of indefatigable Meyer, of his seven sons and their children. In less than a century this family out of a Swiss ghetto had spanned the cycle of business enterprise from crude peddling, through merchandising, through competitive mining and smelting, into the grand era of monopoly finance. Five brothers who, most exceptionally, had shown a monolithic front to the world, had built upon their sturdy father's foundations one of America's great businesses.

And their children? Apparently the mainspring which had pushed old Meyer and his sons into ever new fields, had run down soon. Moreover, Meyer's grandchildren faced a changing world in which emphasis was to be placed on other values. Some might carp at their unwillingness to play the old acquisitive game; others would praise them for their hedonism; perhaps most would agree that the times which called forth a Meyer and a Daniel Guggenheim no longer existed.

The curtain had dropped forever on the Guggenheim era.

ACKNOWLEDGMENTS

I find it difficult to acknowledge the extent of my indebtedness to my wife, Jessie Lloyd, for her assistance in research and in revision of the manuscript. In particular, Chapters 2 and 3 are as much the result of her research as mine.

Much of the material was obtained in a trip through western mining and smelting centers early in 1936. Many engineers, public officials and local writers cooperated but nearly all requested that their names not be used. The *Engineering and Mining Journal*, the *New York Times*, official records and contemporary periodicals have been used extensively. The Messrs. Guggenheim and Mr. Carroll A. Wilson of Guggenheim Brothers were most courteous in granting interviews and in furnishing information requested. Mr. Wilson supplied many valuable criticisms. Naturally, I assume all responsibility for the facts used and the conclusions drawn.—H. O'C.

INDEX

INDEX

tor for Dan, 450; in Chilean nitrate disaster, 452-60; houses, 473; shooting, 473; endows Art Foundation, 475-77

Guggenheim, William, birth, 29, 36, 40; in university, 71, 72; in Pueblo, 83, 87; in Monterrey, 96-97; 100, 103; splits with brothers, 145-46; marriage and divorce, 146-52; and partnership, 152, 154, 157, 163; sues brothers, 356-59; in World War, 365-66; on socialism, 423; philosophic reflections, 481-82; author, 483; and Benjamin Franklin, 483-84

Guggenheim, William, Jr., 149

Guggenheim Brothers (partnership), organized, 355-56; in World War, 362; offices, 398-409; copper sales, 402-3, 405, 407; sells Chile Copper, 413-14; Harry and Edmond resign, 414-15; enters Chilean nitrate business, 417-24; in Morgan pool, 451-52; in nitrate disaster, 452-61; losses in Chile, 461; members of firm, 462

Guggenheim Exploration Company, organized, 109-11; hires Hammond, 128-31; Murry explains success, 131; increases stock, 133; sells to Smelters Securities, 134-36; buys Esperanza, 171-77; in Congo, 179-82; and Nipissing, 184-87; and Yukon Gold, 214-15; Hammond resigns, 214-15; Beatty suit, 216-19; in Utah Copper, 279-80; in Nevada Consolidated, 283, 288; in Chino, 300; in Ray, 301; dissolved, 352-53, 404

Guggenheim family, in Germany, 12-13; in Switzerland, 14-20; "third generation," 355, 424; estimate of wealth, 422; criticism, 422-23; post-depression fortune, 462; divorces, 463

Guggenheim and Pulaski, 38-39, 54, 70, 71, 74

Guiterman, Franklin, 112, 334-35

Haas, Edmund L., 365

Hammond, John Hays, 126-33, 183-84, 186, 187, 188, 190-92, 214-16, 278, 279, 286, 324, 327, 329, 449

Hayden, Charles, 285, 301, 352, 430

Hearst, Mrs. Phoebe, 296

Hebrew Union College, 164, 430

Herbert, Mrs. Grace Brown (Mrs. William Guggenheim), 147-52

Hirsh, Olga (Mrs. Simon Guggenheim), 154, 250-51, 431

Holden, Edward R., 72, 78-82

Howland, Silas W., 451, 462

Huanchaco mines, 346

Industrial Relations Commission, 316-22

Industrial Workers of the World, 308-9, 335

Jackling, Daniel C., 277-80, 283-84, 297, 299-300, 311-15, 387

Jewish Theological Seminary, 164

John Simon Guggenheim Memorial Foundation, 431-33, 476-80

Josephthal, Louis M., 154, 365

Kansas City Smelting and Refining, 86, 90, 110

Kennecott Copper, 342, 351-55, 360, 375-76, 381-84, 404, 407, 416, 437, 461

Kennecott mines, 269, 273

Keystone Canyon case, 255, 258, 263

Kountze, C. B., 72

Labor in A. Y. and Minnie mines, 56-57; in Leadville, 66-68; in Philadelphia smelter, 82-83; in Mexico, 98; Smelters strike of 1900, 112-13; fight for eight-hour law, 232-33; and Meyer Guggenheim, 302; and Smelters Trust, 305-23; and Utah Copper, 311-15; hazards, 315; in Mexico, 325-27; in Aguascalientes, 326; during World War, 380-96; and Kennecott, 381, 84; and Utah, 385-86, 433-34; and Nevada Consolidated, 386; and Ray, 387-88; and A S and R, 392; and Chino, 396

Lautaro Nitrate Co., 420-21, 461

Lawson, Thomas R., 200-12, 218, 287, 297-99

494

495